The Geopolitics of Religious Soft Power

The Geopolitics of Religious Soft Power

How States Use Religion in Foreign Policy

Edited by
PETER MANDAVILLE

OXFORD
UNIVERSITY PRESS

Oxford University Press is a department of the University of Oxford. It furthers
the University's objective of excellence in research, scholarship, and education
by publishing worldwide. Oxford is a registered trade mark of Oxford University
Press in the UK and certain other countries.

Published in the United States of America by Oxford University Press
198 Madison Avenue, New York, NY 10016, United States of America.

© Oxford University Press 2023

All rights reserved. No part of this publication may be reproduced, stored in
a retrieval system, or transmitted, in any form or by any means, without the
prior permission in writing of Oxford University Press, or as expressly permitted
by law, by license, or under terms agreed with the appropriate reproduction
rights organization. Inquiries concerning reproduction outside the scope of the
above should be sent to the Rights Department, Oxford University Press, at the
address above.

You must not circulate this work in any other form
and you must impose this same condition on any acquirer.

Library of Congress Cataloging-in-Publication Data
Names: Mandaville, Peter G., 1971– editor.
Title: The geopolitics of religious soft power : how states use religion in
foreign policy / Peter Mandaville.
Description: New York, NY : Oxford University Press, [2023] |
Includes bibliographical references and index.
Identifiers: LCCN 2023006291 (print) | LCCN 2023006292 (ebook) |
ISBN 9780197605806 (hardback) | ISBN 9780197605820 (epub) |
ISBN 9780197605837
Subjects: LCSH: Religion and international relations. |
Diplomacy—Religious aspects. | Geopolitics—Religious aspects. |
Soft power (Political science)
Classification: LCC BL65.I55 G46 2024 (print) | LCC BL65.I55 (ebook) |
DDC 201/.727—dc23/eng20230711
LC record available at https://lccn.loc.gov/2023006291
LC ebook record available at https://lccn.loc.gov/2023006292

DOI: 10.1093/oso/9780197605806.001.0001

Printed by Integrated Books International, United States of America

Contents

Acknowledgments vii
List of Contributors ix

1. Thinking about Religion and Religious Soft Power in International Relations and Foreign Policy Analysis 1
   Peter Mandaville and Jon Hoffman

2. Tragedy or Irony: Geopolitical Grand Narratives, Religious Outreach, and US Soft Power 19
   Peter S. Henne and Gregorio Bettiza

3. "Putin-Phonia": Harnessing Russian Orthodoxy to Advance Russia's Secular Foreign Policy 41
   Robert C. Blitt

4. Chinese Buddhism and Soft Power: Geopolitical Strategy and Modality of Religion 61
   Yoshiko Ashiwa and David L. Wank

5. Turkey's Ambivalent Religious Soft Power in the Illiberal Turn 79
   Ahmet Erdi Öztürk

6. The Modi Government and the Uses and Limits of India's Religious Soft Power 97
   Sumit Ganguly

7. Shi'i Diplomacy: Religious Identity and Foreign Policy in the Axis of Resistance 113
   Edward Wastnidge

8. Hassan II and the Foundations of Moroccan Religious Soft Power 130
   Ann Wainscott

9. Religious Diplomacy in the Arab Gulf and the Politics of Moderate Islam 151
   Annelle Sheline

10. Indonesian Islam as Model for the World? Diplomacy, Soft
    Power, and the Geopolitics of "Moderate Islam" 169
    James B. Hoesterey

11. Moderation as Jordanian Soft Power: Islam and Beyond 190
    Stacey Gutkowski

12. Israel's Religious Soft Power: Within and Beyond Judaism 211
    Claudia Baumgart-Ochse

13. Soft Power of the Catholic Papacy 232
    Timothy A. Byrnes

14. "Brazil above Everything or God above Everyone?" The
    Sources of Brazil's Religious Soft Power 248
    Guilherme Casarões and Amy Erica Smith

15. Religious Soft Power: Promises, Limits, and Ways Forward 270
    Gregorio Bettiza and Peter S. Henne

Notes 293
Index 305

Acknowledgments

This volume has benefited from the support and insight of numerous individuals and organizations. First and foremost I would like to acknowledge Hillary Wiesner. She and her colleague Nehal Amer at the Carnegie Corporation—whose financial support made this publication possible—have been so supportive at every juncture of the project. It was Hillary who first encouraged me to approach religious soft power as a global phenomenon and to think of this work as an effort to create a new research agenda for the intersection of religion and international relations. I'm also deeply appreciative of the support and guidance provided by Toby Volkman and the Henry Luce Foundation whose partnership enabled some of the preparatory work that led to this volume.

Of the many scholars of religion and international relations who have offered support, feedback, and creative suggestions as the project came together, I would particularly like to thank Scott Appleby, Tom Banchoff, Jose Casanova, Shaun Casey, Jocelyne Cesari, Shadi Hamid, Jeff Haynes, Michael Kessler, Nukhet Sandal, and Annelle Sheline. The staff of the Berkley Center for Religion, Peace, and World Affairs at Georgetown University—where I was in residence during the most active stage of the project—especially Randolph Pelzer, Claudia Winkler, Amy Vander Vliet, and Ruth Gopin, provided invaluable assistance and input across all aspects of the Geopolitics of Religious Soft Power project. In terms of direct research assistance and editorial support for this volume, I owe a particular debt of gratitude to Henry Brill, Mackenzie Poust, Jake Gilstrap, Jon Hoffman, and Fana HaileSelassie.

Contributors

Yoshiko Ashiwa is Professor of Anthropology and Global Studies and the Founding Director of the Institute for the Study of Peace and Reconciliation at Hitotsubashi University, where she also earned her PhD. Her research interests include religion, arts, culture and values, modernity, globalization, and social movements, mainly in Asia, with particular interest in Buddhism's revival in China. She is the co-editor of *Making Religion, Making the State: The Politics of Religion in Modern China* (2009, with David Wank).

Claudia Baumgart-Ochse holds a PhD from Goethe University Frankfurt. She is currently a senior researcher and editorial director of *The Peace Report* at the Peace Research Institute Frankfurt (PRIF). Her research interests include religious conflicts, Middle East conflict, Israel, and Palestinian territories. She is also the author of *Religious NGOs at the United Nations: Polarizers or Mediators?* (2019) and co-editor of *The Role of Religion in Struggles for Global Justice: Faith in Justice?* (2018, with J. Smith, K. Glaab, and E. Smythe).

Gregorio Bettiza is Senior Lecturer in International Relations at the University of Exeter in the United Kingdom where his research focuses on intersections and encounters between liberal and non-liberal ideas in world politics. His 2019 book *Finding Faith in Foreign Policy: Religion and American Diplomacy in a Postsecular World* was singled out for recognition by International Studies Association and the European Academy of Religion.

Robert C. Blitt earned a JD from the University of Toronto. He is currently Toms Foundation Distinguished Professor of Law at the University of Tennessee College of Law, where he focuses on Comparative Constitutional Law, Human Rights Law, International Law, and Religious Freedom Law. Before teaching at Tennessee, Blitt served as an international law specialist for the US Commission on International Religious Freedom. His research interests include issues related to the right to the freedom of thought, conscience, and religion or belief.

Timothy A. Byrnes is the author of *Reverse Mission: Transnational Religious Communities and the Making of U.S. Foreign Policy* (2011), *Transnational Catholicism in Post-Communist Europe* (2001), and *Catholic Bishops in American Politics* (1991), among contributing to numerous other publications. He has a PhD from Cornell University and is currently Charles A. Dana Professor of Political Science at Colgate University, where his research interests include transnational politics, religion, and politics.

LIST OF CONTRIBUTORS

Guilherme Casarões holds a PhD in Political Science from the University of São Paulo. He is currently Vice-Coordinator of Public Administration at the Fundação Getulio Vargas School of Buisness Administration, where he is also Professor of Public Administration, Political Science, and International Relations. He has also previously served as a visiting fellow at Brandeis University (2015) and Tel Aviv University (2011). His most recent publications include *The Place of Israel and Palestine in Brazilian Foreign Policy* (2014) and *Itamaraty's Mission* (2014). More broadly, Casarões' research interests include Brazilian foreign policy, Brazil–Middle East relations, and international relations theory.

Sumit Ganguly is Distinguished Professor of Political Science and serves as Rabindranath Tagore Chair in Indian Cultures and Civilizations at Indiana University. He is also Senior Fellow at the Foreign Policy Research Institute and is a member of the Council on Foreign Relations. His most recent publications include *Ascending India and Its State Capacity* (2017, with William R. Thompson) and the *Oxford Short Introduction to Indian Foreign Policy* (2015). Ganguly earned his PhD in Political Science from the University of Illinois, Urbana.

Stacey Gutkowski is Reader in Peace and Conflict Studies and Deputy Director of the Center for the Study of Divided Societies at King's College London. She was also co-director of the Nonreligion and Secularity Research Network from 2008 to 2020 and now sits on its Advisory Board. She holds a PhD in International Studies from the University of Cambridge and is the author of numerous publications, including *Religion, War, and Israel's Secular Millennials: Being Reasonable?* (2020) and *Secular Wars: Myths of Religion, Politic, and Violence* (2013).

Peter S. Henne earned his PhD in Government from Georgetown University. He is currently Associate Professor at the University of Vermont, where he focuses on the Middle East and global religious politics, specifically investigating how states use religion in their foreign policies and how ties between religion and state affect politics. Dr. Henne's first book, *Islamic Politics, Muslim States and Counterterrorism Tensions* (2017), analyzes how Muslim states' relationship with Islam affects their counterterrorism policies, and his upcoming publication will analyze unpredictable effects of religion in power politics.

James B. Hoesterey is Associate Professor in Emory College's Department of Religion where he also serves as Secretary at the American Institute for Indonesian Studies (AIFIS). His academic research and teaching interests include Islam, popular culture, new media, moral subjectivity, religious biography, and religious authority. Some of these themes are explored in his most recent book, *Rebranding Islam: Piety, Prosperity, and a Self-help Guru* (2015). Hoesterey received his PhD from the University of Wisconsin-Madison.

Jon Hoffman is a political science PhD candidate at George Mason University specializing in Middle East geopolitics and Islam. He is also a foreign policies media editor at *Jadaliyya* and a contributor to *Foreign Policy*.

Peter Mandaville is Professor of Government and Politics in the Schar School of Policy and Government at George Mason University. He is also Nonresident Senior Fellow in Foreign Policy Studies at the Brookings Institution and Senior Research Fellow at Georgetown University's Berkley Center for Religion, Peace, and World Affairs, where he is the founder and director of its Geopolitics of Religious Soft Power project. Dr. Mandaville received his PhD in Philosophy in International Relations from the University of Kent at Canterbury. He is the author or editor of numerous books including *Islam and Politics* (2nd Edition, 2014), *Politics from Afar: Transnational Diasporas and Networks* (2012), and *Transnational Muslim Politics: Reimagining the Umma* (2001). His upcoming publication is entitled *Wahhabism in the World: Understanding Saudi Arabia's Global Influence on Religion*.

Ahmet Erdi Öztürk is Senior Lecturer in Politics and International Relations at London Metropolitan University and Marie Curie Fellow at Coventry University. He is the author of more than 20 peer-reviewed journal articles as well as the editor of the *Edinburgh Studies on Modern Turkey* and *International Journal of Religion*. Additionally, his first solo-authored book, *Religion, Identity, and Power: Turkey and the Balkans in the Twenty-First Century*, was published in 2021. His research interests include, among others, religion, global politics, theories of nationalism, democratization and authoritarianism, East-Southeast Europe, and Central Europe.

Annelle Sheline earned her PhD from George Washington University. She is currently a Research Fellow in the Middle East program at the Quincy Institute and an expert on religious and political authority in the Middle East and North Africa. She has received multiple fellowships from the US government, including a Boren Fellowship and a Foreign Language and Area Studies (FLAS) Fellowship, as well as fellowships from the Project on Middle East Political Science (POMEPS), the Loeb Institute for Religious Freedom, and the Boniuk Institute for Religious Tolerance. Sheline is completing an upcoming book on the strategic use of religious authority in the Arab monarchies since 9/11, focusing on Saudi Arabia, Jordan, Morocco, and Oman, in particular.

Amy Erica Smith received her PhD from the University of Pittsburgh. She is currently Liberal Arts and Sciences Dean's Professor and Associate Professor of Political Science at Iowa State University, as well as the Carnegie Corporation's 2020 Andrew Carnegie Fellows Recipient. Her research investigates how citizens understand and engage in politics in democratic and authoritarian regimes, with a geographic focus on Latin America, specifically Brazil. Her most recent book *Religion and Brazilian Democracy: Mobilizing the People of God* (2019), examines these themes.

Ann Wainscott is Assistant Professor of Political Science at Miami University where her research focuses on religion and politics. She served as the American Academy of Religion Senior Fellow at the United States Institute of Peace from 2017 to 2018 where she helped coordinate a research project on Iraq's religious landscape. Her first book, *Bureaucratizing Islam* (2017), examines Morocco's incorporation of religious institutions into the state as a response to the War on Terror. She holds a PhD from the University of Florida in Political Science and Government.

David L. Wank earned his PhD from Harvard University. He is Professor of Sociology and Global Studies at Sophia University in Tokyo and Dean of its Graduate School of Global Studies. He is the author of *Commodifying Communism* (1999) and co-editor of *Making Religion, Making the State: The Politics of Religion in Modern China* (2009, with Yoshiko Ashiwa), and *Dynamics of Global Society: Theory and Prospects* (2007, with Yoshinori Murai and Tadashi Anno). His areas of interest include culture industries in China and the United States, the global rise of China, globalization, and the revival of Buddhism in China.

Edward Wastnidge is Professor of Politics and International Studies at the Open University. His main area of research explores the politics and international relations of the Middle East and Central Asia, with a focus on contemporary Iranian politics and foreign policy. His additional research interests include the intersection of ideas and foreign policy, soft power, cultural and religious diplomacy, the role of identity in international relations, political Islam, and modern Iranian history. His recent publications include, "Iran's 'War on Terror': Iranian foreign policy towards Syria and Iraq during the Rouhani Era" in *The Foreign Policy of Iran under President Hassan Rouhani* (2020) and *De-securitizing through Diplomacy: De-sectarianization and the View from the Islamic Republic* (2020, with Samira Nasirzadeh). Dr. Wastnidge holds a PhD in Middle Eastern Studies from University of Manchester.

1
Thinking about Religion and Religious Soft Power in International Relations and Foreign Policy Analysis

Peter Mandaville and Jon Hoffman

Religion seems to feature prominently in the international relations of many states around the world today. Whether mobilizing religious affinities as a form of public diplomacy, positioning religion as a force to counteract perceived ideological foes, or creating transnational networks of religious populism to support incumbent regimes—governments clearly perceive geopolitical utility in the power of religion.

The various chapters in this volume explore how states across multiple world regions, and featuring a diverse range of faith traditions, incorporate religion as an aspect of their foreign policy. The volume's contributors explore the role of religion in the global engagement of countries such as Brazil, China, India, Iran, Jordan, Indonesia, Russia, Saudi Arabia, Turkey, and the United States. States such as Israel and the Holy See, which by their nature have a unique relationship with religion, are also included. The various country case studies included in the volume illuminate various cross-national patterns, as well as continuities and discontinuities in the role of religion as a geopolitical tool. A closing chapter looks synthetically across the volume's country case studies to consider both the potential and the limitations of "religious soft power" as a conceptual apparatus for making sense of how governments use religion in foreign policy.

Religion in the External Relations of Modern States

The role of religion in the external relations of modern states was for centuries dominated by "a secularizing set of historical events," namely the secular sovereign state system that was consolidated around the Peace of Westphalia in 1648 (Shah and Philpott 2011). The official treatise marking the end of the Thirty Years' War (1618–1648), the Peace of Westphalia "symbolized the consolidation of the long historical transformation from the authority structure of medieval Europe to that of the modern state system" (Shah and Philpott 2011). This modern, secularized state entailed the subordination of religion to state authority, dramatically reducing the temporal authority of the church. This political secularization would deepen and expand over the next three centuries, compounded by events such as the French and American revolutions. However, religion never did completely disappear from the foreign policies of states. For example, Britain often coupled its colonial endeavors with Christian missionary activities (Porter 2004), and in America, religion featured prominently in the notions of "Manifest Destiny" and "progressive imperialism" abroad in places such as the Philippines (McDougal 1998). Yet, as Haynes (2021) explains, "very few states—especially in the secular West—consistently expressed an organizing ideology which consistently involved religion."

With the twentieth century came the achievement of the Westphalian state system as the commanding organizational structure of the global community as well as the emergence of intense forms of secular nationalism around the world. The Russian Revolution; the Kemalist Revolution in Turkey; German Naziism and Italian Fascism; nationalist revolutions in countries such as Egypt, India, and Indonesia; Communist revolutions in countries such as China and Cuba; all of these events served to further entrench the secular Westphalian state system and subordinate—and at times outright eliminate—religious authority vis-a-vis the state. During this period, "secular ideologies such as liberal democracy, capitalism, socialism, social democracy, and communism were paramount" (Haynes 2021). Again, however, religion did not completely disappear. During the Cold War period pitting the United States against the Soviet Union, America often turned to religious narratives in the fight against "Godless communism." Eisenhower once famously stated that "when God comes in, communism has to go" (Indoben 2008). Moreover, the United States often supported religious groups and organizations in places such as Latin America, the Middle East, Europe, and so forth as a counterweight to Soviet influence. Still, religion was not a central motivating or mobilizing force during this period.

This began to change in the late–Cold War period as religion began to slowly reemerge as a powerful force on the global stage. The Soviet invasion of

Afghanistan led to the United States supporting Muslim Mujahideen forces against the communists, a conflict that served to reignite feelings of a broader pan-Islamic consciousness. The Roman Catholic Church reinvigorated itself through the Second Vatican Council and the papacy of John Paul II. The Islamic Revolution in Iran in 1979 successfully established the world's only theocracy, which was followed by a devastating eight-year war with neighboring Iraq, with both sides seeking to harness religious sentiments and rhetoric in their campaigns against one another. This trend toward a greater role for religion in international politics grew considerably following the collapse of the Soviet Union and the end of the Cold War in 1991. One incident in particular, the eruption of civil war in former Yugoslavia, was "one of the most important events to reignite interest in national and international relations involving culture, ethnicity, and religion" (Haynes 2021). By drawing in so many different ethnic and religious groups, many of whom were supported by external backers abroad, the Yugoslavia conflict raised issues such as religion, culture, and ethnicity at a time when most traditional approaches to International Relations (IR) were ill equipped to account for them.

Then came the September 11, 2001 (hereafter "9/11") terrorism attacks in the United States committed by Al-Qaeda. It is difficult to overstate the tremendous impact 9/11 had on global affairs and how it served to bring religion to the forefront of international politics. Snyder (2011) explains that "since 11 September 2001, religion has become a central topic in discussions about international politics," placing religion directly in the "international spotlight." George W. Bush immediately sought to use religious rhetoric and imagery in his justifications for the "war on terror" and the 2003 invasion of Iraq (Sandal 2016). In the two decades since, the prominence of religion in international politics has increased considerably. Transnational terrorist organizations such as Al-Qaeda and ISIS continue to bring religion to the forefront of discussions of national security. Religious nationalist parties in Europe, Asia, Latin America, and elsewhere have emerged as influential powerbrokers. Leading powers across the world such as the United States, Russia, and China have increasingly turned to religion as a useful tool to use as part of their broader foreign policies. International politics in the post-9/11 era has indeed witnessed what is commonly referred to as a global resurgence of religion (Thomas 2005).

The importance of religion in international politics has received new impetus as the prevailing liberal world order dominated by the West—particularly the United States—begins to deteriorate in the face of growing domestic and international challenges. As Mandaville and Hamid (2018) argue, it is growing more important to "pay attention to the increased salience of culture, religion, and ideas in the context of an emerging post-liberal world order." Indeed, as we increasingly enter what Amitav Acharya (2018) refers to as a "multiplex world order"—a global order in which there is a multiplicity of important international actors (states, transnational corporations, transnational social movements, transnational terrorist organizations, etc.), as well as increased cultural, ideological, and political diversity among these important actors—being able to properly conceptualize the relationship between ideational variables (such as religion) and international politics will remain of paramount importance.

Current Scholarship on Religious Soft Power and Related Themes

Religion is largely neglected by the dominant theories of IR. As Markus Fischer (2006) argues, this is primarily due to the fact that the major paradigms of IR—with some exceptions—primarily follow a logic of Enlightenment rationalism. Such a rationalist, utility-maximizing approach privileges the pursuit of security, material well-being, and self-interest over ideational concerns. Classical realism, Neorealism, Liberalism, Liberal Institutionalism, and Marxism adhere to this rationalist approach. Constructivism on the other hand is more open to considering the role of religion due to its emphasis on ideas, culture, norms, and so forth. As opposed to the more material focus of other theories, this approach is more interested in the construction of the identities and interests of actors, rather taking them as given, arguing that material interests "cannot be understood apart from the cultural or ideological discourses that endow them with concrete meaning in the minds of the agents" (Fischer 2006). Since ideas construct "both identities and interests" (Houghton 2007), the building blocks of international reality are ideational as well as material (Ruggie 1998), and are socially constructed as opposed to the result of some unseen force (Wendt 1999). Though most of the canonical constructivist literature says little to nothing about religion, the importance it ascribes to ideational and identity-based variables provides an initial framework for examining the significance of religion for international politics.

Jeffrey Haynes (2021) explains that "International Relations has long seen the international as a demonstrably secular one. The fundamental norms of international relations were enshrined in the Treaty of Westphalia (1648)—particularly the notion of state restraint in religious matters, and the general privatization of the latter, implying political marginalization." However, the post–Cold War era witnessed a renewed interest in the relationship between religion and IR. The main purpose of these studies was to gauge the applicability and utility of existing IR theories in understanding the relationship between religion and international politics. The most infamous analysis produced on the subject immediately following the end of the Cold War was Samuel Huntington's *Clash of Civilizations* (1996). Huntington posits that with the end of the Cold War era, conflicts between different "civilizations," which he defines as "the highest cultural grouping of people and the broadest level of cultural identity people have short of what distinguishes humans from other species. It is defined by both common language, history, religion, customs, institutions and by the subjective self-identification of people" (Huntington 1996). Although religion is mentioned in conjunction with other factors such as language and history, most of the civilizations Huntington lists—Western, Sino-Confucian, Japanese, Islamic, Hindu, Slavic-Orthodox, Latin American, and "possibly" African—include religion in their definition (Fox and Sandal 2016). Therefore, in essence, Huntington's "clash of civilizations" may be described, largely, as a clash of religious identities (Fox and Sandler 2004).

This endeavor to understand the importance of religion as a significant facet of international politics expanded dramatically following the September 11, 2001, terrorist attacks within the United States, as academics, journalists, and lay individuals scrambled to try and comprehend the religious motivations behind what many viewed as a hostile Islamic tradition that governed the actions and policies of Muslims and Muslim states. The consequences of the 9/11 terrorist attacks and their aftermath were profound on the field of IR, leading to an increased focus on religious ideas and the emergence of a broad body of scholarly works on the subject (Fox and Sandler 2004; Berger 2010; Sandal and James 2010; Snyder 2011; Sheikh 2012; Haynes 2012; Fox and Sandal 2010; Fox and Sandal 2016; Adiong et al. 2018). There has likewise been increased focus on what has been perceived as a shift toward a "postsecular" IR (Thomas 2005; Habermas 2006; Barbato and Kratochwil 2009).

It is within this context that several scholars have begun turning toward Joseph Nye's notion of "soft power" in order to conceptualize how religion impacts international politics. Soft power refers to "the ability to get what you want through attraction rather than coercion or payments," and "arises from the attractiveness of a country's culture, political ideals, and policies" (Nye 2004). Such an approach is more designed to win "hearts and minds" via cooptation as opposed to coercing someone into submission. As Nye (2004) explains, competing soft powers are really competitions for "attractiveness, legitimacy, and credibility." Nye does not discuss religion at length in his analysis, noting only that "for centuries, organized religious movements have possessed soft power" (Nye 2004). Religious traditions certainly possess the ability to attract and legitimize through symbols, narratives, doctrines, and so forth. The use of religion by different actors as a form of soft power represents a more particularized form of Nye's original concept, which will be referred to here as religious soft power. Some of the first literature on religious soft power dealt specifically with transnational religious actors and the influence of these ideologies or movements across national borders (Haynes 2012). Other works have highlighted how if religious actors are able to "get the ear" of foreign policy decision makers, "the former may become able to influence foreign policy outcomes through the exercise of religious soft power" (Haynes 2008). In other words, certain religious groups or actors can seek to influence the foreign policy process by "encouraging policy makers to incorporate religious beliefs, norms, and values into foreign policy" (Haynes 2008).

By focusing so heavily on transnational religious movements/organizations or the ways in which religious actors influence foreign policy while remaining relatively autonomous actors, the early literature on religious soft power tended to neglect a central element of the broader phenomenon of religious soft power: the role of the state. As a result, more recent scholarship has sought to bring the state "back in" to discussions of religious soft power. This is because, as Kristin Diwan argues, states are "competing within a game of established players including both state and non-state actors," such as religious establishments, independent clerics, transnational religious movements, competitor states, and so forth (Diwan 2021). In the effort to recognize the critical importance of the state to discussions of religious soft power, Mandaville and Hamid (2018) turn to questions of how state actors seek to "harness the power of religious symbols and authority in the service of geopolitical objectives." Far from being passive actors, states can seek to harness the power of religion as a source of identification, a tool for legitimization or delegitimization, or a mechanism of mobilization or demobilization. They explain that "whether it is state support for transnational religious propagation, the promotion of religious interpretations that ensure regime survival, or competing visions of global religious leadership," these all embody what they term the "geopolitics of religious soft power" (Mandaville and Hamid 2018).

Religious Soft Power: The Concept and Its Limitations

This volume represents the first, globally comparative study of the varying ways in which states incorporate religion and religious outreach into their external relations. With the exception of one mostly theoretical chapter exploring the promise and limitations of "religious soft power" as a concept, the volume is organized around a dozen detailed country case studies spanning all major world regions. The author of each case study chapter demonstrates how the history, religious culture, and geopolitical orientation of their focus country determine its capacity for using religion as part of a soft power strategy while simultaneously dictating the nature and shape of its religious outreach activities, its intended audiences, and likelihood of success or impact.

Theoretically, this volume augments Joseph Nye's well-known concept of soft power, first elaborated in the early 1990s, by fleshing out a religious dimension previously absent or underdeveloped within existing treatments of soft power. The work presented in this volume also represents an effort to "displace" Nye's primary focus on soft power as means of explaining the persistent appeal of American ideals as a central aspect of US standing in the world. In contrast, the collective thrust of the proposed volume suggests that as we shift toward a "post-Western" world, some states are able to leverage other sources of soft power—and religion in particular—as a means of building and sustaining geopolitically valuable relationships with diverse publics around the world. We argue that paying attention to developments such as religious soft power is particularly significant during periods of time—such as we find ourselves in today—when world order is in flux. The dissolution and consolidation of new world orders are often accompanied by heightened salience of discussions and narratives about identity, values, and meaning. Religion is a major source of all of these and carries unique discursive power.

An Overview of the Volume

The diverse array of cases within this volume are designed to present a broad overview of how religious soft power is utilized by various actors across geographic, cultural, and religious contexts. Peter Mandaville and Jon Hoffman open the volume by . . . .

In Chapter 2, Peter S. Henne and Gregorio Bettiza consider the essential role religion has played in the United States and how it constitutes an important element in US foreign policy. Religious rhetoric and outreach has been utilized throughout American history to increase the attractiveness of its international initiatives and draw allies closer. Though religion has played a prominent role in American foreign policy, the precise nature of such usage has differed as the United States has confronted different challenges during different periods of its history. For example, during the Cold War, the United States used religious language to establish a grand narrative against "Godless Communism," whereas during the post-9/11 era, America has used religious soft power as part of its efforts to combat terrorism. Religious soft power has proved to be a powerful tool of American foreign policy, but it has also generated unpredictable and unintended consequences.

In Chapter 3, Robert Blitt details the Kremlin's embrace of the Russian Orthodox Church-Moscow Patriarchate (ROC-MP) as a lever of soft power, particularly following the significant Russian constitutional amendments ratified in July 2020, arguing that this state-church partnership is poised to grow much stronger and more entrenched moving forward. Blitt explains that the ROC-MP has been a crucial instrument used by Russian President Vladimir Putin in his campaign for a more multipolar international system, Moscow's compatriot policies, and the attempt to burnish Russia's "anti-West" traditional values. The readiness of the ROC-MP to justify Putin's foreign policy decisions highlights the Church's increasing proximity to the Kremlin, thereby challenging its veneer as an autonomous religious actor.

In Chapter 4, Yoshiko Ashiwa and David L. Wank examine how, particularly following the rise to power of Xi Jinping in 2013, the Chinese Communist Party (CCP) has sought to incorporate Buddhism into Beijing's broader great power aspirations. Presenting Buddhism as an essential element of traditional Chinese culture, China under Xi Jinping has sought to integrate religion with its broader economic and political interests. The authors argue that the current use of Buddhism by the People's Republic of China (PRC) is not only unprecedented in both scale and scope, but operates as a mechanism of both soft power designed to further the aims of the CCP's political aims domestically and internationally.

Next, Ahmet Erdi Öztürk investigates how Turkey has emerged as a force of religious soft power, especially following the ascension of the Turkish Justice and Development Party (*Adalet ve Kalkinma Partisi*, AKP). Arguing that religion in Turkey constitutes a component of both state identity and foreign policy, Öztürk examines Ankara's approach to the Balkans, the Middle East, and the world more generally, primarily via the Presidency of Religious Affairs (*Diyanet İşleri Başkanlığı*, Diyanet). The Diyanet has been central to Turkey's religious soft-power efforts, constructing mosques and building schools abroad while offering various forms of humanitarian, economic, and educational assistance. Turkey's use of religion in both its domestic and foreign policies has only increased in prominence amid the rapid shift toward populist authoritarianism under President Recep Tayyip Erdoğan and the power struggle between the AKP and the Gülen Movement.

Chapter 6 by Sumit Ganguly examines India's long tradition of the use of soft power in its diplomacy. Religion, however, was rarely drawn upon by India's early leaders such as Prime Minister Jawahal Nehru, who instead anchored his approach in a vision of Indian nationalism that was quintessentially secular, civic, and plural. This changed with the election of Prime Minister Narendra Modi in 2014, whose nativist Hindu nationalist party, the Bharatiya Janata Party (BJP), has moved in a distinctly ideological direction under Modi, deepening its commitment to a vision of militant Hindu nationalism. Unlike previous governments, Ganguly explains that the Modi administration has explicit religious underpinnings. What remains to be seen is whether Modi will be able to further capitalize on such a soft-power strategy considering India's sharp turn toward illiberalism and marginalization of religious minorities, namely Muslims.

In Chapter 7, Edward Wastnidge examines how Iran's government has sought to harness both universalistic and particularistic Shi'i claims to legitimacy in order to advance their domestic and foreign objectives. Iran's government post-1979 has relied heavily on coupling its foreign policy with religious narratives and symbols. The world's preeminent theocracy, the Islamic Republic of Iran contains a range of parastatal organizations that carry out its religious outreach and soft-power initiatives, using its position as a religious hub of Shi'ism as a vector to enhance its diplomacy. Wastnidge argues that religiously informed notions of justice are foundational in Iran's religious soft power and broader foreign policy conduct. Tehran's Shi'i identity has also been utilized to help provide justification for its strategic and military engagements throughout the region. However, Wastnidge explains that Iran's foreign policy should not be understood in purely ideological terms: it has a pragmatic intent at its core that is guided primarily by geopolitical realities.

The next chapter by Ann Wainscott explores Moroccan religious soft power and how the current endeavors of King Mohammed IV build upon the key initiatives begun by his father, Hassan II. Wainscott argues that contemporary Moroccan religious soft power builds upon the priorities first elaborated by Hassan II's religious policy initially primarily focused on domestic politics, but which came to influence foreign policy, namely Rabat's attempts to position itself as a patron of West African Islam and depict Morocco as a modern, moderate, and tolerant country. Despite there being only a few active initiatives during Hassan II's tenure, Wainscott explains that the long-term consistency with which the monarchy has continued these initiatives has allowed Rabat to establish itself as a center of religious soft power in West Africa and beyond.

In Chapter 9, Annelle Sheline dissects the increased securitization of Islam in the post-9/11 era and how governments in the Middle East—namely US security partners—have sought to capitalize on this image of Islam as a security threat and present themselves as offering the solution: so-called moderate Islam. By blaming violence on a misrepresentation of Islam and offering the solution for such violence as something only they can provide, these governments seek to present themselves to Western security partners as the answer to terrorism. This myth of "moderate Islam" has allowed these governments to demonize political opposition as forms of "extremism" and capitalize on Western fears of Islam, thereby advancing their domestic and foreign objectives. Sheline argues that the legacy of demonizing Islam as the primary causal factor in violent extremism has masked how other factors—such as systemic repression and corruption—have allowed for extremist messaging and actors to gain greater salience.

In Chapter 10, James B. Hoesterey examines the Indonesia's soft-power usage of "moderate Islam" and Jakarta's attempts to demonstrate how Islam and democracy can coexist. Hoesterey explains that the term "moderate Islam" itself is ambiguous and reflects wider geopolitical and historical forces, particularly in the post-9/11 era as Western governments anxious about Islamic extremism have sought partners they perceive as offering an alternative to such ideologies. Indonesia, whose diplomatic agenda has undergone an "Islamic turn" in recent decades, continues to jostle with longstanding domestic concerns about political Islam and theological fault lines between Indonesian traditionalists and Wahhabi detractors, both at home and abroad. Though Western governments have been eager to support and engage Indonesia's religious soft-power diplomacy, Hoesterey argues that it remains to be seen whether Jakarta will have similar success with co-religionists in the Middle East and North Africa.

Next, Stacey Gutkowski analyzes Jordan's strategic deployment of "moderation discourse" as part of Amman's broader nation-branding strategy. Arguing that religious soft power is best understood as a complex set of relationships between actors, Gutkowski explains that within Jordan there is a religious soft-power "ecosystem" operating within two linked but loose policy regimes: one about moderate Islam and the other about interfaith harmony. Such strategies are designed to present Jordan as a haven of Levantine religious coexistence and a reliable counterterrorism partner for the United States post-9/11.

In Chapter 12, Claudia Baumgart-Ochse investigates how Israel, despite its strong emphasis on hard power and matters of national security, employs religious soft power as a tool of foreign policy and an instrument used to shape others' preferences. These efforts have particularly focused on two distinct civil-society audiences within the United States: the US-American Jewish community and Evangelical Christians. Heavily reliant upon the United States for both diplomatic and military support, Israel regards these two communities as being highly influential in setting Washington's political agenda and shaping the preferences of incumbent US administrations. Designed to influence the preferences of these two influential civil societies communities and ultimately the policies of Washington, Israel's religious soft power has been a crucial tool that it has used to address its most pressing political and security concerns.

Next, Timothy Byrnes examines the soft power of the Catholic Papacy following the Church's loss of temporal power in the nineteenth century. In this modern era, Byrnes argues that Catholic Popes have exercised soft power in three closely related ways: to defend the institutional interests of the church; to advance their tradition's moral and social teachings; and to influence political and social processes and structures. Such soft-power initiatives have been exercised through two related channels of influence: direct application of Papal preferences, and indirect application via the broad membership of the global Church. Amid the Church's efforts to reckon with the extent of abusive behavior in its midst, such soft-power initiatives—combined with institutional reforms—have become a critical mechanism through which Pope Francis has sought to reestablish the credibility of the Papacy's moral voice.

Chapter 14 by Guilherme Casarões and Amy Erica Smith explains how Brazil has resorted to soft-power strategies largely because, unlike other emerging nations, São Paulo lacks considerable military capabilities or economic reach. As the world's largest Catholic country and home to the fifth largest Protestant population, presidents of Brazil have previously incorporated religious soft power within their broader policy strategies, but these occurrences have been rare. However, this has changed in recent decades, signified most notably by Jair Bolsonaro's embrace of religion as part of his foreign policy. Amid this significant transition, the authors contend that religion is being used to convey particular national identities or construct specific foreign policy narratives as a tool in their broader struggle for power vis-a-vis other international actors, and in domestic struggles for power between different religious groups.

Gregorio Bettiza and Peter S. Henne conclude the volume by contextualizing the contributions herein to the existing literature on religious soft power, namely bringing questions about power back to the center of the analysis of religion in world politics; broadening the existing research agenda on the entanglements between religion and states' foreign policy; and challenging prevailing secularist assumptions in international relations. These contributions are not without limitations, the authors acknowledge, explaining that there are certain shortcomings of the project, namely the more reductive approach to religion and certain limits surrounding the concept of soft power. The authors complete their conclusion by offering suggestions for future research that directly build on the valuable insights generated by this volume.

Comparing Religious Soft Power Across Global Contexts

The various cases addressed within this volume have several overlapping and connecting themes and patterns. At their core, the religious soft-power efforts of the actors addressed in this project are primarily concerned with framing religious discourse—both popular and scholarly—in a way that amplifies narratives favorable to these actors. Religious narratives, symbols, doctrines, and so forth are marshaled most often as a mechanism of legitimization for the domestic and foreign policies pursued by these different actors.

This can take the form of religious actors associated with the state or the state itself—using religion to outright justify specific policies advanced by the government, or efforts to construct a broader discursive environment whereby the actions of these states are viewed more positively. In many cases, the specific form(s) these religious soft-power efforts assume are often a reflection of the domestic realities within these states, namely competition over religious discourse and state authority. However, the religious soft-power efforts undertaken by these governments are not inflexible: different strategies can be appropriated according to context and the intended target audience(s).

A central element to the religious soft-power efforts of several states addressed within this volume is the building of various cultural, religious, political, and scholarly centers or organizations to influence knowledge production and amplify favorable discourses. These centers or organizations may exist within the host country, but they also often afiliate themselves with academic institutions abroad or other more general "cultural" initiatives, though the overbearing objective most often remains the dissemination of narratives conducive to the interests of these actors. Examples from this volume include China's efforts to establish many Confucius Institutes at universities around the world; various organizations operating on Israel's behalf within the United States to push favorable discourses and policies; Jordan's Royal Aal al-Bayt Institute of Islamic Thought, the Royal Islamic Strategic Studies Center, and the Jordan Interfaith Coexistence Research Center; and Turkey's Diyanet building mosques, schools, and other educational centers abroad.

Additionally, the religious soft-power initiatives pursued by the actors addressed in this volume are often designed to compete with alternative discourses and/or other centers of religious authority. It is critical to recognize that the religious soft-power efforts advanced by the different actors within this volume do not exist within a vacuum, but rather in direct relation—often competition—with initiatives advanced by other actors as well. China has sought to elevate itself as a center of Buddhist teaching and pilgrimage vis-a-vis India. Iran's government has competed with alternative centers of Shi'i authority in Iraq, alternative Shi'i conceptualizations of the relationship between religion and state, and Sunni Saudi Arabia for claims to religious legitimacy. Likewise, those governments championing so-called moderate Islam must compete with alternative religious narratives and claims to Islamic legitimacy, both mainstream and radical.

A central pillar of many of these religious soft-power efforts also includes the attempted courting of fellow co-religionists elsewhere in the world.

Russian religious soft power anchored in Orthodox Christianity has been central to the Kremlin's compatriot policies in its near abroad. Iran's government uses outreach to different Shi'i communities outside its borders in the hopes of finding those sympathetic to its guiding ideology and regional interests. The Vatican wields its Papal authority and much of its influence through Catholics around the world who comprise the global Church. Israel too views outreach to the American Jewish community as central to its religious soft-power efforts. However, the case of Israel also demonstrates how states can also court nonaffiliated demographics who likewise share their interests, namely American Evangelical Christians. Often these efforts to court co-religionists or other sympathetic demographics abroad incorporate religious tourism as a mechanism to further advance mutual ties. Religious tourism to Chinese Buddhist temples has been central to Beijing's religious soft-power efforts as people flock to pray to Buddha, Bodhisattvas, and other deities for health and fortune. Iran's city of Qom serves as a pilgrimage destination for many Shi'i Muslims, for it is home to some of the holiest shrines in Shi'ism and is a hub of Shi'i learning and scholarship. Likewise, Tel Aviv encourages Jews and Christian Evangelicals to pilgrimage to Israel.

Much of the religious soft-power initiatives considered in this volume also have to do with identity. Religion is often used by the actors discussed in this volume as a tool in their efforts to construct a cohesive national identity. Moscow has used religion as part of its strategy to present Russia as a strong civilization and upholder of "traditional values." Brazil has utilized religion as a mechanism to create a cohesive national identity via Catholicism and, more recently under Bolsonaro, a form of Christian nationalism. India under Modi has come to rely upon a nativist, militant Hindu nationalism. Iran's government uses a particularistic Shi'i claim of legitimacy and presents itself as the vanguard of revolutionary Islam and Shi'ism. Israel uses its identity as the holy land for Judaism and Christianity as part of its religious soft-power strategy and outreach to Jews and Evangelical Christians in the United States.

The Global Politics of Religious Soft Power: Looking Ahead

As the contributions to this volume demonstrate, emerging great powers such as China and persistent global players like Russia are incorporating new forms of cultural and religious outreach into their external relations as they seek to shape and influence settings around the world deemed to be strategically significant. In some cases we see new religious manifestations of classic soft-power projection such as, for example, China's efforts to emphasize its Buddhist heritage in countries along the route of the Belt and Road Initiative—Sri Lanka and Thailand, for example—with significant Buddhist populations. Similarly, in a show of pan-Islamic solidarity, Turkey has been building both transportation infrastructure and new mosques in parts of east Africa with significant Muslim populations. In Brazil, conservative groups linked to President Jair Bolsonaro have expanded their transnational ties with like-minded evangelical and Pentecostal groups in Portuguese-speaking African nations.

However, the mobilization and projection of religious or values-based identities can also have a distinct impact on peace and conflict dynamics, particularly in societies with underlying social or intercommunal tensions. In this regard, some of what we see today has started to resemble a religious variant of what Christopher Walker (2018) terms "sharp power." Sharp power—as distinct from either the positive allure of soft power or the use of military force often associated with hard power—refers to the use of information, communication, and technology tools to disseminate ideas and messages likely to sow discord and tension in target societies. Russian efforts to exacerbate political polarization and partisanship via social media platforms during recent US election cycles are but one example.

The results of these new religious sharp power dynamics have manifested across multiple regions, including Africa, the Middle East, South and South-Central Asia, and Southeast Asia. From the cross-regional politics of China's suppression of its Muslim populations in the name of "counter-terrorism," to the role of transnational Hindu supremacist networks organized out of India, today's emerging powers are developing new malignant forms of public diplomacy—often with religious inflections—that, going forward, will likely have major implications for global stability and social cohesion.

Furthermore, while this volume has focused primarily on single-country cases and the role of religion in their respective bilateral relations with other nations, it is worth taking note that religion is also emerging as an important dimension of shifting geopolitical alliance structures. In some cases, such as the 2020 Abraham Accords that normalized diplomatic relations between Israel, the United Emirates, and Bahrain, the religious references appear to mount to little more than rhetoric. In other cases, however, religion features more substantively in the generation of new forms of transnational political cooperation between groups and organizations with close ties to state or state-adjacent structures and political parties. For example, Russia has become a focal point for the transnational mobilization of "traditional values" and "family values," often involving a primary focus on anti-LGBTQ activism (Stoeckl 2014). Through this work, groups connected with the Russian Orthodox Church—often backed by the Kremlin—have succeeded in building ties with like-minded conservative evangelical groups in the United States and Latin America, as well as with organizations on the political right in the Middle East and India.

What emerges from this portrait is a sense that perhaps Samuel Huntington (1996) got something right with his infamous Clash of Civilizations thesis—geocultural fault lines do seem to be emerging as the basis of global conflicts—while at the same time being fundamentally mistaken in his most basic assumptions. It is not discrete and bounded Christian, Hindu, or Muslim civilizations that seem to be at odds with each other—indeed, adherents of those three religions seem very capable of working cooperatively across the borders of world regions. The relevant divisions appear to have more to do with liberal/progressive vs. conservative worldviews within different religion traditions which, in turn, often map very directly onto multiculturalist versus monoculturalist visions of society more broadly. As playing in the global "culture wars" begins to yield increasing geopolitical dividends for states, we should expect to see religious soft and sharp power become an even more prominent aspect of international relations.

References

Acharya, Amitav. 2018. *The End of American World Order*. Cambridge: Polity.
Adiong, Nassef Manabilang, et al. 2018. *Islam in International Relations: Politics and Paradigms*. New York: Routledge.
Barbato, Mariano, and Frederic Kratochwil. 2009. "Towards a Post-Secular Political Order?" *European Political Science Review* 1 (3): 317–340.
Berger, Maurits. 2010. *Religion and Islam in Contemporary International Relations*. Clingendael: Netherlands Institute of International Relations.
Diwan, Kristin. 2021. "Clerical Associations in Qatar and the United Arab Emirates: Soft Power Competition in Islamic Politics." *International Affairs* 97 (4): 945–963.

Fischer, Markus. 2006. "Culture and Foreign Politics." In *The Limits of Culture Islam and Foreign Policy*, edited by Brenda Shaffer, 27–64. Cambridge, MA: MIT Press

Fox, Jonathan, and Shmuel Sandler. 2004. *Bringing Religion into International Relations*. New York: Palgrave.

Fox, Jonathan, and Nukhet Sandal. 2010. "Toward Integrating Religion into International Relations Theory." *Zeitschrift für internationale Beziehungen* 17 (1): 149–159.

Fox, Jonathan, and Nukhet Sandal. 2016. "Integrating Religion into International Affairs." In *Routledge Handbook of Religion and Politics*, edited by Jeffrey Haynes, 270–283. New York: Routledge.

Habermas, Jürgen. 2006. "Religion in the Public Sphere." *European Journal of Philosophy* 14 (1): 1–25.

Haynes, Jeffrey. 2008. "Religion and Foreign Policy Making in the USA, India, and Iran: Towards a Research Agenda." *Third World Quarterly* 29 (1): 143–165.

Haynes, Jeffrey. 2012. *Religious Transnational Actors and Soft Power*. New York: Routledge.

Haynes, Jeffrey. 2021. "Religion and International Relations: What Do We Know and How Do We Know It?" *Religions* 12 (328): 1–14.

Houghton, David. 2007. "Reinvigorating the Study of Foreign Policy Decision Making: Toward a Constructivist Approach." *Foreign Policy Analysis* 3 (1): 24–45.

Huntington, Samuel. 1996. *The Clash of Civilizations and the Remaking of World Order*. New York: Simon and Schuster.

Indoben, William C. 2008. *Religion and American Foreign Policy, 1945–1960*. Cambridge: Cambridge University Press.

Mandaville, Peter, and Shadi Hamid. 2018. "Islam as Statecraft: How Governments Use Religion in Foreign Policy." In *The New Geopolitics: Middle East*. Washington, DC: The Brookings Institution. https://www.brookings.edu/research/islam-as-statecraft-how-governments-use-religion-in-foreign-policy/.

McDougall, Walter. 1998. *Promised Land, Crusader State: The American Encounter with the World since 1776*. New York: Mariner Books.

Nye, Joseph. 2004. *Soft Power: The Means to Success in World Politics*. Cambridge: Public Affairs.

Porter, Andrew. 2004. *Religion Versus Empire? British Protestant Missionaries and Overseas Expansion, 1700–1914*. Manchester: Manchester University Press.

Ruggie, John. 1998. *Constructing the World Polity: Essays on International Institutionalization*. New York: Routledge.

Sandal, Nukhet. 2016. "Religion and Foreign Policy." In *Routledge Handbook of Religion and Politics*, edited by Jeffrey Haynes, 284–298. New York: Routledge.

Sandal, Nukhet, and Patrick James. 2010. "Religion and International Relations Theory: Towards a Mutual Understanding." *European Journal of International Relations* 17 (1): 3–25.

Shah, Thomas, and Daniel Philpott. 2011. "The Rise and Fall of Religion in International Relations: History and Theory." In *Religion and International Relations Theory*, edited by Jack Snyder, 24–59. New York: Columbia University Press.

Sheikh, Mona Kanwal. 2012. "How Does Religion Matter? Pathways to Religion in International Relations." *Review of International Studies* 38 (1): 365–392.

Snyder, Jack. 2011. *Religion and International Relations*. New York: Columbia University Press.

Stoeckl, Kristina. 2014. *The Russian Orthodox Church and Human Rights*. London: Routledge.
Thomas, Scott. 2005. *The Global Resurgence of Religion and the Transformation of International Relations*. New York: Palgrave Macmillan.
Walker, Christopher. 2018. "What Is 'Sharp Power'?" *Journal of Democracy* 29 (3): 9–23.
Wendt, Alexander. 1999. *Social Theory of International Politics*. Cambridge: Cambridge University Press.

2
Tragedy or Irony
Geopolitical Grand Narratives, Religious Outreach, and US Soft Power

Peter S. Henne and Gregorio Bettiza

In 1947, Myron Taylor, the United States' envoy to the Vatican and an ally of President Truman, met with several European religious leaders. In that meeting, Taylor called on "people of all faiths" to "unite upon a universal two-point declaration embodying the spirit of belief in God and belief in human liberty" (Inboden 2008, 124). The political significance of this statement is clear from the context: Taylor held this meeting to gain European support for the emerging struggle between the United States and the Soviet Union. While much of Truman's early Cold War policies involved military and economic might, he also hoped to build up the America's "soft power" by appealing to common religious values and identities among allies.

The role of religion in Truman's diplomacy should not be a surprise to anyone who studies (or engages in) US politics. As observers since Alexis de Tocqueville have noted, religion is an essential element of America. It infuses debates, and influences political struggles, and therefore it ends up also becoming an important element of US foreign policy. The idea of Manifest Destiny, which guided the country's early expansion, included a belief in the providential backing of the new United States of America. Religious rhetoric and imagery popped up repeatedly throughout the Cold War while continuing to influence US priorities in the twenty-first century, from debt relief to religious freedom promotion.

Few, then, would take issue with the claim that religion influences American politics, both domestic and international. But can religion actually be a tool for policymakers? That is, can US leaders draw on faith to advance US interests? If so, is it an effective tool? In this chapter, we argue that the United States has used religion as a form of "religious soft power" in its foreign policy. Building off Nye's (1990) formulation as a state getting others to "want what we want," Mandaville and Hamid (2018) discussed religious soft power as the way states "incorporate the promotion of religion into their broader foreign policy conduct" by "[harnessing] the power of religious symbols and authority in the service of geopolitical objectives." They focused on the Saudi and Iranian examples, but we argue that such religious soft power is also a potential tool for America.

The United States has tried to use religious outreach to increase the attractiveness of its international initiatives, drawing allies closer. This occurred in the early Cold War, when America pointed to shared religious faith to convince Western European societies to join its side in the struggle with the Soviets. America also pointed to common religiosity to build up pro-American voices in non-European countries. After the Cold War, America appealed to religion to gain allies in the struggle against terrorism, both broad religious engagement under Obama and Bush and more explicit civilizational divides under Trump.

These efforts worked, albeit with some complicated side effects. The pro-American factions America established held off Communist influence in crucial countries as the Cold War began. Post-9/11 religious engagement, especially under Obama, increased US standing in the world. However, some of America's Cold War allies established through religious soft power turned out to be unreliable, complicating America's situation in states such as Vietnam. Additionally, the generally inclusive religious language of the Bush and Obama administrations gave way to more antagonistic civilizational divides under Trump, increasing international skepticism of America's intentions.

Despite these mixed results, one cannot argue that religious soft power is irrelevant. States did respond to US religious appeals in ways that tangibly affected their foreign policy. Moreover, the fact that some uses of religious soft power backfired further indicates the potency of religious sources of influence. Its unpredictability is the result of the power of religious beliefs and identities in international relations and demonstrates the importance of attempts to understand how and when states use religious soft power.

This chapter will present evidence of religious soft power's impact in US foreign policy in two time periods. The first is the early Cold War, when the United States was trying to establish its international leadership and form a global coalition against the Soviet Union. We also include brief examples from later in the Cold War to highlight the persistence of such religious elements. The second is the post–Cold War era, in which the United States is struggling against violent Islamist nonstate actors—like al-Qaeda and

Daesh/ISIS—while also trying to define the nature of the international order. There are major differences between these periods, such as the specificity of US initiatives, but both indicate the presence and impact of religious soft power in its foreign policy.

Religious Grand Narratives and Soft Power in the Cold War

Religion played an important, if often underappreciated, role in the US struggle against Communism during the early Cold War. With the end of World War II, the Soviet Union emerged as a threat to US interests. Under Presidents Truman and Eisenhower, the United States tried to hold off Soviet expansion and form an international anti-Communist coalition. As Inboden discusses in his study on faith in the Cold War, religion "functioned" as both a "cause and as an instrument" in the US-Soviet struggle (Inboden 2008, 2). Some of this had to do with the grand narratives through which US leaders justified the conflict and tried to convince other states to side with the United States. It also took the form of specific programs through which the United States drew on religion to strengthen friendly voices in other societies and bind their states to its Cold War effort. While these efforts tended not to be institutionalized—but were rather integrated into various other elements of US statecraft—they had significant impacts on America's attempt to combat Soviet influence.

In this section we begin by discussing the religious grand narratives which shaped Cold War thinking. We then discuss some of the United States' efforts to use religion and craft an anti-Communist alliance first in the context of European Christians. We then explore similar strategies adopted by the United States in non-European contexts, especially with Islamic and Muslim-majority states, Muslim non-state actors, and non-Western Christians.

Grand Narratives in the Cold War

Religious soft power is apparent in the grand narrative underlying US involvement in the Cold War. US Presidents, members of Congress, policy intellectuals, and religious leaders framed the Cold War as a struggle between the forces of freedom and those of totalitarianism. This grand narrative was partly based on religious beliefs of US leaders like Truman. According to

Inboden (2008, 1), Truman saw the Cold War as "nothing less than a religious war." While giving a speech to the Federal Council of Churches in 1946, Truman claimed the "fundamental conflict in the world was between those nations who believed in God and morality, and those who did not" (Inboden 2008, 107). Yet, framing the Cold War as a struggle between faith and atheism was also a way to expand US soft power, convincing the rest of the world that the US cause was just and that they should join its side. According to Kirby (2008, 358–359), Truman "deliberately exaggerated" the Soviet threat "and fashioned a particular brand of anti-Communism, heavily imbued with Christian rhetoric, in order to ease The United States' transition" into international dominance. Similarly, according to Preston, Truman believed religion was "the missing element in US foreign policy and potentially its secret weapon" (Preston 2012, 412). The president also framed US policies in religious terms. For example, when promoting the Marshall Plan—intended to rebuild Europe and hold off Soviet inroads—Truman used religious language. In one speech, he pronounced "through labor and industry, with the blessing of God, these sorely stricken nations shall again become masters of their own destiny" (Inboden 2008, 112). He would also call out Communist repression of religious communities as a way to highlight the threat the Soviets posed (Preston 2012, 432–433).

Such practices persisted past Truman, with several US Presidents referencing faith in their foreign policy rhetoric. Eisenhower drew explicitly on faith to justify the United States' efforts and even existence. In 1956, Eisenhower added "under God" to the pledge of allegiance to the US flag, and shortly thereafter adopted "In God we trust" as the United States' official motto (Canipe 2003). We can find similar examples later in the Cold War. Jimmy Carter drew on his faith when formulating his foreign policy, including his peace efforts in the Middle East and his push for human rights (Smith 2011). He also initiated a public diplomacy campaign to improve Muslim attitudes toward the United States (Guerrero 2017). Likewise Reagan explicitly drew on Christian scripture in his "shining city on a hill" speech (Davis and Lynn-Jones 1987).

US Religious Outreach to Europe and Its Impacts

But religious soft power in the Cold War involved more than just rhetoric. There were specific policies the United States enacted that drew on religion in order to gain an edge in the struggle with the Soviet Union. One important policy was outreach to religious leaders and institutions, intended to convince religious communities to back US Cold War efforts.

The most prominent such effort was Truman's outreach to the Vatican.[1] In the aftermath of World War II the United States did not have formal diplomatic relations with the Vatican, but Truman hoped the Pope could be a powerful ally against Communism. In a 1948 letter to the Pope, Truman described the Cold War in spiritual terms. He expressed hope for a return of peace despite the tensions with the Soviet Union, writing that "we shall strive" to "fulfill the prophecy of unity of world peoples under God" (Inboden 2008, 111). Truman also appointed the aforementioned Myron Taylor as an emissary to the Vatican, moving closer to formal diplomatic ties.

Truman also wanted to create an ecumenical alliance, uniting Catholic and Protestant Churches against Communism. Taylor met with the Archbishop of Canterbury, the Lutheran Bishop of Berlin, and the Catholic Bishop of London in an attempt to convince them of the dire threat posed by the Soviets. He also worked specifically with the Lutheran Bishop of Berlin to help spread anti-Communist messages among his religious community (Inboden 2008, 124–125).

There were other examples of religious outreach. The Patriarch of the Greek Orthodox Church died in 1949, setting off a succession struggle. The United States urged the church to appoint a candidate known for his anti-Communist sympathies, in order to broaden their religious coalition; Taylor also met with the Orthodox Patriarch of Istanbul, who "endorsed" Truman's Cold War efforts (Inboden 2008, 140–142). Additionally, to hold off Communist political gains in Italy and Germany the United States supported these countries' conservative Christian Democrat parties (Preston 2012, 434–435). For example, in the 1948 Italian elections, the Christian Democratic candidate financed his electoral campaign through the sale of US army surplus with the help of the Vatican (Pollard 2003).

The United States also drew on religion in its propaganda efforts. During the Cold War, the United States devoted significant resources to broadcasting positive images of the United States and its policies to the world. This was meant to increase the attractiveness of the United States, and decrease the Soviets' by contrast. Examples include the public diplomacy efforts of the US Information Agency (USIA), and Radio Free Europe, which broadcast to Soviet-controlled countries. Under President Eisenhower, religion was an important part of these efforts. The USIA director believed that religion was "the strongest bond between freedom-loving peoples on both sides of the Iron Curtain" and thus expanded time for religious programming (Inboden 2008, 302). Similarly, Radio Free Europe would broadcast Lutheran and Catholic religious programs into Communist-held societies. Spreading religious messages through its propaganda services gave the United States an opportunity to increase support among religious communities in Europe, undermining the Soviet appeal. Likewise, the United States' Food for Peace program used religious organizations and missionaries to distribute US food surplus abroad (Preston 2012, 431).

Another way the United States drew on religious soft power was its support for religious activities. American missionaries spread throughout the world after World War II, trying to convert non-Christian societies or—in the case of Europe—encourage them to sustain their Christian heritage. While these occurred independently of the US government, US officials at times supported these trips and helped them gain access to high-level officials. For example, famous evangelist Billy Graham—known as "God's machine gun"—often incorporated anti-Communist messages into his sermons when preaching in Europe (Gradert and Strasburg 2018). He also had close ties to the Eisenhower Administration. Secretary of State Dulles saw Graham's trips to Europe as an opportunity to strengthen American alliances; as he said of one trip to England, "the most basic ties that bind our two nations together are religious ties" (Inboden 2008, 244). That is, US officials hoped that religious figures' trips to Europe would promote closer ties between Western European societies and the United States, and clarify the threat Communism posed to their faith.

The United States was clearly attempting to build its religious soft power through such outreach to European audiences. The next question, then, is did this work? The United States did seem to establish some goodwill through its religious outreach. Anecdotal evidence suggests worried Europeans saw the United States as a defender against the threat of Communism, and the United States' anti-Communist efforts resonated most strongly among religious communities. As Kirby (2008, 365) noted, the United States' religiously focused anti-Communism messaging succeeded in establishing "a powerful ideological basis of agreement" with conservative forces in Europe that helped to "legitimize the Cold War." Also, some specific US initiatives seemed to work. The biggest success was the outreach to the Vatican. In July of 1949, the Vatican announced it would welcome an alliance with Protestants to fight back against Communism, and would even excommunicate Communists.

Given the then intense distrust between Protestant and Catholic institutions, Truman's ability to bring them together on anti-Communist efforts represents a significant achievement (Inboden 2008, 141–142). Furthermore US-backed Vatican support for Italy's Christian Democrats helped that party expand their appeal and prevent Communists from gaining power in the aftermath of World War II (Pollard 2003).

Thus, US religious outreach likely contributed to the containment of Communism in Western Europe, ensuring the United States had a robust alliance through which to combat the Soviet Union. Furthermore, by strengthening conservative political forces, US religious soft power helped align Western European states with US interests. But it is not clear whether these efforts had a broader effect on these societies, changing overall perceptions of the United States. Not all segments of European society welcomed US religious outreach or anti-Communist messages. Some saw it as meddling or threatening overtures, resulting in a rise in anti-American feelings (Isernia 2007). Additionally, many specific instances of religious outreach failed. While the Vatican was receptive to a religious coalition against Communism, many Protestant churches were hesitant to work with the Vatican (Inboden 2008, 147–155). The pro-US Orthodox Patriarch of Athens attempted to establish ties with the Russian Orthodox Church and convince it to openly criticize the Soviet Union but failed (Inboden 2008, 141–142).

Additionally, there is some evidence that the United States' religious outreach complicated efforts to craft an anti-Soviet alliance. Some have argued the US Manichean view of the Cold War—as a struggle between faith and godless Communism—led the United States to exaggerate the Soviet threat and take steps against leftist movements that were more aggressive than needed (Alexander 2002; Lebow and Stein 1994; Iber 2017). That is, America's reliance on religion increased the stakes of the Cold War, making it difficult for the United States and Soviet Union to coexist.

Beyond that, there are also signs that the power of religious belief itself undermined US anti-Communist efforts. While Truman managed to establish ties with both Catholic and Protestant leaders in Europe, he struggled to form an ecumenical anti-Communist alliance. As Inboden (2008, 156) argues, "the very potency of religion" was the cause, as "Christian elders' dedication to their own theological convictions finally precluded meaningful cooperation" (also Preston 2012, 413). The United States' religious language also opened it up to charges of hypocrisy. For example, Anglican Bishop George Bell worked with the United States on anti-Communist efforts—he called the Korean War as a "war of faiths"—but also criticized the United States for ignoring poverty and injustice even as they fought the Soviet Union (Kirby 2008, 366). Thus, religious figures could be powerful allies, but their convictions often led them to train their fire on any state deemed immoral.

Cold War Religious Outreach to Non-Western States

American religious outreach efforts were not confined to Western Europe or Christian societies. The United States tried to build up its religious soft power through outreach to states in the Middle East, East Asia, and Southeast Asia. As with European outreach, some of this involved a general recognition of the importance of religion to non-Western societies, and its potential utility in convincing them to side with the United States in the Cold War. Abbott Washburn, a propaganda expert in the Eisenhower Administration, wanted Eisenhower to meet with Muslim leaders; he argued that, "in view of the President's deep convictions regarding the spiritual foundations of our democracy... the hoped for results would be that the Muslims will be impressed with the moral and spiritual strength of America" and resist Communist overtures (Inboden 2008, 290). Eisenhower also recognized the value of religious statecraft when working with non-Western states; he urged the United States to "stress the holy wary aspect of the Cold War" when working with Middle East leaders, and argued the United States "must use a religious appeal to trump Communism's ideological appeal" (Inboden 2008, 294).

The United States also directed religious propaganda efforts toward non-Western societies, and enlisted American religious figures in these efforts. It did so in the Middle East, using a "religious approach to appeal to Arab interest" (Inboden 2008, 295). This extended beyond the Middle East, as the United States broadcast Quran readings on the Voice of America, events from the Washington Islamic Center, and a series on the negative state of Islam under Communism (Inboden 2008, 306). Similarly, just as the United States coordinated with Billy Graham's outreach to Europe, Eisenhower enlisted his pastor—Edward Elson—to conduct informal diplomacy with Jordan and Saudi Arabia while on a Middle East trip (Inboden 2008, 295).

There were also efforts to build up religious soft power with Muslim countries. One was Saudi Arabia, an increasingly important US ally since the establishment of their alliance during World War II. The Eisenhower Administration hoped the Saudis could undermine Communist influence in the region, and tried to establish then-King Saud as an "Islamic Pope" to help enable this outcome (Bronson 2006). As Doran (2016, 164) noted, Eisenhower "suggested to the State Department" that the United States "begin to build up some other individual as a prospective leader of the Arab world," pointing specifically to Saud.

While Islamists were not an important political force in the 1950s, US policymakers did try to work with them and combat the Soviet Union later on in the Cold War. For example, the United States rejuvenated its ties with Pakistan during the reign of military leader Zia ul-Haq. Zia Islamized the country's military and supported the spread of conservative Islamic education. He was also strongly anti-Communist. In response, the United States provided significant military and economic aid to Pakistan, part of a broader effort to "unite a billion Muslims worldwide" to fight the Soviet Union (Ahmad 2012, 276). This took a tangible form when the United States worked with Pakistan and Saudi Arabia to support domestic and foreign Muslim fighters—the *Mujahidin*—in Afghanistan resisting the Soviet invasion.

Another was South Korea, where the United States turned to American missionaries and Korean Christians to gain support for resisting Communist inroads. As Yin and Haga (2012) discuss, there was initial distrust of the US occupation in South Korea after World War II, led by then dominant leftist movements. As the United States increased its power in order to hold off Communist incursions, US policymakers relied on conservative Christians in Korea to govern the country and ensure it remained pro-American. This was enabled by the influx of US missionaries into South Korea after World War II. They helped care for refugees and set up a chaplain core for the South Korea army.

A similar case was Vietnam, where religious forces were being supported in an effort to oppose Communist elements. Charles Lowery, an Eisenhower ally started the Foundation for Religious Action in the Social and Civil Order (FRASCO). This organization wanted to promote spiritual renewal within American society, but Eisenhower also enlisted it to conduct religious outreach abroad. Lowery discussed ways to "use the religious factor to intensify local anti-Communism" in Vietnam, and the Administration discussed using FRASCO to send Catholic priests to Vietnam and work with anti-Communist forces (Inboden 2008, 280–281). The goal was to use religious outreach to increase the strength of pro-US Christian figures in Vietnam, and thus increase US soft power. This seemed to work with the rise of Ngo Dinh Diem. Diem, a Catholic, had a pro-US outlook partly due to ties between his regime and US Catholic organizations (Chapman 2012).

As with religious outreach to Western Europe, US religious soft power had mixed results. There were some success, as in South Korea where Christian outreach established deep ties between that country and the United States, increasing the appeal of the United States in South Korea. These ties helped secure South Korean support for a US military presence, and Christian groups played a key role in this relationship (Yin and Haga 2012, 96). For example, while Members of Congress were debating a bill to continue military aid to South Korea, South Korean churches organized public demonstrations in which people shouted, "we Christians will defend our native land from Communist attack" (Yin and Haga 2012).

Yet, the impacts of American religious soft power was limited in cases, and at times even complicated US interests. This was most apparent in US outreach to Muslims. King Saud of Saudi Arabia never became the much-hoped-for "Islamic Pope." He ended up an ineffective leader who struggled to compete for regional popularity against the popular nationalist Nasser of Egypt, and was ultimately overthrown by his brother Faisal. Eisenhower's emphasis on religious outreach likely led his Administration to exaggerate King Saud's potential effectiveness as an alternative to the region's leftists, giving the Soviet Union greater opportunity to establish an ideological presence in the region. Moreover, while US work with Pakistan did lead to a Soviet defeat in Afghanistan, the support for Islamist fighters led to later threats, such as the rise of the Taliban and al-Qaeda (Coll 2004).

This was also apparent in America's east and southeast Asian efforts. In Vietnam, Diem was pro-American, but struggled to win over the Vietnamese people and his support ended up complicating anti-Soviet efforts. Part of this had to do with Diem's open Catholicism, which many saw as contrary to Vietnamese tradition (Chapman 2012). Diem was especially unpopular given his murderous repressive policies, which further fueled anti-Americanism in Vietnam. Ultimately he alienated much of the population and helped provide a Buddhist opposition movement in the early 1960s (Chapman 2012). The ties between South Korean and American Christians complicated US policy there too. After the Korean War, the United States faced opposition to truce talks from Christian communities upset that the conditions included restrictions on North Korean prisoners of war's right to stay in South Korea after the war (Chapman 2012, 102). Thus, US religious outreach, in a convoluted way, complicated US interests in South Korea by increasing reciprocal identification between Korean and American Christians.

Religious Grand Narratives and Soft Power in the War on Terror

With the end of the Cold War and its Soviet threat, there was considerable uncertainty among American international affairs observers and foreign policymakers about the nature of the international order to come. Scholars like Francis Fukuyama (1992) framed this new era in terms of the "end of history," in which liberalism—in its democratic and capitalist forms—was the last remaining viable ideology. It was at this moment that Joseph Nye (1990) coined the term "soft power," in order to make sense of the attractive power of American culture and liberal values. These ideas were attempts to characterize the post–Cold War order and establish a place for US leadership in it. The Clinton administration's stress on "democratic enlargement" and its active promotion of free trade and globalization were very much informed by such thinking.

Yet, in parallel, American security concerns became increasingly tied to a range of disparate international dynamics seemingly related to what many have called the "global resurgence of religion" (Hatzopoulos and Petito 2003; Thomas 2005; Toft, Philpott, and Shah 2011). On the one hand, these included civil wars and failing states torn apart by conflicts appearing to pit warring parties along sectarian and religious lines, which the collapse of the former-Yugoslavia epitomized in the eyes of many. On the other hand, this extended to religious fundamentalism and mounting violent attacks directed toward American targets by Islamist actors, most dramatically in the case of the September 11, 2001 (9/11), attacks by Al-Qaeda. In such a context, a separate discourse about world order would emerge among US international affairs experts. This was the idea that world politics would come to be defined by wars driven by religious and cultural differences, most notoriously and (in)famously captured by Samuel Huntington's notion of the "clash of civilizations" (Huntington 1996, 1993; Kaplan 2000; Lewis 1990).

In a post–Cold War international context perceived to be marked by rising sectarian conflicts and religious terrorism, the United States' appeal to religiously infused narratives and outreach as a soft power tool did not go away, but shifted form in two important ways. First, US religious outreach would no longer be informed by ideas of a struggle between faith and godless Communism, but rather it would come to be shaped in complex ways by narratives of civilizational struggles and engagements (Bettiza 2014; also Bettiza 2015).

Such narratives took three broad forms. One form represented the United States as the defender and promoter of "civilization," and with it of religious freedom and liberal modernity, against the forces of barbarism, extremism, and violence represented by Islamists—this discourse defined much of America's religious statecraft during the George W. Bush administration. A second form represented the United States as a partner of religious communities in general and "Muslim" ones in particular, seeking engagement and dialogue rather than civilizational conflict and clash. This discourses defined much of the Obama administration's approach. The third, and final, civilizational grand narrative represented the United States as the leader and defender of the "Judeo-Christian West" under assault by "Islam" and "Islamic fundamentalism"—a discourse that defined much of the rhetoric and approach of the Trump administration.

Second, along with a shift in grand narratives, in order to cultivate further religious soft power, there would be a push in the aftermath of the Cold War to operationalize different forms of religious statecraft in more structured and institutionalized ways within the American foreign policy architecture. New offices and policies, constituting a series of distinct *religious foreign policy regimes* (Bettiza 2019), emerged around four major areas: (1) monitoring religious freedom and promoting it globally, (2) delivering humanitarian and development aid abroad by drawing on faith-based organizations, (3) fighting global terrorism by seeking to reform Muslim societies and Islamic theologies, and (4) advancing American national security interests and values worldwide by engaging with religious actors and dynamics. Each of these policy frameworks were themselves shaped by wider grand narratives about civilizational conflicts or dialogues, as we shall see in the following three subsections.

The Bush Administration: Securing and Advancing "Civilization"

The 9/11 attacks and the subsequent War on Terror launched by the Bush administration led religion to become, once again following the Cold War, embroiled in larger geopolitical grand narratives. The Bush administration, heavily influenced by ideas developed within Neoconservative intellectual circles (Lynch 2008), largely framed the conflict in terms of a struggle between liberty and civilization against Islamist barbarism and obscurantism

(Salter 2002). Through such a narrative the United States hoped to attract states to its side and buttress its military and economic might with soft power. "Islamofascism" (Podhoretz 2007), a Neoconservative term that Bush himself came to adopt at one point (*BBC* 2006), was prevalently going to be defeated by promoting freedom and democracy—even militarily if necessary—across the Muslim world. The wars in Afghanistan and thereafter Iraq were presented as the epitome of this strategy.

The "Muslim world" itself was framed in the administration's 2002 National Security Strategy (USG 2002, 31) to be in the midst of a "struggle of ideas" and a "clash inside a civilization" between good/moderate and bad/extremist Muslims. A range of policies were devised intended to support the former, seen as an antidote against the latter (Henne 2017). The promotion of religious freedom, a norm that had been institutionalized in American foreign policy following the passage of the International Religious Freedom Act by Congress in 1998, was increasingly reframed not just as a human right's issue, but as an integral part of Bush's freedom strategy in the War on Terror (USG 2006; see also Bettiza 2019, 74).

Bush's religious rhetoric and statecraft in the context of the War on Terror often backfired, undermining US soft power. The war in Iraq generated greater insecurities, leading to further conflict and terrorism in the Middle East. It also dramatically weakened US standing in the world. Public opinion worldwide turned sharply against the United States, with levels of anti-Americanism in places like Europe and across the Muslim-majority world reaching some of the highest levels ever recorded (Fabbrini 2004; Pew 2006). The Bush administration's divisive and inflammatory language, along with US interventionism and attempts to place practices in the War on Terror outside international law—such as proposing the idea of "preemptive war" in Iraq, or detaining "unlawful combatants" in Guantanamo and subjecting them to "enhanced interrogation"—appeared to many as being driven by a clash-of-civilizations mindset (*The New York Times* 2009).

To little avail were public diplomacy efforts implemented to reassure and build support among Muslims around the world. Whether PR campaigns—led by advertising executive Charlotte Beers first and longtime Bush communication advisor Karen Hughes thereafter—seeking to promote a favorable image of the United States to Muslim audiences around the world; symbolic gestures by President Bush—most notoriously in the case of his visit to an Islamic center in Washington, DC, on September 17, 2001—suggesting that the War on Terror was *not* a war against Islam; or the appointment of America's first-ever Special Envoy to the Organization of Islamic Cooperation (OIC).

Ironically for a Republican presidency, given that conservatives historically have not been major supporters of development and humanitarian aid, the Bush administration was able to cultivate substantial soft power for the United States through its faith-based initiatives instead. Inspired by compassionate conservative ideas, and prompted by his Evangelical voting base, President Bush launched in the early years of his presidency the Faith-Based and Community Initiative (Bettiza 2019, Ch.4). The initiative's intent was, among other things, to give greater opportunities to religious organizations—rather than just secular NGOs—to access US government resources for the delivery of international aid (White House 2001). Partnerships between the federal government and faith-based organizations (FBOs) received a further boost with a multibillion President's Emergency Plan for AIDS Relief (PEPFAR) in 2004.

These activities have certainly been at the center of multiple controversies. For example, they have been critiqued for undermining church-state separation norms or approaching public-health issues through (conservative) theological lenses on issues of family planning and contraception (Evertz 2010; OIG 2009). Nonetheless they would also be generally well-received producing considerable amount of good will and soft power for the United States, especially in Africa where President Bush's popularity continues to be extremely high to this day (Pilling 2019).

The Obama Administration: Engaging Religion and Muslims

Under Barack Obama, the United States took a different approach to religious soft power. First of all, the Obama administration moved away from some of the most controversial aspects of the War on Terror, including forcefully promoting "freedom" around the world. A greater effort was placed on diplomatic engagement, especially with the Muslim world. Religious and civilizational categories still permeated US foreign policy thinking and rhetoric, but this had shifted to a more dialogical approach (Bettiza 2015, 593–599). The gesture that crystallized this shift in thinking as well as in policy practices was President Obama's (2009) Cairo speech, "A New Beginning," addressed to Muslims around the world. Along with reappointing a Special

Envoy to the OIC, the administration created the novel position of Special Representative to Muslim Communities. Bush's highly ideological and inflammatory "war of ideas" was to be replaced by more targeted interventions to counter violent extremism (CVE) and support moderate Islamic actors and voices.

The concept of engagement permeated various aspects of American religious statecraft. Religious freedom issues were partly delinked from democracy promotion activities and tied to notions of tolerance, pluralism, and minority rights against the sectarianism and exclusivism promoted by fundamentalists (Birdsall 2012). The idea of generating soft power for the United States through faith-based development and humanitarian activities led to a continuation of many of the policies that had been in place since the Bush administration (White House 2010). Quite significantly, US outreach to religious actors was further expanded when a novel Office of Religion and Global Affairs (RGA), along with a specific *US Strategy on Religious Leader and Faith Community Engagement*, were launched in 2013.

President Obama's more dialogical approach considerably helped restore America's soft power after Bush. US standing in Muslim-majority states and around the world was partly restored in the aftermath of the Cairo speech as fears of potential civilizational clashes were being addressed and quelled. However, much of the good will that was generated initially among Muslim communities soon started to fizzle away. That's because when the time came to move from rhetoric to action, much of the Obama administration's Muslim engagement activities focused on a series of second-order educational, scientific, and economic programs. More politically and emotionally charged issues of primary concern to Muslims, such as resolving the Israeli-Palestinian conflict or closing Guantanamo, instead never really came to fruition (POMED 2010; also Lilli).

In parallel, the Obama administration did create an important infrastructure that developed a greater and more nuanced appreciation of the role of religious dynamics and actors in world politics, especially in the context of its CVE and the religious engagement/RGA activities. Yet, as many have observed, these policy frameworks were often in need of greater coordination and funding to be effective (Mandaville 2017; Miller and Higham 2015; Zaharna 2009). As a result, while potentially generating some circumscribed policy successes, their overall contribution to American soft power remains unclear, at best, or negligent, at worst.

The Trump Administration: An Explicit Turn to the "Clash of Civilizations"

Donald Trump took a paradoxical approach to religious statecraft and soft power. On the one hand, his administration appeared to adopt at the start a style similar to that of the Obama administration focused on engagement. This was most notable in the case of Trump's first presidential trip abroad where his stops in Saudi Arabia, Israel, and Rome were couched as a message of peace and symbolic pilgrimage to the epicenters of the world's three Abrahamic faiths (CFR 2018).

On the other hand, the Trump administration adopted a brazenly explicit clash-of-civilizations grand narrative (Hirsh 2016), one which most previous administrations were careful to distance themselves—albeit not always successfully—from. Such an outlook has come to shape much of the Trump administration's rhetoric and policies. Abandoning the more neutral language of CVE, President Trump and his advisers repeatedly singled out terrorism as a uniquely Islamic problem. The "Judeo-Christian" West, in their view, is under assault from multiple quarters, including especially from Muslims. The Muslim travel ban was a direct result of such thinking (Haynes 2017).

Likewise is an approach to international religious freedom—a policy that received considerable attention under Secretary of State Pompeo—which put the rights and concerns of Christians first (Bettiza 2019; Henne 2020). President Trump's unquestioned support of Israel and especially its more right-wing and uncompromising stance against Palestinians and their self-determination fits within the same Judeo-Christian conservative logic (Durbin 2020). In the context of a worldview defined by clash, the infrastructure dedicated to religious engagement—including the Office of Religion and Global Affairs—practically disappeared.

Paradoxical were also the effects on American soft power of President Trump's religiously infused rhetoric and policies. On the one hand, Donald Trump presided over yet another dramatic decline in favorable attitudes toward the United States around the world (Pew 2020). Yet, its adoption of a rhetoric and policy orientation inspired by a Judeo-Christian, anti-Muslim, clash-of-civilizations worldview, generated admiration and support among certain foreign leaders and constituencies. This is especially the case among right-wing populists, illiberal strongmen, and religious nationalists like Jair Bolsonaro, Victor Orbán, Vladimir Putin, or Narendra Modi and their supporters. Trump's religious statecraft did not appear to decrease the threat from terrorism, promote religious freedom, or advance Middle East peace. Actually, his rhetoric and policies seem to be quite antithetical to these objectives. What they certainly achieved, though, was exciting and galvanizing a key constituency of his electorate: White Christian Nationalists.

Conclusion

Religious soft power has played an important, if unpredictable, role in US foreign policy. In the Cold War, the United States used religious language to establish a grand narrative of a faithful West versus godless Communism in order to bind states and societies to its side. American policymakers also used specific religious outreach activities to increase America's attractiveness and support pro-American forces in Europe, the Middle East, and East Asia. After the Cold War, and especially after 9/11, the United States' War on Terror and religious soft-power efforts became entangled and embroiled—in one way or another—within a larger grand narrative of civilizational struggles and engagements. In a world seen as experiencing a resurgence—often violent—or religion, policymakers undertook several initiatives designed to manage and marshal the power of faith according to different administrations' understanding of America's national interest.

Religious soft power has been an important and persistent part of US foreign policy, even if it is consistently downplayed in favor of military or economic tools. Yet there have also been some differences between these two eras. During the Cold War religious soft-power approaches were less institutionalized, more covert, and much of it directed toward one main and clear foe. During the post–Cold War period, religious statecraft has taken a more institutionalized form, with the advent of multiple religious foreign policy regimes. While many of these efforts were targeted at fighting Islamist terrorism their objectives also transcended this specific issue and included a more diffused set of targets such as promoting religious freedom, solving religious conflicts, and providing development and humanitarian assistance.

Overall, the impact of the US religious grand narratives and policies has been mixed. While religious soft power did help to craft anti-Soviet alliances during the Cold War, not all of these efforts came to fruition. At times they would also backfire, causing America to prop up repressive leaders—such as Vietnam's Diem—or unintentionally create later threats, like the rise of

Al-Qaeda thanks to its support for Islamic fighters in Afghanistan. In the post–Cold War era Bush's faith-based initiatives in Africa and Obama's religious engagement activities toward the Muslim world, have been praised for producing tangible benefits for people on the ground and enhancing the United States' reputation around the world. These initiatives, however, have taken place against a backdrop of wider clash of civilizational narratives which have shaped US foreign policy and religious outreach in multiple ways, setting back efforts at expanding America's attractiveness or even undermining its national security. In short, religious statecraft has been a powerful tool that has proven effective in particular circumstances, but one which has also generated unpredictable and unintended consequences.

This study is a preliminary exploration of the dilemmas and paradoxes that religious statecraft and soft power produce. Future studies would require more in-depth analysis of specific foreign policy episodes in order to determine the nature and impact of America's religious soft power. They should conduct more rigorous comparison of successful and unsuccessful uses of religious soft power drawing, for instance, on the tools of comparative historical analysis to trace the development of the grand narratives in each period, and their connection to religion.

Additionally, this chapter suggests we may need to move beyond a focus just on soft power when discussing the use of religion in foreign policy. Much of what we found certainly relates to the classical understanding of soft power: America using religious tools to get other states to want what it wants. The United States, however, also used religious outreach and appeals actively, as an instrument of power. US presidents and policymakers used religious arguments to convince Western European states to follow the US lead and undermine the appeal of the Soviet Union and Communism. This use of symbolic instruments of power is often conflated with soft power, but, as Henne discussed in a recent article, it may be better to disaggregate soft power from other nonmaterial instruments of power (Henne forthcoming). Properly defined, "soft power" is a passive attempt to integrate international coalitions by appealing to shared values like religion. But states can also actively appeal to religion in order to integrate alliances or even fragment rival coalitions. Future studies could do more to disaggregate the complex and different ways that states mobilize religion as a source of power and influence in world politics.

This chapter can also provide suggestions for US policymakers. First, policymakers and security studies experts cannot keep ignoring religion's importance when formulating US foreign policy. Religion obviously matters a great deal to both the United States and the countries it deals with. Leaving religion "out of the equation" leads to a faulty analysis of issues and the alienation of global audiences. Moreover, the aforementioned cases show that religious soft power can be a very useful tool when forming international alliances. But we must also be modest with the expectations for this religious outreach and engagement, and be careful of unintended consequences. Future religious soft-power efforts will not transform US relations with other states and societies. They may even be exploited by other states hoping to twist US intentions and enable their own repression and hostility. For example, Hungary—a state quickly sliding into authoritarianism under its current leader—has publicly framed its identity along Christian nationalist lines and endorsed the Trump administration's international religious freedom promotion efforts. This is an easy way by Victor Orbán to deflect criticism of its record, and a good example of the negative, disruptive impacts of religious soft power about which we must be on guard. If policymakers are to pursue religious soft-power strategies, they must ensure they are as carefully crafted (if not more so) than military actions or economic negotiations.

References

Ahmad, Zahid Shahab. 2012. "Political Islam, the Jamaat-e-Islami, and Pakistan's Role in the Afghan-Soviet War, 1979–1988." In *Religion and the Cold War: A Global Perspective*, edited by Philip E. Muehlenbeck, 275–297. Nashville: Vanderbilt University Press.

Alexander, Andrew. 2002. "The Soviet Threat Was a Myth." *The Guardian*, April 18, 2002. https://www.theguardian.com/world/2002/apr/19/russia.comment.

BBC. 2006. "Bush's Language Angers US Muslims." *BBC*, August 12, 2006. http://news.bbc.co.uk/1/hi/4785065.stm

Bettiza, Gregorio. 2015. "Constructing Civilisations: Embedding and Reproducing the 'Muslim World' in American Foreign Policy Practices and Institutions Since 9/11." *Review of International Studies* 41 (3): 575–600.

Bettiza, Gregorio. 2019. *Finding Faith in Foreign Policy: Religion and American Diplomacy in a Postsecular World*. New York: Oxford University Press.

Bettiza, Gregorio. 2019. "Why Does the United States Have a Christian 'Soft Spot' and What to Do about It?" *LSE Religion and Global Society*, December 20, 2019. https://blogs.lse.ac.uk/religionglobalsociety/2019/12/why-does-the-united-states-have-achristian-soft-spot-and-what-to-do-about-it/.

Bettiza, Gregorio. 2014. "Civilizational Analysis in International Relations: Mapping the Field and Advancing a "Civilizational Politics" Line of Research." *International Studies Review* 16 (1): 1–28.

Birdsall, Judd. 2012. "Obama and the Drama Over International Religious Freedom Policy: An Insider's Perspective." *Review of Faith & International Affairs* 10 (3): 33–41.

Bronson, Rachel. 2006. *Thicker than Oil: America's Uneasy Partnership with Saudi Arabia.* New York: Oxford University Press.
Canipe, Lee. 2003. "Under God and Anti-Communist: How the Pledge of Allegiance Got Religion in Cold War America." *Journal of Church and State* 45 (2): 305–323.
CFR. 2018. "President Trump's World Religion Tour." In *Religion and Foreign Policy Conference Call.* Council on Foreign Relations.
Chapman, Jessica M. 2012. "Religion, Power and Legitimacy in Ngo Dinh Diem's Republic of Vietnam." In *Religion and the Cold War: A Global Perspective*, edited by Philip E. Muehlenbeck, 206–229. Nashville: Vanderbilt University Press.
Coll, Steve. 2004. *Ghost Wars: The Secret History of the CIA, Afghanistan and bin Ladin, from the Soviet Invasion to September 10, 2011.* New York: Penguin Press.
Davis, Tami R., and Sean M. Lynn-Jones. 1987. "City upon a Hill." *Foreign Policy* 66 (Spring): 20–38.
Doran, Michael. 2016. *Ike's Gamble: America's Rise to Dominance in the Middle East.* New York: Free Press.
Durbin, Sean. 2020. "From King Cyrus to Queen Esther: Christian Zionists' Discursive Construction of Donald Trump as God's Instrument." *Critical Research on Religion* 8 (2): 115–137.
Evertz, Scott H. 2010. "How Ideology Trumped Science: Why PEPFAR Has Failed to Meet its Potential." *Center for American Progress* January 13, 2010. https://www.americanprogress.org/article/how-ideology-trumped-science/.
Fabbrini, Sergio. 2004. "Layers of Anti-Americanism: Americanization, American Unilateralism and Anti-Americanism in a European Perspective." *European Journal of American Culture* 23 (2): 79–94.
Fukuyama, Francis. 1992. *The End of History and the Last Man.* New York: Free Press.
Gradert, Kenyon, and James Strasburg. 2018. "Billy Graham, Cold Warrior for God." *New York Times*, February 23, 2018. https://www.nytimes.com/2018/02/23/opinion/billy-graham-cold-war.html.
Guerrero, Javier Gil. 2017. "Propaganda Broadcasts and Cold War Politics: The Carter Administration's Outreach to Islam." *Journal of Cold War Studies* 19 (1): 4–37.
Hatzopoulos, Pavlos, and Fabio Petito, eds. 2003. *Religion in International Relations: the Return from Exile.* 1st ed. Basingstoke: Palgrave Macmillan.
Haynes, Jeffrey. 2017. "Donald Trump, 'Judeo-Christian Values,' and the 'Clash of Civilizations.'" *Review of Faith & International Affairs* 15 (3): 66–75.
Henne, Peter. 2020. "Pompeo Investigation Could Undo Religious Freedom Movement's 'Success.'" *Religion News Service*, May 20, 2020. https://religionnews.com/2020/05/20/pompeo-investigation-could-undo-religious-freedom-movements-success/.
Henne, Peter S. 2017. *Islamic Politics, Muslim States and Counterterrorism Tensions.* New York: Cambridge University Press.
Henne, Peter S. forthcoming. "What We Talk about When We Talk about Soft Power." *International Studies Perspectives* 23 (1): 94–111.
Hirsh, Michael. 2016. "Team Trump's Message: The Clash of Civilizations Is Back." *Politico*, November 20, 2016. http://www.politico.com/magazine/story/2016/11/donald-trump-team-islam-clash-of-civilizations-214474.
Huntington, Samuel P. 1993. "The Clash of Civilizations?" *Foreign Affairs* 72 (3): 22–49.
Huntington, Samuel P. 1996. *The Clash of Civilizations and the Remaking of World Order.* New York: Simon and Schuster.

Iber, Patrick. 2017. "Cold War World." *The New Republic*, October 30, 2017. https://newrepublic.com/article/144998/cold-war-world-new-history-redefines-conflict-true-extent-enduring-costs.
Inboden, William. 2008. *Religion and American foreign Policy, 1945–1960: The Soul of Containment*. New York: Cambridge University Press.
Isernia, Pierangelo. 2007. "Anti-Americanism in Europe during the Cold War." In *Anti-Americanisms in World Politics*, edited by Peter J. Katzenstein and Robert O. Keohane, 57–93. Ithaca, NY: Cornell University Press.
Kaplan, Robert D. 2000. *The Coming Anarchy: Shattering the Dreams of the Post Cold War*, 1st ed. New York: Random House.
Kirby, Dianne. 2008. "Bishop George Bell and the Cold War." *Kirchliche Zeitgeschichte* 21 (2): 349–372.
Lebow, Richard Ned, and Janice Gross Stein. 1994. *We All Lost the Cold War*. Princeton, NJ: Princeton University Press.
Lewis, Bernard. 1990. "The Roots of Muslim Rage." *The Atlantic Monthly* 266 (3): 47–60.
Lilli, Eugenio. 2016. *New Beginning in US-Muslim Relations: President Obama and the Arab Awakening*. Basingstoke: Palgrave MacMillan.
Lynch, Timothy J. 2008. "Kristol Balls: Neoconservative Visions of Islam and the Middle East." *International Politics* 45 (2): 182–211.
Mandaville, Peter. 2017. "The Future of Religion and U.S. Foreign Policy under Trump." *The Brookings Institution*, March 7, 2017. https://www.brookings.edu/research/the-future-of-religion-and-u-s-foreign-policy-under-trump/.
Mandaville, Peter, and Shadi Hamid. 2018. "Islam as Statecraft: How Governments Use Religion in Foreign Policy." *Brookings Institution*, November 4, 2018. https://www.brookings.edu/research/islam-as-statecraft-how-governments-use-religion-in-foreign-policy/.
Miller, Greg, and Scott Higham. 2015. "In a Propaganda War, U.S. Tried to Play by the Enemy's Rules." *Washington Post*, May 8, 2015. https://www.washingtonpost.com/world/national-security/in-a-propaganda-war-us-tried-to-play-by-the-enemys-rules/2015/05/08/6eb6b732-e52f-11e4-81ea-0649268f729e_story.html?utm_term=.76cd60e91969.
Nye, Joseph S., Jr. 1990. "Soft Power." *Foreign Policy* 80: 153–171.
Obama, Barack. 2009. "President Obama's Speech in Cairo: A New Beginning." Cairo University, Cairo, Egypt, June 4, 2009. https://obamawhitehouse.archives.gov/the-press-office/remarks-president-cairo-university-6-04-09.
OIG. 2009. "Audit of USAID's Faith-Based and Community Initiatives." In *Office of Inspector General: Audit Report NO. 9-000-09-009-P*. Washington, DC: Office of Inspector General, U.S. Agency for International Development.
Pew. 2006. "The Great Divide: How Westerners and Muslims View Each Other." *Pew Research Center*, June 22, 2006. https://www.pewresearch.org/global/2006/06/22/the-great-divide-how-westerners-and-muslims-view-each-other/.
Pew. 2020. "Trump Ratings Remain Low Around Globe, While Views of U.S. Stay Mostly Favorable." *Pew Research Center*, January 8, 2020. https://www.pewresearch.org/global/2020/01/08/trump-ratings-remain-low-around-globe-while-views-of-u-s-stay-mostly-favorable/.
Pilling, David. 2019. "Why George W. Bush Is Africa's Favourite US President." *Financial Times*, July 17, 2019. https://www.ft.com/content/72424694-a86e-11e9-984c-fac8325aaa04.

Podhoretz, Norman. 2007. *World War IV: The Long Struggle Against Islamofascism.* New York: Doubleday.

Pollard, John. 2003. "The Vatican, Italy and the Cold War." In *Religion and the Cold War*, edited by Dianne Kirby, 103–118. New York: Palgrave Macmillan.

POMED. 2010. "Obama's Cairo Speech, One Year Later." *The Project on Middle East Democracy (POMED)*, http://pomed.org/blog-post/democracy-promotion/obamas-cairo-speech-one-year-later-2/.

Preston, Andrew. 2012. *Sword of the Spirit, Shield of Faith: Religion in American war and diplomacy.* New York: Alfred A. Knopf.

Salter, Mark B. 2002. *Barbarians and Civilization in International Relations.* London; Sterling, Va.: Pluto Press.

Smith, Gary Scott. 2011. "Jimmy Carter: A Progressive Evangelical Foreign Policy." *Review of Faith and International Affairs* 9 (4): 61–70.

The New York Times. 2009. "End of the Clash of Civilizations." *The New York Times*, April 12, 2009. https://www.nytimes.com/2009/04/12/opinion/12sun2.html.

Thomas, Scott. 2005. *The Global Resurgence of Religion and the Transformation of International Relations: The Struggle for the Soul of the Twenty-First Century.* New York: Palgrave Macmillan.

Toft, Monica Duffy, Daniel Philpott, and Timothy Samuel Shah. 2011. *God's Century: Resurgent Religion and Global Politics.* New York: W.W. Norton and Company.

USG. 2002. *The National Security Strategy of the United States of America.* Washington, DC: United States Government, USG.

USG. 2006. *The National Security Strategy of the United States of America.* Washington, DC: United States Government, USG.

White House. 2001. *Unlevel Playing Field: Barriers to Participation by Faith-Based and Community Organizations in Federal Social Service Programs.* Washington, DC: White House Office of Faith-Based and Community Initiatives.

White House. 2010. "A New Era of Partnerships: Report of Recommendations to the President." In *President's Advisory Council on Faith-Based and Neighborhood Partnerships.* Washington, DC: The White House.

Yin, Kai, and Allison Haga. 2012. "Rising to the Occasion: The Role of American Missionaries and Korean Pastors in Resisting Communism Throughout the Korea War." In *Religion and the Cold War: A Global Perspective*, edited by Philip E. Muehlenbeck, 88–113. Nashville: Vanderbilt University Press.

Zaharna, R. S. 2009. "Obama, U.S. Public Diplomacy and the Islamic World." *World Politics Review*, March 16, 2009. http://www.american.edu/soc/faculty/upload/Zaharna-public-diplomacy-islamic-world.pdf.

3
"Putin-Phonia"
Harnessing Russian Orthodoxy to Advance Russia's Secular Foreign Policy

Robert C. Blitt

The 2020 Constitutional Amendments Augur Significant Implications for Kremlin Foreign Policy

In January 2020, President Putin surprised Russians and the world by proposing a sweeping set of constitutional reforms. Despite an apparent emphasis on domestic policy and the welfare state, the push for amendments signaled a distinct preoccupation with Russia's international standing. Putin's proposed reforms began by asserting that "Our nation's sovereignty must be unconditional . . . Russia has returned to international politics as a country whose opinion cannot be ignored" (Presidential Address 2020). Propelled by this outward-facing orientation, Putin's first suggested amendments sought to curb the domestic impact of any decisions taken by international bodies regarding Russia's international obligations.

Putin's traditional allies were quick to embrace his invitation to propose further amendments (Dixon 2020). Among others, Patriarch Kirill, head of the ROC-MP, suggested believers should "pray and work so God would be mentioned in our foundational law . . . through joint efforts and prayers we will help to ensure that such a lofty idea as faith in God . . . [is] included in our constitution."[1] President Putin answered these prayers by endorsing Kirill's proposal and bundling it into the list of revised amendments delivered to the State Duma in March 2020 (AFP 2020). Within a matter of days—and with virtually no opposition—Putin's package of amendments secured the approval of Russia's Duma and Federation Council, all 85 regional parliaments, and finally, Russia's Constitutional Court.[2] In July 2020, citizens overwhelmingly endorsed the 60 pages of amendments in a public vote (Law of the

---

Robert C. Blitt, *"Putin-Phonia"* In: *The Geopolitics of Religious Soft Power*. Edited by: Peter Mandaville, Oxford University Press. © Oxford University Press 2023. DOI: 10.1093/oso/9780197605806.003.0003

Russian Federation 2020), thus blessing the largest overhaul of the Russian constitution since its ratification in 1993.

The approved constitutional amendments cover wide ground, ranging from social and welfare benefits to reorganization of the state's political power structure. But lost in this torrent of reform, certain key amendments—namely those addressing sovereignty, historical truth, Russian compatriots, and traditional values—harbor significant implications for Russian foreign policy.

Perhaps most strikingly, Putin's constitutional amendments offer a muscular assertion of sovereignty aimed at suppressing perceived interference in domestic affairs and invigorating the Kremlin's longstanding campaign for a multipolar international system (Meeting with members 2020). Russia's constitution now enables the Constitutional Court to render unenforceable any international ruling against Russia where the decision is deemed contrary to Russia's constitution (Law No. 1-FKZ Art. 12). A still more sweeping amendment enables rejection of foreign or international judicial or arbitral tribunals based on the decidedly more vague—and likely less onerous—standard that the decision conflicts with Russia's public order (Law No. 1-FKZ Art. 40(d)).

The constitutional amendments prioritizing sovereignty also proclaim that Russia will "tak[e] measures to . . . prevent interference in the internal affairs of the state" (Law No. 1-FKZ Art. 13). This mandate links up with the Kremlin's promotion of "multipolarity" and provides fresh constitutional cover for repudiating the work of international bodies deigning to "interfere" not only in Russia's internal affairs, but the internal affairs of its allies as well.

An additional amendment ensuring the constitutional protection of a particular version of history is inextricably linked to the Kremlin's larger effort to project Russian power and civilization within the international order. President Putin made plain this connection early on during the amendment-drafting period:

> We will put a sock in the rotten mouths that some people abroad keep opening to achieve immediate political goals . . . We will shut them up with true, basic information . . . [about] our heroes who fell dead defending . . . the whole world from the brown plague [fascism]. (RFE/RL 2020)

To validate this decidedly global campaign, Russia's constitution now prohibits questioning Russia's activities during World War II (The State Duma 2020). Elevating this "monolithic, triumphalist [historical] narrative"

(Edele 2017, 109.) to constitutional imperative will embolden the Kremlin's violation of human rights obligations at home.[3] At the same time, the constitutional prohibition will enable the Kremlin to amplify its rhetoric targeting noncompliant states. As Putin has already cautioned, those seeking to tarnish Russia's historical reputation are nothing less than "a threat to the fundamental principles of the world order. . . . Neglecting the lessons of history inevitably leads to a harsh payback" (Putin 2020).

Constitutionalizing a duty to combat falsification positions the Kremlin to open a raft of international challenges, including condoning crimes committed under the Soviet occupation. No less disturbing, leveraging Russia's seat on the United Nations Human Rights Council (UNHRC) to contest sources of factual information risks amplifying the Kremlin's ongoing disinformation (*dezinformatsiya*) campaigns,[4] dividing European states,[5] and undermining the internal stability of vulnerable societies (Ajir and Vailliant 2018, 32).

Much like the prohibition on falsification, a new amendment expanding support to "compatriots living abroad in the exercise of their rights" (Law No. 1-FKZ, Art.1(4)) is similarly linked to Russia's effort to project power abroad (Kudors 2014, 110). President Putin's open-ended definition for "compatriots"—asserting "Everyone is Russian outside of Russia, and everyone who speaks Russian and is steeped in Russian culture is entitled to call themselves that"[6]—strengthens the Kremlin's case for a larger "Russian world" (Russkiy Mir) outside of Russia proper. These compatriots, in turn, "amplify Russia's political influence in the former USSR and provide political, economic, and military intelligence" (Zakem, Saunders, and Antoun 2015) further legitimating Russia's civilizational and great power claims. Enhancing the constitutional status of compatriots in this manner thus reinforces a range of Russia's foreign policy priorities tied to

- entrenching Kremlin-friendly media outlets, the ROC-MP, and Russian culture, including the fight for Russian language use;
- disseminating Russia's official views on history and the fight against falsification; and
- compounding local societal cleavages and alienation, including by influencing other states' sovereign decisions "without obvious intervention by Russia" (Bulakh et al. 2014).

Finally, an array of constitutional amendments focusing on traditional values builds up a key ingredient in the Kremlin's post-Yeltsin civilizational identity-building project and its multipolarity campaign. This campaign relies on a narrative wherein only Russia can thwart the West's effort to impose global "ultra-liberalism." In Putin's words, "[E]fforts are being taken today to ... destroy the traditional values" (Putin Address 2018).[7] This "clash of civilizations" is considered nothing less than a strategic threat to Russia's geopolitical interests:

> [P]romoting the rights of LGBT community and spreading the ideas of radical feminism . . . dilute[e] the notion of sex identity [and] the values of family and marriage ... In fact, the trend is to transform people into ... ideal objects for manipulation . . . [such a] society . . . is a perfect target for so-called coloured revolutions. (Ministry of Foreign Affairs of the Russian Federation 2019)

Regarding the amendments themselves, first and perhaps most curiously, Russia's de jure secular constitution now recognizes "faith in God" as a component part of Russia's unifying thousand-year history (Law No. 1-FKZ, Art. 1(2)). Without irony, Russia's Human Rights Commissioner Tatyana Moskalkova offered her ringing endorsement of the provision, asserting that the appeal to one god "will not encroach on the views of atheists" (Interfax 2020). Moskalkova's assessment, however, belies how this amendment functions to bless Russia's longstanding—but until now only statutory—discrimination between so-called traditional and nontraditional religions (Blitt 2008).

A second traditional values amendment makes good on Putin's pledge that "as long as I am President, we will have no 'parent number one' [and 'parent number two'], there will be a father and a mother" (Meeting with the working group 2020). The new provision, protecting "the institution of marriage as a union between a man and a woman" (Law No. 1-FKZ, Art.1(7)(d)) signals an escalation of the Kremlin's battle against Russia's LGBTQ community and the international human rights regime. Alongside this targeted anti-LGBTQ measure, a third amendment establishes a more general obligation to ensure policies strengthen protection of the family and preservation of traditional family values (Law No. 1-FKZ, Art. 1(35)(a)). In practical terms, this provision affords a catchall constitutional impetus for promulgating "family values" legislation likely to exacerbate discrimination and harm by targeting LGBTQ and other families deemed "nontraditional," as well as other vulnerable individuals, including women and minors, living within "traditional" family structures.[8]

Constitutionalizing these "traditional values" in toto paves the way for additional discriminatory legislation[9] destined to exacerbate the Kremlin's collision course with international human rights mechanisms. But beyond their obvious domestic ramifications, these amendments harbor clear foreign policy implications designed to burnish Russia's bona fides as the vanguard of an anti-West traditional values coalition.[10] As the next section demonstrates, the ROC-MP is a crucial instrument in building international support for this role.

The Constitutional Amendments Redouble the Moscow Patriarchate's Central Role as a Kremlin Soft-power Tool

As Patriarch Kirill reflected in 2016, "it is no longer the West vs. the non-West, but secular liberals vs. adherents of traditional values" (Curanović 2018, 259). To support the Kremlin against this civilizational threat of "mindless multiculturalism" (Roache 2019)—and to prop up its own vision of Russia as "predestined to be the guardian of global balance, not merely in geopolitical but . . . in a moral/ethical sense" (Curanović 2018, 259)—the ROC-MP has long committed itself to advocating for the Kremlin's views on each of the constitutional amendments.

Stalwart Advocate of Russian Sovereignty and Multipolarity

The ROC-MP has consistently reinforced the Kremlin's emphasis on sovereignty and multipolarity. Nearly two decades ago, then Metropolitan Kirill asserted: "Orthodoxy in international politics [can assist] the building up of a multipolar world" (View from Russia 2015). This commitment to multipolarity has continued unabated until today, with one Church hierarch going so far as to claim that "One of the consequences of the current coronavirus pandemic could be the real emergence of a multipolar world" (World Russian People's Council 2020). The ROC-MP has similarly used its platform to echo the Kremlin's rejection of jurisprudence emerging from the European Court of Human Rights (ECtHR) and other human rights bodies, characterizing it as alien and harmful to Russia's sovereignty (Stoeckl 134).

So pervasive is the Church's commitment to multipolarity and Russian sovereignty that it serves as a leitmotif of sorts, hovering around even the most seemingly innocuous exchanges. For example, when asked about how he passed the time during a flight to the United States, Metropolitan Hilarion, head of the Church's external relations department, replied that he read a book exposing China's plan to replace America as the global superpower. As the self-described representative of a multinational church (rather than a representative of the Russian Federation), Hilarion further opined "If this book had been read in America, it would probably have sobered up those who believe that the main threat to the USA comes from Russia" (Metropolitan Hilarion 2019).

Church efforts to deflect attention from Russian misadventures builds on a long parallel history of echoing Kremlin disdain for interference in internal affairs of state. In 1999, then Metropolitan Kirill lamented what he called "new forms of confrontation in which . . . interference in the life of nations have been realized through political and economic actions" (Metropolitan Kirill of Smolensk and Kaliningrad 1999.) A decade later, the ROC-MP adopted a *Statement on Growing Manifestations of Christianophobia in the World*. While the statement plainly intended to draw attention to discrimination and persecution against Christians, it also explicitly disavowed any intention to "interfere in the internal affairs of state" or to "call the world community to do it" (Holy Synod's statement 2011).

The full extent of the ROC-MP's embrace of Kremlin policy in this area, however, is revealed on the occasions when both parties appear willing to set aside their commitment to the principles of sovereignty and nonintervention. For example, the Kremlin has taken an interventionist stance regarding Montenegro's recently enacted *Law on Freedom of Religion or Beliefs* (2019). To justify this inconsistency, Russia's Foreign Ministry offered some impressive verbal gymnastics: "The case in point is a sovereign state's law. This is a prerogative of Montenegro and its people. We are categorically against any interference in internal affairs. [But this law] . . . could affect the interests of the Metropolitanate of Montenegro . . . [Therefore], it goes beyond national boundaries and concerns the unity and cohesion of the Orthodox World" (Zakharova 2019).

The Kremlin's proffered rationale for carving out this exception to noninterference simply doesn't hold water. Rather, it leaves bare the larger campaign to undercut Montenegrin sovereignty and push back against competing western influence in the region. This sense is so acute that President Milo Djukanovic accused Russia of fueling a controversy over the religion law to "undermine [the] country's independence, NATO membership and its attempt to join the European Union" (Reuters 2020).

Through this larger lens, it becomes evident that Kremlin intervention—cloaked in ostensible concern for the Orthodox world—serves to advance Russia's interests relating to multipolarity and global status. These decidedly secular motives have not deterred the ROC-MP from serving as the chief vehicle for reiterating the Kremlin's temporal concerns and fueling the tension in Montenegro. Patriarch Kirill dutifully mobilized his high-level diplomacy and media outlets to echo Kremlin attacks on the religious freedom law and the Montenegrin government. From his perspective, events in Montenegro are akin to a "Ukrainian scenario" that encroaches "on canonical Orthodoxy" (Metropolitan Hilarion 2020c) and accordingly is not subject to the niceties of noninterference. Revealingly, the Patriarch's invocation of a "Ukraine scenario" ties back to the Kremlin's larger concern over Montenegro's political alignment to the West: "The current authorities of Montenegro do not conceal that they are active supporters of eurointegration and isolation from Serbia and for this reason they seek to discredit the common historical spiritual and cultural heritage of the Serbian and Montenegrin peoples" (Archbishop Leonid 2020). The prospect of a loss of Russian influence within this tiny country augurs so deep a blow to the Kremlin that the Patriarch has gone so far as to insinuate that Montenegrin officials have subjected Orthodox faithful to torture (Patriarch Kirill 2020).

The ROC-MP's readiness to justify Russian interference in Montenegro's internal affairs surely evidences an inconsistency with respect to its adherence to the doctrine of noninterference.[11] But the constant drumbeat of its propaganda is rendered more sinister because it feeds domestic friction and plants the seeds for potentially more egregious intervention from Moscow. The Kremlin's view that "Unity and solidarity of the Orthodox world ... are a condition to ensure normal development of society" gels with the Patriarchate's belief that the Orthodox faithful in Montenegro are inexorably connected to Russia.[12] This fact, coupled with Foreign Minister Sergei Lavrov's declaration that Russia "will always defend the interests of Orthodox Churches" and the freshly minted constitutional imperative to protect an elastic concept of "compatriots" makes the possibility of Russia expanding its compatriot umbrella to all eastern Orthodox believers in the region not altogether far-fetched. At a minimum, it is likely that the target population in Montenegro, egged on by interference from the ROC-MP and Kremlin, will still serve Russia's foreign policy interests by ensuring an environment of domestic political and social instability, within which Moscow can continue to advance its own interests while subverting the West.

The case of Montenegro signals that, like the Kremlin, the ROC-MP will vociferously defend noninterference to shield Russia and its allies from international scrutiny, but quickly discard the norm in service of Russia's foreign interests. Syria provides another case in point. Prior to Moscow's own direct military involvement beginning in 2015, the Kremlin worked tirelessly to foreclose effective international intervention through the UN Security Council, including after the Assad regime's use of chemical weapons (Security Council Resolution 2118 2013). Russia premised its opposition to UN-sanctioned intervention on the basis of noninterference.[13] The ROC-MP staked out a similar view disfavoring international intervention, but dramatically changed its tune with Putin's surprise decision to deploy Russian forces to Syria in late 2015. The protection of co-religionist Orthodox faithful and the projection of Russian influence proved so powerful an elixir, that the ROC-MP urged other states to join what it called a "holy war" (BBC 2016). Indeed, the Church's deafening silence in the face of credible reporting on civilian deaths in Syria due to Russian military operations most revealingly betrays the extent of its backing for the Kremlin's view of sovereignty and noninterference.[14] With this complicity, the message communicated to its estimated 100 million Orthodox faithful, to compatriots abroad, and across its global interfaith and diplomatic networks is plain: Russian sovereignty, influence, and projection of power comes first.

Guard Dog for Kremlin Truth

The ROC-MP has consistently echoed the Kremlin's preoccupation with the threat posed by the "falsification" of history (Blitt 2010, 1337). During the late 2000s, Church clergy leveled accusations of falsification at Ukraine's government, mirroring similar Kremlin actions (Bigg 2009). Building on this shared mission, the Ministry of Foreign Affairs and ROC-MP pledged in 2010 to continue their "joint efforts to combat the falsification of history" (Blitt 2010, 1363). With falsification now constitutionally prohibited, the Kremlin is likely to continue relying on the Church's unique position to legitimize its branding of those who question the Soviet Union's legacy as enablers of fascism. Already in early 2020, Sergei Lavrov proclaimed that Russia's "diplomatic service will continue to do its best to counter attempts to falsify history [through] close cooperation with the Russian Orthodox Church and other traditional religions" (Lavrov 2010).

The Moscow Patriarch has taken this cooperative role to heart, marshalling its resources to fiercely reject any position that challenges the Kremlin's narrative of unsullied Russian supremacy. As part of this effort, the Church advocates within the compatriot community abroad to preserve historical memory and oppose attempts to distort history.[15] But more broadly, the Church also wields the Kremlin's historical narrative as a carrot and stick, to both build a common framework for potential alliances and also to exert pressure on foreign governments.

For example, the Church recently lauded Croatian officials for restoring a memorial to Soviet soldiers, calling it "one of these profoundly symbolic actions which help preserve historical memory" (On the eve of Victory Day 2018). In contrast, Patriarch Kirill directed a six-minute long harangue (Moscow Patriarchate 2018) at the Bulgarian president for remarks Kirill deemed "outrages" of historical revisionism that depreciated the primary role of Russian state power and sacrifice (Avramov 2018). In particular, the Patriarch took issue with state representatives who downplayed the fact that "the liberation of Bulgaria . . . was written in bloody letters in the history of Russia. . . . No political correctness can justify the false historical interpretation. And it is a principal message that the Patriarch addresses to Bulgaria, her leadership and people today" (Patriarch Kirill completes 2018).

Through these actions, the Church continually reinforces the Kremlin's view that Russia's reputation is sacrosanct, and that any perceived slight against it, including the "criminal war on monuments" (Zakharova 2020) is tantamount to the glorification of Nazism. Moreover, as in the context of the Kremlin's compatriot policy, here too the Church can act without the diplomatic fetters that might otherwise bind Russia's Ministry of Foreign Affairs. The Patriarch's action in Bulgaria drives this point home, with one observer concluding that Kirill's remarks "aggressively push[ed] the Russian nationalist agenda in a straightforward style, in a way that even the Russian Foreign Ministry avoids when dealing with what it considers 'friendly' nations" (Avramov 2018).

In addition to the Church mirroring the state's conception of historical memory regarding World War II, it also perpetuates the Kremlin's false narrative of Russia as a haven for religious freedom, tolerance, and coexistence. This "falsification"—intended to boost Russia's international image as a civilizational alternative to the West—downplays Russia's current and past human rights abuses, and instead proffers its approach to religious coexistence as an export-ready model for other like-minded states. In echoing this dubious claim, the Church consistently ignores the regime's (and its own) contemporary treatment of "nontraditional" religious groups, while also denying Russia's checkered history of religious persecution. In one speech, for example, Metropolitan Hilarion set aside Russia's ever-increasing antipathy toward Jehovah's Witnesses (Case 2010), its role in the production and dissemination of *The Protocols of the Elders of Zion* (Hagemeister 2011, 243) and the country's forcible expulsion of Muslim Tatars from Crimea (Punished 1999, 38), to boast: "In Russia there have been no religious wars or religious confrontations in our history. People in our country have been able to find a language of mutual understanding ... despite their differences in faith" (Metropolitan Hilarion 2011). The Kremlin invokes a similarly stilted narrative to bolster Russia's international status. For example, Sergei Lavrov has crowed that Russia "[has] accumulated great experience in ensuring the co-existence of people of various creeds" and "protect[ing] true religious values" (Lavrov 2010).

Global Anchor Point for Cultivating Compatriots

As it continues to hammer home the Kremlin's messages on Russian sovereignty and historical truth, the Church's international footprint also positions it to continue playing a central role in realizing the new constitutional obligations toward compatriots. According to Foreign Minister Lavrov, "The tradition of cooperation between national diplomacy and the [ROC-MP] stretches back into centuries. We are still working hand in hand, helping the Russian diaspora and protecting the rights of Russians who have found themselves far away from the Homeland" (Lavrov 2010). President Putin similarly has stressed tight church-state cooperation regarding compatriot policy, celebrating the fact that the ROC-MP's "great spiritual exploits know[s] no state borders. Her canonical territory extends beyond the confines of Russia. You do much for the support of our compatriots and Orthodox communities abroad" (Speech 2017).

The Church's deep involvement with other compatriot-focused organizations confirms its pivotal role in echoing Kremlin messages to this constituency. For example, the World Russian People's Council (WRPC),[16] essentially a Church-directed NGO, functions as a linchpin compatriot-networking organization that seeks to bolster Russia's profile and policy preferences abroad, including through UN lobbying (Curanović 2018, 70).

Similarly, the Church maintains formal cooperation agreements with a range of governmental organizations engaged in compatriot outreach, including Rossotrudnichestvo (the Federal Agency for Compatriots Abroad and International Humanitarian Cooperation) and Russkiy Mir.[17] The ROC-MP's formal agreements with these actors confirm its position as a central nexus for promoting compatriot activities and connections to Russia, unifying this community under the umbrella of Orthodoxy, and echoing the larger message of a clash between Russian and western civilizations (Ćwiek-Karpowicz 2017).

Tapping into the Moscow Patriarchate's religious and cultural terroir provides the Kremlin with two significant advantages: First, the Church can promote Kremlin messages without the conventional baggage that attaches to overtly political channels or state-backed propaganda outlets such as RT and Sputnik. Second, because of the Church's sweeping global engagement, the Kremlin can access broader, more diverse constituencies that transcend the narrow realm of compatriots. This formula—whereby the ROC-MP operates as convenor of compatriots, other clergy, and foreign government officials to discuss interreligious relations and cooperation with state authorities (DECR 2019)—is repeated across the globe, furnishing the Kremlin with a persuasive and seemingly neutral forum for informing worldviews and influencing global and foreign political dynamics.

With the onset of a constitutional obligation to protect compatriots, the Church's role as the Kremlin's spear tip for engagement is poised for expansion. If defending Russian civilization includes the protection of orthodoxy, and compatriots include "individuals who make the free choice of a spiritual, cultural, and legal link to the Russian Federation," it may not be too great a leap to suggest that Moscow may seek to bless Orthodox belief as a basis for passportization (Nagashima 2019). Such a move could be used to deepen instability, enhance Russian influence, or even to justify direct intervention in the name of Christian communities expressing affinity and support for Russia (50,000 2013). Patriarch Kirill already has sought to inculcate goodwill for such intervention abroad. And the mantle of defending persecuted Christians in Syria continues to resonate for the Kremlin. Expanding on this, the Church's outreach to other Orthodox "compatriots" hints at regions and countries where the Kremlin may seek to expand its influence using Orthodoxy as a bridgehead. The view of Catholicos-Patriarch Nerses Bedros XIX, head of the Armenian Catholic Church, is informative here: "Christians in the Middle East looked at Russia as at their defender and their main hope" (His 2015). From this perspective, the constitutional amendment on compatriots may signal additional fuel for Russian messianism and the Kremlin's framing of the country and its civilization as the last bulwark against a godless world overrun by the corrupting influence of the ultraliberal West (Adamsky 2019, 51).

The Moscow Patriarchate's Crown Jewel: Spreading Traditional Values Everywhere

If the constitutional amendments on sovereignty, falsification and compatriots merely portend an enlarged soft-power role for the ROC-MP, the amendments entrenching traditional values render this eventuality inescapable. These amendments—directly attributed to the ROC-MP's lobbying (Metropolitan Hilarion 2020a)—effectively enshrine the Church's function as guardian of Russia's spiritual and moral identity, thus elevating its already central role as a chief exporter of the Kremlin's civilizational vision. In Patriarch Kirill's words, "Mentioning the value of the faith in God in our Constitution . . . solidif[ies] the historical and spiritual continuity of the peoples of our country, who cannot imagine themselves without religion" (Patriarch Kirill 2020).

More accurately, however, the ramifications of constitutionalizing the collection of traditional values amendments go well beyond a harmless nod to history or religious belief. These values now reflect Kremlin norms of the first order to be spread as the mortar for shoring up multipolarity, sovereignty, and opposition to the looming threat of western "ultraliberalism." In fact, the Church has portrayed traditional values as under siege for longer than the Kremlin, and in even broader terms that lack any pretense of diplomatic nicety. For example, in 2004 then Bishop Hilarion warned of a brewing clash of civilizations: "It may well be the case that the entire Western civilization, not only in Europe but also elsewhere, is becoming radically anti-Christian and anti-religious. In this case there is a need of not only a pan-European but also of a universal common front formed by traditional religious confessions in order to repel the onslaught of militant secularism" (Alfeyev 2004).

To strengthen Russia's hand in this conflict, the Church has established and reinforced alliances with a range of religious constituencies. In addition, it has courted conservative activists, compatriots, simpatico foreign governments, and political operatives. Through these alliances and its own efforts, the ROC-MP staunchly opposes any perceived encroachments on traditional values while simultaneously endorsing the Kremlin's international leadership as the most effective guardian of these values.

In the realm of religious outreach, the Church regularly engages with other "fraternal" churches to project its politics outside Russia. These interactions often seek to undercut Western institutions from within. In one visit to Bulgaria—a European Union (EU) member state—Patriarch Kirill used a meeting with the Bulgarian Orthodox Church to appeal directly to Bulgarians to reject the EU for imposing "behaviours believed to be sinful by Christians and ethically unnatural" (Fraternal 2014).[18] Similarly, the ROC-MP invokes traditional values to build common ground with other non-Orthodox religious faiths. As one human rights organization concluded, this "unholy alliance" brings together "traditionalist actors from Catholic, evangelical, Mormon . . . and Muslim faith backgrounds" to "attempt[] to revert feminist and sexual rights gains at the international level" (Observatory 2017).

The 2016 Havana Declaration (Joint 2016) signed by the ROC-MP and the Vatican exhibits this latter type of outreach and also illustrates the ROC-MP's use of traditional values as a tacit springboard for endorsing the Kremlin's larger foreign policy ambitions.[19] Seemingly validating Russia's role in Syria as the best hope for its indigenous Christians, the Declaration calls "upon the international community to act urgently . . . to prevent the further expulsion of Christians from the Middle East." Likewise, the Declaration offers only a generic condemnation of violence in Ukraine (Joint 2016, ¶ 26) that coincidentally aligns with the ROC-MP's effort to portray itself (and the Kremlin) as neutral peacemakers in the conflict. By championing these views as shared, the Declaration propels the Vatican "deep into geopolitics" and effectively functions to condone Russia's foreign policy misadventures while simultaneously critiquing the West (Did the Pope 2016). The ROC-MP's effort to win over the Vatican as an international ally is rendered especially transparent when situated alongside parallel Kremlin efforts to secure the same Papal buy-in for Russia's Syria project and its narrative of Russia "as a bulwark of morality and traditional values" (Barigazzi 2017).

Church hierarchs also conduct myriad meetings and working groups with high-level government representatives in Russia and abroad. During these exchanges, Church officials typically reiterate the importance of joint efforts to defend traditional values and protection of the family (Working 2012), discuss religious cooperation (Negotiations 2020), stress special ties based on faith and spiritual culture (DECR 2020), raise concerns relating to Christian persecution and "problems of the Russian-Ukrainian relationships" (Metropolitan Hilarion 2020b); and use traditional values as a wedge to engage other issues typically falling into the realm of bilateral state relations.[20]

The Church's advocacy on behalf of traditional values—and Russian policy—similarly extends to conservative civil society groups across the globe. For example, C-Fam, a US-based self-described "pro-family" NGO, has fawned over the ROC-MP's rejection of a UNICEF brief calling for the elimination of discrimination based on sexual orientation and gender identity (Gennarini 2014). More explicitly, the International Organization of the Family (IOF) has consistently boosted the international status of the ROC-MP and Kremlin in advancing traditional values. Among other things, the IOF has organized its World Congress of Families gatherings (Gessen 2017) using funding provided by Orthodox oligarch Konstantin Malofeev (Horowitz 2019), endorsed the need to have Russia play "a very prominent role in the matter of family advocacy and moral values on a global scale" (Gais 2019) and has celebrated Russia as "the Christian saviors of the world" (Bertrand 2016).

Through these types of contacts and interactions, the ROC-MP is able to network not only with like-minded civil society,[21] but to "mingle with leaders" from across Europe and "their comrades from the American heartland" (Applebaum 2009). Groups like C-Fam and IOF also echo this shared traditional values agenda—replete with its Kremlin-endorsed prosovereignty and antiinternational human rights law message—in lobbying their own domestic governments. Consider C-Fam's assertion that it "worked for 24 years" to secure US endorsement of the recently signed Geneva Consensus Declaration (GCD) on Promoting Women's Health and Strengthening the Family (Geneva 2020; C-Fam 2020). This document, signed by the Trump administration (but subsequently rescinded by the Biden administration; White House 2021), invoked national sovereignty to reject international protection for the right to abortion and framed women's right to sexual and reproductive health as exclusive of abortion, two hallmarks of the traditional values agenda.

Conclusion

The aforementioned constitutional amendments resonate with implications for Russia's foreign policy. The emphasis on sovereignty, together with the elevation of historical truth, compatriots, and traditional values are all likely to reenergize the Kremlin's global efforts to press for multipolarity as a means of supplanting democratic and liberal values and justifying its relativist war of attrition against the international human rights framework. In addition, given the ROC-MP's longstanding global engagement around these issues, the amendments are further likely to usher in of an even tighter era of church-state integration. This will involve positioning the Church as the Kremlin's primary soft-power instrument for building up Russia's international status as a norm arbiter and policy shaper, and as the deflector in chief of any criticism of Russian adventurism abroad. Consequently, policy makers should take note of the ROC-MP's burgeoning foreign policy role and make necessary adjustments to account for the Church's increasing proximity to the Kremlin and its ongoing interaction and influence campaigns with governmental and nongovernmental actors both here and abroad.

References

Adamsky, Dmitry (Dima). 2019. "Christ-Loving Diplomats: Russian Ecclesiastical Diplomacy in Syria." *Survival* 61 (6): 49–68.
Alfeyev, Bishop Hilarion. 2004. "European Christianity and the Challenge of Militant Secularism." *The Ecumenical Review* 57 (1): 82–91.
Alicja, Curanović. 2020. "The Russian Orthodox Church, Human Security, Migration and Refugees: Concepts, Strategies and Actions." In *Forced Migration and Human Security in the Eastern Orthodox World*, edited by Lucian N. Leustean, 66–105. Abingdon: Routledge.
Andis, Kudors. 2014. "Russian Soft Power and Non-Military Influence: The View from Latvia." In *Tools of Destabilization: Russian Soft Power and Non-military Influence in the Baltic States*, edited by Mike Winnerstig, 71–112. Swedish Defense Research Agency.
AFP. 2020. "Putin Proposes to Enshrine God, Heterosexual Marriage in Constitution." *France 24*, March 2, 2020. https://www.france24.com/en/20200302-putin-proposes-to-enshrine-god-heterosexual-marriage-in-constitution.
Ajir, Media, and Bethany Vailliant. 2018. "Russian Information Warfare: Implications for Deterrence Theory." *Strategic Studies Quarterly* 12 (3): 70–89.
Applebaum, Anne. 2009. "The False Romance of Russia." *The Atlantic*, December 12, 2009. https://www.theatlantic.com/ideas/archive/2019/12/false-romance-russia/603433/.
Archbishop Leonid of Vladikavkaz and Alania. 2020. "Montenegro Authorities Prosecute Orthodox Church according to Ukrainian Scenario." May 25, 2020. Moscow: Moscow Patriarchate Publishers. http://www.patriarchia.ru/en/db/text/5641535.html.
Avramov, Kiril. 2018. "Orthodox Fury: Not-So-Subtle Politics of Patriarch of Moscow and All Rus." *The Globe* Post, March 23, 2018. https://theglobepost.com/2018/03/23/russia-bulgaria-patriarchkirill/.
Barigazzi, Jacopo. 2017. "Why the Pope ♥ Putin." *Politico EU*, August 11, 2017. https://www.politico.eu/article/pope-francis-loves-vladimir-putin-russia-religion/.

Bertrand, Natasha. 2016. "'I Really Believe that Russia Is the Leader of the Free World Right Now.'" *Business Insider*, December 11, 2016. https://www.businessinsider.com.au/russiaconnections-to-the-alt-right-2016-11.

Bigg, Claire. 2009. "Russian Patriarch's Visit Creates Storm in Ukraine." *Radio Free Europe Radio Free Liberty*, July 31, 2009. https://www.rferl.org/a/Russian_Patriarchs_Visit_Creates_Storm_In_Ukraine/1789959.html.

Blitt, Robert C. 2008. "How to Entrench a De Facto State Church in Russia: A Guide in Progress." *BYU Law Review* (3): 708–778. https://digitalcommons.law.byu.edu/lawreview/vol2008/iss3/2/.

Blitt, Robert C. 2010. "One New President, One New Patriarch, and a Generous Disregard for the Constitution: A Recipe for the Continuing Decline of Secular Russia." *Vanderbilt Journal of Transnational Law* 43 (107): 1337–1369.

Blitt, Robert C. 2011. "Russia's Orthodox Foreign Policy: The Growing Influence of the Russian Orthodox Church in Shaping Russia's Policies Abroad." *University of Pennsylvania Journal of International Law* 33 (2): 363, 389–390. https://scholarship.law.upenn.edu/jil/vol33/iss2/2/.

Briefing by Foreign Ministry Spokesperson Maria Zakharova, Moscow, December 18, 2019, https://www.mid.ru/en/web/guest/foreign_policy/news/-/asset_publisher/cKNonkJE02Bw/content/id/3961456.

Briefing by Foreign Ministry Spokesperson Maria Zakharova, Moscow, January 23, 2020, https://www.mid.ru/en/foreign_policy/news/-/asset_publisher/cKNonkJE02Bw/content/id/4004544.

Bulakh, Anna, Tupay Julian, Kaas Karel, Tuohy Emmet, Visnapuu Kristiina, and Kivirahk Juhan. 2014. "Russian Soft Power and Non-Military Influence: The View from Estonia." Tools of Destabilization: Russian Soft Power and Non-Military Influence in the Baltic States. Stockholm: Swedish Defence Research Agency.

Case of Jehovah's Witnesses of Moscow and Others v. Russia, European Court of Human Rights, App. No. 302/02, Judgment (Final), November 22, 2010. Legal ruling. Unsure of publication status.

C-Fam. 2020. "Statement of Austin Ruse, President of C-Fam, on the Signing of the Geneva Consensus Declaration." *Catholic Citizens*, October 22, 2020. https://catholiccitizens.org/news/93078/statement-of-austin-ruse-president-of-c-fam-on-the-signing-of-the-geneva-consensus-declaration/.

Curanović, Alicja. 2018. "Russia's Mission in the World: The Perspective of the Russian Orthodox Church." *Problems of Post-Communism* 66 (4): 253–267.

Ćwiek-Karpowicz, Jarosław. 2012. "Limits to Russian Soft Power in the Post-Soviet Area." *DGAPanalyse*, July 2012. https://dgap.org/system/files/article_pdfs/2012-08_DGAPana_C%CC%81wiek-Karpowicz_www.pdf.

"DECR Chairman Presided over Round-Table Conference on Cooperation between Russian Church and Compatriots Living in Countries of Middle East and Africa." *Russian Orthodox Church*, November 28, 2019. http://www.patriarchia.ru/en/db/text/5539041.html.

"DECR Chairman Meets with the Head of the Greek Diplomatic Mission in Moscow." *Russian Orthodox Church*, October 13, 2020. http://www.patriarchia.ru/en/db/text/5705703.html.

"Did the Pope Just Kiss Putin's Ring?" *The Economist*, February 15, 2016. https://www.economist.com/europe/2016/02/15/did-the-pope-just-kiss-putins-ring.

Dixon, Robyn. 2020. "Putin as Russia's Supreme Leader? A Constitutional Rewrite Brings out Some 'Crazy' Ideas." *The Washington Post*, February 23, 2020. https://www.washingtonpost.com/world/europe/putin-as-russias-supreme-leader-constitutional-rewrite-brings-out-some-crazy-ideas/2020/02/23/1e0187ca-4cf6-11ea-967b-e074d302c7d4_story.html.

Edele, Mark. 2017. "Fighting Russia's History Wars: Vladimir Putin and the Codification of World War II." *History & Memory* 29 (2): 90–124.

European Parliament. 2019. "European Parliament Resolution of 19 September 2019 on the Importance of European Remembrance for the Future of Europe." European Parliament. https://www.europarl.europa.eu/doceo/document/TA-9-2019-0021_EN.html.

Foreign Minister Sergey Lavrov's remarks at the opening of the 28th International Educational Christmas Readings. 2020. "The Great Victory: Heritage and Inheritors," January 27, 2020. Moscow: Ministry of Foreign Affairs. https://www.mid.ru/en/foreign_policy/news/-/asset_publisher/cKNonkJE02Bw/content/id/4005976.

Fraternal Talk between Primates of the Russian and Bulgarian Orthodox Churches, May 27, 2014. https://mospat.ru/en/2014/05/27/news103134/.

Gais, Hannah. 2019. "In Search of the Russian Soul: How Russia Became the U.S. Far Right's Mirror." *The Public Eye*, October 11, 2019. https://politicalresearch.org/2019/10/11/search-russian-soul.

Gessen, Masha. 2017. "Family Values: Mapping the Spread of Antigay Ideology." *Harper's Magazine*, March 2017. https://harpers.org/archive/2017/03/family-values-3/?single=1.

Gennarini, Stefano. 2014. "Russian Orthodox Condemn UN Children's Fund for Promoting Homosexuality." *Center for Family and Human Rights*, December 23, 2014. https://c-fam.org/friday_fax/russian-orthodox-condemn-unicef-childrens-fund-for-promoting-homosexuality/.

"Geneva Consensus Declaration On Promoting Women's Health and Strengthening the Family." 2020. https://aul.org/wp-content/uploads/2021/06/geneva-consensus-declaration-english.pdf.

Hagemeister, Michael. 2011. "The Protocols of the Elders of Zion in Court: The Bern Trials, 1933–1937." In *The Global Impact of the Protocols of the Elders of Zion: A Century-Old Myth*, edited by Esther Webman, 241–253. Abingdon: Routledge.

Horowitz, Jason. 2019. "Italy's Right Links Low Birthrate to Fight Against Abortion and Migration." *The New York Times*, March 27, 2019. https://www.nytimes.com/2019/03/27/world/europe/italy-verona-salvini-world-congress-of-families.html.

Joint Declaration of Pope Francis and Patriarch Kirill of Moscow and All Russia, Havana, Cuba, February 12, 2016. http://www.vatican.va/content/francesco/en/speeches/2016/february/documents/papa-francesco_20160212_dichiarazione-comune-kirill.html and http://p2.patriarchia.ru/2016/02/13/1238676766/eng.pdf.

Lavrov, Sergei. "Speech at the XIV World Russian People's Council." May 25, 2010. Moscow: Ministry of Foreign Affaairs of the Russian Federation.

"Lavrov: Terrorism Has Nothing in Common with Professing True Religious Values." *TASS*, December 11, 2015. https://tass.com/politics/843516.

Russian Federation. Law of the Russian Federation on amendment to the Constitution of the Russian Federation of March 14, 2020 No. 1-FKZ. "On Improving the Regulation of Certain Issues of the Organization and Functioning of Public Authority." Pub. No.

0001202003140001. http://publication.pravo.gov.ru/Document/View/0001202003140001.

Laruelle, Marlene. 2015. "Russia as a 'Divided Nation,' from Compatriots to Crimea: A Contribution to the Discussion on Nationalism and Foreign Policy." *Problems of Post-Communism* 62 (2): 88.

Law No. 1-FKZ. 2020. "On Improving the Regulation of Certain Issues of the Organization and Functioning of Public Authority," Art. 12.

Law No. 1-FKZ. 2020. "On Improving the Regulation of Certain Issues of the Organization and Functioning of Public Authority," Art. 1(4).

Law No. 1-FKZ. 2020. "On Improving the Regulation of Certain Issues of the Organization and Functioning of Public Authority," Art. 1(2).

Law No. 1-FKZ. 2020. "On Improving the Regulation of Certain Issues of the Organization and Functioning of Public Authority," Art. 1(7)(d).

Law No. 1-FKZ. 2020. "On Improving the Regulation of Certain Issues of the Organization and Functioning of Public Authority," Art. 1(35)(a).

"Letter to all Permanent Missions to the United Nations of Signatories to the Geneva Consensus Declaration from the United States Permanent Mission to the United Nations." 2021. *Center for Family and Human Rights (C-Fam)*, February 19, 2021. https://c-fam.org/us-withdrawal-letter-to-gcd-signatories-2-19-2021/.

Luzgin v Russia, European Court of Human Rights, App. No. 17942/17, communicated September 26, 2017. http://hudoc.echr.coe.int/eng?i=001-178086.

Meeting with Members of the Working Group on Drafting Proposals for Amendments to the Constitution, February 26, 2020. http://en.kremlin.ru/events/president/news/62862.

"Memorandum on Protecting Women's Health at Home and Abroad." 2021. *The White House*, January 28, 2021. https://www.whitehouse.gov/briefing-room/presidential-actions/2021/01/28/memorandum-on-protecting-womens-health-at-home-and-abroad/.

"Metropolitan Hilarion: US Secretary of State Pompeo Cancelled the Meeting an Hour Before It, under the Pressure of Ill-Wishers." 2019. *The Russian Orthodox Church*, July 11, 2019, https://mospat.ru/en/2019/11/07/news179812/.

"Metropolitan Hilarion: Transformation of Hagia Sophia into Mosque in Situation of Today Would Be Inadmissible Violation of Freedom of Faith." 2020a. *The Russian Orthodox Church*, June 4, 2020, https://mospat.ru/en/2020/07/05/news185295/.

"Metropolitan Hilarion of Volokolamsk Meets with Ambassadors of Italy, France, Great Britain, Greece, Brazil, Serbia, Bulgaria and Lebanon." 2020. *The Russian Orthodox Church*, October 5, 2020. http://www.patriarchia.ru/en/db/text/5702292.html.

"Metropolitan Hilarion of Volokolamsk: We Have Supported and Will Support the Canonical Church of Montenegro." 2020c. *The Russian Orthodox Church*, August 4, 2020. http://www.patriarchia.ru/en/db/text/5672925.html.

"Metropolitan Hilarion: It Is Urgent that a System of Protecting Christians against Persecution be Organized." 2011. *The Russian Orthodox Church*, May 19, 2011. https://mospat.ru/en/2011/05/19/news41800/.

Montenegro. Parliament of Montenegro. 2019. Law on Freedom of Religion or Beliefs and Legal Status of Religious Communities. Adopted December 24, 2019, https://www.venice.coe.int/webforms/documents/?pdf=CDL-REF(2020)019-e.

Nagashima, Toru. 2019. "Russia's Passportization Policy toward Unrecognized Republics." *Problems of Post-Communism* 63 (3): 186–199.

"Negotiations between Patriarchal Exarch for South-East Asia and Singapore's Minister for Foreign Affairs." September 8, 2020. http://www.patriarchia.ru/en/db/text/5689149.html.

"On the Eve of the Victory Day a Russian Orthodox Church Hierarch Said the Office for the Dead at the Memorial to Soviet Soldiers in Croatian Ilok." 2018. *The Russian Orthodox Church*, May 9, 2018. https://mospat.ru/en/2018/05/09/news159747/.

Orthodox Christianity. 2020. "Patriarch Kirill Proposes Adding Reference to God to Russian Constitution." February 3, 2020. https://orthochristian.com/127683.html.

"Patriarch Kirill Completes His Visit to Bulgarian Orthodox Church." 2018. *The Russian Orthodox Church*, March 5 2018. http://www.patriarchia.ru/en/db/text/5157784.html.

"Patriarch Kirill Insists on Inserting God Reference in Russian Constitution." 2020. *Interfax*, March 2, 2020. http://www.interfax-religion.com/?act=news&div=15500.

"Presidential Address to the Federal Assembly." *Kremlin.RU*, January 15, 2020. http://en.kremlin.ru/events/president/news/62582.

"Protests in Montenegro Carry into New Year over Church Bill." 2020. *Radio Free Europe/Radio Liberty (RFE/RL)*, January 2, 2020. https://www.rferl.org/a/protests-in-montenegro-carry-into-new-year-over-church-bill/30355770.html.

"Punished Peoples of the Soviet Union: The Continuing Legacy of Stalin's Deportations." 1991. *Helsinki Watch*, September 1991. https://www.hrw.org/reports/pdfs/u/ussr/ussr.919/usssr919full.pdf.

"Putin Says He Rejects Soviet-Style Leaders For Life." 2020. *Radio Free Europe/Radio Liberty (RFE/RL)*, January 18, 2020. https://www.rferl.org/a/russia-s-putin-rejects-soviet-style-leaders-for-life/30384778.html.

"Putin Address to World Russian People's Council." November 1, 2018. http://en.kremlin.ru/events/president/news/59013.

Putin, Vladimir. 2020. "The Real Lessons of the 75th Anniversary of World War II." *The National Interest*, June 18, 2020. https://nationalinterest.org/feature/vladimir-putin-real-lessons-75th-anniversary-world-war-ii-162982.

"Reference to God in Constitution Doesn't Encroach on Atheists' Views—Ombudsman." 2020. *Interfax*, March 3, 2020. http://www.interfax-religion.com/?act=news&div=15505.

"Report by Metropolitan Kirill of Smolensk and Kaliningrad, Chairman of the Department for External Church Relations of the Moscow Patriarchate." 1999. *The Russia Orthodox Church*, December 6, 1999. https://mospat.ru/archive/en/1999/12/ne911251/.

"Rights at Risk: The Observatory on the Universality of Rights Trends Report 2017." 2017. *Observatory on the Universality of Rights*, May 22, 2017. https://www.awid.org/publications/rights-risk-observatory-universality-rights-trends-report-2017.

"Russia's Patriarch Kirill Urges 'Holy War' on Terror." 2016. *BBC News*, October 19, 2016. https://www.bbc.com/news/av/world-europe-37702914/russia-s-patriarch-kirill-urges-holy-war-on-terror.

"Russian Orthodox Church Holy Synod's Statement on Growing Manifestations of Christianophibia [sic] in the World." 2011. *The Russian Orthodox Church*, May 30, 2011. https://mospat.ru/en/2011/05/30/news42347/.

Roache, Madeline. 2019. "'Liberalism Is Obsolete,' Russian President Vladimir Putin Says Amid G20 Summit." *TIME*, June 28, 2019. https://time.com/5616982/putin-liberalism-g20/.

"Speech by the President of Russia Vladimir Vladimirovich Putin before the Participants of the Episcopal Council of the Russian Orthodox Church." 2017. *The Russian Orthodox Church*, December 1, 2017. https://mospat.ru/en/2017/12/01/news153708/.

Stabile, Joseph, and Elizabeth Grimm Arsenault. 2020. "Just Security." *Justsecurity.Org*. February 6. https://www.justsecurity.org/68420/confronting-russias-role-in-transnational-white-supremacist-extremism/.

"Statement by Director of the Foreign Intelligence Service of Russia Sergey Naryshkin at the X International Meeting of High-Level Officials Responsible for Security Matters." 2019. *The Ministry of Foreign Affairs of the Russian Federation*. June 18, 2019. https://www.mid.ru/en/foreign_policy/international_safety/regprla/-/asset_publisher/YCxLFJnKuD1W/content/id/3704728.

"Statement of Patriarch Kirill of Moscow and All Russia on the Developments in Montenegro." 2020. *The Russian Orthodox Church*, July 13, 2020. http://www.patriarchia.ru/en/db/text/5662894.html.

Stoeckl, Kristina. 2016. "The Russian Orthodox Church as Moral Norm Entrepreneur." *Religion, State, and Society* 44 (2): 132–151.

"The Russian Orthodox Church foresees the collapse of globalization and the emergence of a multipolar world due to the pandemic." 2020. *World Russian People's Council*, April 30, 2020. https://vrns.ru/news/5430.

"Thousands in Montenegro March Against Religion Law." 2020. *Reuters*, February 29, 2020. https://www.reuters.com/article/us-montenegro-protest-religion-idUSKBN20N0LL.

"View from Russia: The Orthodox Church, State and Europe." 2005. *The Russian Orthodox Church*, Oct. 3, 2005. https://mospat.ru/archive/en/2005/10/27808/.

"What Changes Will Be in the Constitution of the Russian Federation." 2020. *The State Duma*, March 12, 2020. http://duma.gov.ru/en/news/48039/

"Working Group for Dialogue between the Russian Orthodox Church and the Residency of Religious Affairs of the Republic of Turkey Takes Place." 2012. *The Russian Orthodox Church*, December 16, 2012. https://mospat.ru/en/2012/12/16/news77874/.

Zakem, Vera, Paul Saunders, and Daniel Antoun. 2015. "Mobilizing Compatriots: Russia's Strategy, Tactics, and Influence in the Former Soviet Union." Center for Naval Analyses. https://www.cna.org/archive/CNA_Files/pdf/dop-2015-u-011689-1rev.pdf.

"50,000 Syrian Christians ask for Russian citizenship." 2013. *Interfax*, October 16, 2013. http://www.interfax-religion.com/?act=news&div=10818.

4

Chinese Buddhism and Soft Power

Geopolitical Strategy and Modality of Religion

Yoshiko Ashiwa and David L. Wank

Since Xi Jinping became leader of the People's Republic of China (PRC) in 2012, the state has stepped up its global promotion of Chinese Buddhism.[1] Xi has said that Buddhism is an essential element of traditional Chinese culture and has advocated its promotion to spread "excellent" Chinese culture worldwide. The aim is not to spread belief in Buddhism as a religion but rather to further the aspiration of the Communist Party of China (CPC) for China to be recognized as a powerful country that has inherited a great civilization in the context of the modern world. This aspiration is expressed in the "China Dream," Xi's vision of China regaining the glory of the Tang Dynasty (618–907 CE), the time when Buddhism was Sinicized into Chinese culture and flourished in the country. Buddhism has become linked with the Belt and Road Initiative (BRI) that seeks to reconnect China to Europe via trade routes through central Asia and the Indian Ocean. The routes overlap with the historical passage of Buddhism from India to China, but now are spreading Buddhism as religion and culture from China to countries in Asia and beyond.

This chapter's primary claim is that the global promotion of Buddhism operates as both soft power and sharp power (Walker 2018, 9–23). Xi sees Buddhism as a core element of traditional Chinese culture and among China's most profound cultural soft-power strategies. Since taking office, he has advocated using Buddhism to spread "excellent" Chinese culture to explain to other countries' publics that the "rise of China" is benign and will contribute to world peace and prosperity (Jinping 2013). However, we see the state promotion as sharp power as well because it proceeds through the state administrative system that uses religion to further the CPC's political aims domestically and internationally.[2] This administrative system, created after the founding of the PRC in 1949, has been repurposed under Xi to promote

Yoshiko Ashiwa and David L. Wank, *Chinese Buddhism and Soft Power* In: *The Geopolitics of Religious Soft Power*. Edited by: Peter Mandaville, Oxford University Press. © Oxford University Press 2023.
DOI: 10.1093/oso/9780197605806.003.0004

Buddhism globally to support China's political and economic interests. The promotion links Buddhism to such discourses as peace, happiness, harmony, and prosperity that the state can control to further national interests. We see the globalization of Buddhism described in this chapter as broadly analogous to the historical rise of Europe accompanied by Christianity, which used religion and culture to help Europeans fashion and control the global economic and political system.

To clarify the argument, the chapter's first section examines extant perspectives of the promotion of Buddhism under Xi Jinping. We elaborate on the concept of sharp power and describe the state administrative control of religion in China that Xi has reoriented to a global scope. The second section examines the history of the state's Buddhist diplomacy in the PRC from the 1950s to the 2010s. The third section examines the promotion process by focusing on the state-approved modalities of Buddhism and their promotion strategies in specific world regions. The promotion proceeds through the activities of clerics that are both supported by and coopted by the state, as seen in the case of one cleric. The conclusion considers contradictions in globally promoting a nationalistic Buddhism.

Before continuing, it is instructive to note two things. First, rulers have deployed Buddhism for internal legitimacy and external diplomacy throughout its two-thousand-year history. They have used varied techniques, such as exchanges of clerics, Buddha relics, and knowledge, including sutras, rituals, architecture, painting, and medicine.[3] Therefore, in the modern context, it is not surprising that Buddhism is expected to be soft and sharp power. In the early twentieth century, the Empire of Japan used Japanese Buddhism to justify its imperialist ambitions and military actions in East Asia (Victoria 2006). However, we consider the use of Buddhism by the PRC state to be unprecedented in scale and scope.

Second, the PRC is the world's largest Buddhist country. It contains all three Buddhist traditions: Mahayana Buddhism practiced by Han Chinese, Theravada Buddhism practiced by the Dai people, and the Vajrayana Buddhism of the Tibetan and Mongolian peoples. By 2012, China had 33,000 Buddhist temples, 240,000 clerics, and 38 Buddhist seminaries (Zhe 2019). Studies estimate that there are 250 million Buddhists in the PRC, about half the world total (Lugo et al. 2012).[4] However, their numbers are difficult to ascertain. Many Chinese visit Buddhist temples as a custom to pray to the Buddha, bodhisattvas, and other deities for health and fortune, but few have taken vows as Buddhist devotees.

Framework of the Analysis

To illustrate the argument, we examine extant perspectives in the international relations field on the Chinese state's promotion of Buddhism. One perspective embodies Joseph Nye's definition of soft power as a country pursuing its interests through culture rather than military force (Nye, Jr. 2004). The international relations scholar Sudha Ramachandran observes, "The officially atheist Chinese Communist Party has adopted religion for diplomatic purposes: Buddhism's central tenets of nonviolence, peace and tolerance make it a rich source of potential soft power, and the cultivation of Buddhist communities is emerging as an important component of the PRC's initiatives in public diplomacy" (Ramachandran 2019). Other scholars describe the public diplomacy initiatives, including holding Buddhist forums, reviving Buddhist sites, and lending Buddha relics "emphasize themes of shared history, heritage, and culture" between China and other Buddhist countries in Asia (Ramachandran 2019; Scott 2016). Outcomes of public diplomacy include presenting a public image of China as peaceful, competing with other national Buddhisms for status in the world, and winning public goodwill in other countries to overcome the resistance of their populations to BRI projects.

Other scholars see the concept of soft power as inadequate to explain China's use of Buddhism. Raymond argues that state use of Buddhism has "sharpened" under Xi Jinping so that "it is best understood as a type of influence operation rather than merely a form of Chinese soft power" (Raymond 2020, 348). He notes four characteristics of the use of Buddhism that distinguish it from typical soft-power public diplomacy. First, it is conducted by the CPC's United Front Work Department (UFWD) rather than by foreign affairs organs. Second, CPC members are forbidden to practice religion, so Buddhist diplomacy is an "insincere and even Machiavellian" CPC strategy to further its interests. Third, diplomacy is tightly bound to BRI activities in Asian countries that have large Buddhist populations. Fourth, Buddhism is used to support specific political positions of the CPC, such as Chinese sovereignty in the South China Sea (Raymond 2020, 350).

This chapter overarches the soft power and influence perspectives while filling in their explanations. Both perspectives have overly narrow views of the state strategies of promotion and of Buddhism itself. We see promotion as encompassing multiple state-approved modalities of Buddhism reflected in three discourses: Chinese Buddhism (*zhongguo fojiao*), Buddhist culture (*fojiao wenhua*), and Sinicized Buddhism (*zhongguohua fojiao*). These three discourses existed well before Xi Jinping's tenure but have been politically repurposed under him to further China's interests in relations with other countries around the world. The forms are being promoted, not only in Asian countries with Buddhist traditions but also in countries in North America and Europe. The modalities of Buddhism and the promotion strategies vary by a country's relation to the PRC.

Our analytic framework draws on the concept of sharp power, which incorporates both soft power and influence in a broader institutional analysis. According to Christopher Walker, sharp power is a strategy in international relations by which more authoritarian states, such as China and Russia, use the greater "openness" of the societies of other countries to influence their polities. They seek to extend their institutional strategies of state control in their own countries to other countries' discourse-producing sectors of culture, academia, media, and publishing. The purpose is to create a discourse environment favorable to their national interests. The strategies operate through civil society actors so that populations and states in other countries may not initially recognize them as state initiatives. Walker cites the Confucius Institutes, affiliated with the PRC Ministry of Education, as an example of sharp power. Starting in 2004, institutes were set up in universities in other countries to teach Chinese culture, including language and history, but also worked to suppress discussion of topics, such as Tibet and Taiwan, that the CPC considered sensitive (Walker 2018, 9–23). Under Xi, the CPC use of Buddhism increasingly constitutes sharp power. It is reorienting the Chinese state system of internal religious administration to coordinate the external activities of Buddhist clerics and temples to amplify discourses favorable to the priorities of the CPC.

The state system of religious administration was established after the founding of the PRC in 1949. It starts with the constitutional right of "religious freedom" for citizens that protects freedom for individuals to believe or not to believe in religion. The CPC recognizes five religions: Buddhism, Catholicism, Daoism, Islam, and Protestantism. Their precondition for existing in the PRC is to be "patriotic" by placing "love of country" before "love of religion." In practice, patriotism means that followers must obey the CPC. The state system of religious administration was established to mobilize religious followers to work for CPC goals. The system ensures that clerics and devotees confine their collective practices, such as rituals and teaching, to registered temples, churches, and mosques; the religious policy refers to them as "religious activity sites." Such delimitation is justified as protecting the rights of both believers and nonbelievers. The former can freely practice religion in religious activity sites, while nonbelievers outside the temple are free from proselytizing that violates their right to nonbelief.

The system has three main actors, each with central, provincial, and local offices. The most powerful actor is the UFWD, created in 1943 to manage CPC relations with nonparty groups, including religions, ethnic groups, professionals, business people, and the populations of Tibet, Taiwan, and Xinjiang. It develops the CPC's ideological position toward these groups and may create organizations to represent them. The purpose is to coopt their leaders and isolate enemies among the nonparty groups (Van Slyke 1970, 119–135). The second actor is the State Administration of Religious Affairs (SARA),[5] which is part of the government, not the CPC. This bureaucracy was founded in 1953 to control religions administratively. It translates CPC ideology into religious policies and supervises their local implementation at religious activity sites. The third actor is the Buddhist Association of China (BAC) whose members are elite clerics. The BAC adapts state religious policies to Buddhism, disseminates CPC ideology, government policies, approved forms of Buddhism among clerics and devotees, and mobilizes them to support state initiatives.

The UFWD manages the coordination of the system. An essential means is to create and cultivate institutional networks linking all three actors. This ensures consistency of message. For example, leading SARA officials are CPC members, which subjects them to party discipline and ideological training, and they may hold concurrent appointments in the UFWD. Influential clerics are given positions in the legislative organs of the state, which are under the purview of the UFWD and exist at all three levels (national, provincial, and city/county). These organs are the Chinese People's Political Consultative Conference (CPPCC), which drafts laws, and the National People's Congress (NPC), which approves them. These appointments increase the familiarity of clerics with CPC ideology and state policy. They become "bridges" between religion and the PRC state. Their facility in translating between religious teachings and CPC ideology brings state discourses into the religious communities.

Under Xi, the UFWD has played a growing international role (Shiu-Hing Lo 2019).[6] This change is reflected in a 2018 reorganization of the state system of religious administration. SARA, previously part of the government, was absorbed into the UFWD, making it part of the CPC. This may have been because SARA's administrative experience in localized administration of domestic religious activities sites was inadequate for the CPC's global expectations for religion. In contrast UFWD had far more experience dealing with varied social groups holding multiple points of view in China and abroad. Notably, as part of the 2018 organization, the government's Overseas Chinese Affairs Office was merged into the UFWD. This lets the UFWD more tightly control coordination and integrate its work with religion and overseas Chinese communities (Joske 2019).

Overview of State Use of Buddhism in Foreign Relations, 1950s–2010s

The state utilization of Buddhism in international relations consists of three periods. The first is from the 1950s to the outbreak of the Cultural Revolution. Even while suppressing religions domestically, the CPC used Buddhism for public diplomacy toward countries in Asia with large Buddhist populations. Practices included lending Buddha relics for public veneration, funding the renovation of temples, founding bilateral Buddhist friendship associations, encouraging Chinese clerics to lead international Buddhist organizations, and inviting foreign Buddhist leaders and delegations to visit the PRC. The aim of this diplomacy is described by Holmes Welch, a scholar of Chinese Buddhism, as follows: "In any Asian neighbor, whenever a segment of society like the sangha came to look to China as a model or fell under the domination of a pro-Chinese faction, it slightly increased the internal pressure on the government of that country to adopt a pro-Chinese foreign policy" (Welch 1972, 169). However, the diplomacy fell short of CPC expectations because many Asian countries were anticommunist and international Buddhist organizations resisted BAC initiatives (Welch 1972, 213–214). During the Cultural Revolution (1966–1976), Buddhist diplomacy ceased as religions came under political attack. Buddhist clerics were forced to laicize, and many temples were destroyed.

The second period is from 1979, when the CPC launched the Four Modernizations, including creating a market economy, to the early 2000s. During this period, Buddhism recovered from prior decades of suppression and destruction. During the 1980s, overseas Chinese, previously viewed with suspicion as spies, were now seen as useful to reconnect China to the international economy. At the national level, reciprocal visits of

PRC clerics and overseas Chinese clerics helped the PRC deepen ties with Singapore before the two countries had formally established relations. In Southeast China's ancestral homeland regions of overseas Chinese, local governments were especially tolerant toward religion. By encouraging the recovery of Buddhism, as well as Daoism, ancestral halls, and local shrines, they sought to convince overseas Chinese businesspersons to invest in their locales. In the 1990s, the CPC revived earlier practices of Buddhist diplomacy that had been established in the 1950s. In 1994, the BAC initiated the establishment of the China-Korea-Japan Friendship Buddhist Exchange Association, demonstrating that the PRC was again an active center of Buddhism in the world. From 1995, Buddhist relic visits resumed to Southeast Asian countries, along with visits to Hong Kong and Taiwan. These were undertaken to reassure the populations of neighboring countries concerned by China's growing power by emphasizing their shared history of Buddhism.

The third period started in the early 2000s. By then, Buddhism had recovered, with temples expanding beyond their original scale and new temples being constructed. China became the second-largest economy in the world, and the CPC desired a Chinese cultural presence commensurate with this global power. In 2006, Chinese leader Hu Jintao, reflecting the injection of the concept of soft power into PRC policy circles, declared "it to be a paramount state mission to improve China's soft power" (Zhang 2013, 75–97).[7] The following year, the CPC called for "improving China's soft power for the country's peaceful rise" (Zhang 2013).[8] One of the first expressions of this occurred in 2006 with the establishment of the World Buddhist Forum, the first major international religious conference in the PRC. Under the theme "harmonious society," the forum brought together Buddhist delegations of Theravada, Mahayana, and Vajrayana schools from three dozen countries. This demonstrated that China was a vital center of Buddhism in the world. The Chinese state also began helping other Asian countries recover Buddhist sites and restore temples. In 2008, the state authorized the building of the Zhonghua Temple in Lumbini, Nepal, the first time for the PRC state to construct a Buddhist temple outside the country. Other promotion activities used public diplomacy to support growing Chinese investments overseas. For example, in 2011, when anti-Chinese protests erupted in Myanmar over the construction of the Myitsone Dam, the BAC dispatched a Buddha tooth relic on a 48-day tour of the country to generate goodwill (Mon 2011). Other activities were a new emphasis on Buddhism as Chinese cultural practices, including tea ceremony and meditation to appeal to Chinese, as well as people around the world who were not Buddhists.

Since 2013, under Xi Jinping, the state view of Buddhism as a desirable soft power for China has deepened. Xi articulated the link between Chinese culture and the global power of China (Xu 2015, 14–35).[9]

> Throughout the ages, the status and influence of the Chinese nation in the world has depended not on militarism or external expansion but on the strong appeal and attraction of Chinese culture. Our ancestors have long recognized the truth that "if others do not respect [our country], then [we] must cultivate ourselves with culture and morality to attract them."
> (Jinping 2014)

While Xi considered Buddhism, Confucianism, and Daoism as the cultural foundations of Chinese civilization, he was partial to Buddhism for conveying it to the world (Jinping 2014).[10] Daoism held minimal appeal outside of overseas Chinese communities, while Confucius Institutes were becoming controversial. Some universities in North America, Europe and Japan had expelled them on the grounds that they enabled the CPC to culturally control discussions on such sensitive issues as Tibet. Some countries even required them to register as agents of foreign states (Bowe 2018, 12–15). In contrast, Buddhism was already familiar as a religion in many Asian countries and, more recently, had growing appeal as religion and "culture" in western countries.

Under Xi, the BAC has taken the global promotion of Buddhism as a main task. A rationale for the BAC's promotion was expressed by its vice-president Ven. Juexing 覺醒 in a 2014 interview with state media. While the existing strategy of "inviting in" (*qing jinlai*) foreign Buddhists to China, exemplified in the World Buddhist Forum, developed relationships and showed the strength of Buddhism in China, it did little to raise its status globally. In contrast, Juexing noted that Tibetan Buddhism and Theravada Buddhism were distinctive global "brands," while Buddhists from Japan, Korea, and Taiwan had aggressively propagated their Buddhisms abroad. He favored a new strategy for Chinese Buddhists to

> take the initiative to go global (*zou chuqu*), promote Chinese Buddhism, and spread Chinese culture. This is related to the international competitiveness of Chinese Buddhism, improving the ability of Buddhism's

non-governmental diplomacy, enriching connotations in public diplomacy, and expanding the development channels of non-governmental diplomacy. This is necessary to make Chinese culture and values known and accepted by people around the world. (Fang 2014)

He urged Chinese clerics to emulate Buddhists from Taiwan in establishing overseas branch temples. This would "open up overseas bases for the spread of Chinese Buddhism and Chinese culture, which is beneficial to enhancing the country's cultural soft power" (Fang 2014). He saw countries as fertile ground for Chinese Buddhism: "Foreign systems are different from China's system, and there are diverse ideologies. Therefore, as long as the spread of religion and culture in other countries meets the requirements of their laws and regulations, the development space and prospects should be relatively optimistic" (Fang 2014).

In 2015, the BAC Ninth National Congress formally adopted the global propagation of Buddhism as a key activity for the next five years. In his speech, BAC president Xuecheng incorporated Xi's political discourse in describing this new direction. This can be seen in the title of his speech, "Love the Country, Love Religion, be Faithful and Righteous, Promote the Healthy and Comprehensive Development of Buddhism to Contribute to Realizing the China Dream and the Great Rejuvenation of the Chinese Nation." Xuecheng concluded by saying,

> Buddhism is not only a cultural bridge for friendly exchanges between China and the peoples of East, South and Southeast Asia but also a spiritual bond for friendly exchanges with Buddhists all over the world . . . We must consolidate and develop the traditional Buddhist friendship with Buddhist countries and regions in South and Southeast Asia, enhance feelings between their peoples, and promote good neighborliness and friendship. We will further develop friendly exchanges and cooperation with other parts of the world, especially the Buddhist circles in Europe and the United States. We will actively participate in the activities of international Buddhist organizations and religious peace organizations, participate in world religious dialogue, and constantly improve the participation and discourse power of Chinese Buddhist circles in international Buddhist affairs . . . The Buddhist community should give full play to its unique advantages . . . to promote Chinese Buddhism to go global and contribute to implementing the "One Belt and One Road" strategic concept. We will play an active role

in promoting lasting world peace and shared prosperity through friendly exchanges with foreign countries. (Xuecheng 2015)

An article in *Fayin*, the official BAC journal, announced that this was the first time for the BAC to strongly encourage Chinese Buddhism to "go global." This would enable Buddhists to "tell the Chinese story well" to the peoples of other countries so they could realize the PRC's great accomplishments and peaceful character. The article variously referred to these efforts as "soft power" (*ruan shili*), "public diplomacy" (*gongyi waijiao*), and "person-to-person diplomacy" (*renjian waijiao*) (Xingqiao 2015).

Modalities of Buddhism and Strategies of Promotion

The promotion has emphasized three modalities of Buddhism in China. While discourses signifying them have existed for some time, their terms have acquired new political significance under Xi Jinping. The first is "Sinicized Buddhism." The term has long referred to the historical process by which Buddhism from North India adapted to Chinese culture in the Tang Dynasty and began flourishing. Under Xi, it has been politically adapted to refer to incorporating Chinese values in the modern context. Examples are new flag-raising ceremonies in Chinese temples, emphasizing the value of harmony in Tibetan Buddhism, and upgrading Chinese texts and language in scholarship on Buddhism. The second is "Chinese Buddhism." This term has referred to the coexistence of the Mahayana, Theravada, and Vajrayana traditions in China under the umbrella of BAC, but now also refers to Chinese Buddhism as the center of all Buddhisms in the world. The third is "Buddhist culture." This refers to Buddhist-inspired values and practices that people can pursue in their everyday lives, such as clothes fashion and tea ceremony, without learning Buddhist teachings, worshipping statues, or questioning matters of belief. The strategies of promoting these modalities of Buddhism abroad vary locally by such factors as a country's history of Buddhism, degree of economic dependency on PRC, and geopolitical value to the CPC.

Based on preliminary research in several countries, we see promotion varying by three types of countries. First are Asian countries with Buddhist majorities, or significant minorities, that are economically dependent on China, including Cambodia, Myanmar, Mongolia, Nepal, Sri Lanka, and

Vietnam. Key strategies include (1) establishing bilateral Buddhist friendship associations; (2) setting up Buddhist media networks; (3) holding joint religious and cultural rituals, such as praying for peoples' health during the coronavirus pandemic and commemorating historical Buddhist ties; (4) renovating temples and restoring Buddhist sites; (5) inviting foreign Buddhists to BAC-initiated regional Buddhist conferences; (6) joint Buddhist scholarship and clerical exchanges; (7) charity and disaster relief projects; and (8) building Buddhist-themed BRI infrastructure to appeal to populations and enhance the position of leaders (Ashiwa and Wank 2020).[11] These activities seek to engage elite clerics, politicians, and officials, including inviting them to visit the PRC, reflecting the UFWD aim of cultivating elites. Such ties expose persons to Chinese views, amplifying discourses that facilitate Chinese interests (Lulu 2019, 28).[12]

Second are Western countries with recent histories of Buddhism and growing popular appreciation of Buddhism as Asian culture in daily life. Here, we see efforts to build Chinese Buddhist temples, both small and large, that can represent Chinese culture to non-Buddhist populations. An example is the Shaolin Temple in Berlin, which opened in 2004, one of the earliest temples from the PRC to open overseas branches. When we visited in 2018, its members referred to the temple as a martial arts school that taught self-defense, body conditioning, and stress relief, without mentioning Buddhism (Wank 2018).[13] Large temple building projects are visible in Australia and Canada, with sizable immigrant communities from the PRC (at least 3 percent of the population). For Buddhists and Chinese tourists, the projects are sites of worship and pilgrimage, while to the general population, they are Chinese culture theme parks and peace parks. These projects can give the Chinese clerics associated with them greater prominence in the host countries. This can increase the volume of PRC-linked voices in their public spheres, offsetting those of other Buddhists that the CPC considers competitors, such as those linked to the Dalai Lama and Taiwan. Other activities include establishing Buddhist associations and undertaking joint scholarship on Buddhism with universities outside the PRC. Notably, promoting Buddhist culture and temple building in Buddhist-majority Asian countries seems much less common, possibly because this might offend populations with long Buddhist traditions.

Third are strategies for Asian countries—India, Japan, Taiwan—that the CPC sees as geopolitical rivals, and the BAC views as competing for global status in Buddhism. Strategies seek to raise the status of China's Buddhism globally. India, with its long history of Buddhism, competes with China as the center of Buddhism's historical legacy, even though there are few Buddhists in India.[14] To compete, China is establishing Buddhist academies and expanding Buddhist sites in China and other countries. This seeks to elevate China as the center of Buddhist teaching and pilgrimage vis-à-vis India. In Japan, Chinese clerics and devotees are recovering a Vajrayana Buddhist lineage that disappeared in China but still exists at a temple on Mount Koya 高野山. This could reintroduce a Vajrayana Buddhist lineage into China as an alternative to Tibetan Buddhism, possibly diluting its influence in the PRC. Regarding Taiwan, PRC clerics are undertaking charity and cultural activities in other countries that compete with Taiwan-based Buddhist global organizations, such as Fo Guang Shan and the Buddhist Compassion Relief Tzu Chi Foundation.

The visible face of the state promotion are Buddhist clerics. Having studied in Buddhist academies in the PRC, the clerics understand the CPC religious discourse and policy, state expectations toward religion, and how to cooperate with the system. To varying degrees, they accept this cooperation as means to propagate Buddhism. Some of them are elite members of the PRC Buddhist establishment and are primarily based in the PRC. They pursue propagation activities with the backing of state agencies. Other clerics have emigrated abroad after being educated and ordained in the PRC. In their new societies, they receive support from the UFWD and PRC embassies in mobilizing support for their activities from the overseas Chinese communities. This can include considerable funding for new temple construction from overseas Chinese business communities (Groot 2018).[15] The CPC sees these activities as increasing the visibility and soft power of Chinese culture. Clerics who are active and successful in these endeavors may gain enhanced status in the PRC, including invitations to participate in ceremonies and give keynote talks at important Buddhist events.

The alignment of clerics' efforts to propagate Buddhism with the state initiatives and discourses can be observed in the activities of Yinshun 印順.[16] He is best known as the architect of a "South Seas Buddhism" that seeks to expand the influence and reputation of Chinese Buddhism in Buddhist countries along the BRI in South and Southeast Asia. He has promoted all three modalities of Buddhism in projects that further state political and economic interests at national, provincial, and local levels and are integrated with industry sectors, including media, tourism, transportation, and construction.

Yinshun 印順 was born in 1974 into a family of teachers in Hubei Province, studied philosophy at Peking University, was ordained in 2000, and obtained a doctorate in Buddhism from Thailand's Chulalongkorn University. His master was Benhuan 本煥 (1907–2012), the 44th generation of the Linji School 臨濟宗, and among the last living links to the famous master monks in China in the early twentieth century, and honorary president from the BAC (2010–2012). He was also the founder of Hongfa Temple 弘法寺 in the 1980s, the first new temple built by the state in the PRC. The temple added a cultural dimension to the Shenzhen Special Economic Zone, established in 1981 next to Hong Kong at the start of China's market liberalization. In 2008, Yinshun became abbot of Hongfa Temple and was subsequently selected for national and provincial leadership positions, including BAC vice president and representative positions on the CPPCC of Guangdong and Hainan provinces and Shenzhen City (Jiaojiao 2018). He has assumed multiple office-holding positions, skillfully leveraging them to gain cooperation and support from government and party agencies.

One of his earliest accomplishments was helping to develop Lumbini, the birthplace of Siddhartha Gautama Siddhartha in the fifth century BCE, designated as a UNESCO World Heritage site in 1997. In 1999 the Zhonghua Temple (China Temple) 中華寺 was consecrated in Lumbini, with Yinshun becoming abbot in 2001. It was the first large-scale temple authorized by the BAC for construction outside of the PRC and was financed by China to build goodwill with the Nepali government (Yanrong 2015). The temple's construction extended Chinese influence over the Buddhist heritage of Nepal, one of Asia's poorest countries strategically located between China and India. Its construction elevated the status of Lumbini as a pilgrimage site that competes with Bodh Gaya in India, the site of Buddha's enlightenment, as the holiest site in Buddhism (Lam 2018). The temple seeks to build goodwill with the surrounding Nepalese population by disbursing charity and relief aid. China's $3 billion spending in Lumbini was a significant share of Nepal's foreign investment, giving the PRC leverage over its government. Nepal has permitted the PRC to build a rail link between Lhasa and Lumbini to serve Chinese tourists and connect to the BRI. India considers it a security threat and sought permission to connect Nepal to the Indian railway network. The Nepalese government has also discouraged Tibetan refugees from coming to Tibet, which the CPC strongly desires to marginalize supporters of the Dalai Lama. Additionally, Zhonghua Temple can be seen as a base to weaken the Tibetan Vajrayana Buddhism widely practiced among the 10 percent of

Nepalis who are Buddhist by providing a Mahayana Buddhist alternative controlled by the BAC (Jackson 2019).[17]

Another activity of Yin Shun is creating "people-to-people exchanges" among influential clerics, ministers of culture, and retired statespersons from other countries. Such exchanges are the core UFWD strategy of creating networks that amplify discourses conducive to Chinese economic and political interests. He has established the South China Sea Buddhism Shenzhen Round Table 南海佛教深圳圓桌會議 and the Religious Leaders Dialogue session at the Baoao Forum, China's answer to the Davos World Economic Forum. The former was founded in 2016 and convened by Hongfa Temple. It invites clerics from other Asian countries to discuss and adopt shared activities for exchanges of clerics, Buddhist scholarship, and charity. Its discourses help legitimize the "South China Sea" as a region comprising Southeast and South Asia integrated through China. The anodyne theme of each roundtable encompasses both Buddhist teaching and Chinese state discourses. For example, at the 2018 roundtable, under the theme "Welcome the Contributions of All Parties and Build a Common Future," participating clerics from 12 countries signed a document calling for stable peace in the region. At the discussion, the participants denied claims that China was militarizing the South China Sea and attributed regional tensions to an "outside power," most likely an oblique reference to the United States (Ruohan 2018). One monk in the US delegation was quoted as saying, "Sending aircraft and warships will only increase the intensity in the region and trigger unnecessary panic among people living in the region" (Ruohan 2018). This highlights the UFWD technique of cultivating third-party actors in overseas Chinese communities to amplify CPC-approved discursive talking points (Lim and Bergin 2018).[18] The US monk was Huieguang, who founded the International Bodhisattva Sangha in 2006 in San Diego, California. He is a disciple of Hsingyun, the founder of Fo Guang Shan on Taiwan, a visible advocate of close ties between Taiwan and the PRC. Huieguang is also a dharma brother of Yinshun.[19]

A third area of Yinshun's activities has been developing state-approved modalities of Buddhism while establishing China as a world center of Buddhist education. In 2017, he opened the Nanhai Buddhist Academy in China's southernmost province of Hainan. The Chinese media calls it "China's Nalanda," an appropriation of the name of the world's oldest Buddhist school located in India. The academy has an international student body, and its curriculum encompasses all three modalities of Buddhism. It teaches the three traditions of Chinese Buddhism, with Chinese, Tibetan, and Pali as the foundational scholarship languages. Notably, the displacement of Sanskrit challenges the authority of Western Buddhist scholarship and Indo–Sri Lankan Buddhist study, which takes Sanskrit as the authentic language for understanding Buddhism. The displacement also elevates the importance of the Chinese language and Chinese texts. The majority of the departments exclusively teach Buddhist culture, including tea, music, architecture, and charity management. The academy is also a platform for exchanges of clerics, agreed upon at the Shenzhen South China Sea Buddhism Roundtable with slots for specific countries, including 40 for Laos and 60 for Cambodia (Shumei 2019). Additionally, the academy contributes to the large tourism economy of Hainan Province. It lies adjacent to the Nanshan Culture Tourism Zone, a 34.7 square kilometers theme park that includes the Buddhism Culture Park, Nanshan Temple, where Yinshun is abbot, and the Guanyin Park with a 108-meter-high Guanyin statue. The academy's presence helps legitimate the entire zone as a Buddhist religious and cultural site, elevating its soft-power value for the state. Thus, the Hainan Buddhist Academy, the Zhonghua Temple in Lumbini, and the South China Sea Buddhism Shenzhen Roundtable, illustrate how Buddhist clerics from the PRC, with state support, promote Buddhism in projects that create relations, dependencies, and discourses conducive to Chinese political and economic interests.

Conclusion

The career of Yinshun shows how globalizing Chinese Buddhism proceeds through modalities of Buddhism and state strategies in multiple projects. The projects are coordinated through the CPC and integrated with economic and political interests to produce local effects in other countries. Depending on the context and means of promotion, the effects can be soft power or sharp power, or even both, because a project has multiple effects. The involvement of the clerics does not necessarily signify their commitment to CPC ideology but rather their awareness of how religions exist in the PRC and CPC expectations toward Buddhism. Under Xi Jinping, more aspects of CPC's political discourses and state administrative control of Buddhism within the PRC are projected outward via international organizations and to other countries.

On the one hand, Xi Jinping has declared Chinese Buddhism as the "excellent" civilizational culture of the rejuvenated Chinese nation and, on the other, the cultural vehicle for international understanding and universal values of peace and shared destiny. There is an inherent contradiction in the promotion of nationalistic Buddhism in local contexts of other countries. A similar contradiction existed in the earlier promotion by the Empire of Japan of nationalistic Japanese Buddhism to culturally control the populations in East Asian colonies. The historical record shows that this effort contributed to anti-Japanese sentiments in the colonies (Hur 1999, 107–134). An issue is how state-promoted Chinese Buddhism will interact with locally embedded Buddhist traditions in Asian countries and westernized Buddhism seeking ecumenicism while confronting other religions seeking religious dialogue and tolerance. It is undeniable that Chinese Buddhist clerics and organizations at the front lines of projects will be affected by these experiences. Their everyday interactions may alter their thinking and actions for the long term, possibly triggering a transformation in the relations of Buddhism and the state in the PRC (Ashiwa and Wank 2009).[20]

References

Ashiwa, Yoshiko, and David L. Wank, eds. 2009. *Making Religion, Making the State: The Politics of Religion in Modern China*. Stanford: Stanford University Press.
Ashiwa, Yoshiko, and David L. Wank, eds. 2020. "COVID-19 Impacts Chinese Buddhism, State Control, and Soft Power." *Religion & Diplomacy*, April 20, 2020. https://religionanddiplomacy.org.uk/2020/04/20/special-report-impact-of-covid-19-on-chinese-buddhism-and-soft-power.
Bowe, Alexander. 2018. "China's Overseas United Front Work: Background and Implications for the United States." *U.S.-China Economic and Security Review Commission Staff Research Report*, August 24, 2018, 12–15. https://www.uscc.gov/research/chinas-overseas-united-front-work-background-and-implications-united-states.
Chen Xingqiao 陈星桥. 2015. "The Significance, Bottlenecks, and Strategic Thinking of Chinese Buddhism Going Global" (中國佛教走出去的意義、瓶頸及其戰畧思考), *Fayin* 6. www.chinabuddhism.com.cn/yj/2015-07-21/9189.html.
Groot, Gerry. 2018. "Understanding the Role of Chambers of Commerce and Industry Association in United Front Work." *The Jamestown Foundation*, June 19, 2018. https://jamestown.org/program/understanding-the-role-of-chambers-of-commerce-and-industry-associations-in-united-front-work/.
Hur, Nam-Lin. 1999. "The Sōtō Sect and Japanese Military Imperialism in Korea." *Japanese Journal of Religious Studies* 26 (1–2): 107–134.
Jackson, Lauren. 2019. "China Is Winning the War for Nepali Buddhism." *The Diplomat*, March 21, 2019. https://thediplomat.com/2019/03/china-is-winning-the-war-for-nepali-buddhism/.
Ji Zhe, Gareth Fisher and André Laliberté, eds. 2019. *Buddhism After Mao: Negotiations, Continuities, and Reinventions*. Honolulu: University of Hawai'i Press.

Joske, Alex. 2019. "Reorganizing the United Front Work Department: New Structures for a New Era of Diaspora and Religious Affairs Work." *The Jamestown Foundation*, May 9, 2019. https://jamestown.org/program/reorganizing-the-united-front-work-departm ent-new-structures-for-a-new-era-of-diaspora-and-religious-affairs-work/.

Kyaw, Hsu Mon. 2011. "China to Send Sacred Tooth Relic." *Myanmar Times*, August 15, 2011. www.mmtimes.com/national-news/2320-china-to-send-sacred-tooth-relic.html.

Lai, Hongyi. 2012. "Introduction: The Soft Power Concept and a Rising China." In *China's Soft Power and International Relations*, edited by Hongyi Lai and Yiyi Lu, 1–20. Abingdon: Routledge.

Lam, Raymond. 2018. "Chinese Monks Walk from Nepal to Bohd Gaya in Gesture of Ecumenicism." *Global Buddhist Door*, December 5, 2018. www.buddhistdoor.net/news/chinese-monks-walk-from-nepal-to-bodh-gaya-in-gesture-of-ecumenism.

Lim, Louisa, and Julia Bergin. 2018. "Inside China's Audacious Global Propaganda Campaign," *The Guardian*, December 7, 2018. www.theguardian.com/news/2018/dec/07/china-plan-for-global-media-dominance-propaganda-xi-jinping.

Shiu-Hing Lo, Sonny , Steven Chung-Fun Hung, and Jeff Hai-Chi Loo 2019. *China's New United Front Work in Hong Kong: Penetrative Politics and it Implications*. Singapore: Palgrave.

Lulu, Jichang. 2019. "Repurposing Democracy: The European Parliament China Friendship Cluster." *Sinopsis*. https://sinopsis.cz/wp-content/uploads/2019/11/ep.pdf.

Mendis, Patrick. 2013. "China Buddhist Diplomacy: Why Do America and India Entangle with Tiny Sri Lanka?" *Journal of International Affairs*, February 22, 2013. https://jia.sipa.columbia.edu/online-articles/china's-buddhist-diplomacy-why-do-america-and-india-entangle-tiny-sri-lanka.

Nye Jr., Joseph S. 2004. "Soft Power and American Foreign Policy." *Political Science Quarterly* 119 (2): 255–70.

Ramachandran, Sudha. 2019. "Rivalries and Relics: Examining China's Buddhist Public Diplomacy." *The Jamestown Foundation* 19 (5): 15–21. https://jamestown.org/prog ram/rivalries-and-relics-examining-chinas-buddhist-public-diplomacy/.

Raymond, Gregory V. 2020. "Religion as Tool of Influence: Buddhism and China's Belt and Road Initiative in Mainland Southeast Asia." *Contemporary Southeast Asia* 42 (3): 346–371.

Ruohan, Li. 2018. "Buddhist Masters Urge Understanding to Preserve Sea Peace." *Global Times*, October 31, 2018. www.globaltimes.cn/content/1125285.shtml.

Scott, David. 2016. "Buddhism in Current China-India Diplomacy." *Journal of Current Chinese Affairs* 45 (3): 139–174.

Sen, Tansen. 2015. *Buddhism, Diplomacy, and Trade: The Realignment of India-China Relations, 600–1400*. Lanham: Rowman & Littlefield.

Shumei, Leng. 2019. "Monks Offer Peaceful Approach to Enhance Civil Communication in South China Sea Region." *Global Times*, October 22, 2019. www.globaltimes.cn/cont ent/1167611.shtml.

Slyke, Lyman. 1970. "The United Front in China." *Journal of Contemporary History* 5 (3): 119–135.

Strong, John S. 2004. *Relics of the Buddha*. Princeton: Princeton University Press.

Tambiah, S. J. 1976. *World Conqueror and World Renouncer: A Study of Buddhism and Poilty in Thailand against a Historical Background*. Cambridge: Cambridge University Press.

Victoria, Brian Daizen. 2006. *Zen at War*. Lanham: Rowman & Littlefield.
Walker, Christopher. 2018. "What Is 'Sharp Power'?" *Journal of Democracy* 29 (3): 9–23.
Welch, Holmes. 1972. *Buddhism Under Mao*. Cambridge, MA: Harvard University Press.
Xi Jinping. 2013. "Transcript of Xi Jinping's August 19th Speech: In Terms of Speech, We must Dare to Grasp, Dare to Control, Dare to Shine" 傳習近平8•19講話全文：言論方面要敢抓敢 管敢於亮劍, November 4, 2013, *China Digital Times*. https://chinadigitaltimes.net/chinese/321001.html.
Xi Jinping. 2014. 在藝文工作座談會的講話 ["Speech at the Symposium on Literary and Artistic Work"], March 15, 2014. http://cpc.people.com.cn/n/2015/1015/c64094-27699249.html.
Xu Jiaojiao 許嬌蛟. 2018. "Yinshun: I Wish to Spend my Whole Life using Great Love to Comfort People" (印順：我願傾盡一生用大愛撫慰人). CPPCC, September 29, 2018. http://cppcc.china.com.cn/2018-09/29/content_64311809.htm.
Xu, Yihua. 2015. "Religion and China's Public Diplomacy in the Era of Globalization." *Journal of Middle Eastern and Islamic Studies (in Asia)* 9 (4): 14–35.
Xuecheng 學誠. 2015. "Love the Country, Love Religion, be Faithful and Righteous, Promote the Healthy and Comprehensive Development pf Buddhism so as to Contribute to Realizing the China Dream and the Great Rejuvenation of the Chinese Nation" (學誠, 愛國愛教 正信正行 推動佛教事業健康全面發展 為實現中華民族偉大復興的中國夢貢獻力量). *Fayin* 5.
Zhao Yanrong. 2015. "Pillars of the Community." *China Daily Asia*, July 31, 2015. www.chinadailyasia.com/asiaweekly/2015-07/31/content_15298128.html.
Zhang, J. 2013. "China's Faith Diplomacy." In *Religion and Public Diplomacy*, edited by Philip Seib, 75–97. London: Palgrave Macmillan.
Zhou Fang 周芳. 2014. "Chinese People's Political Consultative Conference National Committee member Ven. Juexing: Chinese Buddhism Should 'Go Global'" (全國政協委員覺醒法師：中國佛教應"走出去"). *Zhongguo Minzu Bao*, March 5, 2014. www.cssn.cn/zjx/zjx_zjsj/201403/t20140305_1020038.shtml.

5
Turkey's Ambivalent Religious Soft Power in the Illiberal Turn

Ahmet Erdi Öztürk

This chapter will explore Turkey's position as a religious soft power, a discussion that has risen in prominence during the era of the Turkish Justice and Development Party's (*Adalet ve Kalkınma Partisi*, AKP) political domination and which necessarily entails a more detailed and retrospective analysis. The debate around whether Turkey embodied a soft power was particularly relevant during the 2000s. Some research in this field claims that the relatively positive transformation Turkey experienced in domestic politics between 2002 and 2010 contributed favorably to its positioning as a soft power and, moreover, that its potential in this context grew outward (Oğuzlu 2007; Kalın 2011; Altınay 2008). Parallel to these studies, other discussions proliferated with a comparably positive reading of the soft-power practices that Turkey implemented, in various regions, with its television programs (Yörük and Vatikiotis 2013), business representatives (Özdemirkıran 2015), and the cultural activities of its transnational state apparatuses (Kaya and Tecmen 2011). The research not only pertains to these issues but also varies immensely regarding Turkey's approach to the Balkans, the Middle East and, even, the rest of the world (Candar 2009, Ekşi 2017; Dursu-Ozkanca 2013). It would undoubtedly be misguided to believe that these studies affirmed Turkey and its foreign policy actions, which could be described as soft power. Starting with Turkey's descent into authoritarianism in 2013 (Esen and Gümüşcü 2016, Baser and Öztürk 2017), debates arose regarding the limitations of the instruments of soft power it sought to equip in foreign policy as well as the domains in which it was decidedly inadequate (Altunışık 2008).

Despite the frequent discussions of Turkey and the soft power the country sought to exhibit in various manners, these studies fail to transcend a merely descriptive approach, even though their analyses always examine religious soft power as being interwoven with culture and history (Gözaydın 2010;

Yılmaz and Barry 2020). Nevertheless, when we consider that religion, in Turkey, is a component of both its state identity and its foreign policy (Koppa 2020; Özpek and Park 2020) and that, especially during the reign of the Justice and Development Party (*Adalet ve Kalkınma Partisi*, AKP), Turkey used Sunni Islam to various extents in foreign policy (Öztürk and Sözeri 2018; Bruce 2020), two crucial questions emerge: How does Turkey use Sunni Islam as a tool in foreign policy consistently with its changing and evolving domestic policy, and how can we assess this usage within the concept of religious soft power? The answers to these questions arise from a collective analysis of Turkish domestic and foreign policy, which are certainly advancing in tandem.

With the goal of answering these questions, this study will primarily explain the manner in which the concept of religious soft power is discussed, using the views of a host of thinkers who have published works on the topic. Later, the paper will examine what meaning religion and, especially, Sunni Islam bear for the Turkish state identity and will strive to illustrate Turkey's distinct understanding of laïcité. It will then consider how Turkey wielded religion in foreign policy, starting in the mid-twentieth century up until 2002. And finally—constituting a significant portion of this study—it will discuss how the AKP utilized religion as a soft power in foreign policy throughout its 20-year exploits, offering examples from the Balkans, continental Europe, Africa, and the rest of the world.

The Debates Around Religious Soft Power

Joseph Nye, with the concept of soft power he introduced to the world, articulated changes to his own definition numerous times since the early 1990s. Although he did this by offering examples of a host of actors in the evolving international order, the fundamental characteristic of soft power, according to him, remained fixed. This characteristic was that states, without using direct military intervention or other coercive sanctions, exert relatively positive influence over other states and other societies and increase their persuasive capabilities (Nye 1990, 2004, 2008). The discussions of soft power after Nye proliferated and diversified, and thinkers strove to understand the soft powers of nations other than the United States and Western countries. They sought to elucidate how and in what manner nations such as Japan (Iwabuchi 2015) and even Russia (Stefano 2018) used the concept of soft power. Beyond these country-based studies, more discussions arose around how elements of popular culture (Chu 2012), state identity (Mingjiang 2008), and history (Sancak 2016) were wielded as soft power. Interestingly, other prominent figures—including the founder father of the concept—neglected in the considerably rich and comprehensive discussions of the idea, to scrutinize the relationship soft power constructed with religion. Fundamentally, the pressure of the secularization issue failed to bring together the themes of religion and soft power, even though religion, as Ben-Porat (2013) pointed out, is one of our oldest codes of identity along with ethnicity.

Nevertheless, we slowly began to realize, in the closing decades of the twenty-first century, that global secularization was not the final destination. The 1979 Iranian Revolution,[1] the Bosnian War that broke out in the mid-1990s, the reemergence of religion as a central element in the Balkans, the 9/11 attacks that struck at the turn of the millennium, and the Christian democratic parties that arose immediately afterward communicate to us that the influence of religion, in reality, had never disappeared (Thomas 2005; Fox and Sandler 2004, 4). It also amasses many pejorative ideas, such as the power religion holds over politics and society, and the clash of civilizations (Huntington 1993)—a fundamentally orientalist postulation. Despite the vigorous reiterations that these pejorative arguments lack significant provision in the real world (Cesari and Fox 2016; Haynes 2019), phenomena such as ISIS continually nourish pessimistic scenarios.

Within all this chaos, as philosophers ponder the manner in which religion plays a role in international relations (Fox and Sandler 2004; Mavelli and Petito 2014), figures influenced by variants of theory—primarily the liberal, neoliberal, and English School theories—and the representatives of nearly all subsequent theories began debating whether religion could be used collectively with the concept of soft power that Joseph Nye posited in the late 1980s. Jeffrey Haynes (2007, 2008, 2016) was the first to seriously use this concept in relation to religion. Haynes argues that both religion and religious actors can impact foreign policy and that this influence must be defined as religious soft power. But we can say that this influence reveals itself with great variation—both positive and negative—because religion, as Philpott (2007) specified, is "ambivalent" about politics. Despite the frequency with which the ability of religion and religious institutions and actors to be used as an element of soft power in international politics has been discussed in the past decade (Steiner 2011; Ciftci and Tezcür 2016), limited research has approached the issue with a collective reading of domestic and international politics. Moreover, there is a dearth of studies that examine whether, how, and the manners in which states can use religion as soft power.

As religion has cast about for a new path, intertwined with populist politics, and as we hurtle into the 2020s, it produces a reexamination of its use as an element of power in foreign policy. Mandaville and Hamid (2018), expanding on the groundwork Haynes set out, emphasize the numerous, divergent facets of reliance on the transnational use of religion despite the variant usage of the concept of soft power. They identified three characteristics that states possess regarding transnational religious soft power. First is the institutional and normative capacity of states and their civilizational affinity. Second is the sociopolitical circumstances of states and the aims of those seeking to wield religious soft power. Third is the double-edged sword structure of religious soft power. And finally, as a contribution to the literature, Bettiza (2020) posits that some states have critical religious resources and that we must learn to craft new definitions for the use of these as symbolic, cultural, and network-based religious elements by broadening the limitations of the classic concept of soft power. It is possible to use these definitions in a form of collective synthesis.

The issue here assumes a slightly complicated state when it pertains to a country like Turkey, which, after the Ottoman Empire, was founded by sometimes rejecting and sometimes using its legacy, and the imperative emerges to synthesize and use the explanations mentioned earlier in the chapter. The underlying reason for this is that religion played a critical role in Turkey's evolving and transforming domestic political configuration and that domestic political changes reflected directly in the state's foreign policy behaviors. While it maintains the ability to use religion, consistent with Haynes's suggestion, with soft power in foreign policy, it also boasts the ability to diversify this symbolically, culturally, and in a network-based manner, as Bettiza defined it. Moreover, it has serious institutional power networks it crafted through religious transnational state apparatuses and the state as well as with the religious organizations with which it works in coordination. But because of the state identity that Turkey strove to change as a result of the AKP administration's political maneuvers, especially in the 2010s, this is a multifaceted religious soft power. To put it more explicitly, Turkey, over the past 10 years, has undergone a process of metamorphosis in which religion played a considerable role during the AKP era, and this diversifies and convolutes the use of religion in domestic and foreign policy. From within this diversification, a slew of different actors and historical turning points rise to a determinant position. In sum, if we are to examine Turkey's relationship with religion on a historical and multidimensional plane, stretching from domestic policy to international politics, not only will we see the manner in which such an intricate country wielded religion as an element of soft power, but we can also contribute to the debates around religious soft power.

The Turkish Brand of Secularism and Its Transformation

Although the classic discourse may allege that Turkey was founded as an infant state upon the collapse of the Ottoman state in 1923, the reality is that the situation relies upon multifaceted processes of continuity and denial. We can say that Turkey emerged as a product of the modernization process that began initially with the Ottoman army in the seventeenth century, which continued with the state administration and that ultimately influenced the state identity (Mardin 2000). Turkey's founding cadre may not have expressly underscored this continuity, but another important matter that similarly received no such emphasis was the relationship between state-society and religion. The founder cadre claims that they founded a "secular republic," declaring that the relationships of state and religion in Turkey were discrete from the very beginning of the republic and, constitutionally, starting in 1937. The elimination of the caliphate on March 3, 1924 was a revolutionary decision for both Turkey and the Muslim world, but, with the same decision, the Presidency of Religious Affairs (*Diyanet İşleri Başkanlığı*, Diyanet) was founded to fulfill, on behalf of the state, the regulation and supervision of Sunni Islam in Turkey. As the abolition of the Caliphate and all the activities of religious communities were banned, support was given for the state to manage religious affairs via a bureaucratic institution. The Turkish brand of secularism fundamentally relates not to the separation of religion and state but to the state's control over the influence that religion has on society, in order to advance the interests of the state (Öztürk 2016). And this pattern of intellectual and practical behavior is the continuity of a Byzantine and Ottoman legacy.

But the most critical point at which Turkey deviates from the Ottoman Empire was the nascent country's efforts to Turkify Sunni Islam during the formation of the nation-state and the right of the state to speak, with a universal tone, about Sunni Islam through the Diyanet. In the 1930s, which featured the most intense Turkification efforts, the traces of historical religious organizations were erased from Anatolia and the reading of the Quran was Turkified in this context. In other words, the state wished to absorb Sunni Islam into its own monopoly during what is referred to as the Early Republican Era. While this appears to have been successful, the situation fundamentally culminated with extreme dissatisfaction among significant segments of society, and, starting in 1946 when the political system transitioned to a multiparty structure, politicians in each era have used perpetuated this configuration (Öztürk 2019, 83). This caused the departure of both secularism and religion from the stable use of political institutions.

The instrumentalization of the religious space by a slew of political structures that control the state is, in a sense, consistent methodologically with Turkish laïcité, but over time, the Islamic communal organizations that were initially excluded became actors of paramount influence, along with the Diyanet. These Islamic communal organizations, such as Naksibendi Movement and Nur Movement, have been the historical civic or semicivic structures in Anatolia, and they have been organizing as an alternative Islamic sociopolitical movement in Turkey (Öztürk 2021). Moreover, actors within Turkey, over time, began to export domestic activities with the changing and evolving world order. These circumstances first appeared in continental Europe in the late 1960s. European nations, which hosted numerous Muslim and Turkish migrants within their borders after World War II, started collaborating with Turkey to provide these residents with religious services. Turkish religions organizations during the 1970s and, afterward, the Diyanet began to operate in continental Europe. The coordination between European states and Turkey and Turkish actors originated from Turkey's more similar nature, culturally and politically, to Europe, with its secular state identity. Additionally, Turkey's satiation of the space for religious services would, in a sense, break any potential Wahhabi and Salafi influence; Europe viewed these movements as detrimental to its own social fabric (Öztürk and Sözeri 2018). We see that Turkey was operating in Western societies with the Diyanet, its official religious institution, starting in the early 1970s and with religious organizations that were active as the unofficial yet de facto arms of the state in the late 1980s. Turkey started fostering relations with both its own diaspora and non-Turkish Muslim groups by constructing mosques and offering Quran-reading courses in countries with prominent Muslim and Turkish populations, including Germany, France, and the Netherlands. In those years, when Turkey had not yet begun using the concept of soft power, it was possible to interpret its ingress into foreign nations with religion and religious institutions and its creation of a certain influence over those societies as religious soft power. We can connect Turkey's more active nature, relative to other Muslim-majority nations, to its historical Ottoman legacy, its having a religious institution which the secular state identity supported and maintaining a comparably harmonious understanding of Islam.

We witness the state's expanding use of religion after the implementation of the multiparty system in Turkey. We see that religion and religious actors advance toward the center of state functions, a move that reveals itself with the changing and evolving structure of the international political system in the 1990s (Yavuz 2003). The conclusion of the Cold War and the instrumentalization of religion in countries' domestic political spaces and in international relations paved the way to Turkey's more active engagement beyond its borders with religious institutions. Turkey, especially in the 1990s, began opening foreign missions of the Diyanet in newly founded Turkic republics and in Balkan nations, becoming active in those nations also through religious organizations. For instance, the Turkish Diyanet was operating in Balkan nations such as Bulgaria, Albania, and North Macedonia and in Turkic republics such as Azerbaijan in the 1990s. Differently from European nations, Turkey began to train imams and conduct commercial operations with the religious institutions in those countries.

Starting especially in the early 1990s, the other structure with which Turkey engaged besides the Diyanet was the Gülen Movement. Understanding what the Gülen Movement is and what kind of relationship it cultivated with Turkey's state structure is critical in order to grasp how Turkey was defined as a religious power in the 2000s. The Gülen Movement was a multidimensional religious movement that was organized in Anatolia in the late 1960s by Fethullah Gülen, a retired imam. Fragmenting from the Nur Movement, whose roots date back to before the founding of the modern Turkish republic, this structure, on the one hand, inoculated younger, religious generations in Anatolia with a more moderate and worldly understanding of religion and, on the other hand, sought to gain a foothold within the state mechanism, which was in the hands of the Kemalist and secular elites (Yavuz 2018). Because of this characteristic, we can declare that the Gülen Movement has two distinct faces. The first face relies on education and seeks to engender a new, pious generation, and the other is a parapolitical face striving to function within the state and the state's security bureaucracy (Watmough and Öztürk 2018). While being labeled the enemy by Turkey's secular state elite, it became a protected structure in center-right and conservative spaces. This structure began to open educational institutions, first in the Balkans, Turkic republics, and Africa, and, later, in continental Europe, gaining a transnational character in the late 1990s, and started developing social and political relations by educating the children of elites in these countries. The Gülen Movement founded educational institutions, industrial associations, and media publications such as newspapers and magazines, and it portrayed itself as representative of the moderate Islam that was popular in the 1990s. These actions were no doubt etched into Turkish society and, in a sense, could be identified within religion's soft power.

The period between 1950 and 2000, for Turkey, could be read as the struggle between the secular Kemalist raison d'état and the Islamist political and social actors endeavoring to veer toward the central state that the Kemalists strove to preserve. Despite this struggle and the efforts of many bureaucratic institutions, not the least of which being the military, to preserve Turkish secularism, political elites managed to strengthen religious institutions, primarily the Diyanet and the Gülen Movement, both domestically and internationally. The fundamental reason for this was the use of religion in domestic politics as an instrument that would bring together different segments of society and would be viewed as a potential for amassing votes. Additionally, it maintained a status as the principal actor in foreign policy, both among Turkey's own diasporas and in other Muslim groups.

Turkey's AKP Years and the Use of Religion in Foreign Policy

Turkish Islamists, though seizing the brief opportunity to come to power through center-right parties such as the Motherland Party (*Anavatan Partisi*) and the True Path Party (*Doğru Yol Partisi*) and with parties emerging from Necmettin Erbakan's National Vision (*Milli Görüş*) tradition, they were unable to ascend to the ranks of government as forcefully as the AKP did when it assumed sole control in 2002. The AKP turned the page in this sense and in many more in Turkey with its rise to power. Recep Tayyip Erdoğan, who had been reared in the old National Vision tradition but had pushed religious identities to the background and portrayed himself as a conservative democrat, and his friends came to power immediately after organizing politically in 2002 under the banner of a "catch-all" party (Çınar 2006). Within their rapid ascent to power are several key elements challenging the Kemalist and secular state system. Primary among these are their commitment to solve the economic depression through which Turkey had stumbled in the late 1990s, their articulation of their ability to include in the political system key elements of the public whom the state had been excluded for years, and their outline of decisive steps to take on issues such as religious freedom and the Kurdish question, which had become a chronic problem for Turkey (İnsel 2003). Additionally, one of the most significant reasons that they succeeded in enticing various segments in Turkey and elsewhere in the world was that they declared, contrary to their Muslim identity and Islamist history, that they would integrate Turkey with the West to an extent greater than effecting changes in Turkey's Western-based understanding of civilization. The AKP received optimistic reactions from many Western institutions and organizations, not the least of which being the European Union, and came to power promising full membership for Turkey in the EU and, discretely from similar nations, with an understanding of civilization that was majority Muslim yet maintained a secular constitution and was harmonious with the West.

Despite the Muslim-majority Turkish electorate in 2002 and the political administration leading the AKP with a religious sensitivity, the party enacted numerous legislative changes in the name of democratization and freedom during the initial years of its reign. Additionally, it launched an alliance of civilizations initiative with Spain, as an ideology and political configuration to challenge the clash of civilizations thesis that Samuel P. Huntington posited in a rather orientalist manner in 1996, emphasizing the importance of secularism abroad. The weight of this alliance underscored that there was no need for a normative distinction between the Islamic and Christian worlds, and that this distinction emerged only due to political interests (Balcı and Miş 2008).

The arrival, in a burst of positive upheaval, of the AKP's political dominance—and its exhibition of liberalism domestically and solution-oriented activity internationally—paved the way for Turkish institutions to function more comfortably abroad. And the AKP administration, ensuring economic development fixed to a program previously championed by Kemal Derviş (Erkoç 2019, 143), was functioning more freely and confidently. In addition to all these, bureaucrats who, during this time, defended and discharged Turkey's formulaic visions, both in the foreign ministry and within the Diyanet, began to serve in greater numbers. For instance, Mehmet Görmez, who would lead the Diyanet in a manner that later became quite controversial, served as the deputy director of foreign affairs in the Diyanet. During his tenure, the Diyanet began to print Qurans in close to 60 languages and provide aid to African and Balkan nations, and he allowed the Diyanet to become a more active instrument of Turkey's soft power internationally. Turkey's actions in the West also began to expand, with the number of mosques growing rapidly in places such as Germany, France, and Sweden. Ultimately, the AKP, harmonious with the West, was able to function without facing any obstacles.

One of the most important reasons why AKP administrations occupied such a position in the world in the early 2000s and directly and indirectly implemented policies of soft power by coordinating with religious institutions was the collaborative practices it had maintained with the Gülen Movement. As has previously been noted countless times, the Gülen Movement and the National Vision Movement, which the AKP's founding cadres—including Erdoğan—had cultivated, were not religious and political structures that could interact agreeably (Turam 2007). Nevertheless, it is a fact that these cadres, historically incapable of mutual understanding, collaborated in line with certain objectives and interests a short while after the AKP came to power in 2002—and especially after 2004—both within Turkey and beyond its borders. The essential goal, within Turkey, was to install sovereignty within the state to supplant the Kemalist bureaucracy and, internationally, to be the main representative of Turkey as Muslim structures that were amicable with the rest of the world. While the AKP undoubtedly represented the political wing and popular structure within society in this relationship, the weight of the business world and media were in the hands of the Gülen Movement. While the Gülen Movement had for years maintained the public diplomacy for the AKP's Turkey abroad, through the establishment of networks of social relations in various countries, the AKP had engaged in diplomatic initiatives to propagate the schools and operations of the Gülen Movement in different countries (Watmough and Öztürk 2018). Succinctly, this "win-win" relationship based around mutual interests spawned Turkey's discovery of its own religious soft power and resulted in its mobilization to an extent it had never before experienced beyond its borders with a configuration we can observe as a civil society structure at the hands of the state and of the Gülen Movement. The Turkish Diyanet and Gülen Movement schools functioned in close to 100 nations in 2007 and 2008.

But as of 2008, friction began to appear at some points in Turkey's domestic politics. On the one hand, the Gülen Movement-AKP collective began to create judicial processes aiming to liquidate the Kemalist bureaucracy (Rodrik 2011), and, on the other hand, the 2008 global economic crisis began to indirectly rattle the country (Temiz and Gökmen 2009). These two situations damaged two concepts Turkey had sought to bolster since 2002 under the banner of the AKP: justice and development. But the short-term upheaval that broke out in domestic Turkish politics after 2008 did not constitute an obstacle before the state's direct use of religion as soft power in foreign policy. To the contrary, with Ahmet Davutoğlu's rise, first as adviser and by 2009 as foreign minister, Turkey's religious soft power began to crystallize.

Transformation of the AKP's Religious Soft Power

Although, by 2020, he had been forced to resign as prime minister to which Erdoğan had previously appointed him and later founded a new party by departing the AKP, Ahmet Davutoğlu is an important actor necessary to recognize in order to understand Turkish foreign policy between 2009 and 2016 and the extent to which religion was used as an element of soft power in this policy. Davutoğlu, a professor of international relations, had endeavored throughout his active political career to implement the theory he developed himself called "Strategic Depth." Some theorists prefer to describe this as pan-Islamism or neo-Ottomanism, but Davutoğlu stresses the element of Islam that underpins his ideology. This comparably accurate approach does not, however, offer us the full picture, because Davutoğlu claims, with foreign policy activity comprising history, culture, civilization, and religion, that Turkey has the potential to be a regional and global power. In his opinion, Turkey bears the legacy of not only the Ottoman Empire but of all Muslim countries that were previously influential in the region, and it should embody a more active nation around the world, with its civilizational wealth. Islam is, undoubtedly, inherent to this pattern of civilization. Davutoğlu maintained a divergent foreign policy strategy by harmonizing his ideology with such concepts as "zero problems with neighbors" and "rhythmic diplomacy," and this pushed Turkey to depicting itself as a religious soft power.

Turkey began to use transnational state apparatuses more actively—instruments of public diplomacy—during this period and interacted more prolifically in more than 100 countries, primarily via the Diyanet. In the Balkans as well as in other countries with large Muslim populations and, finally, with a significant Turkish diaspora, Turkey began to provide cultural, educational, and humanitarian assistance under the leadership of, or in coordination with, the Diyanet. In many places, Turkey constructed mosques and built schools while offering various forms of aid to countries of a lower economic status than itself. It operated through TIKA, the Yunus Emre Institute, and similar organizations in numerous countries. It maintained these operations in coordination with the Gülen Movement until early 2014, and this allowed Turkey to exist beyond its own borders with help from the state and civil society.

One can assert, for this period, that Turkey's religious soft power increase positively and that this growth spawned a degree of concern in some regions. And this positively realized advancement certainly was the effect of Erdoğan's direct suggestion to the Muslim Brotherhood "not to shy away from secularism." Turkey demonstrated that it still preserved its secular identity in a manner contrary to its broadened use of religion in a manner that conflicted with its classic understanding of foreign policy, and it was viewed positively in Western nations. Nevertheless, Turkey's inclination toward a foreign policy harboring more Islamic tendencies than previously triggered some concerns, especially in Balkan countries, because the appeal of Turkey's religious soft power. We can assert that Turkey began to use religion after 2011 in a paradoxical manner that would instigate a series of problems in the future.

We can say that the appeal of Turkey's active use of religion and religious apparatuses in foreign policy, consistent with the secular state identity it had developed over the years, deteriorated in the wake of certain incidents that arose after 2013. Turkey, as a reflection of some adjustments in domestic politics, came to occupy a position where it more clumsily wielded religion abroad and, consequently, where the policies it implemented in some regions no longer fit the definition of soft power.

Primary among these factors was rapid shift to a populist authoritarianism that Turkey experienced after 2013. Protest movements that erupted against governments around the world in the summer of 2013 appeared in Turkey as well in the form of the Gezi Protests. In Turkey, individuals who oppose the assortment of disconcerting ideological views in the practices of the AKP government began to criticize government policies with street demonstrations in nearly all the nation's provinces and accuse the government of gradually veering toward rampant authoritarianism (Tuğal 2013). The AKP government, rather than extinguishing these demonstrations in a reconciliatory manner, opted to respond with harsh and repressive policies, setting the stage for the party's burgeoning authoritarian tendencies (Iğsız

2014). Additionally, the sudden reversal of outlook for the Arab Spring and the losses by Muslim Brotherhood–supported structures, with which the AKP governments planned to coordinate, of national power in, primarily, Egypt, precipitated the fizzling, in a sense, of policies the AKP had pursued in its neighboring region and compelled Erdoğan to choose more security-oriented policies. The fuel these two situations added to the party's descent into authoritarianism swiftly eliminated Turkey's proportional growth through the democratization of its soft power.

One other reason for Turkey's rapid, domestic authoritarianization, and its adoption of a more aggressive religious foreign policy was the power struggle fought between the Gülen Movement and the AKP that boiled over in late 2014. To the same degree that these two structures formed an interests-based coalition in the 2000s to seize power from the former Kemalist and secular segments of Turkish society, they hurtled into an interests-based battle that began in 2012 and became public in 2014. While this battle culminated with the AKP's victory and the Gülen Movement being declared traitorous, with exclusion from Turkey after the complicated July 15, 2016 coup attempt— still a dark moment for the country—this process influenced how the AKP administration utilized religion domestically and internationally in terms of the religious perspectives of the two structures. Wishing to incapacitate the Gülen Movement, which had amassed influence in more than 100 countries, the AKP primarily began to use Islam more frequently in regions of considerable Muslim populations, such as the Balkans, and began to portray itself as a more "reasonable" Muslim actor than the Gülen Movement (Watmough and Öztürk 2018). Opening mosques, actions that prioritized religion and providing aid entered into the scope of duties for the Turkey of the AKP. The AKP, wishing to engage in these and similar actions in Western nations that had significant Muslim diasporas, was able to carve out a space for itself. Subsequently, countries including Austria, Germany, and France began to react because Turkey's domestic political interests were transported to their countries by means of religious apparatuses. For instance, while France froze the bank accounts of Diyanet mosque associations in early 2020, since these institutions were often weaponized for political aims and degraded the harmony between Muslims in France, Germany launched a 2017 investigation with the assertion that Diyanet imams were conducting espionage in Germany on behalf of the Turkish government (Öztürk 2020).

The Gülen Movement was certainly not the only actor with which Erdoğan's Turkey engaged in conflict using religion over "reasonable" Islam and domestic interests. While interacting with small but influential groups, such as the Furkan Foundation, that resisted complying with the state domestically, a global struggle erupted. Saudi Arabia, Egypt, Iran, and even the Balkans, which are representative of Islam's various interpretations and which battled during the Ottoman era and the early Turkish republic over religion, have waged war over services and visibility in regions in regions with larger Muslim populations, within the Muslim diasporas of European nations and in other areas where Islam is fundamentally not a determinant actor (Öztürk 2021). Though this fundamentally illustrates how various actors used religion as an element of soft power, it reveals how Turkey, which had historically maintained a degree of soft power with its secularism, now portrayed itself with a different identity. This new trajectory, undoubtedly, fans the flames of Turkey's aggressive foreign policy through religion and results in the export of symbols, nationalism, and populist policies cultivated domestically. The best example, in my opinion, is the reversion of the Hagia Sophia to a mosque and that Erdoğan amplified this as a victory won on behalf of Muslims and Turks both domestically and internationally. However, whether this truly was a victory or merely the use of religion for the perpetuity of the administration is another matter entirely.

Conclusion

It is clear that religion and especially Islam have been utilized for centuries as an element of power in foreign policy. Nevertheless, there remains significant uncertainty over how countries of Islam hegemony evaluated this behavior in the use of religion as an element of soft power, a pattern that has only emerged recently. The ambivalent status of religion certainly convolutes the answer to the question whether religion is a mode of soft power, but the weaponization of Islam today both for peace and for terror propels the issue in several different directions. Moreover, it complicates the discussion in a manner that will not easily be resolved. Turkey confronts us beneath all this complexity as an intriguing example both in contemporary and historical terms. While it is relevant that a nation, founded in the ashes of the caliphate and which has a Muslim population, was accepted globally with its unique understanding of laïcité and that this is inherently soft power, we witness a swift and multifaceted transformation. This transformation materialized, especially after 2010, in the AKP's understanding of foreign policy that synthesized authoritarianism, populism, nationalism, and religion, and in its erasure of Turkey's previous perceptions. But the circumstances by which various segments of Turkish society perceived this transformation is also incredibly relevant. It would be better to underline that a considerable group of Muslims around the world viewed this transformation positively, even as it altered Turkey's identity and caused the country's perception as a nation responsible for a sporadic array of problems. This ensures that we cannot remain under the impression, for Turkey, of solely a positive, religious soft power.

References

Altinay, Hakan. 2008. "Turkey's Soft Power: An Unpolished Gem or an Elusive Mirage?" *Insight Turkey* 10 (2): 55–66.

Altunişik, Meliha Benli. 2008. "The Possibilities and Limits of Turkey's Soft Power in the Middle East." *Insight Turkey* 10 (2): 41–54.

Balcı, Ali, and Nebi Miş. 2008. "Turkey's Role in the Alliance of Civilizations: A New Perspective in Turkish Foreign Policy?" *Turkish Studies* 9 (3): 387–406.

Baser, Bahar, and Ahmet Erdi Öztürk. 2017. *Authoritarian Politics in Turkey: Elections, Resistance and the AKP*. Bloomsbury Publishing.

Ben-Porat, Guy. 2013. *Between State and Synagogue: The Secularization of Contemporary Israel*. New York: Cambridge University Press.

Bettiza, Gregorio. 2020. "States, Religions and Power: Highlighting the Role of Sacred Capital in World Politics." *Berkley Center for Religion, Peace, and World Affairs*, March 30, 2020. https://berkleycenter.georgetown.edu/publications/states-religions-and-power-highlighting-the-role-of-sacred-capital-in-world-politics.

Bruce, Benjamin. 2020. "Imams for the Diaspora: The Turkish State's International Theology Programme." *Journal of Ethnic and Migration Studies* 46 (6): 1166–1183.

Çandar, Cengiz. 2009. *Turkey's" Soft Power" Strategy: A New Vision for a Multi-Polar World*. Halle: Universitäts-und Landesbibliothek Sachsen-Anhalt.

Cesari, Jocelyne, and Jonathan Fox. 2016. "Institutional Relations rather than Clashes of Civilizations: When and How Is Religion Compatible with Democracy?" *International Political Sociology* 10 (3): 241–257.

Chu, Yun-han. 2012. "China and East Asian Democracy: the Taiwan Factor." *Journal of Democracy* 23 (1): 42–56.

Ciftci, Sabri, and Güneş Murat Tezcür. 2016. "Soft Power, Religion, and Anti-Americanism in the Middle East." *Foreign Policy Analysis* 12 (3): 374–394.

Cinar, Menderes. 2006. "Turkey's Transformation under the AKP Rule." *Muslim World* 96 (3): 469–486.

Dursun-Ozkanca, Oya. 2013. "Turkish Foreign Policy and the Balkans: Implications on Transatlantic Security," London School of Economics. https://www.lse.ac.uk/LSEE-Research-on-South-Eastern-Europe/Assets/Documents/Events/Presentations/2013-May-Oya-Dursun-Ozkanca-LSEE-Presentation.pdf.

Ekşi, Muharrem. 2017. "Turkey's Cultural Diplomacy and Soft Power Policy towards the Balkans." *Karadeniz Araştırmaları* 55: 189–208.
Emre Erkoc, Taptuk. 2019. "Islam and Economics in the Political Sphere: A Critical Evaluation of the AKP Era in Turkey." *Southeast European and Black Sea Studies* 19 (1): 139–154.
Esen, Berk, and Sebnem Gumuscu. 2016. "Rising Competitive Authoritarianism in Turkey." *Third World Quarterly* 37 (9): 1581–1606.
Fox, Jonathan, and Shmuel Sandler, eds. 2004. *Bringing Religion into International Relations*. New York: Springer.
Gözaydın, İştar. 2010. "Religion as Soft Power in the International Relations of Turkey." *Political Studies Association. IPSA Paper*.
Haynes, Jeffrey. 2008. "Religion and Foreign Policy Making in the USA, India and Iran: Towards a Research Agenda." *Third World Quarterly* 29 (1): 143–165.
Haynes, Jeffrey. 2019. "Religion, Education and Security: The United Nations Alliance of Civilisations and Global Citizenship." *Religions* 10 (1): 51.
Haynes, Jeffrey. 2007. *Introduction to International Relations and Religion*. New York: Routledge.
Haynes, Jeffrey. 2016. *Religious Transnational Actors and Soft Power*. New York: Routledge.
Huntington, Samuel P. 1993. "The Clash of Civilizations?" *Foreign Affairs* 72 (3): 22–49.
Iğsız, Aslı. 2014. "Brand Turkey and the Gezi Protests: Authoritarianism in Flux, Law and Neoliberaiism." In *The Making of a Protest Movement in Turkey: #occupygezi*, edited by Umut özkirimli, 25–49. London: Palgrave.
Insel, Ahmet. 2003. "The AKP and Normalizing Democracy in Turkey." *The South Atlantic Quarterly* 102 (2): 293–308.
Iwabuchi, Koichi. 2015. "Pop-Culture Diplomacy in Japan: Soft Power, Nation Branding and the Question of 'International Cultural Exchange.'" *International Journal of Cultural Policy* 21 (4): 419–432.
Kalin, Ibrahim. 2011. "Soft Power and Public Diplomacy in Turkey." *Perceptions* 16 (3): 5–11.
Kaya, Ayhan, and Ayşe Tecmen. 2011. "Turkish Modernity: A Continuous Journey of Europeanisation." In *Europe, Nations and Modernity*, edited by Robin W. Winks and Joan Neuberger, 13–236. London: Palgrave.
Koppa, Maria Eleni. 2020. "Turkey, Gulf States and Iran in Western Balkans: More than the Islamic Factor?" *Journal of Contemporary European Studies* 29 (5): 1–13.
Mandaville, Peter, and Shadi Hamid. 2018. "Islam as Statecraft: How Governments Use Religion in Foreign Policy." *Brookings Institution*. https://www.brookings.edu/research/islam-as-statecraft-how-governments-use-religion-in-foreign-policy/.
Mardin, Serif. 2000. *The Genesis of Young Ottoman Thought: A Study in the Modernization of Turkish Political Ideas*. New York: Syracuse University Press.
Mavelli, Luca, and Fabio Petito. 2014. "Towards a Postsecular International Politics." In *Towards a Postsecular International Politics*, edited by Luca Mavelli and Fabio Petito, 1–26. London: Palgrave.
Mingjiang, Li. 2008. "China Debates Soft Power." *The Chinese Journal of International Politics* 2 (2): 287–308.
Nye, Joseph S. 2008. "Public Diplomacy and Soft Power." *The Annals of the American Academy of Political and Social Science* 616 (1): 94–109.
Nye, Joseph S. 2004. *Soft Power: The Means to Success in World Politics*. New York: Public Affairs.

Nye, Joseph S. 1990. "Soft Power." *Foreign Policy* 80: 153–171.
Oğuzlu, Tarik. 2007. "Soft Power in Turkish Foreign Policy." *Australian Journal of International Affairs* 61 (1): 81–97.
Özdemirkıran, Merve. 2015. "Soft Power and the Challenges of Private Actors: Turkey-Kurdish Regional Government (KRG) Relations and the Rising Role of Businessmen in Turkish Foreign Policy." *European Journal of Turkish Studies: Social Sciences on Contemporary Turkey* 21 (1): 1–21.
Özpek, Burak Bilgehan, and Bill Park, eds. 2020. *Islamism, Populism, and Turkish Foreign Policy*. New York: Routledge.
Öztürk, Ahmet Erdi, and Semiha Sözeri. 2018. "Diyanet as a Turkish Foreign Policy Tool: Evidence from the Netherlands and Bulgaria." *Politics and Religion* 11 (3): 624–648.
Öztürk, Ahmet Erdi. 2021. *Religion, Identity and Power: Turkey and the Balkans in the Twenty-First Century*. Edinburgh: Edinburgh University Press.
Öztürk, Ahmet Erdi. 2019. "An Alternative Reading of Religion and Authoritarianism: The New Logic between Religion and State in the AKP's New Turkey." *Southeast European and Black Sea Studies* 19 (1): 79–98.
Öztürk, Ahmet Erdi. 2021. "Islam and Foreign Policy: Turkey's Ambivalent Religious Soft Power in the Authoritarian Turn." *Religions* 12 (1): 2–16.
Öztürk, Ahmet Erdi. 2016. "Turkey's Diyanet under AKP Rule: From Protector to Imposer of State Ideology?" *Southeast European and Black Sea Studies* 16 (4): 619–635.
Öztürk, Ahmet Erdi. 2020. "The Many Faces of Turkey's Religious Soft Power." *Berkley Center for Religion, Peace & World Affairs*, August 26, 2020, 1–21. https://berkleycenter.georgetown.edu/publications/the-many-faces-of-turkey-s-religious-soft-power.
Philpott, Daniel. 2007. "Explaining the Political Ambivalence of Religion." *American Political Science Review* 101 (3): 505–525.
Rodrik, Dani. 2011. "Ergenekon and Sledgehammer: Building or Undermining the Rule of Law?" *Turkish Policy Quarterly* 10 (1): 99–109.
Sancak, Kadir. 2016. "Soft Power as an Effect Instruments in Foreign Policy: Turkey's Soft Power Analysis and the Assessment of Its Soft Power Capacity on Azerbaijan." *Turkish Economic Review* 3 (1): 225–234.
Sandal, Nukhet, and Jonathan Fox. 2013. *Religion in International Relations Theory: Interactions and Possibilities*. New York: Routledge.
Stefano, Giulia. 2018. "Russian Soft Power in the Balkans: Bosnia and Serbia, Two States in Comparison." *Centar za Sigurnosne Studije*, 1–21.
Steiner, Kerstin. 2011. "Religion and Politics in Singapore: Matters of National Identity and Security? A Case Study of the Muslim Minority in a Secular State." *Osaka University Law Review* 58 (1): 107–134.
Temiz, Dilek, and Aytac Gokmen. 2009. "The 2000–2001 Financial Crisis in Turkey and the Global Economic Crisis of 2008–2009: Reasons and Comparisons." *International Journal of Social Sciences and Humanity Studies* 1 (1): 1–16.
Thomas, Scott. 2005. *The Global Resurgence of Religion and the Transformation of International Relations: The Struggle for the Soul of the Twenty-First Century*. New York: Springer.
Tuğal, Cihan. 2013. "'Resistance Everywhere': The Gezi Revolt in Global Perspective." *New Perspectives on Turkey* 49 (1): 157–172.
Turam, Berna. 2007. *Between Islam and the State: The Politics of Engagement*. Palo Alto: Stanford University Press.

Watmough, Simon P., and Ahmet Erdi Öztürk. 2018. "The Future of the Gülen Movement in Transnational Political Exile: Introduction to the Special Issue." *Politics, Religion & Ideology* 19 (1): 1–10.

Yavuz, M. Hakan. 2018. "A Framework for Understanding the Intra-Islamist Conflict between the AK Party and the Gülen Movement." *Politics, Religion & Ideology* 19 (1): 11–32.

Yavuz, M. Hakan. 2003. *Islamic Political Identity in Turkey*. New York: Oxford University Press.

Yilmaz, Ihsan, and James Barry. 2020. "Instrumentalizing Islam in a 'Secular' State: Turkey's Diyanet and Interfaith Dialogue." *Journal of Balkan and Near Eastern Studies* 22 (1): 1–16.

Yörük, Zafer, and Pantelis Vatikiotis. 2013. "Turkey, the Middle East & the Media—Soft Power or Illusion of Hegemony: The Case of the Turkish Soap Opera 'Colonialism.'" *International Journal of Communication* 7 (1): 25–41.

6
The Modi Government and the Uses and Limits of India's Religious Soft Power

Sumit Ganguly

Background

India has a long and mostly honorable tradition of the use of soft power in its diplomacy. In the wake of its emergence as an independent nation from the detritus of British colonialism it had few material assets that it could effectively deploy to support its foreign policy goals. Consequently, its policymakers, most notably Prime Minister Jawaharlal Nehru, relied heavily on the power of moral suasion in the conduct of India' foreign policy. Accordingly, he pursued a highly ideational foreign policy that sought to shape international norms in a range of issue areas. These ran the gamut from the pursuit of global disarmament to the quest to end the apartheid regime in South Africa.

However, rarely, if ever, did Nehru draw on India's many religious traditions in his attempts at norm entrepreneurship. Instead, his vision of Indian nationalism was quintessentially secular, civic, and plural. Consequently, he had cast his arguments in humanistic and universalistic terms (Kennedy 2011). During much of his long term in office (1947–1963) he tirelessly worked to promote a range of challenging foreign policy goals. His efforts, though far from wholly successful, did usher in a modicum of changes in the global arena. Among other matters, there is little or no question that he played a vital role in delegitimizing colonialism. He was also at the forefront of opposing the racist regime in Rhodesia and in the apartheid regime in South Africa. Furthermore, despite India's significant material weaknesses he was instrumental in placing global disarmament on the international agenda (Latham 1998, 129–158).

Nehru, of course, was the exponent of the doctrine of nonalignment which served as the basis of India's grand strategy during his term in office.

Under the aegis of this doctrine Nehru had also promoted the concept of "Panchshila" or the "five principles of peaceful coexistence." However, the ideas embodied in these principles had made no explicit reference to India's various religious traditions. They had, of course, drawn upon India's extensive civilizational heritage (Hause 1960, 70–82). That said, Nehru, a staunch believer in a particular conception of secularism that accorded respect toward all faiths, had a complex relationship with religion. In the final analysis, he never attempted to introduce it let alone impose it on public life.[1] More to the point there is evidence that he actively shunned the use of religious rituals in the public sphere.[2]

His successors, while often relying on much of his ideational rhetoric, for all practical purposes, ceded India's moral leadership in most global arenas. They, for the most part, lacked his moral stature because they had squandered his legacy through their flawed policies both at home and abroad (Ajami 1980/1981). Consequently, their attempt to draw on his intellectual inheritance mostly rang hollow and contributed little to meaningful changes in the global order. India's hoary statements in support of a New International Economic Order (NIEO), its long-standing opposition to apartheid and periodic attempts to resurrect various proposals for global disarmament all amounted to little more than a form of "metaphysical pathos" (Duffin 1980, 267–281). For all practical purposes India's voice counted for next to nothing in international affairs during the 1970s and 80s. Its pronouncements were seen as moralistic and devoid of any substance especially as the country wielded little material clout (Thakur 1997, 15–22). At worst, these gestures were viewed across the global community as little more than quixotic.

Its real clout was mostly confined to South Asia. This was amply demonstrated when India successfully intervened in the East Pakistan crisis of 1971 and broke up Pakistan. The collapse of Pakistan albeit with India's assistance underscored the hollowness of Pakistan's founding myth: namely, that Islam alone could serve as the basis of state construction in South Asia. Even though East Pakistan had a larger Muslim population than West Pakistan, it seceded on the grounds of linguistic (and other forms) of discrimination (Chopra 1974).

Indeed, it was not until the Cold War's termination, the dissolution of the Soviet Union, and the end of India's hoary commitment to nonalignment, along with its fitful embrace of market-oriented economic policies that it would emerge, once again, as a somewhat influential actor in the global arena. However, its leaders, for the most part, did not seek to resurrect the

Nehruvian approach to foreign policy. More to the point, the country was preoccupied at home with the needs of liberal economic reforms and the demands of ethnic strife. On the international front it was adjusting its foreign policy to a vastly changed international order (Ganguly 1992, 173–184). The exigencies that the country faced, both at home and abroad, consumed the energies of its political leadership. Consequently, they could not mount a concerted effort to mobilize and deploy the country's significant soft-power resources whether religious or secular.

The country did have a venerable organization, the Indian Council for Cultural Relations (ICCR), which had been founded as early as 1950 with a noted Indian nationalist and India's first Minister of Education, Maulana Abul Kalam Azad, as its president. However, its activities were mostly hobbled owing to a very limited budget. Despite its financial constraints, the ICCR did try to promote cultural diplomacy through the disbursement of a range of scholarships mostly to students from other developing states, the creation of Indian cultural centers abroad and the launching of chairs of Indian studies abroad in a range of fields. Later, especially under Prime Minister Indira Gandhi and several of her successors, New Delhi did launch various "Festivals of India" designed to showcase its cultural heritage abroad. It should be underscored that these activities did not have explicit religious overtones. Subsequently, the Indian Ministry of Tourism launched a massive global campaign, "Incredible India" designed to highlight India's cultural diversity (Isar 2017). What impact these activities had in terms of boosting India's image and standing abroad, however, remains an open question.

The first, novel, institutional effort, of any consequence, came well after the end of the Cold War. It involved the creation of a new Division of Public Diplomacy in the Ministry of External Affairs during the second iteration of the Indian National Congress-led United Progressive Alliance (UPA) government in 2014.

By this time, the Indian economy was on an even keel, and the country had dramatically altered its foreign policy. Also, it had successfully weathered a raft of international sanctions that it had faced in the aftermath of its nuclear tests in May 1998. The motivation to create this new division, it is widely believed, came from a perceived need to compete with the growing influence of the People's Republic of China (PRC) in Asia (Hall 2012, 1089–1110).

The efforts that this new division undertook in short order were substantial. Among other matters it inaugurated a new web portal for Indian Public Diplomacy, released a series of videos on YouTube and launched a dedicated Facebook page. Also, in conjunction with the Center for Media Studies Academy in New Delhi it held its first conference on the theory and practice of public diplomacy in 2010 (Hall 2012). Yet there was a curious ambivalence about its overall mission. While primarily focused on global public diplomacy it also had a significant domestic component. To that end, one of its tasks was also to educate the Indian public at home about the goals and objectives of Indian diplomacy. Accordingly, part of its efforts involved giving talks at universities and other educational settings at home.

Indeed, by the time the UPA government left office in 2014, India already had a substantial infrastructure in place to deploy soft power in the conduct of its diplomacy. Consequently, the new National Democratic Alliance (NDA) government of Prime Minister Narendra Modi, which assumed office became an important beneficiary of the prior efforts of the UPA government.

Narendra Modi and the Use of Indian Religious Soft Power

The election of Prime Minister Narendra Modi to the premiership in 2014, with a clear-cut majority for his nativist, Hindu nationalist, Bharatiya Janata Party (BJP), marked a watershed in Indian politics. The Indian National Congress, which had mostly dominated Indian politics since independence, had to varying degrees adhered to the distinctly Indian understanding of secularism based upon notions on religious inclusivity. Its record on secularism was hardly flawless but, at least in principle, the party had upheld secular values. The BJP, and its predecessor, the Bharatiya Jana Sangh, on the other hand, had always been a right-of-center, Hindu chauvinist party. When in the opposition, the party had claimed that it believed in "positive secularism," accusing the Congress of simply pandering to minorities under the guise of secularism (Malik and Singh 1992, 318–336).

However, the ideological underpinnings of the party underwent a steady transformation under Modi's leadership. He effectively moved the party in a distinctly ideological direction, deepening its commitment to a vision of militant Hindu nationalism.[3] Part of this enterprise involved the invocation of a mythical Indian past.[4] In fact, it appears that Modi and the BJP now seem intent on transforming the very basis of Indian nationalism—moving India away from its commitment to civic nationalism to a form of muscular, assertive ethnic nationalism based on a particular vision of Hinduism. This nationalist agenda also neatly dovetails with the country's increasing economic prowess, thereby facilitating its efforts to enhance its standing in the global arena.[5]

Shortly after his election, in an interview that he gave to the prominent Indian national newspaper, *The Indian Express*, Modi provided the first inkling between his vision of Hindutva ("Hinduness") and foreign policy. He asserted that certain precepts drawn from the well-springs of Hindu beliefs could prove useful in the shaping of foreign policy. To that end he argued that the ancient Sanskrit dictum, "vasudeva kutumba" (the world is one family) could serve as a useful guiding principle. He also paid tribute to an earlier BJP stalwart and prime minister, Atal Behari Vajpayee, arguing that his predecessor had relied on the concepts of "shakti" (strength) and "shanti" (peace) in the conduct of foreign policy (Panda 2014).

Furthermore, his second electoral victory in 2016 marked a decisive end to the long-term dominance of the professedly secular Indian National Congress (INC). The results of the election saw its parliamentary presence reduced to a mere 44 seats in a 545-seat parliament. The weakness of the parliamentary opposition, along with an absolute majority in parliament, with no need to rely on allies, gave Modi virtually free rein to pursue the politics of Hindu nationalism.

Apart from some allusions to illegal Muslim immigration from Bangladesh, a well-worn Hindu nationalist trope, his 2014 election campaign had focused almost entirely on issues of lagging economic growth and lackadaisical governance under the UPA government. Issues of foreign policy were hardly remarked upon during the campaign. Furthermore, questions lingered about his ability to travel extensively abroad because in 2005 Modi, who was then the Chief Minister of the state of Gujarat, had been denied a visa to the United States. The United States had turned down his visa request because of his government's failure to prevent mass attacks on Muslim communities in the wake of an attack on a train that had led to the deaths of a group of Hindu pilgrims (Mann 2014).

Consequently, the flurry of diplomatic activity that he embarked on after assuming office proved to be a surprise to many observers. Among other matters, in a historic move, he invited all the premiers of the South Asian Association for Regional Cooperation (SAARC) to his inauguration. Within weeks thereafter he made his first foreign visit to the Himalayan kingdom of Bhutan in June 2014. Indeed, his new government evinced a keen interest in matters of foreign policy as exemplified in the announcement of his "neighborhood first" policy—one designed to improve ties with India's smaller neighbors (Kaura 2018).

Within months of assuming office Modi went on a two-day state visit to Nepal. While there he went to the noted Hindu shrine, the Pashupatinath Temple in Kathmandu, and offered prayers. In an important gesture he also donated 2,500 kilograms of sandalwood, which is used in various Hindu religious rites (Parashar 2014). The visit to this temple was laden with significance. It obviously appealed to a significant domestic constituency which would be impressed with the Prime Minister's overt display of such piety. Beyond addressing this domestic audience, however, this gesture was also squarely directed at Nepal. It constituted an attempt on Modi's part to draw on a shared religious heritage to emphasize India's organic ties to Nepal.

International Day of Yoga: Indian Global Branding or Nativist Dog-Whistle?

Beyond these initiatives Modi also moved swiftly to deploy what could be considered as a use of religious soft power in the conduct of diplomacy. This shift on Modi's part is hardly inconsequential as its marks a significant break from the past. Even a BJP-led coalition government under Prime Minister Atal Behari Vajpayee, between 1998 and 2004, had made no overt effort to deploy religious soft power in its foreign policy strategy. Modi's adoption of this project is nothing short of novel.

His first foray into this arena came in the form of an address to the United Nations General Assembly in September 2014 where he called on the body to declare an international yoga day. Shortly thereafter Indian diplomats made a concerted effort to generate sufficient support for such a declaration. Their efforts proved to be successful and in December 2014 the United Nations formally declared June 21 to be the International Yoga Day (Press Trust of India 2014). Obviously, large numbers of yoga aficionados across the world practice yoga for its therapeutic benefits. For them it is simply another form of physical training and exercise bereft of any particular religious significance. For millions of Indians and Modi, in particular, the practice of yoga, however, cannot be severed from its religious moorings in Hinduism. While much of the world embraced Modi's espousal of yoga, religious minorities, especially Muslims, India's largest minority, expressed unhappiness with his efforts precisely because of the religious roots of the practice (Burke 2015).

Buddhism as a Soft-Power Resource for India's Relations with Asia

Interestingly enough, Modi also chose to draw on another important Indian religious tradition, Buddhism. His choice of Buddhism was hardly surprising for at least two compelling reasons. First, the faith had its origins as a reform movement of Hinduism designed to challenge sacerdotal authority. Subsequently, one sect of the faith, Mahayana (the greater vehicle) Buddhism, actually came to be incorporated into the Hindu fold with the Buddha seen as the ninth incarnation of one of the key members of the Hindu pantheon, Lord Vishnu, the preserver.[6] Buddhism's organic kinship with Hinduism no doubt rendered it attractive to Modi.

Second, India's proximity to Nepal, Burma/Myanmar, and Sri Lanka, all three countries with substantial Buddhist populations, with the latter two actual Buddhist-majority states, no doubt played a role in his calculations to boost Buddhism. More to the point, it could also prove useful in deepening the cultural dimensions of India's burgeoning and multifaceted relationship with Japan. It could also foster better ties with other Buddhist nations such as South Korea and Thailand and thereby dovetail with another strand of Modi's foreign policy, namely the "Act East" initiative designed to bolster India's links in a range of areas with the states of East and Southeast Asia.[7]

Yet it does need to be underscored that Modi's decision to embrace Buddhism does mark an important historical discontinuity. Two of the most important exponents of the BJP's ideological underpinnings, Madhav Sadashiv Golwalkar and Vinayak Damodar Savarkar, had expressed considerable misgivings about Buddhism in their copious writings (Hall 2019). Consequently, Modi's decision to draw on Buddhism's teachings and appeal probably reflect a clear-cut instrumental strategy to boost his national agenda.

This historical and intellectual anomaly notwithstanding, Modi has also sought to boost Buddhism in myriad ways. Even though the original idea had been discussed under a UPA government, he seized on the plans to resurrect the Nalanda University, an ancient center of Buddhist learning in India. The university had existed as early as the fifth century and had lasted until 1193 when it had been destroyed following a Turkish invasion. In September 2014, a new university was opened at the original site (Krishna 2014). Since the launch of this university was a pan-Asian initiative the Modi government has sought to highlight its Buddhist origins and India's concomitant contribution to Asian civilization (Kishwar 2018).

Beyond the revival of the university, the government has also actively sought to promote prominent Buddhist sites across the country as part of a tourism drive directed toward predominantly Buddhist nations across Asia. The goal of this effort, obviously, is to attract a range of pilgrims from across Asia and highlight India's substantial Buddhist heritage. To that end, the government has created a tourist circuit that would enable visitors to travel to a series of prominent historical and cultural sites associated with the life of Gautama Buddha (Kishwar 2018).

Despite being fraught with some risk, given the Peoples' Republic of China's extreme sensitivities on the subject, the Modi government adopted a different stance than previous governments toward the presence and activities of the Dalai Lama, the spiritual and temporal head of Tibetans. Other governments, fearful of invoking the wrath of the PRC had, for the most part, avoided granting the Dalai Lama much leeway despite continuing the long-standing policy of providing him and his followers asylum in India. The Modi government, however, chose to take a more expansive view of the activities that it deemed permissible. To that end, it allowed the Dalai Lama to inaugurate a seminar on "Buddhism in the Twenty-First Century" in March 2017 (Aneja 2017). In April of the same year, it also allowed him to visit a prominent Buddhist monastery in Tawang in the northeastern state of Arunachal Pradesh. The latter decision was fraught with particular significance because it is not only part of the PRC's territorial claims but also the birthplace of the sixth Dalai Lama (Press Trust of India 2017).

Leveraging India's Jewish Legacy in Relations with Israel

Finally, Modi's attempts to draw on India's religious traditions, as long as they do not involve Islam, have been nothing short of relentless. This is evident from Modi's decision to highlight India's Jewish heritage in forging a strategic partnership with Israel. While India had recognized Israel as early as 1950 it had kept the country at an arm's length until it accorded full diplomatic ties in

1992. India had limited its ties to Israel for a complex array of reasons ranging from its involvement in the Non-Aligned Movement, its perceived need to avoid alienating its own substantial Muslim population, and out of concerns about provoking the Arab world. After full diplomatic ties with Israel had been established the relationship had made steady progress. Indeed, it received a significant boost after the BJP first came to power in a coalition government in 1998. However, Modi was the first Indian prime minister to visit the country (Malhotra 2020).

Following the creation of the state of Israel, India's once-thriving and robust Jewish community steadily dwindled owing to their emigration. This, however, did not prevent Modi from seizing upon and underscoring India's substantial Jewish heritage as he has pursued a strategic partnership with Israel.[8] As the first Indian prime minister to visit Israel in 2017 he did not lose an opportunity to highlight that Jews had historically found India to be a safe haven when they faced persecution in various other parts of the world. Prime Minister Benjamin Netanyahu, in turn, has also recognized the significance of this heritage. Not surprisingly, he stressed this dimension of the Indo-Israeli relationship during his visit to India in 2018 (Weil 2018). It is, of course, entirely possible that the two leaders find each other on the same page for another reason: they are both unabashed ethnic nationalists who wish to turn their respective countries into religiously based states and have little regard for religious minorities.

India and the Geopolitics of the "Muslim Question"

There is little question that Modi has sought to capitalize on particular strands of India's religious heritage in his foreign policy outreach. Islam, however, is the one faith that he really has not sought to draw on in his conduct of religious diplomacy. For example, his visits to mosques, whether at home or abroad, have been quite limited. He did visit the Sheikh Zayed mosque in Abu Dhabi during a visit to in 2016. This move apparently stemmed from mixed motives. Beyond showing goodwill toward Muslims it was also with an eye to toward prodding Abu Dhabi allow the construction of a Hindu temple, a matter dear to many in the substantial Indian expatriate community (Gupta 2019). Also, while in Jakarta in 2018, he went to the Istiqlal mosque. In the latter case it is believed that it involved an attempt to flatter President Jokowi (PTI 2018).

One of his few attempts to reach out to the Indian Muslim community was his willingness to host the World Sufi Forum in 2016. At this meeting he gave a speech extolling the virtues of this particular sect of Islam (Ghosh 2016). His choice of Sufism was hardly accidental. It is widely believed that this particular, mystical sect of Islam is known for its commitment to peace. Despite this nod toward the Indian Muslim community a number of Muslim leaders expressed ambivalence about the sincerity of his outreach (Malhotra 2016).

His government's intransigence toward Muslims, the few cosmetic gestures of amity that have been noted notwithstanding, is likely to undermine his foreign policy goals toward significant parts of the Muslim world. Despite having made considerable headway, for example, with the states in the Persian Gulf, including Iran and Saudi Arabia, there are troubling signs that some of these ties are at the risk of fraying. India has also seen its relations strained with Malaysia and Turkey. In the case of Malaysia, the tensions have arisen from Prime Minister Mahathir Mohammed's comments on the India's passage of the Citizenship Amendment Act as well as its human rights record in Kashmir (Cherian 2020). Relations with Turkey have also been strained over its stance on developments in Indian-controlled Kashmir (Pubby and Chaudhurry 2019).

A series of domestic policy initiatives that have been undertaken, and some political lapses, that have taken place, especially during Modi's second term have caused a rift with parts of the Arab world and beyond. Among these has been the Citizenship Amendment Act (CAA) that will expedite applications for citizenship from Buddhists, Christians, Hindus, Jains, and Parsis from a number of India's neighboring countries. This list, however, quite conspicuously does not include Muslims. Coupled with the CAA India is also creating the National Register of Citizens (NRC), which threatens to disenfranchise a significant segment of India's Muslim community. Among other matters the NRC requires all residents of India's northeastern state to demonstrate that they were citizens of India before March 24, 1971 (a day before the infamous Pakistani military crackdown in the then-East Pakistan, which led to the flight of some 10 million refugees into India) with appropriate documents or face deportation (Merelli 2019). The BJP has made clear its intent to expand the writ of this law to the rest of the country. Since much of India's poor and marginalized are Muslims there is every likelihood that significant numbers of them will be caught in this dragnet as they may not have suitable documents.

The event that probably triggered the adverse reactions of the Muslim/Arab world, however, was the brutal police crackdown on students at a predominantly Muslim university in New Delhi, Jamia Milia Islamia, in December 2019. The students had been protesting the both pieces of aforementioned legislation on the grounds that they were highly discriminatory (Prasad 2020). In its wake a number of commentators in the Gulf and elsewhere expressed their concerns about the treatment of Muslims in Modi's India (Ganguly and Blarel 2020). A number of astute Indian political analysts have also highlighted the tensions between India's domestic policies and its attempts to court the Muslim Arab world.[9] The Modi government will probably take diplomatic steps to assuage the concerns of the Arab world. However, it is far from clear that these criticisms will lead it to genuinely rein in its domestic ideological agenda either in whole or part.

Marginalizing Christians and Christianity?

India has a minuscule Christian community even though its antecedents are often traced to the arrival of Saint Thomas, the apostle (Zakaria 2016). Despite its very small numbers, the BJP and particularly the members of its militant affiliate, the Rashtriya Swyamsevak Sangh (RSS), have long viewed the community with considerable suspicion and distrust. Much of the hostility stems from Christianity's commitment to proselytization. This hostility reached its apogee during the first BJP-led coalition government. During its term in office, in January 1999, members of a militant Hindu organization, the Bajrang Dal, in the eastern coastal state of Orissa (later Odisha) brutally attacked and killed Graham Staines, an Australian missionary and his two children (Singha 2020). This was perhaps the most egregious case of hostility toward Christians that resulted in lethal violence. Beyond this particular episode, however, there have been other cases of attacks on churches across the country leading a prominent former police official, Julio Rebeiro, to publicly express his misgivings about the safety of religious minorities in India (Ribeiro 2015). Against this backdrop it is not especially surprising that despite his stated interest in visiting India, the Modi government has not responded favorably to Pope Francis (The Catholic Herald 2020).

It should, however, be noted, that this vilification of Christians has also been accompanied with some efforts, perhaps quite cosmetic, to exemplify India's Christian heritage. To that end, Modi had sent his then Minister for External

Affairs, Sushma Swaraj, to the canonization of Mother Teresa, the Catholic nun who had spent the bulk of her professional life in missionary activity as well as caring for the poor and the destitute in Calcutta (PTI "Sushma" 2016). Also, Modi had spoken quite approvingly of Mother Teresa's work in one of his regular nationwide radio addresses (PTI "Sainthood" 2016).

These gestures aside, the failure to guarantee the rights of Christians in India could have significant adverse repercussions abroad and especially in the United States where evangelical Christians enjoy significant political clout in the US Congress. In this context it should be highlighted that in 2020 the Congressionally mandated body, the US Commission on International Religious Freedom, issued a harsh report on the state of religious freedom in India. Quite predictably, India's spokespersons dismissed the contents of the report (Boorstein and Slater 2020). Nevertheless, it clearly underscored that India's image as an open and plural society had taken a significant battering. If attacks on the Christian community continue India's efforts at projecting religious soft power will be further undermined.

Conclusions

As the foregoing discussion shows, unlike previous governments the Modi administration has explicit religious underpinnings. More to the point it has substantial constituencies both at home and abroad who look upon its unabashed embrace of Hinduism with considerable favor.

Consequently, it is hardly surprising that it has chosen to utilize and emphasize particular aspects of India's religious heritage in its soft-power strategy.

Despite its fervid attempts to draw on some of India's religious traditions to boost the India's standing and to render the country more attractive to prospective partners it is far from evident that this strategy has yielded significant, tangible benefits. At best, it may have had a marginal, positive impact on relations that were already on the upswing, for example, with Japan. It has, however, had no discernible effect on India's relations with India's immediate neighbors. For example, its dealings with Sri Lanka have remained focused on more quotidian issues such as those of trade, investment and security. Similarly, the invocation of India's Jewish heritage has not really moved the needle on India's expanding ties with Israel. Instead more tangible matters, such as arms sales, intelligence cooperation, and counterterrorism, have remained at the forefront of this strategic security partnership.

Whatever initial benefits that Modi's religious diplomacy had initially yielded in Nepal were swiftly squandered as a consequence of the informal blockade that followed not long thereafter. In 2020, the relationship has reached a particularly low ebb (Shakya 2020).

It is also unclear that the Modi government will be able, in the foreseeable future, to further capitalize on its soft-power strategy. In considerable part, Modi's attempts to burnish India's image abroad through the use of religious soft power will be tarnished because of the sharp turn toward illiberalism in India under his watch (Ganguly 2020, 193–202). As the government hounds and marginalizes its largest religious minority, Muslims, and fails to protect other, smaller religious groups, it is hard to see how the highlighting of selective aspects of India's religious heritage is likely to acquire traction in its dealings with a range of countries. The jarring juxtaposition of harsh domestic realities with the attempts to promote a vision of religious amity and harmony are unlikely to be lost on much of the world.

Acknowledgments

Rajesh Basrur, Shibashis Chatterjee, Ian Hall and Chris Ogden provided thoughtful criticisms and suggestions on an earlier draft of this chapter. The usual caveats apply.

References

Ajami, Fouad. 1980/81. "The Third World Challenge: The Fate of Nonalignment." *Foreign Affairs*.

Aneja, Atul. 2017. "China 'Strongly Dissatisfied' with India for Inviting Dalai Lama to Buddhist Meet." *The Hindu*, March 20, 2017. https://www.thehindu.com/news/international/china-strongly-dissatisfied-with-india-for-inviting-dalai-lama-to-buddhist-meet/article61804092.ece.

Boorstein, Michelle, and Joanna Slater. 2020. "Religious Freedom in India Deteriorated Last Year, US Government Watchdog Says." *The Washington Post*, April 28, 2020. https://www.washingtonpost.com/religion/2020/04/28/india-receives-low-rating-us-government-watchdog-religious-freedom/.

Burke, Jason. 2015. "Modi's Plan to Change India and the World through Yoga Angers Religious Minorities." *The Guardian*, June 6, 2015. https://www.theguardian.com/world/2015/jun/06/narendra-modi-yoga-india.

Cherian, John. 2020. "Troubled Relations Between India and Malaysia." *Frontline*, February 14, 2020. https://frontline.thehindu.com/world-affairs/article30652433.ece.

Chopra, Pran Nath. 1974. *India's Second Liberation*. Cambridge: MIT Press.
Duffin, Kathleen. 1980. "Arthur O. Lovejoy and the Emergence of Novelty." *Journal of the History of Ideas* 41 (2): 267–281.
Ganguly, Sumit. 1992. "South Asia After the Cold War." *The Washington Quarterly* 15 (4): 173–184.
Ganguly, Sumit. 2020. "An Illiberal India?" *Journal of Democracy* 31 (1): 193–202.
Ganguly, Sumit, and Nicolas Blarel. 2020. "Why Gulf States Are Backtracking on India." *Foreign Policy*, May 5, 2020. https://foreignpolicy.com/2020/05/23/india-china-border-skirmishes/
Ghosh, Abantika. 2016. "Narendra Modi at World Sufi Forum: Terror Fight Not Against any Religion." *The Indian Express*, March 18, 2016. https://indianexpress.com/article/india/india-news-india/modi-at-world-sufi-forum-terror-fight-not-against-any-religion-says-pm-modi/.
Gupta, Shishir. 2019. "Abu Dhabi's 1st Hindu Temple to be Opened by PM Modi by Video or in Person." *The Hindustan Times*, April 8, 2019. https://www.hindustantimes.com/india-news/pm-narendra-modi-to-take-a-call-this-week-on-visiting-uae/story-F7ibKwZtkYiouLO7RSfPiI.html
Hall, Ian. 2012. "India's New Public Diplomacy." *Asian Survey* 52 (6): 1089–1110.
Hall, Ian. 2019. *Modi and The Reinvention of Indian Foreign Policy*. Bristol: University of Bristol Press.
Hause, E. Malcom. 1960. "India: Noncommitted and Nonaligned." *Western Political Quarterly* 13 (1): 70–82.
Isar, Yudhishthir Raj. 2017. "Cultural Diplomacy: India Does It Differently." *International Journal of Cultural Policy* 23 (6): 705–716.
Kaura, Vinay. 2018. "Grading India's Neighbourhood Diplomacy." *The Diplomat*, January 1, 2018. https://thediplomat.com/2017/12/grading-indias-neighborhood-diplomacy/.
Kennedy, Andrew. 2011. *The International Ambitions of Mao and Nehru: National Efficacy Beliefs and the Making of Foreign Policy*. Cambridge: Cambridge University Press.
Kishwar, Shantanu. 2018. "The Rising Role of Buddhism in India's Soft Power Strategy." *ORF Issue Brief* 228: 1–12.
Krishna, Rai Atul. 2014. "Nalanda University Reopens After 800 Years." *Hindustan Times*, September 1, 2014. https://www.hindustantimes.com/india/nalanda-university-reopens-after-800-years/story-ysbIgYUq4LXA9U8k0vLSVP.html#:~:text=Around%20800%20years%20after%20it,of%20an%20international%20knowledge%20destination.
Latham, Andrew. 1998. "Constructing National Security: Culture and Identity in Arms Control and Disarmament Practice." *Contemporary Security Policy* 1 (1): 129–158.
Malhotra, Divya. 2020. "India, Israel and the Myriad Connections." *The Jerusalem Post*, March 25, 2020. https://www.jpost.com/opinion/india-israel-and-the-myriad-connections-608049.
Malhotra, Jyoti. 2016. "The Parameters of Modi's Muslim Outreach are Finally Becoming Clear." *Scroll.in*, March 28, 2016. https://scroll.in/article/805691/the-parameters-of-modis-muslim-outreach-are-finally-becoming-clear.
Malik, Yogendra, and V. B. Singh. 1992. "Bharatiya Janata Party: An Alternative to the Congress (I)?" *Asian Survey* 32 (4): 318–336.
Mann, James. 2014. "Why Narendra Modi was banned from the US." *The Wall Street Journal*, May 2, 2014. https://www.wsj.com/articles/why-narendra-modi-was-banned-from-the-u-s-1399062010.

Merelli, Annalisa. 2019. "The BJP's threat to restrict Indian Citizenship unmasks the Ugliest Side of Nationalism." *Quartz India*, April 11, 2019. https://qz.com/india/1591557/bjp-threat-to-restrict-indian-citizenship-targets-muslims/.

Panda, Ankit. "Modi: Hindutva Will Be an Asset in Foreign Policy." *The Diplomat*, April 24, 2014, https://thediplomat.com/2014/04/modi-hindutva-will-be-an-asset-in-foreign-affairs/.

Parashar, Utpal. 2014. "PM Narendra Modi visits Pashupatinath temple, offers 2,500 kilograms of sandalwood." *The Hindustan Times*, August 4, 2014. https://www.hindustantimes.com/india/pm-narendra-modi-visits-pashupatinath-temple-offers-2-500-kg-of-sandalwood/story-ygxo9wPUPA6Q6wOfrqv8DL.html.

Prasad, Shubha Kamala. 2020. "India Is Cracking Down on University Protests. Here's What You Need to Know." *The Washington Post*, January 10, 2020. https://www.washingtonpost.com/politics/2020/01/10/india-is-cracking-down-university-protests-heres-what-you-need-know/.

Press Trust of India. 2014. "UN declares June 21 as International Yoga Day at Modi's Suggestion." *India Today*, December 11, 2014. https://www.indiatoday.in/world/americas/story/modi-un-declares-june-21-as-international-yoga-day-230828-2014-12-11.

Press Trust of India. 2016. "Sushma Swaraj Attends Mother Teresa's Canonization at Vatican." *The Indian Express*, September 4, 2016. https://indianexpress.com/article/india/india-news-india/sushma-swaraj-attend-mother-teresas-canonisation-at-vatican-3013328/.

Press Trust of India. 2016. "Sainthood for Mother Teresa Proud Moment: PM Modi." *The Indian Express*, September 5, 2016. https://indianexpress.com/article/india/india-news-india/sainthood-for-mother-teresa-proud-moment-pm-modi-3013343/.

Press Trust of India. 2017. "Dalai Lama Reaches Tawang, to Start Religious Discourses." *The Hindu*, April 7, 2017. https://www.thehindu.com/news/national/other-states/the-dalai-lama-reaches-tawang/article61798223.ece.

Press Trust of India. 2018. "PM Mdi, Prez Widodo visit Grand Istiqlal Mosque." *The Asian Age*, May 31, 2018. https://www.asianage.com/world/south-asia/310518/pm-modi-prez-widodo-visit-grand-istiqlal-mosque.html.

Pubby, Manu, and Dipanjan Roy Chaudhury. 2019. "India Cuts Defence Exports to Turkey over Pakistan Nexus." *The Economic Times*, October 24, 2019. https://economictimes.indiatimes.com/news/defence/india-cuts-defence-exports-to-turkey-over-pakistan-nexus/articleshow/71714590.cms.

Ribeiro, Julio. 2015. "As a Christian, Suddenly I Am a Stranger in My Own Country, Writes Julio Ribeiro." *The Indian Express*, March 17, 2015. https://indianexpress.com/article/opinion/columns/i-feel-i-am-on-a-hit-list/.

Shakya, Sujeev. 2020. "There Is a New Nepal; India Hasn't Kept Up." *The Hindustan Times*, January 19, 2020. https://www.hindustantimes.com/analysis/there-is-a-new-nepal-india-hasn-t-kept-up/story-2Iyuyo6XWT4KyLjgJFzcZN.html.

Singha, Minati. 2020. "21 Years on, Odisha Village Still Weeps for Graham Staines." *The Times of India*, January 23, 2020. https://timesofindia.indiatimes.com/india/21-years-after-his-killing-odisha-village-says-it-still-weeps-for-staines/articleshow/68666096.cms.

Thakur, Ramesh. 1997. "India in the World: Neither Rich, Powerful, Nor Principled," *Foreign Affairs* 76 (4): 15–22.

The Catholic Herald. 2020. "Modi Has Nothing to Fear from a Papal Visit." *Catholic Herald*, January 23, 2020. https://catholicherald.co.uk/modi-has-nothing-to-fear-from-a-papal-visit/.

Weil, Shalva. 2018. "The Indian Jews at the Heart of the Netanyahu-Modi Love Affair." *Haaretz.com*, January 14, 2018. https://www.haaretz.com/israel-news/.premium-the-indian-jews-at-the-heart-of-the-netanyahu-modi-love-affair-1.5730732.

Zakaria, Paul Zakaria. 2016. "The Surprisingly Early History of Christianity in India." *Smithsonian Journeys Quarterly*, February 19, 2016. https://www.smithsonianmag.com/travel/how-christianity-came-to-india-kerala-180958117/.

7
Shi'i Diplomacy

Religious Identity and Foreign Policy in the Axis of Resistance

Edward Wastnidge

Introduction

Since the founding of the Islamic Republic, Iran's leaders have sought to harness both universalistic and particularistic Shi'i claims to legitimacy in the Muslim world. Beginning with attempts to actively export the Islamic revolution in the 1980s, Iran has invested in building its diplomatic and religious infrastructure, expanding its religious outreach activities across the Shi'i world, drawing on its position as something of a Shi'i metropole in a demonstration of its growing soft power. This chapter will explore how religious identity informs the diplomacy of the world's preeminent theocracy, the Islamic Republic of Iran, focusing on how religiously grounded notions of justice have informed its foreign policy thinking and diplomatic reach.

As readers of this volume will be aware, the notable works of Mandaville (2001, 2014, 2018), Telhami and Barnett (2002), and others have thus sought to unpack the various identity currents inherent in the politics of the Middle East and wider Muslim world. Studies rooted in identity considerations have also found fertile ground for exploring state behavior and foreign policy-making by engaging with the concept of soft power (Haynes 2008, 2016; Mandaville and Hamid 2018; Farquhar 2017; Wastnidge 2015), highlighting how states in the Middle East have utilized their religious influence to expand their reach.

The Islamic Republic contains a range of parastatal organizations that carry out religious outreach and soft-power projection across the Shi'i world. These not only take the form of traditional "religious" activities affiliated to the *hawza* (Shi'i seminaries) but also involve the educational and diplomatic missions undertaken abroad by the Iranian government. Thus, one can see how the transnational linkages that Iran has as a result of its position as religious hub are used as vector to enhance diplomatic relations and deepen ties with communities across the Shi'i world. This chapter starts by contextualizing Iran's religious soft power through exploring the role of religiously informed notions of justice that are foundational in the Islamic Republic's foreign policy. It will then go on to examine how religious identity informs the foreign policy and diplomacy of Iran. The subsequent analysis of the role of Shi'i identity in Iranian foreign policy looks at two broad aspects. First, it illustrates how elements of Iran's Shi'i identity are utilized to help provide a justification for its strategic and military engagements in the Middle East. Second, the chapter examines Iran's cultural diplomacy and soft-power strategies, as evidenced through the examples of various state-sponsored outreach and development initiatives including the work of the Imam Khomeini Relief Foundation (Emdad) and Islamic Culture and Relations Organization (ICRO) in Lebanon. Finally, to show that the use of such identity narratives is not purely a "one way street" emanating from Tehran, but in fact a partnership with local allies, the cultural production work of Iran's partner Hezbollah in Lebanon, is briefly explored.

The Religious Aspect of Iranian Foreign Policy: Seeking Justice, Resisting Oppression

This section explains how a specific Shi'i conception of justice provides a contextual basis for understanding the role of religion in Iran's foreign policy. Starting with the idea of justice in Islam, it is important to note that what is explained in the following is a particular take on justice as espoused by the Islamic Republic, and especially Ayatollah Khomeini, its founder and leader of the revolution in 1979. In a similar vein to Rawls, domestic notions of justice need to be understood and explained first to explain how it operates between nations (Bahrani 2013, 34). It is therefore a particularistic Shi'i interpretation, and a politicized one because of Iran's revolutionary experience, and the idiosyncrasies of clerical rule there. The Islamic Republic's views on justice are informed by its perception of injustice. This is due to two interrelated points: first, the historical framing of Iranian political Islam as an ideal that draws on the religio-philosophical heritage of Shiism, and with it the idea of rallying against injustice; and second, the subsequent position of the Islamic Republic as a historically revisionist power, that has often been isolated in the past and chaffed against Western-defined norms in the international system. Justice can be seen as a continual thread that has been maintained in Iran's foreign policy and international diplomacy since 1979. This evidences a continued desire to maintain the ideological heritage of the revolution, and also highlights the continued importance of the Supreme Leader as the embodiment of revolutionary ideals who has final say in all matters of the state.

Notions of justice and injustice can be seen as playing a central role in Islam. The schism that occurred in Islam in the years after the Prophet's death are important also for understanding how this has gone on to affect thinking around justice in Iran as the world's only Shi'i theocracy. For Sunnis "political justice lay in acknowledging legitimate authority through community consensus . . . [for the Shia] it lay in the strict perpetuation of the line of legitimate succession" (Rosen 2000, 7). Thus for the Shia, authority rested with a line of Imams who drew direct descendance from the Prophet—whereas the Sunni leadership was based on the "chosen" or best candidates for succession. Some of the foundational ideas on justice are drawn from the first Imam of the Shi'i tradition, also the fourth caliph, Imam Ali. It was his son, and the Prophet's grandson, Hossein who led a revolt against the then-ruling Umayyad dynasty in 680, which laid the foundations for Shi'i thinking on oppressive rulers. The Shia were, as they are now, a minority in the Muslim world and the fight against tyranny, oppression, and ultimately injustice are often linked to this formative experience.

Imagery and emotional resonance are utilized by the Islamic Republic from this time to legitimize their stances in terms of the injustice of the world system as they see it. Hence its use by Khomeini with reference to the Shah of Iran who was deposed following the revolution in 1979, and also in the Iran-Iraq war where Saddam was painted as a tyrant with the superpowers' resources at his disposal while Iran gamely fought on, outnumbered as the Shia had been at the battle of Karbala where Hossein was martyred. Such historical reference points therefore have a long-standing tradition in the political Shiism of the Islamic Republic, and the clergy has a long-standing role in the affairs of the Iranian state. Iranian politics has been made in coordination with the clergy, since Shiism became the state religion under Safavids in 1501 (Khalaji 2011, 131). While the Islamic revolution was therefore not the beginning of clergy's relationship with politics, a tradition of quietism historically predominated until Khomeini's coming to prominence, from which he sought to bring clergy into politics in a much more activist sense.

Hence the revolutionary interpretation of Hossein's death is a relatively recent, twentieth-century phenomenon that finds its roots in the writings of key Shi'i scholars such as Musa al-Sadr and Ali Shariati (Louer 2012, 12). Therefore, once the Islamic Republic was established, we see religiously defined notions of justice as constituting a key part of the Islamic Republic's worldview, which remain relevant today.

Khomeini's most famous writings were about challenging the despotism of Shah Mohammad Reza Pahlavi, the ruler of Iran from 1941 to 1979 and a key Western ally in the region. In doing so, he formulated his idea of Islamic government based on the principle of *velayat-e faqih* ("guardianship of the jurist"). Although the clerical hierarchy in Shi'ism is not institutionally defined in a way such as the papacy in Catholicism, it still provides a model for leadership of the Shia worldwide through the principal of *marja'iyat*, whereby a number of high-ranking clerics act as spiritual or "sources of emulation" to Shia worldwide. In the case of Khomeini and Iran, this guidance took on a political hue as well, combining religious and political authority within the Islamic Republic. It should be noted that *velayat-e faqih* is peculiar to political Islam from Khomeini onwards, and as Baktiari (2012, 36) notes, the model does not exist in the literature of classical Shi'i jurisprudence.

The formation of the Islamic Republic institutionalized clerical rule, and with it Khomeini's ideas on justice, which translated to its international outlook also. Justice can be seen as providing a "meta-discourse" that gives meaning to Iranian foreign policy in general (Moshirzadeh 2007, 528). The fight against oppression is therefore key in Khomeini's thinking on justice in which he encouraged an Islam that "repudiates oppression and an Islam in which the ruler and the people from the lowest walk of life are equal before law" (Khomeini 1979, 425). Key to his political thought was emphasizing a type of Islam "whose standard-bearers are the bare-footed, oppressed and poor people of the world" (Khomeini 1968, 204). This was a form of political Shi'ism that drew on the intellectual heritage of Shi'i modernizers, including figures such as Ali Shariati. A key ideologue whose ideas directly influenced the course of the revolution, Shariati (d. 1977) advocated a populist form of Islam, not dissimilar to the so-called liberation theology that was popular in Latin America during his years of political activism. His emphasis on populist egalitarianism saw him reviving and invoking of the originally Quranic term of the *mostazafin* (the "oppressed"), a term which went on to play a key role in the Iranian revolution (Arjomand 2016, 410–411). The idea of supporting the *mostzafin* became key in Khomeini's worldview and was important in shaping Iran's subsequent foreign policy outlook. Thus, there was a strong "third worldist" hue that heavily influenced the ideological course of the revolution and the Islamic Republic's self-perception on the world stage, which has important corollaries for the way in which it enacts its cultural and religious diplomacy.

Religious Identity in Iranian Foreign Policy and Diplomacy

The idea of supporting the oppressed and seeking justice is something that is foundational in Iranian foreign policy, regardless of the different political hues of successive Iranian administrations, because it forms part of the Islamic Republic's constitutionally defined foreign policy objectives. Two articles of the constitution spell this out explicitly: article 3.16 describes the Islamic Republic as "framing the foreign policy of the country on the basis of Islamic criteria, fraternal commitment to all Muslims, and unsparing support to the mostazafin of the world"; while article 154 states,

> The Islamic Republic of Iran has as its ideal human felicity throughout human society, and ... considers the attainment of independence, freedom, and rule of justice and truth to be the right of all people of the world. Accordingly, while scrupulously refraining from all forms of interference in the internal affairs of other nations, it supports the just struggles of the *mostazafin* against the *mostakbirun* [tyrants] in every corner of the globe.

Khomeini believed that the interests of hegemonic powers were based on politically, economically, and culturally subjugating the underprivileged nations, through a plundering of their resources and confiscating their territorial independence (Salamey and Othman 2011, 201). This found its expression in his famous maxim of "Neither East nor West but Islamic Republic," something that was particularly important in guiding Iranian foreign policy in the first decade of the revolution, and manifested itself in what Ramazani (1990) considers as a justice-seeking bent within its foreign policy. As Moshirzadeh (2007, 533) argues, the justice discourse "gave the Islamic Revolution its transnational appeal as a result of it being articulated with elements of Islamic universalism, leftist internationalism, and liberal internationalism." This was used to delegitimize idea of hierarchy in the international system, thus focusing on the perceived unjust actions of powerful states and emphasizing double standards in international relations (Moshirzadeh 2007, 533). Chehabi and Mneimneh (2006) schematize the ways in which the Islamic Republic put this thinking into action in its foreign policy by referring to three concentric circles. Support for the oppressed starts with an outer circle of third-world countries and liberation movements, a middle circle comprising the Muslim world, with the Shi'i Muslims forming the inner circle (Chehabi and Mneimneh 2006, 33). The ways in which this support continues to be articulated to this inner circle can be seen in its well-documented, recent military engagements in the Middle East, and in its religious and cultural diplomacy in the region, both of which are discussed below. These are examples of where Iran's religious identity intersects with elements of its core foreign policy and diplomatic concerns in various articulations of soft power that often have a strong geopolitical flavor.

Iran's Religious Power and Conflict in the Middle East

The earliest manifestation of religious identity in Iranian foreign policy came in the early years of the Islamic Republic following the revolution in 1979, manifesting itself in the patronage of Hezbollah in Lebanon and support for Shi'i communities across the Muslim world. It is in these early efforts that one can see a narrative emerging of support for oppressed groups that chimed with revolutionary Iran's first leader Ayatollah Khomeini, which as noted above invoked a strong emphasis on combating injustice in the international system. Thus, the practice of Iranian foreign policy in the 1980s was framed in terms of exporting the revolution. However, Islamic Republic's attempts to preach Islamic solidarity were partly stymied by its particularistic Shi'i and Iranian nature (Wastnidge 2015, 367), though some scholars from Iran have noted that this was indeed a fertile time in terms of Iran's soft-power projection on account on the perceived "ethical" dimension of Khomeini's foreign policy outlook (Jafarpanahi and Mirahmadi 2012). The Islamic Republic of Iran, as the most populous Shi'i nation, and in its position as a center of religious learning and theology, naturally sees itself as a leader of the Shi'i world.

Iran acting as the protector of the Shia is an important aspect of its foreign policy—something that dates back to its patronage of Hezbollah from the

1980s onwards. This is an outlook that has shaped Iran's more recent military engagements with Syria and Iraq. First, in terms of Iran's involvement in Iraq, while the primary concern was about keeping the so-called Islamic State as far from its borders as possible, providing support to its co-religionists is also a consideration. Though far from a monolithic whole, Iraq's Shi'i population has been cited as a natural, ally for Tehran (Esfandiary and Tabatabai 2015, 3), and with the so-called Islamic State and other Sunni extremist groups in the region espousing a sectarian narrative that seeks to carry out massacres against the Shia, Iran felt duty-bound to act in its very own "War on Terror" (Wastnidge 2020). This sectarian targeting taps into a wider Shi'a experience of being persecuted by Sunni Wahhabi extremist forces in the Middle East, particularly in Iraq, as summed up by Ayatollah Ali Sistani's representative in Iran, Javad Sharestani, stating that "we've been fighting Wahhabis in the region for more than 100 years."[1]

As a result of the existential threat to Iran from Sunni extremist groups operating in Syria and Iraq, Iran committed its Special Forces and military advisors to both countries. In Syria, the Shi'i population (in terms of adherents to Twelver Shi'ism as practiced in Iran) is far smaller, and emphasis has been instead on defending Shi'i religious sites, most notably the Sayidah Zaynab shrine in Damascus. As stated by IRGC Major General Rahim Nowi-Aghdam, in encouraging members of Iran's Basij to volunteer, "If you do not volunteer to fight in Iraq and Syria, I will go myself, and I will martyr myself in the defence of Sayyida Zeynab or the Shia shrines in Iraq" (Spada, quoted in Wastnidge 2020).

It is important to note that the sectarian narrative that is currently prevailing across the region as articulated in much of the media analyses is problematic in terms of its equating of geopolitical competition with centuries old, immutable sectarian tensions between Sunni and Shia. Despite the appeals to Shi'i identity by the Islamic Republic, their current use in the region is borne primarily of realpolitik considerations in countering Saudi hostility and the aims of extremist groups that it is combating. Iran's involvement in these two conflicts has a strong geopolitical, strategic rationale in terms of preserving its interests and maximizing its influence in both states (Wastnidge 2019). However, religion does have a useful role to play in terms of attracting volunteer fighters to help in defending Shi'i shrines. This can be seen in the channeling of Shi'i volunteers from Iran's large Afghan diaspora and the alleged facilitation of Shi'i volunteers from further afield in Pakistan and Iraq (Nada 2015). What can be observed therefore in this military involvement, is Iran's use of religious 'overlays' to serve as a justification for its actions (Wastnidge 2020), drawing on its transnational linkages in an instrumental way.

Cultural Diplomacy and Exchange: Religious Soft-power Channels

Iranian cultural diplomacy is particularly active in countries, or among communities where it has a combination of shared strategic objectives and cultural links, which in turn help service its geopolitical aims. As shown in the examples pertaining to Lebanon discussed in further detail below, this draws upon a long-standing religious link with Lebanese Shia, and is furthered through the shared aims of promoting a form of "resistance culture" to combat Israel and the United States. Organizations such as the Imam Khomeini Relief Foundation (Emdad), the ICRO, and other parastatal organizations also play an important role in helping cement links between Iran and the wider Muslim world. These are reinforced through Iranian tourism and investment in Shi'i shrine cities in Syria and Iraq, and the historical and cultural links that are maintained with other Shi'i communities, such as the Hazara in Afghanistan, Shia in Pakistan, and others (Wastnidge 2015, 7).

Iran's transnational religious links are not only restricted to the activities of the *hawza*, which arguably act as a form of soft-power projection their own right. The clerical training provided in centers of religious learning such as Qom allow the Islamic Republic to shape the religious education for thousands of religious scholars and aspiring clerics from across the globe every year. Supplementary to this transnational religious soft power is the work undertaken by the educational and diplomatic missions of the Iranian government abroad as discussed in the following. Thus, one can see how the transnational linkages that Iran has as a result of its position as religious hub are used as vector to enhance diplomatic relations and deepen ties with communities across the Shi'i world.

As a means of demonstrating how Iran's international cultural and religious outreach work can be thought of a form of religious soft power, the final substantive section of this chapter outlines three examples where international charity and outreach work, cultural diplomacy, and cultural production work intersect with the wider geopolitical aims and outlook of the Islamic Republic and its regional allies.

The Imam Khomeini Relief Foundation: *Emdad*

Emdad is one of the largest charitable foundations in Iran, primarily focusing on domestic charitable work, but also with an active international arm carrying various development projects across the world. Its charity boxes are an ubiquitous presence across Iran, and also in predominantly Shi'i neighborhoods in Lebanon. However, it does not have an inherently sect-based focus in its work, having historically carried out projects across the Muslim world regardless of the prevailing sectarian affiliation of the countries in which it operates. For example, it has been active in Gaza, undertaking charitable initiatives such as distributing *Iftar* meals during the month of Ramadan,[2] and has contributed toward numerous development projects in Sunni-majority countries.

However, despite its cross-sectarian aid work efforts, *Emdad* has been the focus of some controversy in terms of its activities and offices becoming targets of anti-Iranian and/or anti-Shi'i sentiment in certain host countries. This is something that has coincided with the worsening of Iran-Saudi ties, particularly in the years following the Arab Uprisings where religion and geopolitics became entangled in a struggle for hegemony.[3] For example, in Tajikistan, its offices were closed down because of a rupture in relations following Tehran's hosting of a Tajik opposition figure in 2015. Saudi Arabia was quick to take advantage and offer its own development aid as a result of this deterioration in bilateral ties between the two Persian-speaking nations.[4] The Comoros Islands also shut down *Emdad* and other Iranian charitable foundations following its expulsion of Iranian diplomats in 2016 This breakdown in relations followed a period of growing ties between Iran and the Comoros Islands, helped in part by the former Comorian president (2006–2011) Ahmed Abdallah Mohamed Sambi's religious studies in Qom, and former Iranian president Mahmoud Ahmadinejad's visit to the island nation in 2009. In 2016, however, Comoros sided firmly with Saudi Arabia in its dispute with Iran following the attack on the Saudi consulate in Mashhad in the wake of Riyadh's execution of Shi'i cleric, Nimr al-Nimr. Its president was keen to point out Iran's alleged proselytizing activities on the archipelago in an interview with the Saudi-owned *al-Sharq al-Awsat* publication.[5]

Reports and information on *Emdad*'s international outreach work have been removed from its current website, which previously listed all of its overseas operations in terms of offices, development projects, and some budgetary information. At the time of writing, the foundation has drawn down most of its more overt foreign operations, but it appointed a new director of international affairs in 2019 with an emphasis on greater involvement of "local" organizations in international operations,[6] and continues to be active in organizing development assistance projects and distribution of the voluntary contributions that fund its work in Lebanon and Iraq. It is also now placing a greater emphasis on coordinating charitable donations among the Iranian diaspora, as recent communications via Iranian embassies abroad have highlighted.[7]

The Islamic Culture and Relations Organization (ICRO) and Its Work in Lebanon

The ICRO is a particularly significant actor in terms of projecting Iranian soft power among Shi'i communities worldwide, as it is the main channel for Iran's cultural diplomacy initiatives (see Harsij, Toyserkani, and Jafari 2012; von Maltzahn 2013; Wastnidge 2015), which helps further Iran's diplomatic reach. It runs Iran's cultural bureaus abroad, with a particular focus on the Muslim world, but also operates in non-Muslim contexts. In the host countries, the ICRO acts as the base from which Iranian cultural attachés (known as "cultural counselors") carry out their work. It is important to note too that the ICRO operates separately from the diplomats employed by the Ministry of Foreign Affairs of Iran who run the country's embassies abroad. Rather, the ICRO reports directly to Iran's Supreme Leader, Ayatollah Ali Khamenei. It "operationalizes" Iranian soft power (Wastnidge 2015) through sponsoring cultural events and collaborations in the countries in which it operates.

According to the Iranian cultural attachés office in Lebanon, a country where the ICRO has an active presence on account of long-standing ties between Iran and Lebanon's large Shi'i population, the ICRO is responsible for "managing cultural relations with countries and cultural propaganda activities of the Islamic Republic of Iran abroad."[8] The activities the ICRO will undertake in its host country and include: Persian language teaching; promotion of religious and cultural dialogue; supporting cultural needs of Iranian expats and students living in the host country; implementing cultural agreements between the Iran and the countries; cooperation with cultural, educational, literary, and artistic institutions; holding cultural weeks, festivals, and exhibitions; communication with cultural and scientific elites; and attending various cultural events in the host country. It has a fairly flexible remit in terms of the outreach work and communities it targets and has "complete freedom" to cooperate with whomever it chooses,[9] so long as they do not explicitly conflict with the Islamic Republic's declared foreign policy aims. The ICRO is most active in countries with large Shi'i communities, such as Iraq, Lebanon, and Pakistan, fellow Persian-speaking nations such as Tajikistan, and close strategic allies such as Syria. Von Maltzahn's (2013) study of Iranian cultural diplomacy in Syria through the ICRO is especially instructive in showing how this type of cultural relations are primarily carried out at the official level and with limited popular uptake, save student exchanges and Iranian religious tourism to Shi'i shrines in Syria.

An example of the kind of work done by Iran's cultural diplomacy arm can be seen in the activities of the ICRO cultural center in Beirut, which sponsors numerous cultural and artistic events in Lebanon. Though much of their work is based on religious events, they are also highly active in cultural production that reinforces the idea of the Axis of Resistance—the alliance of Iran, Hezbollah, Syria, and also at times certain Palestinian factions, against Israel and the United States. These efforts highlight the continued significance of core revolutionary ideals around fighting injustice that are rooted in the political Shi'ism of the Islamic Republic. For the ICRO in Lebanon, "the cultural dimension of the idea of resistance is part of Iran's foreign policy and relations between the two countries."[10] This is a repurposing of the revolutionary vanguard role that Iran cultivated in the early years of the Islamic Republic, with Iran crafting a role that sees itself constituting the hub of resistance to Israeli and US policies in the region (Wastnidge 2019). Indeed, looking beyond Lebanon, one can see the ICRO's continuing role in helping to maintain the resistance axis with its 2020 "conference of resistance scholars" in Baghdad, where both Sunni and Shi'i ulema from across the Middle East were present.[11]

Other activities involve regular ICRO sponsorship of various arts activities, often working in conjunction with Shi'i communities in southern Lebanon. The cultural events and exhibitions aimed at the Lebanese Shi'i community are very much based around the resistance theme. Examples in recent years include revolutionary art exhibitions in Nabatieh, a resistance art event held at the UNESCO Palace in Beirut,[12] arrangement of reciprocal cultural weeks in Iran and Lebanon, art and poetry of the Iranian and Palestinian revolution events held at the "Iranian garden" on the Lebanese-Israeli border at Maroun el-Ras. This is a site of extraordinary Iranian territorial largesse, given as a gift by the Iranian government to the people of southern Lebanon following the Israeli war against Hezbollah in 2006. It hosts resistance-themed cultural events ran under ICRO auspices, and also hosts visiting Iranian dignitaries when they visit southern Lebanon. The ICRO is also keen to reach out to other denominations in Lebanon, particularly if relations can be couched in terms of a shared outlook toward the Palestinian cause.[13]

Hezbollah's Cultural Production Work in Lebanon

Hezbollah is a key ally of Iran in the Middle East, a significant regional player in its own right and arguably the main power broker in Lebanese politics. While much media and academic analysis tends to focus on the shared strategic outlook and activities of Iran and its ally, the cultural relations between the two, and development of Hezbollah's cultural production work has been less well-examined, save for the notable work of Alagha (2011, 2104, 2016). In terms of spiritual leadership, Hezbollah defers to Ayatollah Khamenei, the current Iranian Supreme Leader, and prior to that Khomeini. Hence their views on the use of culture are important in any discussion of the cultural production work of Iran and its allies. Key to this is the theological concept of *maslaha* (meaning the common good or public interest). Alagha (2016, 170–172) highlights how for Khomeini, *maslaha* is a result of action in the domain of justice, and that it has a prominent role in relation to art. Khamenei sees cultural work as a precursor to political and military work, and therefore views it in instrumental terms as a means of promoting the Islamic Revolution (Alagha 2011). Therefore, all artistic and cultural production has to be "purposeful art" that abides by Islamic sensibilities and has a mission. In the case of Hezbollah, this means taking a modern interpretation of Shi'i jurisprudence and relating *maslaha* to resistance and political struggle, thus making all art "resistance art" (Alagha 2016, 177–178).

Hezbollah's cultural work can be seen within the wider context of its social programs targeted at helping disadvantaged Lebanese. Indeed, its widespread social provision provided a solid base for its transformation from a purely resistance, revolutionary vanguard movement to key political actor in Lebanon. Through its social and educational programs it gains a wider legitimacy, contrary to the well-worn terrorist designation that colors much Western media analysis. Hezbollah also has its own important media outlets such as the *al-Manar* news network, *al-Ahed* newspaper, and also has perceived support from sections of the print media like *al-Akhbar*, which help its popular reach. The combination of social provision and its resistance to Israeli aggression against Lebanon has arguably been instrumental in helping it gain political prominence as seen through its parliamentary victories, with the group now acting as the key power broker in Lebanese politics. As Saad (2019) notes, the movement has transformed from one focused on resisting Israel in the Lebanese context to becoming a regional power in its own right, thus challenging the well-worn "sponsor-proxy" model of understanding the Iran-Hezbollah relationship.

Risalat, Hezbollah's cultural production arm, is responsible for a range of productions. It was established in 2007, following the 2006 Israeli war on Lebanon and according to its director, Sheikh Ali Daher, *Risalat* was founded on a desire to establish a well-managed cultural front of the resistance.[14] The visions of Khomeini and Khamenei are seen as the main inspiring thoughts behind its formation,[15] thus building on the idea that culture and the arts can be useful and sanctioned by Islam if they are purposeful, in this case serving the resistance. *Risalat* operates as a highly professional, well-supported outfit, with public relations strategy that actively seeks effective partnerships with individuals and establishments that can provide moral, human, and financial resources to the organization.[16] It has a clear administrative structure, with an active marketing and social media section. Its artistic section deals with the production work, which is divided into theater, film, music, visual arts, and literature. When asked about collaborating beyond the Shi'i community, Sheikh Ali emphasized that they seek to embrace any communities that find common cause with the resistance,[17] however, while such openness in principle exists, their output is very much aimed at their core constituency. *Risalat* has a substantial base in the Dahiyeh area of southern Beirut, serving the largely Shi'i community there, which hosts studios, a cinema, and puts on theatrical performances. The emphasis in terms of films, musical performances, and plays is very much based on the resistance narrative. Religious themes also predominate, with a range of artistic productions related to important Shi'i religious events such as Ashura and Arbaeen. Such religious festivals are of great significance in Shi'ism, and in their expression are often also tied to the resistance narrative. Such activities highlight the importance of developing a resistance culture that draws on these important foundational beliefs and cultural symbols. This was emphasized by Sheikh Ali when discussing whether one can conceive of an idea of "resistance culture," stating, "We can speak of a resistance culture: The actions of Imam Hussein constitute the first resistance. He planted a culture of resistance and we are the fruits of these ideas."[18] When asked about the significance of key Shi'i historical experiences, notably the experience of Hussein at Karbala, he noted that "from Hussein we learn how to fight injustice. The secret of resistance is from Hussein—he showed how the weak can defeat the strong. Harnessing the legacy of Karbala is very important in resistance culture—perhaps the defining feature."[19]

The links with Hezbollah's allies in Iran are an important feature too, with *Risalat* organizing events in Lebanon involving key Iranian cultural and religious performers, which as the Tehran Symphony Orchestra and performances by notable Iranian *maddah* (Islamic religious singers or "eulogists"). Iranian diplomats are often in attendance at *Risalat* productions, which often feature as news items on the ICRO Beirut office's website.

Conclusion

Iranian foreign policy has undergone notable shifts in emphasis in the last 40 years, beginning with its role as vanguard of revolutionary Islam following the establishment of the Islamic Republic. It tempered this following the death of Khomeini, with its abandonment of active export of the revolution, and instead focused on more pragmatic aims to rebuild its shattered economy after the Iran-Iraq war. It has since vacillated between conciliatory and more conservative interpretations of its role, particularly in relations with the West and regarding its disputed nuclear program, as well as in relations with neighboring states. It has utilized various roles, all of which place Iran at the center of wider transnational identities, which can be nonreligious also—such as acting as the cultural center of the Persianate world. These are articulated through foreign policy narratives that emphasize Iran's role at the center of these wider transnational identity claims (Wastnidge 2019), and they serve useful material objectives as well, as seen in the religious justification utilized for its involvement in the Syria conflict and its investment in shrine cities across the Shi'i world. Despite the varied hues of Iranian foreign policy since the revolution, religiously defined notions of (in)justice are a constant feature, and provide a wider, metanarrative to guide the Islamic Republic's activities globally.

Building on this, the resistance narrative feeds into many aspects of its foreign policy in terms of its cultural diplomacy activities and military engagements in the Middle East. This can be seen in its harnessing of the resistance narrative, and its promotion of its role as a model of religious democracy to be emulated. This latter aspect was key in Iran's approach toward the Arab Uprisings in 2010–2012, where its leaders viewed the uprisings taking place across the region as a form of "Islamic Awakening," thus realizing a new phase in the Islamic Revolution.

Despite regular referral back to core revolutionary ideas, Iranian foreign policy need not be understood in purely ideological terms. It has a pragmatic intent at heart and is more guided by geopolitical realities than any kind of sectarian or religious crusade. This can be seen in the continued hostilities with Saudi Arabia, which are about geopolitical rivalry in the region rather than a deep-seated, historical sectarian rivalry. Iran's emphasis on resistance, while using Shi'i identity reference points as conduits, is generally framed as opposing the interests of Israel and the United States (and their allies) in the region. The religious reference points that are found in Iranian foreign policy, as shown in a small way through the lesser-explored examples of development work, cultural diplomacy, and cultural production work, are more about providing meaning to foreign policy and can also serve as a useful justification when overlaid upon regional dynamics.

References

Akbarzadeh, S., and J. Barry. 2016. "State Identity in Iranian Foreign Policy." *British Journal of Middle Eastern Studies* 43 (4): 613–629.

Alagha, J. 2011. "Pious Entertainment: Hizbullah's Islamic Cultural Sphere." In *Muslim Rap, Halal Soaps, and Revolutionary Theater: Artistic Developments in the Muslim World*, edited by K. van Nieuwkerk, 149–176. Austin: University of Texas Press.

Alagha, J. 2014. "G. Banna's and A. Fadlallah's Views on Dancing." *Sociology of Islam* 2 (1–2): 60–86.

Alagha, J. 2016. "Shi'a Discourses on Performing Arts: Maslaha and Cultural Politics in Lebanon. In *Islam and Popular Culture*, edited by K. van Nieuwkerk, M. Levine, and M. Stokes, 167–186. Austin: University of Texas Press.

Arjomand, S. A. 2016. "Shi'ite Islam and Revolution in Iran." In *Sociology of Shi'ite Islam: Collected Essays*, edited by S. A. Arjomand, 391–492. Boston: Brill. (Originally published as a 1981 journal article in *Government and Opposition* 16 (3): 293–316.)

Article 3.16 of Constitution of the Islamic Republic of Iran. Available online at https://faculty.unlv.edu/pwerth/Const-Iran(abridge).pdf.

Bahrani, M. 2013. "Political Rationality of the Islamic Republic of Iran in Comparison with Contemporary Fundamentalism." In *Iran and the International System*, edited by A. Ehteshami and R. Molavi, 33–42. Abingdon: Routledge.

Baktiari, B. 2012. "The Islamic Republic of Iran: Shari'a Politics and the Transformation of Islamic Law." *The Review of Faith and International Affairs* 10 (4): 35–44.

Chehabi, H. E., and Mneimneh, H. I. 2006. "Five Centuries of Lebanese-Iranian Encounters." In *Distant Relations: Iran and Lebanon in the Last 500 Years*, edited by H. E. Chehabi, 1–51. London: I.B. Tauris.

De Cordier, B. 2007. "Shiite Aid Organizations in Tajikistan." *ISIM Review* 19: 1–11.

Esfandiary, D., and Tabatabai, A. 2015. "Iran's ISIS policy." *International Affairs* 91 (1): 1–15.

Esposito, J. (ed.). 1990. *The Iranian Revolution: Its Global Impact*. Miami: Florida International University Press.

Farquhar, M. 2017. *Circuits of Faith: Migration, Education and the Wahhabi Mission*, Stanford, CA: Stanford University Press.

Harsij, H., M. Toyserkani, and L. Jafari. 2012. "The Geopolitics of Iran's Soft Power (*in Persian*)." *Political Science* 4 (2): 225–269.

Haynes, J. 2008. "Religion and Foreign Policy-Making in the USA, India and Iran: Towards a Research Agenda," *Third World Quarterly* 29 (1): 143–165.

Haynes, J. 2016. *Religious Transnational Actors and Soft Power*. London: Routledge.

Huntington, S. P. 1997. *The Clash of Civilisations and the Remaking of World Order*. London: Simon and Schuster.

Jafarpanahi, M., and Mirahmadi, M. 2012. "Elements of the Islamic Republic of Iran's Soft Power with an Islamic Approach (*in Persian*)." *Journal of Political Knowledge* 4 (2): 105–122.

Khalaji, M. 2011. "Iran's Regime of Religion." *Journal of International Affairs* 65 (1): 131–147.

Khomeini, R. 1990. "Letter to Mr. Mohammad Reza Kazemi, on Hussein and Sharia, 25th October, 1968." In *Sahife-ye Imam, Volume 2* (in Persian). Tehran: The Institute for Compilation and Publication of Imam Khomeini's Works (International Affairs Department).

Khomeini, R. 2008. "Speech in Commemoration the 17th Shahrivar (Black Friday massacre), Qom, 1979." In *Sahife-ye Imam: An Anthology of Imam Khomeini's Speeches, Messages, Interviews, Decrees, Religious Permissions, and Letters, Volume 9*, (English translation). Tehran: The Institute for Compilation and Publication of Imam Khomeini's Works (International Affairs Department).

Louer, L. 2012. *Shiism and Politics in the Middle East*. London: Hurst & Co.

Mabon, S. 2015. *Saudi Arabia and Iran: Power and Rivalry in the Middle East*. London: I. B. Tauris.

Mandaville, P. 2001. *Transnational Muslim Politics: Reimagining the Umma*. London: Routledge.

Mandaville, P. 2014. *Islam and Politics*. London: Routledge.

Mandaville, P., and Hamid, S. 2018. "Islam as Statecraft: How Governments Use Religion in Foreign Policy." In *Brookings New Geopolitics of the Middle East Report*. Washington, DC: Brookings Institute.

Mervin, S. 2010. "Introduction." In *The Shi'a Worlds and Iran*, edited by S. Mervin, 9–26. London: Saqi Books.

Moshirzadeh, H. 2007. "Discursive Foundations of Iran's Nuclear Policy." *Security Dialogue* 38 (4): 521–543.

Nada, G. 2015. "Iran's Growing Toll in Syria." *The Iran Primer—United States Institute of Peace*. http://iranprimer.usip.org/blog/2015/oct/26/iran%E2%80%99s-growing-toll-syria.

Spada, A. 2015. "Iran: General Nowi-Aghdam Urges Recruits to Fight in Syria as Assad Stumbles." *Islam Media Analysis*, June 2015. http://www.islamedianalysis.info/iran-general-nowi-aghdam-urges-recruits-to-fight-in-syria-as-assad-stumbles/.

Ramazani, R. K. 1985. "Iran's Islamic Revolution and the Persian Gulf." *Current History* 84 (498): 5–10.

Ramazani, R. K. 1990. "Iran's Export of the Revolution: Politics, Ends, and Means." In *The Iranian Revolution: Its Global Impacts*, edited by J. Esposito, 40–62. Miami: Florida International University Press.

Rosen, L. 2000. *Islamic Concepts of Justice and Injustice: Comparative Perspectives on Islamic Law and Society*. Oxford: Oxford University Press.

Saad, A. 2019. "Challenging the Sponsor-Proxy Model: The Iran–Hizbullah Relationship." *Global Discourse* 9 (4): 627–650.

Salamey, I., and Othman, Z. 2011. "Shia Revival and Welayat Al-Faqih in the Making of Iranian Foreign Policy." *Politics, Religion & Ideology* 12 (2): 197–212.

Tagliabue, S. M. 2015. "Inside Hezbollah: The al-Mahdi Scouts, Education and Resistance." *Digest of Middle Eastern Studies* 24 (1): 74–95.

Telhami, S., and Barnett, M. 2002. *Identity and Foreign Policy in the Middle East*. New York: Cornell University Press.

Von Maltzahn, N. 2013. "Iran's Cultural Diplomacy." In *Iran and the Challenges of the Twenty-First Century: Essays in Honour of Mohammad-Reza Djalili*, edited by C. Therme, H. E. Chehabi and F. Khosrokhavar, 205–221. Costa Mesa, CA: Mazda.

Wastnidge, E. 2015. "The Modalities of Iranian Soft Power: From Cultural Diplomacy to Soft War." *Politics* 35 (3–4): 364–377.

Wastnidge, E. 2019. "Transnational Identity Claims, Roles, and Strategic Foreign Policy Narratives in the Middle East." *Global Discourse* 9 (4): 605–625.

Wastnidge, E. 2020. "Iran's Own 'War on Terror': Iranian Foreign Policy towards Syria and Iraq during the Rouhani Era." In *The Foreign Policy of Iran under President Hassan Rouhani*, edited by L. Zaccara. Palgrave MacMillan.

Wastnidge, E. 2020. "Iran-Saudi Rivalry and Central Asia." *POMPES Studies* 38.

Wastnidge, E., and Mabon. S. 2021. *Saudi Arabia and Iran: The Struggle to Shape the Middle East*. Manchester: Manchester University Press.

Wyatt, C. 2016. "Syrian Alawites Distance Themselves from Assad." *BBC News*, April 3, 2016. http:// www.bbc.co.uk/news/world-middle-east-35941679.

8
Hassan II and the Foundations of Moroccan Religious Soft Power

Ann Wainscott

> All surrender to beauty
> willingly
> and to power
> unwillingly.
> —Hazrat Inayat Khan[1]

Introduction

Morocco is well known as a contemporary leader in religious soft-power initiatives. With its imam-training center, innovative Countering Violent Extremism (CVE) approach, scholarship programs for sub-Saharan African students, mosque-building initiatives, and other ventures, it effectively projects religious soft power on the African continent and beyond. But the current king Mohammed VI's prowess in the soft-power domain builds on key initiatives begun by his father, including the Hassan II Mosque in Casablanca, the Dar al-Hadith al-Hassaniya, a state-sponsored institution of higher Islamic learning in the country's capital Rabat, and less-well known, but perhaps the true foundation for the country's soft-power initiatives, the *Durus Hasaniya* or Hassanian Lectures, established even before the young monarch had consolidated his throne in 1963, and continued annually to the present day.

Beyond these key institutions, contemporary Moroccan religious soft power also builds on priorities first elaborated by Hassan II's religious policy, including a focus on the relationship between Morocco and West African Muslims and Senegal in particular, the depiction of Morocco as a modern and moderate country especially as regards to the inclusion of women in the

Ann Wainscott, *Hassan II and the Foundations of Moroccan Religious Soft Power* In: *The Geopolitics of Religious Soft Power*. Edited by: Peter Mandaville, Oxford University Press. © Oxford University Press 2023.
DOI: 10.1093/oso/9780197605806.003.0008

religious life of the country and Morocco's leadership in interfaith efforts, and finally, the domestication of the 'ulama, both foreign and domestic, to the benefit of the monarchy's religious authority.

This chapter explores the context in which Hassan II began to lay the foundation for contemporary Moroccan religious soft power, arguing that much of the current success of the strategy has relied on patiently continuing initiatives that at first appeared to not have much impact on the legitimacy of the regime, but have long-term yielded tangible benefits in terms of the country's reputation and foreign policy objectives.

The Concept of Religious Soft Power

In the quote that begins this chapter from the nineteenth century mystic, Hazrat Inayat Khan, beauty is differentiated from power. But contemporary theorists, perhaps learning from the mystics, have realized that beauty is better understood as a form of power, soft power. This is a relatively recent development. In 1950, the political scientist (and, notably, spy for the Soviet Union) Franz L. Neumann lamented, "It is difficult, perhaps impossible, to add any new idea to a discussion of political power" (Neumann 1950, 161). And yet, 40 years later, Joseph Nye did broaden our ability to analyze political power through the development of the concept of soft power (1990).[2] It is not that Neumann was unaware of the softer side of power. He discussed it directly: "those who wield political power are compelled to create emotional and rational responses in those whom they rule, inducing them to accept, implicitly or explicitly, the commands of the rulers." And, like Nye, Neumann understood that soft power was intimately related to violence: "Failure to evoke emotional or intellectual responses in the ruled compels the ruler to resort to simple violence, ultimately to liquidation."

What Neumann seems not to have anticipated is the role that soft power would play not only in the relationship between ruler and ruled but also in a state's foreign relations. For that, we are indebted to Joseph Nye. Nye first developed his concept of soft power as "the ability to get what you want through attraction rather than coercion or payments" (Nye Jr. 1990). He later elaborated the application of this concept to foreign affairs (Nye 2004). Nye was interested in describing how the nature of power in foreign affairs was changing, while once measured in population and natural resources, in the twenty-first century, he argued that power is measured in a state's ability to change the behavior of other states.

Nye's analysis of soft power called for deep attention to context. He explained, "Power always depends on the context in which the relationship exists" (1990, 2). He cautioned, "Before you judge who is holding the high cards, you need to understand what game you are playing and how the value of the cards may be changing" (1990, 4). This is perhaps the most complicated task for assessing a soft-power project—what game do the actors believe that they are playing, how do you know, and by what metrics might they be evaluating the value of their own resources and their competition with other actors?

This chapter explores these dynamics in the case of Morocco, where the early years of its religious soft-power project were characterized by extensive use of violence and coercion by the regime against its population. Nevertheless, the patient development of both a domestic and foreign religious soft-power policy and its increasing integration eventually facilitated a dramatic reduction in the level of violence required to rule, especially when compared to the strategies of other states in the region. In its initial phase, from 1963 to 1981, the project was largely focused on domestic politics, the arena from which the monarchy faced the most serious threats to its own legitimacy. But even in this phase the initial outlines of a foreign policy strategy are in evidence, with a focus on positioning Morocco as a patron of West African Islam. In the second phase, from 1981 to 2003, the country patiently continued many initiatives that had not yet born much fruit and sought out more substantial engagement with Senegal, the main recipient of its patronage. In contemporary times, Morocco's investment in its religious soft-power projects have yielded tangible results including reducing resistance to its territorial claims to Western Sahara, the expansion of the Moroccan banking sector in West Africa, and Morocco's increased leadership on the African continent. What is most impressive about the Moroccan soft-power project is that the regime seems to have understood very well the changing nature of the game it was playing, maintaining initiatives that seemed to yield little results until they were eventually leveraged for broader foreign policy objectives.

1963–1981

The Moroccan religious soft-power project was initiated at a key moment in Hassan II's rule. He took power in 1961 after the unexpected death of his father, Mohammed V, the beloved King at the time of Morocco's independence from France in 1956, who had literally become a symbol of resistance to French rule. The main independence party had split into two factions in 1959, only two years prior. Hassan II established the Hassanian Ramadan lessons (*Durus Hasaniya*), a lecture series held during the holy month of Ramadan, prior to the birth of his first son, so as yet had no heir to the throne. He was faced with serious mobilization of leftist actors, which culminated in the 1965 Casablanca riots, leading the young king to suspend the country's constitution, dissolve parliament, and act as the country's prime minister (much as his own father had done in 1960; Waterbury 1970). In the following decade, Hassan II survived coup attempts in 1971 and 1972. The soft-power project, initiated in 1963, was therefore established prior to regime consolidation, in the midst of great political instability in the country.

The religious soft-power project was meant to strengthen and diversify the sources of the regime's legitimacy at a fragile political moment. The establishment of the Hassanian lessons in 1963 corresponded to the adoption of the first Moroccan Constitution in December of 1962 and the institution of a bicameral parliament. The vote on December 7, 1962 in favor of the Constitution was the first national-level election the country had held. The lectures were held seven weeks later, from January 27 to February 25. The scholar Willard Beling, commenting on the new constitution in 1964, explained,

> the constitution itself seemed hardly the issue of the referendum on December 7. Instead, it appeared that the institution of the monarchy itself and Islām were the real issues to be decided upon. Although the Monarch had changed his title [from Sultan to King] in 1957, campaign references were made to the religio-political institution of the sultanate. It was noted in one address, for example, that "His Majesty the King is the Amīr of the Believers. He can get the opinion of the doctors of the Law to see whether this or that text is contrary to the spirit of Islām." In the same vein, the pro-constitution press headlined the fact that the constitution which the King had prepared for his people declared Islām the state religion. (170)

Observers agreed that voters passed the new Constitution (at more than 97 percent) not on its own merits but for three other reasons: "for the monarchical institution, the King's caliphal authority, or for Islām itself" (Beling 1964, 173). And indeed, Article 19 of the 1962 Constitution was the first to officially give the king an Islamic title, Commander of the Faithful (*amīr al-mu'minīn*). The strong support for the Constitution seems to have indicated strong support for the religious identity of the state and the king's religious authority.

While 1963 was certainly a watershed year for the country's religious soft-power project, in that it codified the king's religious position and established a focus of his patronage, it appears that the young, secular king had virtually no interest in religion's mobilizing force. It is reported that he included article 19 only after being encouraged to do so by independence leaders 'Allal al-Fasi and Abdelkrim Khatib (Zeghal 2003, 2). Al-Fasi was himself an Islamic scholar who was trained at and later employed by Qarawiyyin University in Fez and also served briefly as the Minister of Islamic Affairs from 1962 to 1963 (Park and Boum 2006, 121). It seems likely, therefore, that the king also began the lecture series on al-Fasi's recommendation.

Though largely secular in orientation, and early on oblivious to the role of religion as a resource, the young king did have some characteristics that contributed to his legitimacy as a religious figure, both at home and abroad. As described by one reporter, the king had impressive control of classical Arabic: "Arabs from the heart of the Middle East, who tend to be a bit snobbish on the subject, concede that Morocco's king is probably the most effective orator around in classical Arabic; he sprinkles his discourses with learned or riddlelike allusions to the Koran." While Hassan II made no claims to being a religious scholar, he could perform the part if necessary.

While Hassan II was not particularly interested in religion for its own sake, he saw religious elites as a counterweight to the strength of leftist and socialist opposition activists. He used the Hassanian lectures as a means of amplifying the voice of major Islamists, such as Abd al-Fattah Abu Ghuddah (1917–1997). In the first year of the Hassanian lessons, the monarchy invited Abu Ghudda to give a lecture. At the time, Abu Ghuddah was a recently elected member of the Syrian parliament, the future leader of the Syrian Muslim Brotherhood, and the Mufti of Aleppo (Moubayed 2006, 130). The invitation to him presages Hassan II's later policy of encouraging the mobilization of Islamist actors to combat radical leftist activists. During this time, the spread of leftist ideologies was seen as a threat to the country's Islamic identity of which Hassan II positioned himself as the protector (Slimane 2011).

Hassan II's concerns about the left began not as an ideological dispute but rather out of concern for the stability of the throne, as leftist actors were the most vocal supports of a reduction in the powers of the monarchy.

In response to the new constitution, parliamentary elections were held later that year in May 1963. Following the elections, the regime arrested 104 opposition activists, including 24 deputies-elect from the *Union Nationaliste des Forces Populaires* (UNFP), a faction that had split from 'Allal al-Fasi's *Istiqlal* party. The main cause of the dispute between the two factions was over the power of the monarchy. While Istiqlal was willing to accept a promise for later democratization, the UNFP wanted the monarchy reduced to a symbolic institution with no real political power immediately (Beling 1964, 165). The UNFP also controlled a labor union (the UMT) believed to have nearly 900,000 members at the time of the referendum (Beling 1964, 167). The arrest of the UNFP members was likely retribution for their role in sponsoring an unsuccessful boycott of the 1962 Constitutional referendum and a statement that the monarchy intended to maintain its dominant position in the political system. One observer of the events of 1963 concluded that "the referendum results seem to have given Hasan II a supreme sense of self-assurance. Thereafter, he saw no reason to fear—or court—the opposition" (Beling 1964, 177). The monarchy's aggressive actions toward the opposition activists presaged the brutal years that were to come, where coercion was the primary approach that the monarchy took to managing any perceived threats.

Though coercion was the monarchy's primary method for dealing with the opposition, it also continued to lay the foundation for its religious soft-power project. In the 1964 Hassanian Lectures, the king announced the Founding of Dar al-Hadith al-Hassaniya.[3] In the speech, he connected the need for experts trained in the Islamic sciences for both "Moroccan society and state institutions," demonstrating that the king foresaw the need for state-trained religious bureaucrats decades before the expansion of the state's religious ministries. The royal decree formally founding the institution came later, in 1968, and it officially opened its doors in 1975.

The founding of "Dar al-Hadith" is a significant step in the Morocco religious soft-power project. The institution, which can be literally translated as "Hassan's House of Hadith," is a university that provides training and credentials in the Islamic sciences. The creation of Dar al-Hadith was meant to move the center of religious authority (and therefore the religious scholars or *'ulama*) from Qarawiyyin Mosque University in Fez, where it had been difficult to control for centuries, to the capital city of Rabat, closer to the seat of the monarchy and easier to monitor. Graduates of the university can be enlisted in the state's religious bureaucracy. The Minister of Islamic Affairs from

1985 to 2002, Abdelkébir Alaoui M'Daghri, completed a PhD in Islamic sciences at the institution.

The monarchy chose another Syrian member of the Muslim Brotherhood, Mohammad Farouk al-Nabhan, to lead Dar al-Hadith in its early years. He remained in his position from 1977 to 2000. It is believed that he was chosen because he militantly opposed Nasserism, which by the 1970s had become the foundation for the left across the Middle East (Howe 2005, 127). The institution was useful for a variety of purposes, including in at least one case allowing the regime to plant a Syrian refugee who was a monarchical advisor as a fake professor at the institution in order to gather information on an Islamist organization (Park and Boum 2006, 185). The incident demonstrates that the regime sought to monitor all opposition movements, not just leftist ones.

Long term, the existence of a state-sponsored institution of higher Islamic learning allowed the regime to move processes of change at their preferred pace. When the regime desired to see more women in positions of religious leadership, it hired women to teach at Dar al-Hadith. In 2003, when the King was in the midst of proposing a reform to the country's family code, he enlisted a female faculty member from Dar al-Hadith, Rajaa Naji Mekkaoui, to be the first woman to give a Durus Hassaniya lecture before the king and a largely male audience. In doing so, the king achieved multiple objectives. Not only did he signal the reforms to the family code that would be implemented later that year, but he also signaled to the 'ulama that he expected women to play a greater role in the religious sector. He also implicitly reinforced the authority of Dar al-Haidth, by honoring one of its graduates. The content of the lecture presaged changes to the family code. She spoke on the topic of "The System of the Islamic Family Compared with the Situation of the Family in Western Societies" (*al-Niẓām al-Usrī al-Islāmī Muqārana bimā 'alayhi al-Waḍ' al-Usrī fī al-Mujtama'āt al-Gharbiyya*).[4]

This period also marked the beginning of the projection of Moroccan religious soft power in sub-Saharan Africa, a regional focus that has become dominant in the twenty-first century. Hassan II's first major act of religious patronage was the sponsorship of the Great Mosque of Dakar (La Grande Mosquée de Dakar) inaugurated on March 27, 1964, by King Hassan II and President Léopold Sédar Senghor of Senegal. The King's words that day did not portray the Moroccan regime as a patron but as a fellow participant in a shared independence struggle: "Rare are the generations like ours that have seen three stages of their lives: the stage of combat, the stage of victory, and the stage of rebuilding. Our generation knows what it has lost, knows even better what it has found. It therefore understands the price of its future heritage. But future generations will be born in peace" (Seck 1968, 31).

Although funds were originally solicited by a local organization of religious elites who called themselves "L'association pour l'édification de la Grande Mosquée de Dakar" [The Association for the Construction of the Great Mosque of Dakar], the mosque was built by 135 Moroccan craftsmen and financed by Morocco and Egypt, suggesting that Morocco responded with the most generosity to the association's general call for funds (El Hadj 2010). The mosque contains an Islamic Institute funded by Morocco, Saudi Arabia, Kuwait, Tunisia, Qatar, Bahrain, Iraq, Jordan, Libya, the United Arab Republic, and Syria (Seck 1968). This broad sponsorship was seen as symbolic of the unity of Islam. The mosque, located in Senegal's capital, was built in the style of the Mohammed V Mosque in Casablanca with a square minaret in the style of the Koutoubia Mosque in Marrakesh.[5] The construction of the mosque was a physical embodiment of the close relationship between the two countries, largely mediated by the dominance of the Tijaniyya Sufi brotherhood in both countries.

Two years after the first lectures, events on the ground in Morocco convinced Hassan II that political movements from the left had become too powerful: the 1965 Casablanca riots. Prior to the riots, the Moroccan monarchy ignored politics on university campuses. The Moroccan left, composed of communists and socialists, controlled the powerful student union, UNEM, and dominated internal university politics. The riots of 1965, led by university students, significantly altered the relationship between the regime and universities as well as between the regime and opposition political parties. Because there was only one university in the early years after independence, the institution provided a meeting ground for activists from across the country. The protests demonstrated that the students, upon returning home, could lead countrywide demonstrations. Scholars agree that it was these riots that thrust the significance of university-level politics onto the national agenda, ending the relative autonomy exercised by parties on campus and instigating a series of reforms led by the monarchy intended to control, contain, and structure the internal politics of the university, as well as the opposition.

In addition, threats from the military manifested in coup attempts in 1971 and 1972 that led the king to even greater paranoia and coercion. In response, he sponsored a "Green March" into a disputed territory in the south of the country, leading 350,000 Moroccan citizens across the border, carrying Moroccan flags and Qurans (Hamdoui 2003). The territorial dispute was a convenient way to maintain a distance between the majority of the country's military and the palace. The march dramatically altered the political landscape, whereas the early 1970s were marked by a unified opposition and multiple coup attempts, by the late 1970s, the monarchy was firmly in control of the country.

By 1980, Hassan II had come to appreciate the role that religion played in the life of his people and in his style of rule. While his understanding of this fact appears to be growing throughout this time period, it was cemented by the Iranian Revolution of 1979.[6] James Markham, a reporter for the New York Times, reported,

> Conversing with this reporter in a bungalow office complex set amid a grove of palm trees in Marrakesh, the king [Hassan II], relaxing in a tweedy jacket, observed: "His [the Shah's] first error of analysis—I told him so—was not to have been able to appreciate the place of religion in social life. He wanted to reign as an emperor, but as a lay emperor." (Markham 1980, 29)

Hassan II, by contrast, had already learned that religion was an indispensable resource to rule.

But religion was not sufficient to maintain Hassan II's hold on power. This period, known as the Years of Lead (*les années de plomb/sanawāt ar-rassas*), was characterized by state-sponsored violence against opposition activists, torture, disappearances, and other violations of human rights. The years are named after the lead bullets that plagued those who dared to protest (Amine 2016, 121–141). Amnesty International first documented torture in the country in 1963, and recorded that torture increased in severity in the 1970s, when many detainees were tortured to death (Amnesty International 2014). The years of lead would continue well into the 1990s. The high levels of violence suggest that the young religious soft-power project was too weak to support the monarchy's legitimacy without the threat of coercion.

1981–2003

The second period was initiated by the Casablanca bread riots of 1981, caused by a dramatic rise in the price of basic commodities reflecting strain on the Moroccan economy following six years of war in the south (The New York Times 1981, 4). What was originally planned as a strike evolved into rioting.

The police fired on the rioters. While the estimates of those dead vary dramatically between less than a hundred to more than six hundred, it is clear that the "Years of Lead" were in full force.

A major change in religious policy that took place at this time was the creation of the High Council of 'Ulema (*Conseil supérieur des Oulémas*). In announcing the council, Hassan II framed it as necessary to involve religious scholars who were "absent from daily Moroccan life" (Markham 1980, 401). He called for a more robust involvement, similar to the speech his son would give in September of 2008 calling for the 'ulema to "make a more efficient contribution" and to "focus, in particular, on helping to strengthen the spiritual security of the nation."[7] Hassan's call on the scholars demonstrates that in the wake of the Casablanca riots, the monarchy would rely increasingly on its religious soft-power project to strengthen the monarchy's legitimacy.

The creation of the council marked the beginning of a formal hierarchy of religious scholars that was a necessary first step to the reorganization that would later characterize twenty-first century Moroccan religious policy. While in 1981 there was a regional council to represent each of Morocco's formal regions, and one high council composed of the presidents of those regional councils, these councils were greatly multiplied in the reforms of 2004 where 68 local councils were created.[8] In 1981, the heads of regional councils were all appointed to the national council, formalizing a hierarchy of religious scholars in Morocco for the first time.

This period also marked an expansion in the country's employment of religious soft power in foreign policy. Morocco's formal religious outreach to West Africa actually began in the previous period, with the construction of the Grand Mosque of Dakar. But beginning in the 1980s, Moroccan religious soft power began to expand beyond patronage to sponsor forms of interaction and cooperation. In 1981, Morocco began funding "Islamic cultural days" in Dakar, Senegal, a tradition that in 2021 completed its fortieth gathering, via an online platform due to restrictions posed by the Coronavirus.[9]

Similarly, the founding of the League of Scholars of Morocco and Senegal (la Ligue des oulémas du Maroc et du Sénégal) in 1985 presaged later policy of focused religious outreach to sub-Saharan African Muslim scholars and West African religious elites in particular. The head of this organization, Ibrahim Mahmoud Diop (d. 2014), is credited with the idea of the organization, which Hassan II welcomed and funded.[10] In 1984, Hassan II invited "Barham" Diop to give a Durus Hasaniya lecture on the theme of "the Truths of the contemporary Islamic Call" (Des vérités sur l'appel islamique contemporain).

Some say that it was the erudition of this lecture that led Hassan to call for the creation of the league the next year. Whatever the cause, the sequence of inviting the scholar to give a lecture and then giving him a position of leadership over an organ of Moroccan religious soft power illustrates the way in which the lectures are integrated into broader initiatives to vet potential collaborators and also to reward allies with the prestige of having given a lecture in the presence of the king. In 2005, as an attendee at the lectures, he was invited to read the letter on behalf of all participants at the conclusion of the lectures to his Majesty Mohammed VI, an honor certainly meant to convey the monarchy's intentions to turn toward sub-Saharan Africa in the coming decade. By inviting Diop to read the letter, it was also assured that Diop had publicly addressed both Hassan II and his son, Mohammed VI during their reigns.

As of 2014, at the time of Diop's death, he was the only Senegalese scholar to have been invited to give a Durus Hasaniya lecture (a fact that was prominently mentioned in obituaries). He was a strategic choice to lead the league as one of the key disciples of the popular Tijani Sheikh Ibrahim Niasse (d. 1975) of Senegal. His appointment therefore strengthened the already strong ties between Morocco and one of the major branches of the Tijani brotherhood in Senegal. Diop served as the secretary general of the league from 1985 until his death in 2014. The proximity of his death to the establishment of another Moroccan institution, the Mohammed VI Foundation for African 'Ulama, the next year, suggests that the League is now defunct, as its functions have been absorbed by the Foundation, which is committed to building collaboration between sub-Saharan and Moroccan religious scholars.[11]

Hassan II's use of religious soft power was not limited to outreach to coreligionists. He was also interested in positioning himself as a moderate king who mediates interfaith harmony, particularly with Abrahamic religions. To that effect, he hosted a convention of Moroccan Jews in 1983, inviting many Jews and their descendants who had fled Morocco after the establishment of Israel in 1948 to return. The initiative built on his father's reputation of protecting the country's Jewish population during World War II. Hassan II visited Pope John Paul II at the Vatican in 1981 to discuss peace in the Middle East, and the pope reciprocated with a visit to Casablanca in 1985, the first time a head of state of a Muslim country had received the Pope and the first time the Pope had visited a Muslim country (Yamani 1999; Iraqi 2019, 893).[12] The Vatican opened an embassy in Rabat in 1988 and

Morocco reciprocated opening an embassy to the Vatican in 1997 (Alaoui 2019). Contemporary Moroccan religious policy has expanded on both of these efforts, with continued outreach to the Moroccan Jewish diaspora.[13] Similarly, King Mohammed VI visited the Vatican in the year 2000 to meet with John Paul II, and he welcomed Pope Francis to Morocco in 2019.

The other major soft-power project during this period was the construction of the Hassan II Mosque in Casablanca, which began in 1986 and was the highest minaret in the world at the time that it was completed in 1993. Today it is the second tallest minaret. The style is traditional Moroccan, but its location on the Atlantic coast is an innovation. Scholar Jennifer Roberson explains, "Historically, mosques had been located in densely urbanized settings, so that little of the building was visible other than the minaret and exterior decoration was limited. It was not until one entered the courtyard that high levels of ornamentation were found. The highly visible location of the Hassan II Mosque makes it visible throughout much of Casablanca so that it acts as a constant reminder of the king" (Roberson 2014, 76).

Many aspects of Moroccan religious policy that would later be developed in greater detail were present in the mosque project. The location of the mosque in urban Casablanca and the public relations campaign that accompanied the opening of the mosque suggested that the mosque captures Morocco's modern identity. Mohammed Abderrahim, the chief spokesman at the information Ministry at the time of the opening, explained, "The mosque is intended to present an image of a Muslim country that is open, that is tolerant, that is cosmopolitan and that is modern" (Cohen 1993, A4). The technological features of the mosque, which include a laser beaming toward Mecca and a retractable roof, underscore Morocco's technological sophistication. Also presaging later Moroccan religious policy, Hassan II invited a female poet, Amina Mrili, to recite verses at the inauguration of the mosque (Cohen 1993, A4).

Finally, in 1990, Hassan II established the Hassan II Foundation for Moroccan Foreign Residents, an organization that seeks to maintain the King's religious leadership over the Moroccan diaspora. The organization provides Arabic language and Moroccan cultural lessons to the children of the Moroccan diaspora. Moroccan efforts to reach out to the diaspora have greatly expanded in recent years. In 2021, during the month of Ramadan, the country sent more than 700 imams and female preachers to provide religious services to members of the Moroccan diaspora living abroad. More than 250 of the imams were sponsored by the Hassan II foundation.[14] By claiming religious leadership over members of the diaspora, the Moroccan monarchy signals that its authority extends well beyond its territorial borders.

The Durus Hasaniya or Hassanian Lectures

Under Hassan II, and continuing to the present day, the centerpiece of the Moroccan religious soft-power project is the *Durus Hasaniya*, a lecture series hosted by the Moroccan monarch during the holy month of Ramadan. The King of Morocco invites Moroccan and foreign religious clerics to address him and an audience of distinguished guests. The lectures are broadcast on domestic TV channels as well as satellite channels around the world.

During the month of Ramadan, Muslims fast from sunrise to sunset. The month commemorates the first revelation to the Prophet Mohammed, in the year 610 AD, and therefore the Quran is emphasized during this season. Muslims also believe that there is greater spiritual benefit to religious practices undertaken during this period, so there is generally an increase in religious fervor in the global Muslim community (*umma*) during this month. It is therefore a strategic time to broadcast religious lectures, taking advantage of the increased interest in religion while orienting viewers' toward an interpretation of their faith that is consistent with the monarchy's vision of itself as the leader of the moderate umma.

An invitation to speak at the lectures is an honor. Given that the lectures are broadcast internationally, it is one of the few ways to address the global Muslim community. One Senegalese scholar, Abdul Aziz Kébé, put it this way in an editorial in a Senegalese newspaper, the Durus Hasaniya are "one of the rare spaces where Islam is expressed in its universal dimension, that is to say in its legal and theological plurality and in its cultural diversity, in a climate of remarkable tolerance, characterized by respect for difference, in accordance with the Qur'anic principle of convincing argument" (Kébé 2015, 5). The lectures underscore the diversity of Islam, with many lectures coming from scholars from different Muslim countries.

Giving a lecture is also an honor because the lecture is given in the presence of the King of Morocco, who has claim to the title *Amir al-Mu'minin*, commander of the faithful. This title is significant in Islamic history as the name traditionally given to the Caliph, or the leader of the entire Muslim community on Earth. When Kemal Ataturk abolished the institution of the Caliphate in Turkey, that left the umma without a Caliph. Only a few living individuals can lay claim to this title, through descent from the prophet Muhammad and other requirements. The Moroccan king is one such individual who can lay claim to this title. Meanwhile, the location of the lectures, within one of the royal palaces, strengthens the image of the Moroccan king as a religious authority and patron of the Islamic sciences.

Similarly, an invitation to attend the lectures is also an honor. Guests include distinguished scholars of Islam from around the world, the prince(s), the King's advisors, members of the government including the prime minister, as well as leaders from the Moroccan parliament, leading military officials, and Moroccan religious scholars (Slimane 2011). King Mohammed VI distinguished himself by inviting even religious scholars leading opposition movements, such as Ahmed Raïssouni who was at that time the leader of the Movement for Unity and Reform (MUR), the social movement of the Party of Justice and Development (Slimane 2011). Visiting dignitaries, whether speakers or attendees of the lectures, travel throughout Morocco and often give talks at other institutions such as universities. The lectures are thus an opportunity for real scholarly engagement for local Moroccan scholars with leading Islamic scholars from around the world.

The lectures are highly ceremonial. The first lecture of the month is generally given by the Moroccan Minister of Endowments and Islamic Affairs, which has been Ahmed Toufiq since 2002. He is generally followed by a visiting dignitary or high ranking cleric from another country. High ranking invitees have included the Pakistani Islamist and scholar Abu al-A'la al-Mawdudi and the Egyptian Gad al-Haq 'Ali Gad al-Haq who was then serving on Gamal Abdel Nassar's Supreme Council for Islamic Affairs and would later go on to serve as the Grand Sheikh of al-Azhar and the Grand Mufti of Egypt. In 2005, then Grand Sheikh of al-Azhar, Sheikh Mohamed Sayed Tantaoui, gave the second lecture. In recent years, a local Moroccan scholar and a woman are generally also invited to participate.

Each lecture follows a similar format: it is framed around a verse from the Quran or a Hadith and addresses only one topic. The topics tend to be politically relevant to the monarchy's policy priorities. The lecture series concludes with a letter written on behalf of all those scholars who were in attendance at the lectures. Being selected to read the letter is also a way to honor significant scholars. The lectures position the Moroccan King as a patron of the Islamic sciences who is conferring honor upon his carefully selected guests.

Tables 8.1 and 8.2 present the titles of presentations from the 2005 and 2006 lectures that were collected in a bound volume to commemorate the lecture series (Rabat 2005). Because Morocco initiated major changes in religious policy in April of the previous year, the 2005 lectures were one of

Table 8.1 The 2005 Lectures

Speaker	Position	Country	Topic
Ahmed Toufiq	Minister of Endowments and Islamic Affairs	Morocco	"On the Role of 'Ulemas (Scholars) in the Management of the Prophet's Tradition"
Sheikh Mohamed Sayed Tantaoui	The Grand Sheikh of the Azhar as-Shareef	Egypt	"A Strong Believer is Goodlier (in the Sight of Allah) and more Beloved to Him than a Weak One"
El-Yazid Radi	Head of the Religious Council at Taroudant	Moroccan	"Islam, the Religion of Natural Disposition"
Professor Mohammed Nassr 'Arif	Professor and Head of the Department of Arabic and Islamic Studies at Zaid University	The United Arab Emirates	"*Kheiriah* (Preeminence) and *Ikhrāj* (the Act of Evolving a Community): A Cognitive Approach to the Relations between Islam and the World"
Professor Farida Zumru	Professor at Dar al-Hadith al-Hassaniah	Morocco	"Woman in the Noble *Qurān*: Her Nature and Function"
Professor Mohammed Er-Rougui	Professor at Jami'al-Qarawiyeen in Fez and Mohammed V University in Rabat	Morocco	"On the Benefits of Erudition in the *Malekite* [Maliki] Rite"
Professor Mahmud Ibrahim Diop	Secretary General of the League of Scholars of Morocco and Senegal	Senegal	Read The Speech of the Participating Scholars

Table 8.2 The 2006 lectures

Speaker	Position	Country	Topic
Ahmed Toufiq	Minister of Endowments and Islamic Affairs	Morocco	"The Future of Mankind Lies in the Golden Mean and Moderation"
Sheikh Mohamed Sayed Tantaoui	The Grand Sheikh of the Azhar as-Shareef	Egypt	"On the Good Conduct of Prophet Sayyiduna Muhammad"
Professor Mustapha Benhamza		Morocco	"On Social *Fiqh* (Jurisprudence) in Islam: Consecration and Explanation"
Sheikh Ayatollah Mohamed Ali Taskhiri	Secretary General of the World Academy for the Rapprochement between Madhabs (or, Classical Islamic Religious Schools of Law)	Born in Najaf, Iraq but an Iranian citizen	"The Movement of Rapprochement between *Madhabs* (Rites): Fundaments and Future Perspectives"
Professor Saadia Belmir	Adviser at the Diwān of the Minister of Justice	Morocco	"Notifying Judgements and the Responsibility of Choice and Implementation, from the Vantage-Points of *Sharī'ah* (The Revealed Law of Islam) and Positive Law"
Dr. Mohammed Haytham al-Khayyāt	Senior Adviser to the Regional Director of the World Health Organization in the Middle East	Syria	"The motivation of Creeds and Prescriptions in Islam"
Professor Mohammed Iqbal Aroui	Religious Scholar	Kuwait-Morocco (?)	"Arts and Beauty from the Vantage-Point of Islamic Civilization"

Kingdom of Morocco. Ministry of Waqfs and Islamic Affairs. 2006. *The Hassanian Lectures: Lectures on topics related to the exegesis of the Holy Qur'an and Noble Tradition delivered before His Majesty King Mohammed VI May Allah Grant Him Support and Glory over the holy month of Ramadan 1427 A.H.* (2005). Rabat: Edition impression Bouregreg.

the earliest opportunities to see how the new direction in religious policy could be supported by the lectures. The presenters follow the general pattern described above. Ahmed Toufiq's lecture on the 'ulema presaged a major shift in orientation toward the scholars that would be formally announced in 2008, but which had been signaled since the 2004 speech announcing the reforms to the religious field. The speech was clearly meant to encourage the scholars to take greater ownership in the reforms being initiated. The speech suggested that 'ulama who cooperate with the state are fulfilling their true duty to safeguard Islam.

The lectures reflect the themes originated under Hassan II's reign. The effort to present Morocco as a modern Islamic country interested in interfaith work and reconciliation is evident in Ahmed Toufiq's topic in 2006 as well as in the invitation to Sheikh Ayatollah Mohamed Ali Taskhiri who heads the World Academy for the Rapprochement between Madhabs. The priority given to West Africa and Senegal in particular is represented by the invitation to Ibrahim Diop to read the letter from participants to the king in the 2006 lectures. The inclusion of women in both years reflects the desire to include more women in Moroccan religious policy. This priority is also represented by the *Mourchida* program, another program of the Moroccan Ministry of Endowments and Islamic Affairs, which trains lay female religious leaders (El Haitami 2012, 227–240). The first class of *mourchidat* graduated in 2006.

The lectures have taken on new functions since the dramatic increase in the size of the religious bureaucracy initiated in a reform to the religious field in 2004. The lectures now allow for a kind of integration of the various institutions that now populate the Moroccan religious bureaucracy. At a 2012 lecture, Abdul Ghafoor Kmich, a 13-year-old from the Moroccan city of Kenitra, was invited to recite the Quran for the participants. Kmich had recently won the well-named Mohammad VI National Prize for Quranic recitation (administered of course by the Mohammed VI Foundation for Quranic Recitation). The lectures can be used to draw attention to newer initiatives, to announce important policy changes, reward loyal religious scholars, and perform religious authority. This integration between initiatives is the strength of contemporary Moroccan religious policy. Building on a foundation laid by Hassan II, current Moroccan religious policy has found ways to leverage these initiatives to draw attention to other newer initiatives and to continue to represent the country as modern, inclusive, and tolerant.

Conclusions

Morocco's current soft-power project builds on the legacy built by Hassan II. While there were relatively few initiatives during his tenure, the long-term consistency with which the monarchy continued these initiatives has contributed to Morocco's reputation as a religious leader in West Africa and beyond. With time, these individual initiatives began to integrate and reinforce one another. Contemporary priorities also find their genesis in the rule of Hassan II, especially Morocco's outreach to West Africa and Senegal in particular, the focus on depicting Morocco as both moderate and tolerant, and the emphasis on the 'ulama as key actors in religious policy.

In contemporary times, Morocco's religious soft-power project has strengthened its relationships with allies, alliances which have in turn yielded real benefits toward its foreign policy priorities. In early 2017, Morocco rejoined the African Union (AU) after an all-out multiyear diplomatic effort in sub-Saharan Africa that included religious cooperation but also extended into other domains.[15] This effort included visits from the King and high-ranking dignitaries, the opening of new embassies, and the signing of agreements in wide-ranging domains from religion to agriculture. *Jeune Afrique* counted an astonishing thirty-nine visits by the king to sub-Saharan Africa in the first sixteen years of his reign.[16] These visits often include forms of religious outreach and diplomacy. In the two-year period leading up to the vote, the king publicly performed Friday prayer in African countries thirteen times including in Senegal, Mali, Gabon, and Nigeria (Hmimnat 2018, 18). Several countries including Gabon, Senegal, and Niger announced or reiterated their support for Morocco's membership in the AU after these state visits. Religious cooperation has been a centerpiece of outreach efforts in each of these countries. While not sufficient on its own, the combination of religious cooperation with the country's longstanding religious legitimacy in the region and expanded economic cooperation has been well-received by recipient countries (Wainscott 2018, 1–26).

Morocco has also dramatically expanded economic outreach in countries it has targeted with religious cooperation. Three main Moroccan banks have expanded in sub-Saharan Africa: Attijariwafa Bank, BMCE Bank of Africa, and Banque Centrale Populaire (CBP). These banks are present in 27 African countries, including ten in West Africa (Berrada 2019). Beyond the private sector, more than 85 percent of Moroccan foreign-direct investment goes to sub-Saharan African countries (Economist 2018). While it is impossible to untangle the degree to which these various forms of outreach have contributed to Morocco's reputation in the region, it is clear that Morocco and Moroccan investment are welcomed in the religious sector and beyond. Morocco's foreign policy, often framed as "south-south cooperation" by the kingdom, appears to be much more a form of power, soft power.

In fact, Joseph Nye's description of soft power seem to describe Morocco perfectly:

A state may achieve the outcomes it prefers in world politics because other states want to follow it or have agreed to a situation that produces such effects. In this sense, it is just as important to set the agenda and structure the situations in world politics as to get others to change in particular cases . . . *If a state can make its power seem legitimate in the eyes of others, it will encounter less resistance to its wishes. If its culture and ideology are attractive, others will more willingly follow."* (Nye 2004, 166–167, emphasis mine)

References

Alaoui, Mohamed. 2019. "Pope Francis's Visit to Morocco Constitutes Important Step in Dialogue of Civilisations." *The Arab Weekly*, March 24, 2019. https://thearabweekly.com/pope-franciss-visitmorocco-constitutes-important-step-dialogue-civilisations.
Amine, Khalid. 2016. "After the 'Years of Lead' in Morocco: Performing the Memory." *New Theatre Quarterly* 32 (2): 121–141.
"A la Grande mosquée de Dakar, les prières surérogatoires jettent des ponts de communion entre Marocains et Sénégalais." 2019. *Agence Marocaine De Presse*, Mai 14 2019. http://www.mapexpress.ma/actualite/opinions-et-debats/grande-mosquee-dakar-les-prieres-surerogatoires-jettent-ponts-communion-marocains-senegalais/.
"As Morocco Starts to Gain in War, Nation Erupts." 1981. *The New York Times*, July 4, 1981. https://www.nytimes.com/1981/07/04/world/as-morocco-starts-to-gain-in-war-nation-erupts.html.
Abdelhakim Yamani. 1999. "Moroccans Mourn King Hassan's Death." *AP News*, July 24, 1999, https://apnews.com/article/4893d9f0de8f5493ea99dea4c7c7bf95.
Beling, Willard A. 1964. "Some Implications of the New Constitutional Monarchy in Morocco." *Middle East Journal* 18 (2): 163–79.
Berrada, El Mehdi. 2019. "Growth Slows in Africa for Moroccan Banks." *The Africa Report*, July 29, 2019. https://www.theafricareport.com/15775/growth-slows-in-africa-for-moroccan-banks/.
Cohen, Roger. 1993. "Casablanca Journal; World's Tallest Minaret, but Short on Popularity." *The New York Times*, October 5, 1993. https://www.nytimes.com/1993/10/05/world/casablanca-journal-world-s-tallest-minaret-but-short-on-popularity.html.

El Haitami, Meriem. 2012. "Restructuring Female Religious Authority: State-Sponsored Women Religious Guides (Murshidat) and Scholars ('Alimat) in Contemporary Morocco." *Mediterranean Studies* 20 (2): 227–240.

Hamdaoui, Neijma. 2003. "Hassan II Lance La Marche Verte." *Jeune Afrique*, October 31, 2003. https://web.archive.org/web/20060103155727/https://www.jeuneafrique.com/jeune_afrique/article_jeune_afrique.asp?art_cle=LIN02113hassaetreve0.

Hmimnat, Salim. 2018. "Morocco's Religious 'Soft Power' in Africa As a Strategy Supporting Morocco's Expansion in Africa." *Moroccan Institute for Policy Analysis*. https://mipa.institute/wp-content/uploads/2018/05/Hmimnat-Morocco%E2%80%99s-Religious-%E2%80%9CSoft-Power%E2%80%9D-in-Africa.pdf.

Howe, Marvine. 2005. *Morocco: The Islamist Awakening and Other Challenges*. 1st edition. New York: Oxford University Press.

Iraqi, Ahmed. 2019. "L'articulation de la dimension sécuritaire et religieuse dans la politique étrangère du Maroc en Afrique subsaharienne: Branding religieux à double face." *International Journal of Innovation and Applied Studies*, 25 (3): 890–899.

Kébé, Abdoul Aziz. "La Coopération Religieuse et Spirituelle Pour Un Monde de Paix: L'exemple Du Maroc." *Le Soleil*, July 28, 2015. https://www.academia.edu/37631776/Morocco_model_of_moderate_Islam_and_intercultural_dialogue_docx.

"Le Maroc envoie 700 imams de par le monde pour encadrer le ramadan de sa diaspora." 2019. *Telquel.ma*, May 6, 2019. https://telquel.ma/2019/05/06/france-canada-gabon-le-maroc-envcie-pres-de-700-psalmodieurs-et-predicateurs-encadrer-le-ramadan-de-sa-diaspora_1637471?fbrefresh=3.

"Maghribīyāt Yalqīn Durūsān Dīniyya Fī Ḥaḍrat Jalālat Al-Malik." 2010. *Al-Itiḥād Al-Ishtirākī*, April 9, 2010. http://www.maghress.com/alittihad/114213.

Markham, James M. 1980. "King Hassan's Quagmire." *The New York Times*, April 27, 1980. https://www.nytimes.com/1980/04/27/archives/king-hassans-quagmire.html?smid=url-share.

Moubayed, Sami M. 2006. *Steel & Silk: Men and Women Who Shaped Syria 1900–2000*. Cune Press.

Neumann, Franz L. 1950. "Approaches to the Study of Political Power." *Political Science Quarterly* 65 (2): 161–180.

Nye, Joseph S. 1990. *Bound to Lead: The Changing Nature of American Power*. New York: Basic Books.

Nye, Joseph S. 2004. *Soft Power: The Means To Success In World Politics*. New York: Public Affairs.

Park, Thomas Kerlin, and Aomar Boum. 2006. *Historical Dictionary of Morocco*. Lanham, MD: Scarecrow Press.

El Hadj, Samba Diallo. 2010. *La Tijaniyya sénégalaise. Les métamorphoses des modèles de Succession*. Paris: Publisud.

Kingdom of Morocco Ministry of Waqfs and Islamic Affairs. 2005. *The Hassanian Lectures: Lectures on Topics Related to the Exegesis of the Holy Qur'an and Noble Tradition Delivered before His Majesty King Mohammed VI May Allah Grant Him Support and Glory over the Holy Month of Ramadan 1426 A.H*. Rabat: Edition impression Bouregreg.

Roberson. J. 2014. "The Changing Face of Morocco under King Hassan II." *Mediterranean Studies* 22 (1): 57–87.

Seck, Charles Babacar. 1968. *La Grande Mosquée de Dakar: Suivie d'une Étude Sur l'islam Au Senegal*. Impricap.

Slimane, Rachid. 2011. "Al-Durūs al-Ḥasaniyya . . . Ẓurūf al-Nash'a Wa-'Ālamiyyat al-Ta'Thīr Wa Āfāq al-Mustaqbal." *Al-Tajdīd*, November 2, 2011 http://www.maghress.com/attajdid/20684.
"Stop Torture Country Profile: Morocco." 2014. *Amnesty International*, May 13, 2014. https://www.amnesty.org/download/Documents/8000/mde290042014en.pdf.
Wainscott, Ann Marie. 2018. "Religious Regulation as Foreign Policy: Morocco's Islamic Diplomacy in West Africa." *Politics and Religion* 11 (1): 1–26.
Wainscott, Ann Marie. 2017. *Bureaucratizing Islam: Morocco and the War on Terror*. Cambridge: Cambridge University Press.
Waterbury, John. 1970. *The Commander of the Faithful: The Moroccan Political Elite—A Study of Segmented Politics*. New York: Columbia University Press.
"Why Morocco Is Cosying Up to Sub-Saharan Africa." 2018. *The Economist*, July 19, 2018. https://www.economist.com/middle-east-and-africa/2018/07/19/why-morocco-is-cosying-up-to-sub-saharan-africa.
Yamani, Abdelhakim. 1999. "Moroccans Mourn King Hassan's Death." *Associated Press*, July 24, 1999. https://apnews.com/article/4893d9f0de8f5493ea99dea4c7c7bf95.
Zeghal, Malika. 2003. "Religion et politique au Maroc aujourd'hui." *Institut français des relations internationales*. https://www.ifri.org/sites/default/files/atoms/files/dt_3_zeghal.pdf.

9
Religious Diplomacy in the Arab Gulf and the Politics of Moderate Islam

Annelle Sheline

Introduction

The 9/11 attacks significantly increased the securitization of Islam. Americans already feared so-called radical Islam, but the attacks launched a massive investment in resources to combat and prevent acts of violence committed by Muslim individuals. The governments of US security partners in the Middle East embraced this image of Islam as a security threat to promote themselves as offering a solution—"moderate Islam"—in order to benefit from the associated resources. By blaming violence on a misinterpretation of Islam and framing the remedy for violence as something only they could provide, these governments bolstered their own utility in the eyes of their American security guarantor. They also simultaneously demonized Islamists—their primary source of political opposition—as responsible for spreading these incorrect versions of Islam. The production of moderate Islam primarily represented a signal to the Americans and a means of enhancing a given Arab government's soft power as an alleged purveyor of the solution to terrorism.

Because moderate Islam primarily served as a signaling mechanism, its effectiveness at actually addressing violence was largely beside the point. For the United States and its client Arab governments, the myth of moderate Islam allowed them to maintain their partnerships without acknowledging how both of their actions contributed to the likelihood of terrorist violence. As a result, neither Arab partners nor the Americans showed particular interest in evaluating the impact of the multitude of programs, declarations, and conferences that claimed to encourage moderation, religious tolerance, sectarian harmony, et cetera. International recognition marked an initiative as successful, rather than a decline in the frequency of attacks or the number of individuals who renounced jihadi ideology. And recognition was granted merely for launching an initiative, rather than for its effects. The soft power inherent in a reputation for moderate Islam constituted the driving incentive.

This chapter details claims related to the use of Islam as a means of preventing violence in the early twenty-first century, highlighting the impact of 9/11 on the relationship between the governments of the United States and certain Central Asian and Arab states, including Pakistan, Jordan, the United Arab Emirates, and Saudi Arabia. Although the use of a discourse of moderate Islam was not limited to these contexts, over time, it became more closely aligned with US security partners. The chapter also examines how America's use of religious discourse shifted during the presidencies of George W. Bush, Barack Obama, and Donald Trump.

Why Moderate Islam?

The 9/11 attacks occurred when the United States, the globe's preeminent military and economic power at the time, lacked a clear adversary. Following the establishment of the post–World War II liberal internationalist order and the eventual defeat of the Soviet Union, some American policymakers anticipated a comfortable slide into the "end of history" characterized by the inevitable spread of democratic capitalism. The shock of 9/11 therefore came partly from the realization that America's exertion of military dominance around the world had produced resistance: one of Osama bin Laden's primary grievances was the stationing of US troops in Saudi Arabia during the first Gulf War.

When Americans asked, "Why do they hate us?" the response was, "They hate our freedoms." The real reasons, including frustration with American support for anti-democratic and abusive Arab governments as well as for the state of Israel, proved awkward for US leadership to acknowledge. Grappling with the fact that Al-Qaeda might have legitimate grievances would have required a fundamental shift in America's role in the world as well as the recognition that America's self-image did not necessarily correspond to how it was perceived internationally. Rather than question how the presence of the US military abroad and its willingness to prop up despotic regimes were driving terrorism, the United States doubled down on these policies by expanding its military footprint in the region and bolstering relationships with Arab security partners.

Bewildered by the 9/11 attacks, the American public supported the launch of the Global War on Terror (GWOT), which quickly came to resemble a global war on Islam. Americans did not question the resources pouring into the military's counterterror efforts. Few acknowledged that the 9/11 attack constituted a black swan event unlikely to reoccur, and therefore that it did not merit the massive build-up of military capacity as well as the costly military interventions it spurred. The rise in the number of Islamist terrorist organizations after 9/11 served to justify further expansion of counterterror efforts, rather than being understood as at least partially caused by these efforts.

To be clear, the United States had maintained a substantial military presence in the Middle East after the first Gulf War. Prior to that, the United States had established security partnerships with many of the Arab states, including the members of the Gulf Cooperation Council (GCC), Egypt, and Jordan. The close relationships with the GCC members largely reflected the desire to maintain US control of oil resources as spelled out in the Carter Doctrine of 1980, while those with the latter resulted from these two countries' eventual willingness to enter peace treaties with Israel in 1979 and 1994, respectively: oil and Israel being the United States' primary concerns in the region.

Following 9/11, terrorism was added to the list of urgent regional priorities, and the United States reoriented much of its military posture and resources around the conflicts fought as part of the GWOT, primarily the wars in Afghanistan and Iraq as well as counterinsurgency (COIN) operations around the Middle East, Central Asia, and Africa. A military built for COIN prioritizes different capacities than one prepared to fight a great power war: at the time of writing, Congress has addressed these simultaneous concerns by adopting a military budget of $768 billion for FY2022, despite the multitude of security threats that military funding can do little to address, from pandemic disease to climate change.

America's partners in the Middle East were eager to demonstrate their commitment to the global military hegemon's security agenda of countering terrorism. Authoritarianism throughout the region contributed to the likelihood of terrorist violence. Therefore, participating in the GWOT not only expressed allegiance to the United States, but also distracted from the ways in which corrupt and abusive governments spawned sometimes violent resistance.

Early in the GWOT, the Bush administration identified the lack of democracy, rule of law, and good governance as factors driving dissatisfaction and in some cases violence. The need to "impose" democracy was one of the various justifications given for the US invasion of Iraq in 2003: Bush saw Iraq as the first domino in a chain reaction that would see democratic transitions throughout the region, perhaps similar to what his father had witnessed during his presidency, as nominal democracies emerged from the former Soviet Union (The Christian Science Monitor 2003). Yet there was a crucial difference: as early as March 2003, commentators acknowledged that democracy in the Middle East could empower actors that might be less amenable to US interests, namely Islamists (Miller 2003).

During the Cold War, Arab governments had used fears of Communism to justify the dismantling of Leftist opposition groups, and in some cases encouraged Islamism as a means of reducing the influence of Gamal Abdel Nasser's Arab Socialism and other Marxist-Leninist visions.[1] Yet the Arab governments soon learned that the political quietism of Islamist groups was fleeting. The Muslim Brotherhood, founded in Egypt in 1928, had inspired the establishment of similar groups throughout much of the region. The Brotherhood spread further due to the need for educated professionals to staff the newly modernizing societies of the Arab Gulf countries during the oil boom years of the 1970s and 1980s: many of the Gulf's first bureaucrats, teachers, and engineers were Brothers in exile from Egypt, Syria, and Palestine. In general, the Brotherhood believed that economic and political justice could be achieved through greater piety and institutional adherence to Islamic edicts, yet some individuals viewed such transformations as only possible through violence.

By 2001, Islamist groups of various ideologies dominated the ranks of political opposition groups throughout much of the region: if the ruling regimes fell, Islamists would likely replace them. The thought of an Islamist takeover of the Middle East seemed undesirable for US interests from a rational perspective and unacceptable from an emotional one, as Iran's Islamic Revolution in 1979 and subsequent hostage crisis remained an indelible memory for many Americans. After 9/11, the primary fear was that Islamist terrorists would acquire weapons of mass destruction and use them against the United States. Twenty years into the War on Terror, policymakers began to acknowledge that terrorism did not pose an existential threat to the United States; yet in the aftermath of September 11th, the possibility of Al Qaeda acquiring and launching nuclear weapons seemed plausible.

Arab rulers benefitted from these fears and were eager to reinforce the narrative that Islam was responsible for terrorism, rather than the factors for which they themselves bore responsibility, like the lack of economic and political opportunity, corruption, and the brutal repression of dissidents. Scapegoating Islam for terrorism rather than acknowledging the role of state repression and US military hegemony in provoking violent responses allowed both to continue their existing practices.

The idea of "moderate" Islam, therefore, represents a foil for the version of Islam scapegoated by Arab rulers. To be clear, however, the notion predated 9/11. A rise in the salience of Islamic religious identity in the late twentieth century both drove and resulted from the increasing prominence of Islamist organizations in Muslim majority societies and throughout Muslim diaspora communities.

Some members of the Muslim diaspora felt pressure to identify as "moderates" in part to distinguish themselves from high-profile events seen as incompatible with the mores of their adopted societies, especially in Europe and North America. For example, a British Muslim cited the Salman Rushdie affair as when he began to self-describe as a "moderate" (Manzoor 2015). Both the Quran and the hadith celebrate the notion of *wasatiyya*, or centrism; the Prophet Mohammed explicitly told his followers that "Moderation is the best course," and warned them not to engage in the sorts of extreme behaviors that characterized devout Christianity, such as extreme fasting or celibacy.[2] Many Muslims found the idea that Islam would drive someone to violence as primarily revealing ignorance of Islam as well as Islamophobic biases. Yet over time, especially as acts of violence committed by Muslims continued to receive disproportionate press coverage, many people bristled at the phrase for the implication that their faith required modification.

Some strains of scholarly discourse problematized the ways in which ideas related to toleration reinforced Orientalism, asking, "How might liberal tolerance discourse function not only to anoint Western superiority but also to legitimate Western cultural and political imperialism?" (Brown 2008). The construal of the threat posed by "political Islam," a term coined in the 1970s, demonstrated that the Euro-American insistence on secularism constituted "a form of political authority" (Hurd 2008). The portrayal of Islam as incompatible with Western liberal values of tolerance, equality, and democracy reinforced Western supremacy, even when the West failed to live up to these values itself. Yet despite criticism, a reputation for moderation continued to constitute a valuable form of soft power for governments, and so became an increasingly common strategy.

Pakistan and "Enlightened Moderation"

After 9/11 precipitated the invasion of Afghanistan, Pakistan became one of the first countries to deploy the notion of moderation as a means of courting US favor. Pervez Musharraf, president of Pakistan from 1999 to 2008, introduced the concept of "enlightened moderation" in December 2002 at a meeting of the Organization of Islamic Cooperation (OIC) in Malaysia. Eighteen months later, he published "A Plea for Enlightened Moderation" as an op-ed in the *Washington Post*. In this, he defined "enlightened moderation" as having two components: the first involved Muslims "shunning militancy" while pursuing "socioeconomic uplift." The second called on the United States to "to seek to resolve all political disputes with justice and to aid in the socioeconomic betterment of the deprived Muslim world" (Musharraf 2004). In this, Musharraf reinforced America's self-image as the global arbiter of justice, as well as the state bearing responsibility for the rest of the world. Musharraf makes no mention of Pakistan, his own responsibility as president, or his country's role in providing a haven for Taliban fighters escaping US forces in neighboring Afghanistan. Instead, he speaks in broad generalities and on behalf of all Muslims, describes their allegedly pitiful plight, and begs for US assistance.

Unsurprisingly, his piece provoked pushback. Khurshid Ahmad, a prominent Pakistani economist who had overseen the Islamization of the economy under Zia ul Haq's administration (1977–1988), characterizes Musharraf's goal as trying to "superimpose the West's liberal socioeconomic order over the world at large." Ahmad cites Joseph Nye's description of soft power and interprets Nye's wistfulness that "opposition to American culture limits its soft power [in the Middle East]" as representing nefarious American imperialism.

From Ahmad's perspective, Musharraf's "Enlightened Moderation" seeks to spread Western liberal values into societies previously immune to them. Ahmad quotes the following passage from Fareed Zakaria, editor of *Newsweek* at the time, who said: "We can fund moderate Muslim groups and scholars and broadcast fresh thinking across the Arab world, all aimed at breaking the power of the fundamentalists" (Zakaria 2002). Ahmad (2004) describes Zakaria's suggestion as intended to "systematically eliminate those whom they view as fundamentalists and 'Jehadis' capable to resist and replace them by those whom they think are 'endowed' with the 'liberal vision of Islam.'" He was not wholly incorrect in this interpretation, as Zakaria's suggestion closely aligned with subsequent efforts to prevent violent extremism by highlighting the work of Muslim religious scholars who were seen as moderates.

Despite Ahmad's scorn, Musharraf's sycophancy to American self-aggrandizement exhibited savviness: just a year before, Saddam Hussein had demonstrated what could happen to a Muslim ruler who defied the American military juggernaut. Musharraf clearly wished to signal his compliance with American objectives. Although some continued to push the image of Pakistan as moderate, relatively soon it became clear that the attention of the Bush administration had shifted away from Central Asia to the Middle East (Yousaf and Li 2014).

Jordan and "True Islam"

Acts of terrorism throughout the Middle East in the early 2000s contributed to the urgency these governments felt in exerting greater control over religious actors and spaces. Meanwhile, the language of "moderation" remained primarily directed at an external, foreign, and largely American or European audience, while messaging directed at internal, domestic, Arabic speaking audiences focused less on "moderation" and more on "obedience to the ruler." Jordan offers an example of this trend.

Since its establishment by the United Kingdom in 1921, the Hashemite Kingdom of Jordan had to remain attuned to the goals of its patron states: by the early twenty-first century the United States had taken that role, and so Jordan sought to present itself as a key counterterrorism partner. Jordan demonstrated its commitment to the US security agenda by sending peacekeeping troops to Afghanistan under the auspices of the United Nations. Despite condemning US plans to invade Iraq in 2003, Jordan later provided tacit and covert support.[3]

Jordan also sought to bolster its soft power as a bastion of moderate Islam, basing its status on the religious authority of the Hashemite dynasty, the historical sharifs of Mecca prior to their ouster by the House of Saud after World War I. In 2004, King Abdullah II of Jordan convened Muslim scholars from around the world to produce the "Amman Message," which highlighted the tenets of Islam shared by all Muslims in an effort to reduce declarations of apostasy (*takfir*), a tactic used by extremists to justify violence against other Muslims.[4] Jordan also issued "A Common Word" in 2007, which emphasized similarities between Islam and Christianity, and successfully established "Interfaith Harmony Week" through UN Resolution A/RES/65/5 in 2010, observed each year by the United Nations. As wittily described by Stacey Gutkowski (2015), Jordan portrayed itself as "the very model of a moderate Muslim state."[5]

Yet in the messaging directed at the Jordanian population, the emphasis centered less on religious tolerance, and more on the Hashemites' legitimacy as descendants of the Prophet Mohamed, and their role in safeguarding "true" Islam. Analysis of a textbook issued by the Ministry of Education to help students prepare for the *tawjīhī* (the exam taken by Jordanian public-school students at the end of high school) demonstrates the content of religious education. The text described King Abdullah's efforts to defend the image of Islam and to overcome its distortion by its "enemies" as well as its "delinquent sons."[6] The textbook repeatedly referenced the Hashemites' "inherited legitimacy" and the responsibility passed down from the "Prophet of peace" to explain why Jordan had undertaken the responsibility to promote "true" Islam. Yet this "true" Islam was not characterized as "tolerant" or "moderate": the text seems to assume that the student already knows what is implied by the notion of "true Islam" and does not define it.

Although Jordan possessed a head start in the field of establishing its religious soft power as a result of its various initiatives throughout the 2000s, the government shifted from international messaging around tolerance to a more security-centric approach preferred by the General Intelligence Department (Abu Rumman and Abu Hanieh 2013). Given that Jordanians eventually constituted one of the highest numbers of foreign fighters for the Islamic State, the Jordanian government may have decided that they needed to actually address the issue of violent extremism, rather than merely cultivating an international reputation for religious tolerance.

The Obama Administration and "Muslim Outreach"

Even by the end of the Bush administration, there was increasing recognition of the need for "moderate" Muslim partners (Rabasa et al. 2007). Under the Obama administration, US demand for Muslim interlocutors increased, and the competition to speak for moderate Islam rose. Obama came to power determined to improve America's image in the Middle East, as manifested in his famous Cairo speech in June 2009; that year witnessed the emergence of "a veritable cottage industry of Muslim engagement activities in U.S. foreign policy" (Mandaville 2020). Obama's team emphasized the imperative to develop more robust relations with religious communities beyond an existing White House office established by the Bush administration and focused on outreach to Muslims. New positions were established, such as the State Department's special representative for Muslim communities, Farah Prandith, as well as the special envoy to the Organization for Islamic Cooperation, Rashad Hussein.

Yet outreach to religious communities sometimes had unintended effects. For example, it often reinforced the authority of formal religious institutions and actors. This reified the power of individuals who typically represented codified religious doctrine—who tended to be older and overwhelmingly male—rather than those pushing the boundaries of religious belief, who were more likely to include people who were younger, more marginalized, and sometimes female.

The pitfalls of this approach became apparent in Obama's second term, after the turbulence of the Arab uprisings in 2011 eventually resulted in the rise of the Islamic State in Iraq and Syria (ISIS) in 2014. The group claimed to represent the reincarnation of the Prophet Mohamed's caliphate in its adherence to the most "authentic" interpretation of Islamic law, a notion of authenticity grounded in decades of Saudi propaganda that intolerance corresponded to the most orthodox form of Islam. The group's declarations to have established a true Islamic state appealed to many, especially the young and marginalized, and thousands traveled to join them. The members of the formal religious establishment had few tools to compete with a social media savvy group of young and savage zealots.

Nevertheless, religious figures or their advocates reached out to the Obama administration with claims that they could "solve ISIS" (Mandaville and Nozell 2017). Governments in the Middle East, Europe, and North America scrambled to find a means of repudiating the group and earned plaudits for establishing centers dedicated to countering violent extremism or holding conferences of Muslim religious scholars to repudiate their ideology. The field of individuals and governments that claimed to embody moderate Islam was growing more crowded, yet ISIS continued to attract followers: again, the incentive structure tied to moderate Islam related to enhancing soft power rather than effectively addressing the factors driving extremist violence. In many instances, the Muslim religious figures calling for moderation were not so well known as to have much impact, or they were associated with regimes that lacked legitimacy, so their espousal of moderation further undermined their message (Sheline 2019).

In general, the Obama administration's efforts at Muslim outreach appeared somewhat clumsy. Furthermore, few efforts were made to address Islamophobia in the American public consciousness, such that when Trump took office in 2017, his imposition of a policy known as the "Muslim ban" was contested but remained in place throughout his presidency.

The Trump Administration and "Religious Freedom"

The use of religious freedom as a justification for denying the rights of women and members of the LGBTQ community had become particularly apparent under Obama, primarily as a means of resisting policies advanced by the administration, including the provision of contraception under the Affordable Care Act and the right to marriage equality. In 2016, Obama's chair of the US Commission on Civil Rights, Martin Castro (2016), wrote that "the phrases 'religious liberty' and 'religious freedom' will stand for nothing except hypocrisy so long as they remain code words for discrimination, intolerance, racism, sexism, homophobia, Islamophobia, Christian supremacy or any form of intolerance." Trump's win exacerbated anxieties about the use of "religious freedom" as a means of promoting the interests of Christians at the expense of other groups both in the United States and abroad.

In March 2017, early in the Trump administration, the Religious Freedom Institute held a public event in Washington DC titled "U.S. Foreign Policy and International Religious Freedom: Recommendations for the Trump Administration and the U.S. Congress." During the question-and-answer period, several members of Muslim civil society groups expressed concerns about the Trump administration's agenda. A representative of the Muslim Affairs Council made the following statement:

> Recent policies, like the Muslim Ban, single out a particular faith in this country, and give certain quarters of the American population the idea that Muslims pose a threat, which also feeds into the ISIS narrative. Speaking about so-called Islamic extremism as being a threat to American security validates what they [ISIS] are saying.

The audience member pointed out that given the wave of attacks on synagogues, mosques, and churches throughout 2016 (and subsequently much of Trump's presidency), it seemed hypocritical to talk about religious liberty as a priority for the Trump administration. She also made the prescient observation that the FBI and the Department of Justice had stated that the most significant security threats in the United States came from rightwing extremists rather than Muslims.[7] Former Congressman Frank Wolf (VA-10), one of the speakers at the event, responded by trying to repudiate the audience member's statement about the FBI's findings. The other speakers joined in to push back against her point, asserting that the United States had an obligation to promote religious liberty even if it did not always perfectly enforce it at home.

At the time of the event, the Trump administration's agenda remained somewhat unclear. Yet it soon became apparent that reassuring the American Muslim community was not high on Trump's priorities. Instead, many of his administration's acts pertaining to religion appeared intended to appeal to Trump's Evangelical base, for example, appointing Evangelical Christians to high-level positions. In addition to Mike Pence as Vice President, evangelical members of Trump's cabinet included his first Attorney General Jeff Sessions, Secretary of the Interior Ryan Zinke, Secretary of Health & Human Services Tom Price, Secretary of Housing and Urban Development Ben Carson, Secretary of Transportation Elaine Chao, Secretary of Energy Rick Perry, Secretary of Education Betsy DeVos, Secretary of Agriculture Sonny Perdue, EPA Director Scott Pruitt, as well as Mike Pompeo, who in 2018 became Trump's Secretary of State.

Many of Trump's evangelical cabinet members took part in a weekly Bible study led by Evangelical pastor Ralph Drollinger. Drollinger established Capitol Ministries in 1997, an organization intended to influence political leaders toward his Evangelical beliefs. With the support of the Trump administration, Drollinger established Bible study groups in 24 countries (Schwartz 2019). He is one of the many figures who publicly expressed commitment to advocating for an evangelical Christian agenda that rejected the rights of women and queer people. To the extent that such individuals discussed Islam, their comments were largely Islamophobic; their emphasis primarily centered on bolstering "traditional" or "family" values.

Other Trump appointments of evangelicals included Sam Brownback, the former governor of Kansas, to serve as the Ambassador-at-Large for International Religious Freedom in the State Department's Bureau of

Democracy, Human Rights, and Labor. Yet by many accounts, Brownback's commitment to his Evangelical agenda did not impede his efforts to call for an end to international religious persecution. At the end of the Trump administration, during the weekly virtual meeting of the International Religious Freedom Roundtable convened by the US Commission on International Religious Freedom (USCIRF), global activists expressed gratitude for Brownback's efforts, including advocating for Muslims persecuted in China, India, and Myanmar.[8] Note that although USCIRF officially supports the rights of atheists, agnostics, and individuals who do not identify with a faith tradition, the vast majority of activists coordinated under its umbrella advocate on behalf of people targeted due to faith, rather than its absence.

Yet while the office of the Ambassador-at-Large for Religious Freedom appeared to have maintained its institutional commitment to advocate for all religions, other members of the Trump administration more blatantly prioritized a pro-Christian agenda. Mike Pompeo, who took control of the State Department in April 2018, used his position to redefine the US commitment to human rights. In 2019, he established the Commission on Unalienable Rights, a separate office from the existing Bureau of Democracy, Human Rights, and Labor. The commission was chaired by Mary Ann Glendon, a conservative legal scholar known for her opposition to reproductive freedom.

Meanwhile, at Pompeo's State Department, Morse Tan, Ambassador-at-Large for Global Criminal Justice (GCJ), doubled his office's small staff by hiring nine new individuals, many of whom were graduates of Wheaton College, his alma mater, an evangelical Christian university (Lynch and Gramer 2021). The GCJ usually focused on US determinations of war crimes and genocide, but the individuals hired did not possess expertise in these areas. The move belied Pompeo and the Trump administration's stated commitments to address injustices such as the persecution of the Rohingya Muslims. In general, critics feared that Pompeo sought to use his powerful position at the State Department to align the United States with authoritarian Christian groups in Russia,[9] Poland, Hungary, and elsewhere, as part of a global conservative movement dedicated to Christian supremacy, even at the expense of democracy (Stewart 2020).

Pompeo frequently made headlines for unabashedly publicizing his faith as motivating his actions as well as US policy. In a speech to the American Israel Public Affairs committee in March 2019, Pompeo stated, "As secretary of state and as a Christian, I'm proud to lead American diplomacy to support Israel's right to defend itself" (Wong 2019). Many of the Trump administration's decisions pertaining to Israel aimed to please evangelical Christian Zionists, who believed that the second coming of Jesus would occur once the Jews have returned to Israel.[10]

The Abraham Accords and Moderate Islam

Despite the Trump administration's general prioritization of evangelical priorities, some of America's security partners in the Gulf Cooperation Council (GCC) found that the emphasis on international religious freedom could align with efforts to bolster their religious soft power, specifically tied to the idea of moderate Islam.

Prior to the Trump era, Qatar represented one of the early members of the GCC to cultivate a reputation for liberalization. For example, creating the Al Jazeera news network in 1996 earned Qatar accolades for press freedom, as the platform broke barriers by criticizing the rulers of other Arab countries rather than repeating state-sponsored pablum like most official media channels. Qatar had long sponsored influential Egyptian cleric Yusuf al-Qaradawi, his International Union for Muslim Scholars, and his emphasis on the Quranic notion of centrism/*wasatiyya* (Sheline 2020). Qatar was one of the first Gulf countries to invite American universities to open satellite campuses in its territory. Georgetown, Northwestern, and Carnegie Mellon, as well as influential think tanks like the Brookings Institution, had established a presence in Doha by the early 2000s. Given its relative press freedoms and sponsorship of notions of centrism as well as Western-style education, Qatar had a reputation for being one of the more open and liberal Gulf states. By the early 2000s, Qatari society had gone from being one of the more conservative among the Gulf states to one of the more open.

Dubai, one of the United Arab Emirates, had a different reputation for liberalism, one built on tolerance of un-Islamic practices like drinking alcohol and gambling, in contrast to Qatar's more scholarly mien. After the Arab Spring, the United Arab Emierates began to compete with Qatar for the mantle of moderate Islam in the Gulf, as Abu Dhabi, the capital of the United Arab Emirates, pursued an approach that was closer to Qatar's: it established the Muslim Council of Elders in 2014, strengthened ties with Al-Azhar, created a Ministry of Tolerance in 2016, and began exporting its preferred interpretation of Islam abroad through imam training programs (Worth 2020). According to a scholar of Islamic affairs at the Royal United Services Institute in London, the Muslim Council of Elders, headed by prominent Mauritanian religious scholars Sheikh Bin Bayyah, did exactly the same thing as Sheikh Qaradawi, Qatar's prominent Egyptian scholar of Islamic centrism.[11] Abu Dhabi needed a means of distinguishing itself from Qatar.

Under the leadership of Crown Prince Mohamed bin Zayed, the United Arab Emirates had grown increasingly frustrated with Qatar's support for Islamist groups during and after the 2011 uprising, while Saudi Arabia had long resented Qatar's willingness to engage with Iran (Freer 2018). March 2014 saw a diplomatic dust-up, with the United Arab Emirates, Saudi Arabia, and Bahrain suddenly announcing the withdrawal of their ambassadors from Qatar; after eight months of mediation by Kuwait, diplomatic relations were reestablished.

Once Trump came into office, both the Emiratis and the Saudis saw an opportunity to marginalize Qatar, despite its close security partnership with the United States as the host of CENTCOM's forward headquarters. Trump's first sojourn abroad as president was to Saudi Arabia and Israel. On the trip, Emirati and Saudi officials convinced American officials that Qatar presented a greater regional threat than Iran. When they initiated the blockade of Qatar in June 2017, they had a green light from Trump (Ulrichsen 2020). With Qatar effectively marginalized and its reputation for religious moderation tarnished by allegations of support for Islamists and Iran, the United Arab Emirates had more leeway to bolster its own credentials.

During the Trump presidency, the United Arab Emirates expanded its religious outreach from promoting moderate Islam to interreligious dialogue. The United Arab Emirates hosted Pope Francis early in 2019; allowed a synagogue to open; and invited the Church of Latter-Day Saints to establish itself in the emirate. The most significant indication of the United Arab Emirates' embrace of the US agenda was the decision to normalize relations with Israel in August 2020. The signing of the Abraham Accords firmly established the United Arab Emirates as the Gulf's paragon of religious tolerance and a crucial security partner to the United States. With this move, the United Arab Emirates both cemented its close relationship with the Trump administration and hedged its bets for the possibility that a new US administration would take control in 2021, which ultimately occurred.

Saudi Arabia also partnered closely with the Trump administration but did not go as far as the United Arab Emirates in acceding to US preferences. Saudi Arabia had long derived its Islamic authority from the custodianship of Mecca and Medina, and its promotion of and adherence to a deeply conservative interpretation of Islam. King Abdullah (r. 2005–2015) initiated some of the shifts that became more noticeable under his successor Salman, including relaxing certain laws on gender segregation and participating in international efforts to address the issue of violent extremism.

Under King Salman and Crown Prince Mohammed bin Salman (MBS), the official Saudi stance shifted: as MBS stated in fall 2017, "I will return Saudi Arabia to moderate Islam" (Chulov 2017). Muhammad al-Issa, Secretary General of the Muslim World League, became one of the public faces of this new Saudi Islam, generating headlines with visits to Auschwitz and acknowledgements of the Holocaust, stances that were previously anathema to the Saudi religious establishment.

Saudi Arabia attempted to shift its existing religious authority into a shape better suited for non-Muslim consumption, but its efforts have been largely superficial. Whether MBS, upon his ascension to the throne, would be willing to risk alienating his own population and risking condemnation from Muslims around the world by normalizing with Israel in order to affirm his utility in the eyes of a skeptical Biden administration, remains unknown.

Conclusion

Early reports on the Biden administration's relationship to religion highlighted Biden's Catholic faith, but during his first hundred days, his religious agenda remained subjugated to the many other concerns he faced. Veterans of the Obama administration have written to advise Biden to stay away from the "global Muslim engagement business," and given the prevalence of Obama administration personnel, perhaps Biden will learn from Obama's mistakes (Mandaville 2020).

The legacy of the United States seeking moderate Muslim partners contributed to a shift in geopolitics in the Gulf and the wider region. Unfortunately, the demonization of Islam as the primary causal factor in violent extremism remained a strategy deployed by US security partners in the

Middle East, who continued to avoid scrutiny of how systemic repression and corruption contributed to despair and created conditions for violent extremist messaging and actors to gain greater salience than they otherwise might. Helen Lackner (2017), an expert on Yemen, expressed her frustration with the willingness to attribute blame to Islam. The following passage pertains to Yemen, but her insights apply more broadly:

> Presenting jihadism as a threatening monster only serves the interests of these movements, providing them with the propaganda and media exposure they relish. It also serves the interests of those who need jihadism as a bogeyman, to spread fear among ordinary people everywhere so as to keep the "security" business growing and expanding... They use it to maintain an ideological grip on populations at home who turn to Populist politicians, while the "security" industry and arms dealers profit.

Twenty years after 9/11, some members of the American foreign policy establishment began to acknowledge the mistakes that were made in the aftermath of the attacks. Unfortunately, much of the legacy of US efforts to encourage so-called moderate Islam negatively impacted political opposition in the Middle East, Islamist or otherwise, which undermined the likelihood of improved governance or democratization. As long as the United States remains the security partner for authoritarian regimes in the region, these and other pernicious effects of US policy are unlikely to change.

References

Abu Rumman, Mohammed, and Hassan Abu Hanieh. 2013. *The Islamic Solution in Jordan*. Amman: Friedrich-Ebert-Stiftung.
Ahmad, Khurshid. 2004. "'Enlightened Moderation' Or The New US 'Religious Order.'" https://jamaat.org/Isharat/ish0704.html.
Brown, Wendy. 2008. *Regulating Aversion: Tolerance in the Age of Identity and Empire*. Princeton: Princeton University Press.
"Bush's Domino Theory." 2003. *The Christian Science Monitor*, January 28, 2003. https://www.csmonitor.com/2003/0128/p08s02-comv.html.
Castro, Martin. 2016. "Peaceful Coexistence: Reconciling Nondiscrimination Principles with Civil Liberties." *United States Commission on Civil Rights Briefing Report*, September 7, 2016. https://www.usccr.gov/files/pubs/docs/Peaceful-Coexistence-09-07-16.PDF.
Chulov, Martin. 2017. "'I Will Return Saudi Arabia to Moderate Islam' says Crown Prince." *The Guardian*, October 24, 2017. https://www.theguardian.com/world/2017/oct/24/i-will-return-saudi-arabia-moderate-islam-crown-prince

Freer, Courtney. 2018. *Rentier Islamism: The Influence of the Muslim Brotherhood in the Gulf Monarchies*. New York: Oxford University Press.

Gutkowski, Stacey. 2015. "We Are the Very Model of a Moderate Muslim State: The Amman Message and Jordan's Foreign Policy." *International Relations* 30 (2): 206–226.

Hurd, Elizabeth Shakman. 2008. *The Politics of Secularism in International Relations*. Princeton: Princeton University Press.

Lackner, Helen. 2017. *Yemen in Crisis: Autocracy, Neoliberalism, and the Disintegration of a State*. London: Saqi Books.

Lynch, Colum, and Robbie Gramer. 2021. "State Department Office Sees Last-Minute Surge of New Evangelical Appointees." *Foreign Policy*, January 7, 2021. https://foreignpolicy.com/2021/01/07/state-department-office-sees-last-minute-surge-new-evangelical-appointees-global-criminal-justice-pompeo-trump/.

Mandaville, Peter. 2020. "Why the Biden Administration Should Stay Out of the Global 'Muslim Engagement' Business." *The Brookings Institution*, December 14, 2020. https://www.brookings.edu/blog/order-from-chaos/2020/12/14/why-the-biden-administration-should-stay-out-of-the-global-muslim-engagement-business/.

Mandaville, Peter, and Melissa Nozell. 2017. "Engaging Religion and Religious Actors in Countering Violent Extremism." *The United States Institute of Peace*, August 30, 2017. https://www.usip.org/publications/2017/08/engaging-religion-and-religious-actors-countering-violent-extremism.

Manzoor, Sarfaz. 2015. "Can We Drop the Term 'Moderate Muslim'? It's Meaningless." *The Guardian*, March 16, 2015. https://www.theguardian.com/commentisfree/2015/mar/16/moderate-muslim-devout-liberal-religion.

Miller, Greg. 2003. "Democracy Domino Theory 'Not Credible.'" *Los Angeles Times*, March 14, 2003. https://www.latimes.com/archives/la-xpm-2003-mar-14-fg-domino14-story.html.

Musharraf, Pervez. 2004. "A Plea for Enlightened Moderation." *The Washington Post*, June 1, 2004. https://www.washingtonpost.com/archive/opinions/2004/06/01/a-plea-for-enlightened-moderation/b01ff08e-f0c5-4ad5-8e96-b97a32ec084e/.

Rabasa, Angel, Cheryl Benard, Lowell H. Schwartz, and Peter Sickle. 2007. *Building Moderate Muslim Networks*. Santa Monica, CA: RAND Corporation.

Schwartz, Matthias. 2019. "How the Trump Cabinet's Bible Teacher Became a Shadow Diplomat." *The New York Times Magazine*. October 29, 2019. https://www.nytimes.com/2019/10/29/magazine/ralph-drollinger-white-house-evangelical.html.

Sheline, Annelle. 2019. "Declaration Proliferation: The International Politics of Religious Tolerance." *Berkley Center for Religion, Peace & World Affairs*, July 11, 2019. https://berkleycenter.georgetown.edu/posts/declaration-proliferation-the-international-politics-of-religious-tolerance.

Sheline, Annelle. 2020. "Shifting Reputations for 'Moderation': Evidence from Qatar, Jordan, and Morocco." *Middle East Law and Governance* 12 (1): 109–129.

Stewart, Katherine. 2020. *The Power Worshippers: Inside the Dangerous Rise of Religious Nationalism*. New York: Bloomsbury Publishing.

Ulrichsen, Kristian Coates. 2020. *Qatar and the Gulf Crisis*, London: Hurst Publishers.

Wong, Mike. 2019. "The Rapture and the Real World: Mike Pompeo Blends Beliefs and Policy." *The New York Times*, March 30, 2019. https://www.nytimes.com/2019/03/30/us/politics/pompeo-christian-policy.html.

Worth, Robert. 2020. "Mohammed bin Zayed's Dark Vision of the Middle East's Future." *The New York Times Magazine,* January 9, 2020. https://www.nytimes.com/2020/01/09/magazine/united-arab-emirates-mohammed-bin-zayed.html.

Yousaf, Salman, and Huaibin Li. 2014. "Branding Pakistan as a 'Sufi' Country: The Role of Religion in Developing a Nation's Brand." *Journal of Place Management and Development* 7 (1): 90–104.

Zakaria, Fareed. 2002. "Why Muslims Hate the West and What We Can Do About It." In *Re-Ordering the World*, edited by Mark Leonard. London: The Foreign Policy Center.

10
Indonesian Islam as Model for the World?

Diplomacy, Soft Power, and the Geopolitics of "Moderate Islam"

James B. Hoesterey

With the 1998 fall of Suharto, Indonesia's authoritarian ruler of three decades, Western diplomats, journalists, and political pundits anxiously observed as Indonesia emerged from three decades of dictatorship. Despite some optimism about the reform (*reformasi*) movement, many foreign observers fretted about the imminent "Balkanization" of an Indonesia without a strongman ruler. Indeed, this was the bargain Western diplomats brokered during the decades of Suharto's rule: economic development at the expense of political repression. As ethnic and sectarian violence spread in parts of the country, complicated by the re-emergence of armed Islamic militia groups like Laskar Jihad, the path ahead for democratic consolidation seemed perilous. Especially after the 9/11 attacks in the United States and the 2002 bomb blast in Bali, Indonesia, Western governments (especially America) became increasingly anxious of the rise of Muslim politics, the formation of Islamist political parties, and the apparent spread of Islamic extremism in Indonesia. Would Indonesia become yet another failed state where oligarchs and Islamists ruled the people and split the spoils? Would older ideologies such as communism resurface?

A decade later, the global brand narrative of Indonesia looked much different, at least through Western eyes and interests. In 2010, Barack Obama took his much-anticipated first presidential visit to Indonesia, the world's most populous Muslim majority nation he called home for several years of his childhood.[1] He was in Indonesia to celebrate the bilateral "comprehensive partnership" being negotiated between the two countries. During a speech at the University of Indonesia, Obama was welcomed with uproarious applause when he spoke Indonesian: "*Pulang kampung, nih!*" (I've come back

James B. Hoesterey, *Indonesian Islam as Model for the World?* In: *The Geopolitics of Religious Soft Power*. Edited by: Peter Mandaville, Oxford University Press. © Oxford University Press 2023.
DOI: 10.1093/oso/9780197605806.003.0010

home!).[2] To get a sense of just how much had changed about Indonesia's geopolitical narrative over the course of a decade, consider these excerpts where President Obama waxed nostalgic about his childhood years:

> Because Indonesia is made up of thousands of islands, and hundreds of languages, and people from scores of regions and ethnic groups, my time here helped me appreciate the common humanity of all people. And while my stepfather, like most Indonesians, was raised a Muslim, he firmly believed that all religions were worthy of respect. And in this way, he reflected the spirit of religious tolerance that is enshrined in Indonesia's Constitution, and that remains one of this country's defining and inspiring characteristics... *Bhinneka Tunggal Ika*—unity in diversity.

Later in his speech Obama noted that religion "is fundamental to the Indonesian story." The homecoming of Indonesia's adopted son seemed to solidify Indonesia's image as a Muslim-majority democracy where "moderate Islam" flourished. So, what happened to drastically change global perceptions about Indonesia from the fears of the early 2000s? Yes, Indonesia successfully conducted national direct elections, relaxed most media restrictions, and began to combat rampant corruption. These political and economic dimensions notwithstanding, we cannot begin to understand the rebranding of democratic Indonesia without attending to the rise of soft-power diplomacy that championed Indonesia as the home of "moderate Islam" and proof that Islam and democracy can coexist.

American praise of Indonesia's "moderate Islam" reflects wider geopolitical and historical forces. In one sense, Western governments and think tanks have created this very category of "moderate Islam," an integral component of colonial and postcolonial projects of deciphering the "good Muslims" from their "bad" co-religionists (Mamdani 2004). In the wake of 9/11, various pundits and think tanks went, once again, in search for the "good Muslims." Perhaps not surprisingly, think tanks such as the RAND Foundation suggested partnering with those Muslim "moderates" who reflect Western liberal secularism and embody (Orientalist) notions of gentle, peace-loving Sufis (Corbett 2017). Critiques of the concept of "moderate Islam" as construed by the West provide important historical and political correctives to Western misunderstandings of Islam and politics. At the same time, the Islamic notion of moderation—*wassatiya*—has a long history *within* Islamic thought. Although some Muslim leaders remain sharply critical of the English phrase "moderate Islam," diplomats and religious leaders in Indonesia (and elsewhere) have embraced the term and subsequently designed public diplomacy efforts to position themselves as exemplars of religious moderation and bearers of "true" Islam (Umar 2016). To better understand this diplomatic strategy, I bridge anthropological emphases of the politics of piety (Mahmood 2006) with conversations in international relations about religion, soft power, and public diplomacy (Haynes 2011; Nye 1990).

Over the last couple decades Indonesia's diplomatic agenda has undergone an "Islamic turn." While political Islam has been the focus of abundant scholarship in recent decades, Peter Mandaville and Shadi Hamid note that "much less attention . . . has been paid to the ways in which a number of governments—including some that are frequently the focus or target of Islamic activism—have opted to deploy Islam as a component of their own foreign policy conduct" (2018, 2). As we will see, Indonesia's foreign policy abroad is also closely connected with its religious statecraft at home. Mandaville and Hamid also observe that, at least in the cases of other Muslim-majority countries such as Jordan, Morocco, and Egypt, "the transnational projection of religion—far from representing a monolithic and deliberate expression of foreign policy intent—often tells us a lot about the balance of power between competing social and political forces *within* the country from which it emanates" (2018, 3). Likewise, the search for (and articulations of) an authentic "Indonesian" Islam has also become a cornerstone of its foreign policy abroad—albeit not without contestation at home.

The Islamic turn in Indonesia's foreign policy has refigured long-standing domestic concerns about political Islam and theological fault lines between Indonesian traditionalists and their Wahhabi detractors at home and abroad. After providing brief historical and political context for the Islamic turn in Indonesia's foreign policy, I examine public diplomacy initiatives that have brought together state and civil society religious leaders eager to define and defend the idea of "moderate Islam." The focus of even more contention, however, has been the extent to which an "Islam of the Archipelago" (*Islam Nusantara*) as the traditionalist organization Nahdlatul Ulama has coined, might be exported to the rest of the Muslim world (Sahal and Aziz 2015; Affan 2015).

A cottage industry has developed (in both Jakarta and Washington, DC) around the role of soft power and the place of Southeast Asia—specifically, Indonesia—in the "war on terror." As Bond and Simons contend, "The fact that Islam in Southeast Asia, although under rising fundamentalist pressure, is not yet in crisis, should be all the encouragement the United States needs to step up to the challenge by putting what foreign policy experts know as 'smart power' to work in the region" (2009, 13). Western government officials have been eager to support and engage Indonesia's soft-power diplomacy (while also pursuing hard-power approaches of weapons sales and military training). Less clear, however, is whether Indonesia can leverage its newfound brand with coreligionists in the Middle East and North Africa.

The Islamic Turn in Indonesian Foreign Policy

The fact that Indonesia is the world's most populous Muslim country—with centuries of trade, religious, and political networks scattered throughout the Indian Ocean, Middle East, and North Africa—does not necessarily mean that Islam has played an important role in Indonesia's foreign policy. Notwithstanding Kevin Fogg's (2015) important observation that Muslim networks were an important element of Indonesia's late colonial and revolutionary periods, most scholars of Indonesia's postindependence foreign policy argue that Islam (and Indonesia as a Muslim-majority country) played very little role in the "active and free" (*aktif-bebas*) foreign policy under President Sukarno (1949–1965) and President Suharto (1966–1998). For example, Leo Suryadinata argues that Indonesia's policy to not maintain diplomatic relations with Israel was motivated by Sukarno's devotion to the Non-Aligned movement, not by any primordial bonds of Muslim brotherhood: "This policy has often been seen as reflecting Indonesia's close association with its Islamic brothers, but if the situation is studied more closely it can be seen that these relations were based on Third World nationalism rather than co-religious solidarity" (Suryadinata 1995, 292). Sukarno's fiery rhetoric was about postcolonial justice, and his dedication to the Africa-Asia Conference held in Bandung, Indonesia in 1955 was informed by these antiimperialist aims, not any religious impulse or felt brotherhood among Muslim-majority countries.

During the authoritarian New Order regime (1966–1998), Suharto depoliticized Islam in both domestic politics and foreign policy. Although Indonesia was officially a member state of the Organization for Islamic Cooperation (OIC) since its inception, Suharto instructed diplomats to extend support based on the UN Charter, not religious allegiance (Suryadinata

1995). Even then, in 1972 Indonesia refused to sign the Charter that declared all members were Islamic states. During the New Order, Suharto was about power and control. Regarding the role of Islam in Indonesia's foreign policy, Indonesian scholar-turned-ambassador Rizal Sukma puts it succinctly (2012, 85):

> Before 1998 Islam was never a determining factor in Indonesia's foreign policy, because neither Sukarno nor Suharto would allow foreign policy to be dictated by Islamic considerations. Islam became part of the national identity only after *reformasi*, when the rise of several Islamic-based political parties placed political Islam at the centre of national politics. The effect on foreign policy has been most evident in the attempts to shape Indonesia's image as a moderate Muslim country.

After the fall of Suharto in 1998, Islam would play a much greater role in the idea of governance and political reform, *reformasi*. "Islam is the Solution" became the mantra for the Muslim Brotherhood–inspired Islamist political party, The Prosperous Justice Party (*Partai Keadilan Sejahtera*); Islamic television programming proliferated with the privatization of media; Islamic corporate training promised an ethical, disciplined workforce (Rudnyckyj 2010); and, the public performance of piety accrued its own political currency.

Senior diplomats at the Indonesian Ministry of Foreign Affairs had become accustomed to pursuing foreign policy largely based on national interest. The turbulent early years of democratic reform in Indonesia witnessed the rise of Islamic militia deployed to fight Christians in eastern Indonesia in 1999–2000. The following year, the events of 9/11 shifted the outlook for priorities in US diplomacy. Subsequently, the 2002 (and later again in 2005) bomb blast in Bali, killing hundreds of Western tourists and Indonesians, made violent extremism a top priority of bilateral military and diplomatic relations between Indonesia and Western governments. As Indonesia successfully weathered these tests of democratic reform, the story of democratic consolidation in the world's largest Muslim-majority country started to look like a success story.

Dr. Hasan Wirajuda played an in invaluable role in Indonesia's rebranding. During his tenure as foreign minister between 2001 and 2009, Wirajuda popularized his soft-power philosophy of "total diplomacy." In 2002 he established the directorate of public diplomacy. Wirajuda's "total diplomacy" resonated well with President Susilo Bambang Yudhoyono's (SBY) interest to promote Indonesia as the home of "moderate Islam." Despite his own position as a secular-leaning diplomatic elite, Wirajuda understood the importance of religious diplomacy—and Indonesia's own story—as a corrective to global narratives about clashes of civilizations and the compatibility of Islam and democracy. These efforts bore fruit as Western politicians, diplomats, and pundits began to laud Indonesia as the exemplar where Islam, democracy, and modernity coexist. As Secretary of State Hillary Rodham Clinton noted in 2009, "If you want to know whether Islam, democracy, modernity and women's rights can coexist, go to Indonesia."[3]

As an example of Wirajuda's soft-power strategies, consider one backstory to this declaration. One of his close advisors described how the Indonesian foreign ministry coordinated with the State Department, expressing their hopes that Secretary Clinton publicly declare that Indonesia was evidence of the compatibility of Islam, modernity, and democracy. So how, then, was women's rights added to the checklist of modernity? As this aid recalls, he and Wirajuda were going through final preparations for an official dinner with Secretary Clinton. They wondered what else they might include to make Secretary Clinton's dining experience reflect the newly projected values of Indonesian democracy. As they browsed the seating chart, reflecting on the fact that Indonesia had several high-ranking female cabinet members, they decided to seat these women next to Secretary Clinton. While difficult to prove any causal connection, the story was proudly told as an example of how total diplomacy caused Secretary Clinton to take her own initiative to add "women's rights" to Islam, democracy, and modernity as the hallmark of Indonesia's exemplary status.

Wirajuda keenly understood Indonesia's strategic position as the world's largest Muslim-majority democracy. He launched an ambitious plan for person-to-person diplomacy that connected a range of religious and civil society organizations across a diverse group of countries and multilateral organizations. Wirajuda himself was not well connected with the religious and civil society leaders, so he needed help launching his public diplomacy vision. He began hosting foreign policy breakfasts to forge relationships with journalists, religious leaders, and civil society actors. The Director of Public Diplomacy at that time, Umar Hadi, established the domestic networks necessary to create interfaith programming, promote Indonesian Muslim intellectuals, and showcase Indonesian Islam as modern and "moderate."

Joining Wirajuda's vision, the traditionalist organization Nahdlatul Ulama (NU) and the reformist organization Muhammadiyah each played pivotal roles.[4] Both are important modern Islamic organizations, founded in the early twentieth century, who together have over 100 million members. One such example of collaboration between the foreign ministry and these civil society organizations, the International Conference on Islamic Studies (ICIS), provided extensive funding for leading scholars around the world to convene in Indonesia to discuss the state of Islamic studies in Indonesia and around the world. Given the geopolitical climate of the mid-2000s, fear of terrorism and calls for "moderate" Islam figured heavily in both academic discussion and Indonesian public diplomacy. In addition to invoking the English phrase "moderate Islam," diplomats also conjured the Qur'anic injunction that Islam had come as a blessing for all worlds, or "*Islam Rahmatan lil al-Amin.*" By the mid-2000s, and at the behest of NU leader K. H. Hasyim Muzadi, "*Islam Rahmatan lil al-Amin*" had become Indonesia's mantra for religious diplomacy.

Indonesian total diplomacy resonated well with the geopolitics and foreign policies of America's war on terror. Near the end of his tenure as foreign minister, Wirajuda affirmed Indonesia's standing at the Carnegie Endowment for International Peace:

> President Barack Obama, in Cairo a few days ago, invited the peoples of the Muslim world to a partnership to address an array of critical issues: violent extremism, the Middle East situation, nuclear disarmament, democracy, religious freedom, women's rights, and economic development and opportunity. I am here to tell you that Indonesia, the country with the world's largest Muslim population, has long prepared itself to answer President Obama's call for partnership.[5]

In 2008, Wirajuda and several prominent politicians and diplomats (including then-President SBY and presidential spokesperson Dr. Dino Patti Djalal) founded the Institute for Peace and Democracy (IPD). When Wirajuda stepped down as foreign minister in 2009, IPD provided yet another avenue for Track II diplomacy. As the Arab Uprising was gaining strength in 2011–2012, Wirajuda (who previously served as ambassador to Egypt) was keen to take advantage of that moment to share lessons from Indonesia's arduous path toward democratization and demilitarization. IPD and Wirajuda hosted four seminars—three in Indonesia, another in Cairo—that brought together journalists, civil society leaders, and politicians from Egypt and Tunisia. Despite Wirajuda's efforts to "share lessons" from Indonesia's difficult path of democratization, this form of "total diplomacy" found it difficult to escape deep distrust and political acrimony between some participants (Wirajuda 2011). Despite the limited success of this Track II diplomacy, IPD was serving its purpose as a platform for Indonesia's Track II diplomacy.

The Bali Democracy Forum: Islamic School Tours as Public Diplomacy

The IPD was the hosting agency for Indonesia's diplomatic experiment—the Bali Democracy Forum (BDF)—where politicians, diplomats, and civil society leaders from approximately 100 countries gathered to discuss a range of issues from democratization and global trade to extremism and religious pluralism. Whereas President SBY promoted Indonesia as an important success story of global importance, Jokowi was less attentive to foreign policy and did not even attend his first BDF as president. Unlike SBY, Jokowi was disinterested in leveraging "moderate Islam" a broader soft-power diplomatic strategy. When bombs struck Jakarta in 2016, however, Jokowi began to take religious statecraft more seriously. As part of that shift, Jokowi delivered the opening keynote address for the BDF in December 2016, its theme "Religion, Democracy, and Pluralism." During his opening address, Jokowi embraced the soft power of religious diplomacy:

> Distinguished delegates,
> ... The theme for this year's Bali Democracy Forum, "Religion, Democracy, and Pluralism" is very relevant with the current regional and global situation
>   because we are convinced that religion is Allah's mercy and blessing for all worlds, or *Rahmatan lil al-Amin*, because we are optimistic that democracy embodies the will of the people and brings greater good to the human race, because we realize that tolerance is needed since we all are different [...] Indonesia is home to more than 1,300 ethnic groups [and] the largest Muslim population in the world. Around 85% of more than 252 million population of Indonesia are Muslim. [...] The history of Indonesia teaches us that Islam spread to Indonesia through peaceful means. And it is this value of peace that continues to be upheld to this day by Indonesia's *umma*

[...] I have been informed that there will be a visit tomorrow to an Islamic Boarding School [...]. You can only imagine how, without the value of high tolerance, an Islamic boarding school can possibly live securely and serenely amid a majority Balinese-Hindu society. All these values have promoted a natural synergy between religion, democracy, and pluralism in Indonesia.

Despite his initial reluctance, Jokowi had clearly learned the soft-power mantra of "moderate Islam."

Religious soft power is not just discursive, but also experiential. On the second day of the BDF, Indonesia's foreign minister Retno Marsudi escorted diplomats to the Bina Insani Islamic school. As delegates descended from luxury tour buses, they were welcomed by an ensemble of Balinese gamelan music (Figure 10.1), then were guided to their seats of honor in the front rows of an outdoor covered stage with a huge red backdrop welcoming BDF delegates (Figure 10.2). Rather than emphasize local Balinese Hindu traditions of tolerance, the foreign ministry opted to promote "moderate Islam" through the story of an Islamic school in Hindu-majority Bali. The official program opened with a young female student reciting (in eloquent Arabic) a Quranic passage about ethnic and religious pluralism and God's

Figure 10.1 Islamic school students welcome BDF delegates with gamelan music, Qur'anic recitation, and personal testimonies about religious tolerance and pluralism.

Figure 10.2 Saudi Arabia's ambassador to Indonesia, Osama Mohammad Abdullah Alshuaibi, congratulated the Islamic school as an exemplary model of religious coexistence and pledged a donation of $50,000. For decades, Saudi Arabia has deployed their own soft power strategies to influence the trajectory of Islam in Indonesia.

decree for people to come to know each other (Sura 49, Verse 13). This passage has been invoked time and time again in a wide range of Indonesia's diplomatic events from Bali and Jakarta to London and Washington, DC.

Indonesia's public diplomacy frequently relies on personal testimonial to showcase ethnic and religious diversity. After welcoming remarks by the foreign minister and head of school, a Hindu woman who taught there shared her story of what it was like, how she was welcomed by the Muslim community, and how the Islamic school was greatly respected by Hindu neighbors. She was followed by young female boarding school students who recited—with great dramatic effect and in both English and Arabic—poems about tolerance and pluralism. The headmaster shared stories about his childhood in Bali, then pursuing higher education at the esteemed National Islamic University in Jakarta, and eventually coming back home to found the Islamic school, part of his vision to bridge the Islamic ideal of bringing mercy to all worlds with Indonesia's national motto "unity in diversity."

Once the program concluded, the Saudi Arabian ambassador to Indonesia, Osama Mohammad Abdullah Alshuaibi, rose to his feet to congratulate the Islamic school on being such an exemplar of the Qur'anic injunction that

Figure 10.3 Over thirty Muslim leaders from the Middle East, North Africa, and Europe gather on stage in Jakarta for the International Summit of Moderate Islamic Leaders, ISOMIL.

Islam was brought as a mercy for all worlds. Ambassador Alshuaibi began by scolding the headmaster for not translating for guests the Arabic-language name of the Islamic School, which refers to the cultivation (literally the building) of a person. With dramatic flair, Alshuaibi exclaimed, that he so impressed that Saudi Arabia would donate $50,000. (Figure 10.3) A certain unease followed the polite clapping and remarks of astonishment and gratitude. Although Indonesians have great reverence for Saudi Arabia as the guardian of Islam's holiest sites, there exists a longer colonial and postcolonial ambivalence surrounding the Arabization of Indonesian Islam, understood by many to constitute a new form of colonial domination. Many Indonesians are wary about Saudi influence and gifts. Since the 1970s Saudi Arabia has offered scholarships for Indonesians to study in Saudi Arabia. During King Salman's visit to Indonesia in early 2017, he pledged to help Indonesia spread "moderate Islam." After then signing what many Indonesians felt was a measly bilateral economic package, King Salman and his entourage spent the rest of their vacation in the high-end resorts of Bali, certainly not visiting the Bina Isani Islamic school. Though popular among Western governments, Indonesian Islamic soft power evidently fares less well with Middle Eastern countries who deem themselves—not Indonesians—to reflect the real, authentic Islam.

Indonesian foreign policy finds itself at a crossroads. Whereas Western diplomats appear relatively enthusiastic about Indonesia's "moderate Islam," such an approach complicates Indonesia's bilateral relations with Muslim-majority countries. Partnerships to promote "moderate Islam" do not necessarily imply that each country perceives the other's practice of Islam as authentic or rooted in authoritative tradition. On the bus back to the BDF, I sat next to the Saudi Ambassador. Recounting the visit, I asked if he took issue with the musical instruments, female students dancing, and relaxed standards of gender segregation. Looking a bit disappointed, Ambassador Alshuaibi lamented the use of music and mixing of genders, then proceeded to explain to me that most Indonesians had yet to practice "authentic" Islam. "But," he proceeded, "it would be rude to publicly declare such things. We must realize that this is their culture and how they understand Islam. Remember, Islam has only been here for a few centuries." His remark combined the linguistic finesse of a diplomat with the inexorable scorn of a colonial officer. Despite Ambassador Alshuaibi's ostensible support to help Indonesia promote "moderate Islam," he has long scorned the traditionalist organization Nahdlatul Ulama and would scoff at the very notion of an "Indonesian Islam," much less that the wider Muslim umma could and should learn from its example. In the next section, I examine the tensions created by Indonesian soft-power diplomacy through debates about the idea of an Indonesian Islam, and whether it represents a viable model to be exported globally.

Track II Diplomacy: Islam Nusantara and the Question of Indonesian Exceptionalism

In the lead-up to Nahdlatul Ulama's 2015 national congress, held approximately every five years to elect new leadership, senior NU leadership created quite a hullabaloo when they announced the congress theme of *Islam Nusantara*, or "Islam of the Archipelago." This term has been in popular usage for a couple decades, even beyond the circles of NU's traditionalist membership. Put simply, the concept acknowledges diverse histories of how Islam came to the archipelago and melded with local belief and custom. An especially important part of this understanding emphasizes the role of the "nine saints" (*wali songo*) who preached Islam through Sufism, the arts, and careful respect of local traditions that did not contradict Islamic teachings.

Moreover, the concept is a celebration of Indonesian Islam, a declaration of sorts that authentic Islam is more easily found in Indonesia than the Middle East.

Shortly after NU announced the congress theme of *Islam Nusantara*, several Muslim organizations, celebrity preachers, and conservative leaders bashed the concept. Much of the critique played out on digital and social media with sharp criticism from many that there could even be an "Indonesian Islam" somehow separate from the one, "true" Islam. In a televised tirade that went viral, popular television preacher Mama Dedeh proclaimed the concept has no basis in Qur'anic scripture or the prophetic tradition. Even an NU-affiliated popular preacher cleverly chastised the appeal of *Islam Nusantara* as "pig wrapped in goat meat." Creative memes accused NU leaders (such as chairman Dr. Sa'id Aqil Siraj) of being too liberal, referring pejoratively to proponents of the concept as members of the "Islam Nusantara Network" (*Jaringan Islam Nusantara*). Critics deployed the coy acronym JIN to evoke the Islamic belief in otherworldly beings, or *jinn*. This acronym also uses word play that connects JIN with JIL (*Jaringan Islam Liberal*, or Liberal Islam Network), a now-defunct group of young NU intellectuals in the early 2000s, whose critical exegesis made them suspect among theologically conservative Muslims. In 2005, the Indonesian Council of Ulama rebuked the Liberal Islam Network with a fatwa that decries secularism, pluralism, and liberalism—referred to in Indonesian by yet another pejorative acronym (*sipilis*) intended to conjure the moral abhorrence of the venereal disease syphilis.

One of the great ironies of this particular battle over *Islam Nusantara* is that NU's Chairman and champion of this concept, Dr. Sa'id Aqil Siraj, lived and studied in Saudi Arabia during his undergraduate education through his doctoral degree, compliments of a scholarship program aligned with Saudi Arabia's soft-power strategies. Fluent in Arabic and connected with various leaders of a global *umnma*, Siraj was nonetheless committed to the idea that saints and Sufis forged a distinct form of Islam in Indonesia—though he was emphatic it was not to be considered a new school of law (Indonesia mostly follows Shafi'i law). Siraj was also wary of what he views as the cultural "Arabization" (*Arabisasi*) of Islam in contemporary Indonesia. He relished in provocative critiques of aimed at what he viewed as mindless mimicry of Arab cultural mores, such as one phrase (that made him both hero and villain on social media): "the longer the beard, the more stupid the person."

Beyond trends of Arabization in Indonesian Islam, among many Indonesians there was a sense of increasing confidence and optimism about

Indonesian Islam as the model for the authentic, everyday practice of Islam. In this respect, "moderate Islam" Along with other senior NU leaders such as Yahya Staquf and Mustofa Bisri, Siraj was an active public diplomat who often traveled abroad to convey the message that *Islam Nusantara* was an exemplary model for "moderate Islam" and an antidote to violent extremism. Some of these NU programs were at the impetus of the foreign ministry, while others (such as their longstanding mission in Afghanistan) were in the name of NU. The 2016 bomb blast in downtown Jakarta (just blocks away from the presidential palace, foreign ministry, and NU headquarters) created a renewed sense of urgency to promote *Islam Nusantara* at home and abroad. Eager to improve Indonesia's standing within the global umma, and well aware that Indonesians were considered peripheral by many countries in the Middle East, Siraj and NU leaders decided to convene an international summit that positioned *Islam Nusantara* as the exemplar of "moderate Islam." (Figure 10.4)

With these theological and diplomatic goals in mind, NU leadership hosted the "International Summit of Moderate Islamic Leaders" (ISOMIL) in Jakarta on May 9–11, 2016. As Mandaville and Hamid (2018) have astutely observed, soft-power diplomacy has both global and domestic audiences in mind. In terms of the domestic context, some among NU leadership viewed *Islam Nusantara* as a strategy to implement at the state-level by NU

Figure 10.4 As a symbolic gesture to religious pluralism, a Balinese gamelan ensemble welcomes BDF delegates upon their arrival at the Islamic school.

coordination with the ministries of foreign affairs, religious affairs, and education. At the same time, President Jokowi also found a political expediency in supporting the concept. He often referred to *Islam Nusantara* during speeches and encouraged state patronage on several levels. Indeed, one of the sponsors of ISOMIL was Indonesia's National Agency for the Eradication of Terrorism, BNPT. With respect to the global Muslim community, Siraj wanted to make the case that Indonesia remained the best exemplar of the compatibility of Islam and democracy. With the political changes in Turkey and the Arab Uprising turning into an Arab Winter, Siraj was even more strident in his desire to promote—and defend—the idea of *Islam Nusantara*. The summit brought together over thirty ulama from across the Middle East and North Africa, mostly part of NU's existing global networks who were already sympathetic to NU's theological arguments in favor of Sufism and national citizenship.

Without the space to discuss all of the events, speakers, and ethnographic spaces at ISOMIL, I would like to focus our attention on Siraj's hour-long keynote address, quoted at length to better understand how *Islam Nusantara* engages both domestic and global concerns. With no small amount of nostalgia, and in eloquent Arabic, Siraj regaled the audience with a story about the peaceful spread of Islam across the archipelago, the key influence of NU founder KH Hashim Asy'ari who provided theological cover for national struggles against colonial rule, and the lessons that *Islam Nusantara* provides lessons for an Arab world still reeling from the postcolonial tensions between secular Arab nationalism and political Islam. With a slightly revisionist history, and narrow account of political Islam in contemporary Indonesia that disregards domestic factors, Siraj argued that recent terrorism and intra-religious conflict in Indonesia began only when "transnational" extremist discourses entered Indonesian religious and political life. Below, I include only those segments related to public diplomacy and the position of Indonesia within the global umma:

> [. . .] Respected guests, religion and nationalism represent the principal factors that have brought the nation of Indonesia together. Together, they are important pillars that nurtured along the existence of Indonesia and nourished the continuity of the history and civilization of the Indonesian people. [. . .] Colonialism used every means and device possible to separate Islam and nationalism. Even to this moment, the strength of aggressors still takes the form of fracturing the people into conflicting ethnic groups.

[...] Today our people are experiencing several ominous crises: political, economic, social, and environmental that threaten the existence of our people and their future. Even more, this backdrop of crises has been taken advantage of by false voices here and there with various propaganda to split religion from nationalism, with the potential of dividing the people. This propaganda is supported by foreign powers that continuously strive to separate the two. We greatly need to rethink [matters] and return to strengthening the pillars of religion and nationalism [...]

On account of this, in this address I will attempt to focus on the thinking of a leader who has already poured his strength to safeguard religion and nationalism on account of his deep awareness of the urgency of them both. [...] This was one of the pioneers of reform in Indonesia, K.H. Muhammad Hasyim Asy'ari, who played an important role in safeguarding the relationship between religion and nationalism. [...]

KH Hasyim Asy'ari serves as an exemplary model of one who sensed the poisons of colonialism in this context [separating religion and nationalism] and to confront this before it became a dangerous and growing threat. In the majority of Muslim and Arab countries, for example, there has already been a polarization between religion and nationalism such that we see religious experts who typically have a weak nationalist spirit, and then nationalists who frequently do not have a strong commitment to religion. For example, Michael Aflaq (1910–1989) ... who successfully produced young cadre who would later become leaders in the Middle East, such as: Abdul Karim Qasim and Hafez al-Asad in Syria, Hasan al-Bakr and Saddam Hussein in Iraq, Habib Burghibah in Tunisia, Jamal Abdun Nasser of Egypt, Muhammad Qadafi in Libya, and others. All of them are leaders who succeeded in freeing their countries from colonial powers, even though they felt religion was not important for confronting colonial powers. [...] K.H. Hasyim Asy'ari invited the Indonesian people to be resolutely committed to Islam as a way to safeguard the people and homeland. In this way Islam contributes to sustaining feelings of togetherness among the Indonesian people (Hoesterey 2022, 19–20).

Siraj carefully crafted this retrospective glimpse into the various anticolonial and postindependence moments in various Muslim-majority countries. During this part of his speech, Siraj performed a scholarly affect that was didactic, but also sympathetic to the historical separation of Islam and nationalism in the Middle East. By teaching about NU founder

Asy'ari—who framed the anticolonial struggle as a form of *jihad* while also insisting on the Islamic basis for nationalism—Siraj is crafting Indonesia's (relative) success story with what is characterized as the dire straits of monarchies and authoritarianism in the Middle East. As he shifts his attention to a comparative analysis of Indonesia and the Middle East, Siraj's performance begins to feel even more didactic, with a hint of pity, at the very different paths of religion and governance in Indonesia and the Middle East:

> Let us compare the realities between Indonesia and the Middle East, where the differences of opinion concerning religion and nationalism drove Egyptian president Jamal Abdun Nasser to execute Muslim Brotherhood *ulama* in the city center of Cairo. [. . .] Alhamdulillah such events did not occur in Indonesia on account of the presence of NU, founded by K.H. Hasyim Asy'ari who proved that religious leaders can simultaneously be those who struggle for the nation, as was also the case with other Indonesian *ulama* such as KH Ahmad Dahlan, KH Agus Salim, Abdul Halim, Abdurrahman Baswedan, and others who were both religious and nationalist leaders.[6] *This* is the characteristic of Islam in Indonesia that we call *Islam Nusantara*—an Islam of the archipelago with an ironclad positive relationship with nationalism. Concerning this, KH Hasyim Asy'ari held the viewpoint that whoever was killed defending their homeland would die a martyr, and vice versa that the blood of whoever defended the colonists would be *halal*, even though they are not a *kafir* (unbeliever). [. . .] the time has come to transfer these principles and concepts to the wider Muslim world so that the causes of conflict and division can be wiped out. We see in Afghanistan, for example, the spirit of nationalism has vanished among Muslims, and so too in Somalia, Iraq, and Syria. [. . .] With the rise of ISIS in some of our nations we can still see that the ranks of Muslims and Muslim nations in the Middle East is still fragile and weak on account of the failure of Muslims to understand their religion in one respect, and their nationalism in the other.

With the remainder of his speech, Siraj told the story of Indonesia's successful transition to democratic rule by adhering to neither secular liberalism nor an Islamic state. If one considers democratic liberties, economic development, and the (relatively successful) removal of the military from political power, it would be difficult to argue that Indonesia is not, in fact, in a better position than most Muslim-majority countries in the Middle East.

However, it remains unclear whether Indonesia's success story—and its formula of Islamic nationalism without an Islamic state—will resonate with co-religionists elsewhere. Those foreign ulama in attendance, to be sure, were already enmeshed in different NU networks worldwide and were already sympathetic to the importance of Sufi thought in NU's brand of traditionalism. As I consider in the concluding reflections below, it remains doubtful that Indonesia's success story has had any effect on military rule in Egypt or the future of Wahhabi thought in Saudi Arabia. Further still, Indonesia's story is still unfolding, its democratic success not guaranteed.

Conclusion

Indonesia's revamped image of "moderate Islam" plays much better with Western governments anxious about Islamic extremism than with the monarchies of the Middle East anxious about their power and wealth. When King Salman visited Indonesia just a couple months after the 2016 Bali Democracy Forum, he signed a meager economic deal and promised to "help" Indonesia promote "moderate Islam," but then escaped with his entourage to the beaches of Bali. King Salman never visited the Islamic school Bina Insani that his ambassador raved so much about. As Rizal Sukma cautions, "It is not immediately clear how attractive Indonesia's brand of Islam is to its co-religionist partners in the Arab Muslim world" (2012, 87). Putting it more forcefully, Martin van Bruinessen argues that "the Arab world has shown a remarkable lack of interest in Asia in general, let alone in the social and cultural forms of Islam in Southeast Asia" (2012, 117). Pleasantries of public diplomacy notwithstanding, it remains unfathomable that the king of Saudi Arabia would embrace *Islam Nusantara* or that the Egyptian military is willing to give up power as did the Indonesian generals in 1998.

Given this lack of authority in the Middle East, Indonesia has struggled to assume any significant role as peace broker. Indonesian scholar Azyumardi Azra laments that, "Despite renewed Indonesian activism in Middle Eastern affairs, the hopes that Indonesia can be a bridging and mediating force among the conflicting parties in the Middle East seem to be very difficult to realize" (2015, 151). This is certainly not due to any lack of effort. In March 2016, Indonesia hosted the OIC's extraordinary summit for Palestine, yet the much-heralded "Jakarta Declaration" has certainly not brought about any real political change. Despite their "great power aspirations" (Fealy and

White 2016), Indonesia has yet to project any serious power or influence that in the Middle East.

With respect to Western governments, the viability of Indonesia's brand as the home of democracy, modernity, and "moderate Islam" will not depend on slick slogans or diplomatic stunts. It will largely be contingent on how Indonesia continues to manage the fragile balance of religious liberty and democratic rule. As Andreas Harsono of Human Rights Watch argued in an Op-ed in the *New York Times*, Nahdlatul Ulama and the Indonesian state cannot always be viewed as the model of "moderate Islam" (Harsono 2012). As but one example, scholars have noted that the former NU spiritual leader and current Indonesian Vice President, K. H. Ma'aruf Amin, actually played a central role in anti-Shi'a and anti-Ahmadiyah sentiment when serving as advisor to President Yudhoyono (Bush 2015). Indonesia's soft-power branding strategies thus run the risk of over-promising and underdelivering. As Indonesian public intellectual Dewi Fortuna Anwar cogently argued:

> Indonesia's efforts to promote a new face for Indonesia which is moderate, democratic and progressive will be meaningless and futile if the international news on Indonesia is dominated by stories about the burning of churches, attacks against groups accused of deviating from Islam, such as Ahmadiyyah, women being forced to wear the jilbab [headscarf] and other non-democratic and non-progressive acts... Indonesia's public diplomacy would be received with a degree of cynicism by the international community. (2008, 11; cited in Sukma 2012, 87)

Whereas the limits of the concept of *Islam Nusantara* have been established, both domestically and abroad, the broader idea of religious moderation continues to gain traction in the foreign ministry, several domestic ministries, and with leaders of other Muslim-majority countries such as Morocco, Egypt, and Jordan. In late 2019, Indonesia's Ministry of Religion published a book titled "Religious Moderation" (*Moderasi Beragama*) that touted examples of moderation and tolerance found in Indonesia's many religious traditions. Likewise, the foreign ministry published a book whose title refers to religious pluralism as the "jewel of the nation." The concept of moderation—often phrased with the Arabic-Indonesian gloss *wassatiya*—continues to work its way into not just democratic discourses, but also more authoritarian voices calling for the banning of hardliner groups. In terms of public diplomacy and soft power, the Indonesian state and civil society organizations like NU continue to promote "moderate Islam" and look for ways to partner with other countries who have developed similar soft-power strategies. Considering the prospect of a long Arab Winter ahead, continuing uncertainty about Turkey's democratic future, democratic setbacks in Tunisia, and increasing racialized and religious bigotry in America and Europe, Indonesia's promotion of civic religious pluralism and "moderate Islam"—notwithstanding the political and theological challenges at home and abroad—continues to be an important endeavor for Indonesia's sense of self at home and abroad.

References

Affan, Hayder. 2015. "Polemik di Balik Istilah Islam Nusantara [The Polemics behind the concept of Islam Nusantara]." *BBC Indonesia*, June 15, 2015. http://www.bbc.com/indonesia/berita_indonesia/2015/06/150614_indonesia_islam_nusantara.

Azra, Azyumardi. 2015. "Indonesia's Middle Power Public Diplomacy: Asia and Beyond." In *Understanding Public Diplomacy in East Asia: Middle Powers in a Troubled Region*, edited by Jan Melissen and Yul Sohn, 131–154. New York: Palgrave Macmillan.

Bond, Christopher S., and Lewis M. Simons. 2009. *The Next Front: Southeast Asia and the Road to Global Peace with Islam*. Hoboken, NJ: John Wiley & Sons.

Bush, Robin. 2015. "Religious Politics and Minority Rights during the Yudhoyono Presidency." In *The Yudhoyono Presidency: A Decade of Stability and Stagnation*, edited by Edward Aspinall, 239–257. Singapore: ISEAS.

Carnegie Endowment for International Peace. "Indonesian Foreign Minister Wirajuda on the U.S.-Indonesian Comprehensive Partnership." Carnegie Endowment for International Peace, June 8, 2009. https://carnegieendowment.org/2009/06/08/indonesian-foreign-minister-wirajuda-on-u.s.-indonesian-comprehensive-partnership-event-1356.

Corbett, Rosemary R. 2017. *Making Moderate Islam: Sufism, Service, and the "Ground Zero Mosque" Controversy*. Stanford: Stanford University Press.

Fealy, Greg, and Hugh White. 2016. "Indonesia's 'Great Power' Aspirations: A Critical View." *Asia and the Pacific Policy Studies* 3 (1): 92–100.

Fogg, Kevin. 2015. "Islam in Indonesia's Foreign Policy: 1945–1949." *Al-Jami'ah: Journal of Islamic Studies* 53 (2): 303–335.

Formichi, Chiara. 2012. *Islam and the Making of the Nation: Kartosuwiryo and Political Islam in Twentieth-Century Indonesia*. Leiden-Boston: Brill.

Harsono, Andreas. 2012. "No Model for Muslim Democracy." *The New York Times*, May 21, 2012. http://www.nytimes.com/2012/05/22/opinion/no-model-for-muslimdemocracy.html.

Haynes, Jeffrey, ed. 2011. *Religion, Politics, and International Relations: Selected Essays*. New York: Routledge.

Hoesterey, James B. "Globalization and Islamic Indigenization in Southeast Asian Muslim Communities." *Journal for the Study of Islamic History and Culture* 3, no. 2 (July 2022): 19–20. https://journal.unusia.ac.id/index.php/ISLAMNUSANTARA/article/download/370/288.

Landler, Mark. "Clinton Praises Indonesian Democracy." *New York Times*, February 18, 2009. https://www.nytimes.com/2009/02/19/washington/19diplo.html?_r=0.

Mahmood, Saba. 2006. "*Secularism*, Hermeneutics, Empire: The Politics of Islamic Reformation." *Public Culture* 18 (2): 323–347.

Mamdani, Mahmood. 2004. *Good Muslim, Bad Muslim: America, The Cold War, and the Roots of Terror*. New York: Three Leaves Press.

Mandaville, Peter, and Shadi Hamid. 2018. "Islam as Statecraft: How Governments use Religion in Foreign Policy." *The New Geopolitics: Middle East*. Washington, DC: The Brookings Institution. Available at: https://www.brookings.edu/research/islam-as-statecraft-how-governments-use-religion-in-foreign-policy/.

Nye, Joseph S. Jr. 1990. "Soft Power." *Foreign Policy* 80 (Autumn): 153–171.

Obama, Barack. 2010. "Speech given at University of Indonesia." November 10, 2010. https://obamawhitehouse.archives.gov/the-press-office/2010/11/10/remarks-presidentuniversity-indonesia-jakarta-indonesia.

Rudnyckyj, Daromir. *Spiritual Economies: Islam, Globalization, and the Afterlife of Development*. Ithaca: Cornell University Press, 2010.

Sahal, Akhmad, and Munawir Aziz, eds. 2015. *Islam Nusantara: Dari Ushul Fiqh Hingga Paham Kebangsaan*. Bandung: Mizan.

Sukma, Rizal. 2012. "Domestic Politics and International Posture: Constraints and Possibilities." In *Indonesia Rising: The Repositioning of Asia's Third Giant*, edited by Anthony Reid, 77–92. Singapore: ISEAS.

Sukma, Rizal. 2011. "Soft Power and Public Diplomacy: The Case of Indonesia," In *Public Diplomacy and Soft Power in East Asia*, edited by Sook Jong Lee and Jam Melissen, 91–116. New York: Palgrave.

Sukma, Rizal. 2003. *Islam in Indonesian Foreign Policy*. New York: Routledge Curzon.

Umar, Ahmad Rizky Mardhatillah. 2016. "A Genealogy of Moderate Islam: Governmentality and Discourses of Islam in Indonesia's Foreign Policy." *Studia Islamika* 23 (3): 399–434.

Van Bruinessen, Martin. 2012. "Indonesian Muslims and Their Place in the Larger World of Islam." In *Indonesia Rising: The Repositioning of Asia's Third Giant*, edited by Anthony Reid, 117–140. Singapore: ISEAS.

The White House. "Remarks by the President at the University of Indonesia in Jakarta, Indonesia." The White House, November 10, 2010. https://obamawhitehouse.archives.gov/the-press-office/2010/11/10/remarks-president-university-indonesia-jakarta-indonesia.

Wirajuda, Hassan J. 2011. "Seeds of Democracy in Egypt: Sharing is Caring." *Strategic Review* 1 (1): 147–158.

11
Moderation as Jordanian Soft Power
Islam and Beyond

Stacey Gutkowski

Introduction

The current international relations (IR) debate on religious soft power presents an opportunity to revisit Jordan's strategic deployment of moderation discourse and how religion does and does not function within it. Since the 1950s, the Kingdom of Jordan has asserted its political "moderation" as part of a nation-branding strategy, with Islam playing a greater if complicated role in foreign policy discourse and practice since the 2000s (Gutkowski, 2016). Jordan's moderation discourse is part of a multivectored small state strategy of "omni-balancing" (Ryan 2009) among states upon which the ruling Hashemites depend for support in maintaining regime stability. To contribute to comparative discussion of religious soft power *as* a relationship, this chapter analyzes four pillars of Jordan's foreign relations over the past 20 years: relations with the United States, Europe, Israel, and GCC states. It draws on fieldwork in Jordan in 2013 and 2018, analysis of US religious freedom and relevant European reports 2002–2019, analysis of bilateral aid to Jordan over the same period, media sources, and policy commentary.

This chapter distinguishes between nation branding via a religious idiom as a one-sided, transmission phenomenon and religious soft power as multifaceted relationship between two or more actors. A dance analogy helps illustrate some dynamics of religious soft power as a relationship. We can think of the international system as a ballroom. States are dancers. At moments that are strategically advantageous for both, two states choose to dance with each other. There are different dance steps (foreign policy tactics) to choose from. Depending on what music is playing sometimes states choose to engage in what I call a religious soft-power dance. The right music needs to be playing in the ballroom of international relations for them to choose this dance step.

Stacey Gutkowski, *Moderation as Jordanian Soft Power* In: *The Geopolitics of Religious Soft Power*. Edited by: Peter Mandaville, Oxford University Press. © Oxford University Press 2023. DOI: 10.1093/oso/9780197605806.003.0011

That dance has an end and beginning, may go on for several songs, or may be interrupted by a break and then resume. If the music changes, they may do a different dance step but still together. Dancers may dance with multiple dance partners or refuse an invitation to dance. Finally, many things happen in a ballroom besides dancing (eating, drinking, flirting, gossiping). The same is true in international affairs.

This chapter concludes with some comparative theoretical insights. In addition to the ontological argument that religious soft power is best understood as a relationship, I suggest we might also consider the following.

- A religious soft-power "dance" should be analyzed holistically. We as analysts must account for the full context of interstate relations and engage in two-way process tracing of both states' decision-making, insofar as data gaps allow. The purpose of this methodologically taxing process is to avoid over interpreting the causal role of "religion" or to reproducing Western, Protestant assumptions about what "religion" is.
- Where "religious" activity or discourse is a long-standing part of a diplomatic relationship, we must first determine what is the preexisting baseline for such activity, to understand any divergence, allowing us to determine when a religious soft-power "dance" commences and ends.
- Religious soft-power dances are not always as cooperative as the metaphor implies. We must also account for states simultaneously competing with one another, violently or nonviolently. Indeed, a "hard" and "soft" power distinction often breaks down entirely.

The study of religious soft power would benefit from greater attention to various audiences in the ballroom: state's citizens and also those states not participating in a particular religious soft-power "dance" but keeping close watch on the rhythms of others.

Jordanian Context

In Jordan, there is a small religious soft-power "ecosystem" comprised of institutions and individuals, either parts of the state or working in conjunction with it (Mandaville and Hamid 2018, 10). This "ecosystem" operates within two linked but loose policy regimes of religious soft power, one about moderate Islam and one about interfaith harmony. The traditional Christian churches cluster around the latter. A network of actors, comprised of the royal family, a set of royal institutions, prominent individuals, civil society institutions, and organizations operating under royal ascent have engaged on these issues since the 1980s. There have been several, more intense periods of activity: in the mid-1990s with the signing of the 1994 Wadi Arab treaty with Israel, after 9/11 in the midst of security cooperation with the United States on Iraq and terrorism, and after 2014, accompanying Jordan's participation in the US-led coalition in Syria.

There are several institutions formally dedicated to the promotion of Islamic moderation and positive interfaith relations. Three have royal affiliation: the Royal Aal al-Bayt Institute of Islamic Thought (founded in 1980 to promote Islamic understanding); the Royal Institute for Interfaith Studies (founded in 1994, to promote Christian-Muslim Relations and create a climate for peace following the 1994 treaty with Israel); and the Royal Islamic Strategic Studies Center (founded in 2007 as part of the Royal Aal al-Bayt Institute of Islamic Thought). These institutions have been strongly shaped by the interests and energy of members of the Royal family, particularly a cousin of the King, Prince Ghazi bin Muhammad bin Talal, the former Crown Prince (and uncle of the King) Prince El Hassan bin Talal, and the King himself.

The Royal Aal al-Bayt Institute has a 40-year, distinguished history of Islamic scholarship, publishing and cataloguing important Islamic manuscripts in Arabic, and hosting prominent Islamic thinkers as fellows. Since 1994, the Royal Institute of Interfaith Studies (RIIFS) has run a series of long-term programs and short-term projects. Examples include programs on peace and the arts and on encouraging religious leaders from around the world to support interreligious harmony. RIIFS has also taken a leading role in role in promoting the Amman Message outside Jordan, including training imams and waʿethat in its precepts. The Great Tafsir Project, the publication of translations into English of the great commentaries on the Quran, is one of the most prominent projects of the Royal Islamic Strategic Studies Centre, part of the Royal Aal al-Bayt Institute. Other internationally high profile Royal initiatives include ongoing support for the restoration, maintenance, and promotion of the *Baptism Site of Jesus Christ—Bethany Beyond the Jordan* as a National Park and pilgrimage site (1994–); publication of *The Muslim 500* (2009–), a who's who of globally prominent Muslims; the instigation and annual promotion of UN World Interfaith Harmony Week through events and activities (2010–); publication of a book *Common Ground between Islam and Buddhism* (2010); and initiation of the *Arab-Iberian-American Divan for*

Thought and Cultural Exchange (2017–), a cultural collaboration between Jordan, Spain, and Latin American countries. The Royal Court has also periodically organized ad hoc initiatives related to Islamic moderation and interfaith harmony (Sheline 2020, 122).

There are a handful of notable civil society organizations who are particularly active on interfaith harmony issues. These include the Jordanian Interfaith Coexistence Research Centre, the Catholic Center for Media Studies, which is affiliated with the Roman Catholic Church, and the Community Ecumenical Center. Much of this work is personality-driven, with individuals, many with strong connections to transnational networks including regional church networks (such as the Middle East Council of Churches) and Western churches, playing an important role. The small-scale, elite-driven interfaith harmony regime among civil society consists of a range of annual and ad hoc activities, from interfaith dialogue among clerics, to hosting international visitors, to youth education programs, to social events such as iftar dinners. Funding and the energy of individuals facilitates and limits how much can be done on a regular basis.

Civil society activism by the traditional churches as well as individual Muslim clerics shapes Jordan's engagement in religious soft-power dances transnationally. However, Mandaville and Hamid (2018, 12, 14–15) have noted that what comes out of the Saudi da'wa ecosystem does "not necessarily reflect[. . .] a coherent policy impulse," with some results the product not so much of intended planning but "broad convergence among stakeholders." The same is true in Jordan. These are very small networks of people and there are highly porous boundaries between the official, royal activities and civil society efforts. Because NGOs are not permitted by law to engage in religious activities, civil society activity in this arena is, by definition, state sanctioned. Efforts by Christian clergy are part of a web of long-term interaction with the state, shaped by soft bargaining for policy changes that would benefit and protect Christians, such as the inclusion of Christian history in the official school curriculum. It is a mutually beneficial dynamic: a sufficiently satisfied Christian population is also an important part of Jordan's national brand as a moderately Islamic, religiously plural state (Gutkowski 2016). Still, money and context are paramount. While the Royal Court and parts of civil society may agree that promoting interfaith harmony at home and abroad is a "good thing," the reality is that a long-term economic crisis restricts what is possible. A post-2015 Islamic revival in the public sphere beyond the official state narrative, discussed below, has complicated matters further.

Jordan's claims to moderate Islamic legitimacy are part of a multilevel game in its foreign and domestic policy. The Jordanian policy establishment has mobilized four dimensions of Islamic legitimacy as part of its nation branding. Two interlocking dimensions have been particularly successful with Western audiences: first, Jordan's post-9/11 commitment to countering salafi-jihadist activism at home and abroad and second, Jordan's mobilization of its identity as a haven of Levantine religious coexistence where minorities are protected and celebrated under the paternal, Islamic authority of the King. In turn, two other dimensions target Arab audiences: other states, Arab populations abroad, and its own population. The first dimension is the Hashemite family's claim of Ahl al-bayt (direct descent from the Prophet). This along with Jordan's long-standing custodianship, since 1924, of the Al-Aqsa mosque, support Jordan's claims to moral legitimacy in the Arab world, part of a larger web of highly complex claims to support Palestinian interests. To a population that includes both Palestinians and Transjordanian East Bankers, this strategic narrative serves two purposes. It appeals to broad popular support for Palestine as well as what Sheline (2020, 124) describes as national pride in King Abdullah II as a leader of a state with important religious status.

As a state where 93 percent of citizens are Sunni Muslim, shared social mores and the Islamic legitimacy of Hashemite rule helps underpin national unity in the Kingdom, which has cleavages along class, national (Palestinian–Transjordanian), geographic, and tribal lines. Islamism also remains the primary strand of "loyal" opposition within the Kingdom, though this has begun to slowly evolve since the Arab Spring, with the broadening of youth activism including through the Hirak movement (Ryan 2018). Still, an Islamic milieu saturates even seemingly unrelated policy areas such as refugee policy because it is part of the taken-for-granted fabric of everyday life.

However, there are also myriad, if largely "soft," official state efforts to actively define and monopolize what counts as Islamic legitimacy (*din aldawla*). These are part of long-standing efforts to closely monitor and control religious public space, religious education in public and private institutions, and preaching in mosques, in light of competition from actors representing myriad vernacular conceptions of Islam (*din al-milla*), including competing political parties Islamic Action Front, Du'a party, and the Wasat Party; Hizb al-Tahrir, the traditional Salafists, jihadist Salafists, and da'wa groups; and piety movements (Abu Hanieh 2008). Gradual bureaucratization (Wainscott 2017) and state co-option of Islam culminated in a 1986 royal edict declaring state control and monitoring over all religious instruction in schools and preaching in the kingdom's mosques. This has progressively tightened through the Ministry of Islamic Affairs since 2005, growing stricter since 2015. Still, while Islamists may disagree over *din aldawla* or the direction of state politics, the idea of national unity maintains strong if vague popular legitimacy in Jordan. In turn, the regime has left significant space for Islamists to operate politically. More recently, it has stood back and watched post–Arab Spring fractures within the Muslim Brotherhood and among Islamists, splits which have left those actors capable of winning seats in national elections but not threatening regime stability (Ryan 2018, 73–76) or undermining *din aldawla*.

Using Islamic legitimacy as part of a multiaudience national brand has several in-built structural limitations. First, such branding is a low-impact way of sustaining Jordan's omni-balancing (Ryan 2009) in its interstate relations, without irritating its benefactors. Following a nadir in Western relations in 1991, when King Hussein supported Saddam Hussein during the Gulf War, Jordan has substantially increased its market share of United States and to a lesser extent European overseas funding in the 2000s and 2010s, capitalizing on its consistently pro-Western stance. It has done so by proving itself to be a reliable, amenable partner on both US post-9/11 security goals[1] and European fears of mass refugee flows across their borders, despite substantial drain on the Kingdom's limited monetary and natural resources. Relationships with the United States and European states are based in shared interests—not moderate Islamic religious legitimacy or interfaith aspirations.

Second, such nation branding has had no appreciable impact on Arab interstate relations. Indeed, Jordan's efforts to market a moderate Islamic identity internationally have been surpassed in recent years by better-funded states such as Turkey (Kayaoglu 2015),[2] Qatar, Morocco,[3] and Egypt. Still, Jordan has avoided getting caught out financially after 2011 by the demonization of the Muslim Brotherhood by key allies, including Saudi Arabia (Sheline 2020). Since the Arab Spring and rising Iranian activity in the region, Jordan has successfully cooperated more closely on security issues with its Arab funders in the GCC.

Third, despite state efforts to promote a particular version of Islam domestically, vernacular conceptions of practice and social mobilizations (*din al milla*) have flourished. Ethnographic research shows that the Amman Message have had a limited impact within Jordan (Tobin 2018; Markiewicz

2019; Adely 2012), despite its formal integration into the national school curriculum. Where every day religious toleration or moderation exists, it is a product of quotidian Levantine life at the grassroots, rather than something engineered from above.

In the late 2000s and early 2010s, despite occasional bursts of international activism (such as Prince Ghazi's successful campaign to get the UN to adopt World Interfaith Harmony week, which became the vector for Jordan's activities after its adoption in October 2010), its official efforts at home and abroad suffered "neglect" (Sheline 2020, 123–124). The intersection of long-term economic mismanagement and the strain of the refugee crisis eclipsed "nice to have" policy activity. As Sheline also notes, tension between the General Intelligence Directorate's security-focused approach and the impulses of the religious soft-power ecosystem have also limited official efforts if not good intentions (Abu Rumman and Abu Hanieh 2013, 69–73).

Daesh military successes in neighboring Iraq and Syria in 2014, however, brought new challenges in Jordan. Within Jordan, after brief latitude, there was a swift crackdown on pro-Daesh rallies and individuals, with four pro-Daesh imams banned from preaching in mosques for life (Ryan 2018, 201). The 2016 murder of Nahed Hattar, a journalist from the Christian community known for his pro-Ba'ath views, as he was heading into his trial at the Palace of Justice for insulting Islam showed the regime and Jordanian society how views sympathetic to Daesh had spread, including through the internet. In addition to five attacks by gunmen inspired by Daesh between November 2015 and December 2016, normalization of anti-Shi'a and anti-Christian hate speech on Jordanian social media was part of a broader trend of reassertion of austere Islamic identity in the public sphere beyond the official state narrative. The state responded to this environment through a series of "hard power" security imperatives to contain the reinfiltration of jihadi-salafist activity within Jordan's borders and "soft-power" management techniques to counter online hate speech.

Since Jordan joined the US-led coalition in Syria in September 2014 in response to the rise of Daesh across its border, there have been two subtle shifts within its religious soft-power ecosystem. The first shift is discursive. There has been a revival of Jordan's externally facing Islamic moderation branding alongside a more robust assertion domestically than since the immediate aftermath of the 2005 Al Qaeda attacks in Amman. In 2014, following Daesh's declaration of a caliphate, Prince Ghazi helped to organize an open letter by leading religious scholars to Abu Bakr al-Baghdadi, refuting Daesh's claims

(Mandaville and Hamid 2018, 21). Justifying Jordan's entrance into the Syrian civil war as part of the anti-Daesh military coalition, King Abdullah distinguished between moderation and extremism in speeches to both the UN and Jordan's House of Representatives (Ryan 2018, 44) Addressing the Jordanian people on state television, following the release of the video of the tragic death of Jordanian Air Force pilot Muath al-Kasabeh, burned alive by Daesh in Syria in January 2015, the King argued, "we are waging this war to protect our faith, our values and human principles" (al-Khalidi 2015).

The second shift is institutional. This post-2014 phase in response to Daesh has been marked by a secularization of Jordan's overall approach, with greater state efforts to control and curtail forms of independent religious expression seen as potentially encouraging jihadism. Long-standing state efforts to control preaching in informal and formal mosques intensified after the passing of a new counterterrorism law in 2014, with even tighter, more intrusive guidance from the ministry of Islamic Affairs on mosque sermons (Ryan 2018, 205) and increased surveillance of social media and Islamic religious charitable activity. The General Intelligence Directorate and security services took the lead institutionally rather than religion-related state institutions or civil society, in an expression of hard over soft domestic power. In addition to arresting perpetrators for incitement, the regime also released two leading Salafist ideologues, Muhammad al-Maqdisi and Abu Qatada from prison, in what some analysts have seen as an attempt to divide the movement, eventually reimprisoning al-Maqdisi (Ryan 2018, 204).

Having already positioned itself as moderately Islamic and committed to *wasatiyya* (centrism) prior to the rise of Daesh, Jordan was one of several states in a strong position to attract a new round of Western funding for countering violent extremism (Sheline 2017). A shift is obvious at the discursive level, where a Western discourse of countering violent extremism is visible among a range of Jordanian civil society organizations, including charities and dawa groups. This mirrors what Bettiza (2019) points out about the inculcation of the United States countering violent extremism logic into its religious soft-power activity under the Obama administration.[4] As in the West, this has securitized civil society work which is not security related. For the regime, this has provided an opportunity to kill two birds with one stone. Deepening economic crisis and high unemployment set off a new round of street protests in December 2018, signaling popular discontent with the economy, the pace of post–Arab Spring political reform, and endemic corruption among elites and state institutions. Youth unemployment has climbed to new highs and young people have been at the forefront of pro-reform activism. Western funding for initiatives such as youth social entrepreneurship helps to, as what one Ministry of Youth official quoted by Tauber (2020, 171) called "keep[...] the youth busy," simultaneously offering a narrative to counter Daesh and providing an outlet for middle class aspirations.

Four Religious Soft-Power Dances

Bearing in mind the political and security context, the chapter now turns to four, simultaneous religious soft-power dances that Jordan has engaged in during the 2000s and 2010s. The example of the United States shows Jordan's early energy for "inviting others to dance" in the mid-2000s, while the example of Europe shows the continuation of the dance in the late 2000s and early 2010s, albeit with much-reduced vigor from Jordan. Both of these are cooperative dances. The cases of Israel and GCC states are instances where the two sides grit their teeth and "just dance" with each other on religious matters. They do this across the range of their interstate relations, which precede and will outlast the Western-facing nation-branding exercise.

United States

When considering when religious soft-power dances (relationships) begin and the dynamics of power within them, the order of events matter. The 9/11 attacks led to an almost immediate intensification of US-Jordanian security relations, particularly intelligence sharing on international jihadists, the positioning of troops and equipment, and US training of Jordanian and other militaries and Syrian opposition forces on Jordanian soil. This cooperation explains the trajectory of US aid to Jordan, 2002–2018, and its spikes, as well as the 2001 ratification and 2010 implementation of the US–Jordan Free Trade agreement.

US religious freedom reports on Jordan, 2000–2003, show no real change in US activity beyond its standard human rights advocacy, liaison with the government and civil society organizations, and occasional sponsorship of US-based academics traveling to Jordan to hold workshops on interfaith matters. This is the baseline for diplomatic engagement on religion. The

2004 report (US State Department 2004), however, notes a subtle uptick in Jordanian activity: a 2002 interfaith conference in Amman hosted by Prince Hassan, focused on interfaith dialogue among religious communities in Iraq and the autumn 2003 founding of a new civil society entity, the Jordan Interfaith Coexistence Research Centre. It also notes a new set of US interfaith activities: sponsoring six visitor visas to the United States to engage with civil society there on interfaith matters.

Two Jordan-specific events as well as a third unrelated to both states triggered an intensification of US-Jordanian engagement on religious matters. The first was the first 2004 Amman message. Beginning its life as a sermon given by Jordan's chief justice, Sheikh Iz al-Din al-Tamimi at Amman's al-Hashimiyyin mosque on Laylat al-Qadr, the Amman Message is a statement endorsed by over 500 scholars and political leaders, which defines who is a Muslim under the eight *madhahib* (schools of Islamic jurisprudence); declares illegitimate any declarations of *takfir* (apostasy) against adherents of the eight schools; and declares qualified muftis under the eight schools to be the only legitimate issuers of fatwas (Gutkowski 2016, 211). Its promotion has since helped to facilitate increased US-Jordanian security and political cooperation (Gutkowski 2016, 218). However, Markiewicz (2019, 260) notes that the trigger for the first Amman Message was King Abdullah II's visit to Russia during the Beslan massacre (so not US related). In October 2005, the US government responded to Jordan's "invitation to a religious soft power dance" by funding a conference to commemorate its first anniversary and funding more international visitor programs, including sponsoring a visit by the Supreme Mufti to the United States. The 2005 Religious Freedom report obfuscates the issue of whose initiative was at work, saying that the United States was continuing its multistage program of facilitating the visits of US religious leaders to Jordan and vice versa. However, the reports indicate that prior to this point, exchanges had largely been US religious leaders coming to Jordan, but the Amman message increased reciprocity. The second Jordanian event was the November 9, 2005 Al Qaeda bombings in of three hotels in Amman, which were a seismic shock in Jordan, prompting a wave of anti-jihadist popular sentiment and government activity, deepening US-Jordanian security cooperation. However, a third event entirely separate to Jordan or the US—Pope Benedict XVI's Regensburg lecture on Islam in September 2006—set in motion for Jordan a series of events which led to the 2007 open letter, "A Common Word Between Us and You," reaching out to Christian leaders globally.

During these periods of religious soft-power engagement, how much influence did the United States and Jordan have on one another? In terms of US influence on Jordan, US government Religious Freedom reports produced between 2002 and 2018 provide a running commentary on the ways in which Jordan had or had not progressed in terms of law and practice, from an American perspective. The reports show an intensification of interaction on religious matters, above the 2002 base line. But they also reveal limited US "wins." For example, the Church of Jesus Christ of Latter Day Saints was formally recognized. Jordan also permitted higher numbers of visas for students at evangelical seminaries and has adopted a somewhat more accommodating attitude in practice toward unrecognized Christian evangelical churches, even though legal and social prohibitions to Muslim conversion remain in place. It is hard to discern though to what extent this more accommodating approach is the result of US lobbying or evolving toleration among the traditional Jordanian churches to the presence of new competitors. What is clear from the reports is the extent to which public opinion sets the parameters of policy change in Jordan. For example, proposed changes to the education curriculum to include Christian history, long pursued by Jordanian churches, were blocked in 2019 in response to a public uproar among the Muslim majority. Where there is public outcry or the regime is concerned about calls for political and economic reform, it adopts a status quo approach to religious matters. In turn, a dramatic peak in violent assaults against Muslims in the United States in 2016 (Kishi 2017) and the Trump administration's controversial pursuit of tougher border policies toward travelers and migrant from some Muslim-majority states, starkly show the limitations of Jordanian rhetoric about influencing Islamophobia in the West.

Europe

Since 2004, European partners, particularly in Germany, Denmark and the United Kingdom, have also taken Jordan up on the invitation to engage in a similar religious soft-power dance, funding "religious moderation" initiatives as part of long-term objectives to encourage political liberalization and support independent economic development. For example, between 2007 and 2009, the British Council funded a capacity-building project with the Ministry of Awqaf, targeting Ma'an, a traditional hub of counterregime activism, with the stated aim of "building resilience" among the community and male and female preachers (Markiewicz 2019, 262). Then between 2012 and 2014, a European-Jordanian initiative, though driven by the EU, aimed to spread awareness of the Amman Messages in Europe and the Middle East. The project involved conferences held in five European countries and in Jordan, workshops and trainings for media, projects in schools, two exchanges of imams from the United Kingdom to Jordan and in reverse, and capacity-building programs for Jordanian civil society.

Who impacted whom? On one hand, the Amman Message has been translated from Arabic into five European languages: German, English, Greek, Italian, and Danish (Markiewicz 2019, 264–265). However, with rates of Islamophobia in Europe climbing, and far-right attacks on Muslims escalating from 2018 (Bayrakli and Hafez 2019), Jordan's ability to impact European internal dynamics has been limited (cf. Catto 2017). Jordan's hosting of 2.8 million Syrian and Iraqi refugees who might otherwise make their way to Europe has also helped Jordan evade sharper criticism of its civil and human rights record by European NGOs and IGOs. This, rather than Jordan's ability to project its politically moderate brand, have been the source of what Brannagan and Giuliannotti (2018, 1144) writing about Qatar call a "credible attraction filter." This has allowed Jordan to resist relatively mild European diplomatic pressure regarding political and economic reform and skirt under the radar of European civil society organizations engaged on human rights issues. Analysis of bilateral state funding from the EU and the United States to Jordan, 2002–2018, suggests that neither have financially sanctioned Jordan on matters of religious freedom, despite, for example, on-going concerns regarding issues such as social discrimination against Druze and non-Muslims (US State Department 2017).

Gulf States and Intra-Arab Politics

Since the 2000s, Jordan has had asymmetric relationships with its main Gulf funders, Saudi Arabia, United Arab Emirates, and Qatar (relations with Qatar have declined somewhat though not disappeared since 2017). These have been defined by Jordan's fundamental dependence on Gulf funding to provide public services and service its high public debt. However, in 2004, Jordan invited regional actors, including its funders, to do a new religious soft-power dance step in the region. It neither suffered ill effects from doing so nor made appreciable gains in inter-Arab bilateral relations. Jordan's ability to attract 206 signatories from across 16 Arab states plus Turkey and Iran for its 2004 Amman Message within a one-year window (Grand List 2006) is one example. That state leaders such as then-Egyptian President Hosni Mubarak, then-Iranian President Mahmood Ahmedinejad, and the United Arab Emirates' Shaykh Khalifa bin Zayed Al Nahyan are signatories shows their staff saw little harm in backing a show piece. As Markiewicz (2019, 268) notes, at least one Egyptian signatory did not properly read what he was signing. But his comment "I have confidence in them (the ones who wrote it)" shows that Jordan has successfully socialized itself into some level of long-term, intra-Arab legitimacy in this particular area. Jordan's level of influence is evident in the adoption by other states of its tools of moderate nation branding such as Morocco's 2016 Marakech declaration which echoes themes of the 2004 Amman Message and 2007 A Common Word. But states also come to similar independent conclusions simultaneously. For example, like Jordan, Morocco has also attempted to curtail independent preaching, which deviates from *din aldawla*,[5] including through formal training of imams in "moderate" interpretations of Islam (Boum 2016). However, in the 2010s, Jordan was outspent by regional competitors who also tried to fly the flag of Islamic moderation with mixed success (Sheline 2020).

Post–Arab Spring, Jordan reverted to refugee hosting and military cooperation (backing Saudi counterrevolutionary efforts in Bahrain in 2011–2012 and after 2014 in a US-led coalition involving other Arab states in Syria) as its main dance steps with Arab partners in the international ballroom. From 2011 to 2019, Jordan's primary foreign policy concern was spill over from the war on its border in Syria, followed closely by that in Iraq. Jordanian policymakers feared multiple outcomes: collapse of the Assad regime and "Islamist ascendency in Damascus"; attacks by some of the 2,000 Jordanian salafi-jihadist fighters who had joined Jabhat al Nusra or Daesh in Syria and were poised to return; or infiltration of Jordan by Ba'athist sleeper agents keen to wreak revenge for Jordan's military intervention in Syria, following its alignment with Saudi Arabia and the UAE against the regime (Ryan 2018, 179–187).

As Mandaville and Hamid (2018, 22) have pointed out, promoting Islamic moderation to counter Daesh and Al Qaeda brands of salafi-jihadism has also provided Jordan and other states "with a more palatable message for pushing back against Wahhabi influence—and one less likely to ruffle feathers in Riyadh." This has been particularly important since 2014 when Jordan "expected massive infusions of Saudi aid and investment money"

(Ryan 2018, 186) in exchange for military support and hosting of Syrian and Iraqi refugees. But occasionally political disputes erupt through a religious idiom. One example is a 2019 dispute between Saudi Arabia and Jordan over who should be legitimate custodian of Al-Aqsa. This dispute is a product of Saudi's role in the US Palestinian-Israeli "Deal of the Century," declining Gulf aid to Jordan, and Jordan's unwillingness to fully align itself with Saudi Arabia against Qatar during the blockade (Ayesh 2018). The dispute will almost certainly have no real bearing on long-term arrangements in Jerusalem (cf. Reuters 2017; Times of Israel B 2019). But it shows the parameters of where and how Jordan is willing to mildly assert itself against a major Arab funder, when it feels confident of ongoing cash flow and its indisputable religious legitimacy.

Israel

A religious soft-power dance need not be solely persuasive or cooperative—it may be simultaneously competitive or sometimes exclusively so. Since Israel's capture of the Haram al Sharif in Jerusalem during the 1967 war, Jordan and Israel have been locked together in a long-term religious soft-power dance over the site. Both Jordan and Israel claim international and domestic moral legitimacy from so-called guardianship of the Haram al Sharif—Jordan through its customary custodianship of Al-Aqsa and Israel *de facto* through its territorial state sovereignty and everyday policing of Muslim and non-Muslim entrance to the site. Since the mid-1990s, religious activism at the site by both Palestinian *al murabitun* and *al murabitat* (defenders of the faith) activists, mobilized particularly by the Islamic Movement in Jerusalem in defense of Al-Aqsa and Jewish-Israeli "Third Temple" proponents has increased (Schmitt 2018).

Though a cold peace has held since 1994, the 2014 Israel-Gaza war on the twentieth anniversary of the treaty again inflamed public opinion in Jordan, with a knock-on effect on Jordanian-Israeli relations. Relations experienced a further nadir 2017–2019 (cf. Times of Israel 2019 A), with the Trump administration's move of the American embassy to Jerusalem and the announcement of the "Deal of the Century," terms of which were weighted to Israel's advantage. Contentions over the Haram al Sharif played an outsized symbolic role. The March 2017 stabbing of two police officers at the site and Palestinian protests against Israeli proposals to install security cameras at the site came on top of a series of Israeli proposals in late 2016 and early 2017, which aggravated relations and prompted a Jordanian diplomatic response. Jordan's recall of its ambassador in 2019 over Israel's detention of two Jordanians, as well as Jordan's detention of two Israeli citizens adds to this context (Kavaler 2019), with the run up to the announcement of the Trump administration's "peace" proposal putting additional pressure on parties to take a less conciliatory stance toward each other to gain legitimacy among domestic constituencies. In 2020, the Royal Aal al-Bayt Institute issued a White Paper (in English) on the history of Hashemite custodianship of the Holy Sites and protection of both Muslim and Christian locales, a subtle, "soft" reminder to the world of Jordan's stake in Jerusalem, without the formal, more pointed use of its foreign policy apparatus. The stability and regularity of the competitive religious regime which keeps Jordan, Israel, multiple constituencies of Palestinians and the Waqf locked together in Jerusalem is maintained by the ever-presence of a captive international audience in Western and Arab states who care deeply about symbolic events in the Old City. So, the long, weary dance continues.

Reflecting on Religious Soft Power

What does the case of Jordan suggest for the comparative study of religious soft power? Bettiza (2019, 22) has recently robustly theorized what he calls "an evolving US foreign policy regime complex on religion," expanding midrange IR theory on the subject. First, I briefly consider how his frame could or could not be mobilized for the study of religious soft-power relations in the Middle East. Then I offer some additional reflections for the comparative study of religious soft power in international affairs, integrating insights from Jordan.

Drawing on the IR literature on domestic and foreign policy regimes, Bettiza identifies four US foreign policy regimes regarding religion which emerged in the late 1990s.[6] These four "nested" (overlapping) regimes address religious freedom around the world, faith-based foreign aid, US engagement with the "Muslim world," and religious engagement defined more broadly, with a wider range of states. These mark an important shift in the US approach historically. Prior to the late 1990s, the logic of legal/constitutional/institutional separation of church and state within the context of a highly religious society seeped into policy making, acting as a check on the foreign policy establishment's involvement in religious issues abroad. Bettiza points to a series of events (foreign and domestic "critical junctures") which made possible the successful intervention of what he calls "desecularizing actors" within government and civil society and the evolution of this regime complex. He argues that four logics have driven this process over time: US national interest, the "political-ideological proclivity" of whatever administration is in power, "the United States' own distinctive religious demographics, history and normative arrangements," and the particular interests of "faith-based activists, experts and policymakers that support a particular religious foreign policy regime" (Bettiza 2019, 49–50). These regimes have contributed to what he calls the institutional, epistemic, and ideological desecularization of US foreign policy (Bettiza 2019, 45–46) but also to the wider "religionization" of world politics, due to the sheer weight of the United States in global affairs.

Several of Bettiza's points apply well to a study of religious soft power among Middle Eastern states. These are (1) that policies are a product of short-term events and long-term trends, (2) that path dependency governs policy making, (3) that multiple policy logics shape foreign policy regarding religion, and (4) that American and local actors mutually socialize one another. In this chapter I have problematized slightly Bettiza's assumption that the United States as the stronger state more powerfully socializes others by showing how Jordan, undoubtedly small in global affairs, has been able to capitalize on regional events to gently woo a willing hegemon.

Bettiza's regime framework also has some limitations when applied to Middle Eastern states. Regional powers such as Saudi Arabia and Iran could be said to have formal, multi-strand policy regimes in this area. But for Jordan, a small state with a much more limited set of foreign policy objectives or indeed actors, the term regime can only be used in the loosest sense, as the use of a particular set of discourses and institutions regarding interfaith matters and moderate Islam to further what are its core policy objectives regarding economic survival, internal security, and the survival of the Hashemite regime.[7] Since the 1950s Jordan has periodically used moderation and since 9/11, Jordan has used Islamic moderation, as a wide-ranging "calling card" to the West, to facilitate financial and security support to maintain the regime (Gutkowski 2016). While my analogy of a dance here is not as robust in IR theoretical terms as Bettiza's concept of a regime, its addition captures such important, nuanced dynamics that do not fit neatly into an IR conception of regime.

Beyond Bettiza's starting points, there are several other useful insights from the comparative literature on soft power which could be more fully integrated into midrange theories of religious soft power. First, soft power is, as Brannagan and Giulianotti (2018, 1151) put it, "relational and intersubjective." Religious soft power *is* a relationship, within the context of long-term interstate interaction. It is not something actors can wield or value that they can accrue in the right context, nor is it simply the tactics of cultural diplomacy as a domain of state activity. Wastnidge (2015) has, for example, skillfully disaggregated cultural diplomacy as one domain of Iran's foreign policy activities. Cultural diplomatic methods are undoubtedly one component of a transnational religious soft-power dance. But to see the dance as a whole, to see the full interstate relationship, we would also need to look to other dynamics as well, such as Iranian funding, political support, training or mobilization of nonstate actors around the region. Sometimes Iran has mobilized a shared Shi'a identity construction to partially justify such support, even eliding differences between Iranian Twelver Shi'ism and Alawism or Zaydism to justify support for the Assad regime in Syria or the Houthis in Yemen respectively (Sadeghi-Boroujerdi 2017). At the same time, support for "resistance" factions is determined geostrategically and goes beyond shared Shi'ism, as in Iran's support for Sunni group Hamas (El Husseini 2010) or the secular Ba'ath party in Syria. A more holistic study of foreign policy in the Middle East is more persuasively explanatory than narrowing the lens to "religious" dynamics (cf. Kourgiotis 2020).

This point is related to the as-yet unresolved debate over where or whether to draw a line analytically in the hard–soft power continuum. The literature on religious soft power has thus far focused mainly on nonviolent persuasive activities (cf. Mandaville and Hamid 2018, 7), in line with Nye's original, liberal conceptions of soft and later smart power. Nye has recently introduced a conception of "sharp" power, which includes support for violence and the combination of persuasion and coercion (Nye 2019), but it does not apply well to states like Jordan which are minnows in the pond of international affairs. But as Baldwin (2016) has put it, we are often looking at "a single dimension of something." For example, in Jordan's relations with the United States, Europe, GCC states, and Israel, there is a fundamental blurring between sociocultural dynamics, financial incentives, and security interests, and, perhaps with the exception of Europe, a blurring of cooperative and competitive religious soft-power dances, because Jordan's relations with these states is fundamentally a mixture of cooperation and competition, even if Jordan struggles as an economically weak, small state to make its impact felt.

Religious soft-power relationships also develop within a context of multivectored mobilization of religious symbolism by state and nonstate actors. For example, writing about the Syrian civil war, Pinto (2017) has rightly pointed out that the sectarianization of the conflict unfolded on multiple levels: (1) top down by the Syrian regime, (2) bottom up by society, (3) outside in by regional forces (including Iran), and (4) inside out, spreading sectarianization beyond Syria's borders. Pinto's four-part model is also a useful way of understanding how religious soft-power legitimacy flows. Any account of religious soft power in IR must take into account complexity, accounting for both the multiple "production" and "reception" sides of religio-political discourse, to understand how it is interpreted by and reacted to on both sides of diplomatic activities (Mandaville and Hamid 2018, 13; Koppa 2020) and also by citizens. Citizens confer legitimacy on foreign policy actions, whether it be at the ballot box, online, or in the streets. A religious soft-power dance is seen as legitimate when "citizen[s] rall[y] to" a cause, even if religion plays a latent or taken-for-granted role among all the various, everyday "diverse identities of a citizen" (Harik 2003, 35)—for example, gender, employment, geography, and social class. We can think of legitimacy as conferred when religious or sect identity becomes a "tag identity" (Harik 2003, 35) for citizens. But the dance can just as quickly become illegitimate where people's everyday material needs (for food and shelter) are threatened by the dance. For Jordan, its citizens may rally around Islamic moderation in a time of crisis, such as the murder of Lieutenant al-Kasabeh. But their main demands are for economic growth and political reform, not religious engagement by the state at home or abroad.

Finally, assessing impact of a religious soft-power dance between states is difficult due to data gaps. Properly accounting for impact requires two-way process tracing of (1) all aspects of interstate relationships; (2) decisions to engage in a religious soft-power dance; and (3) possible reasons behind any visible "impacts" of religious soft power, such as shifts in public opinion (cf. Cifti and Tezkür 2014), transfer of funds, or the staging of a public event, as well as process tracing the intersection of these with civil society activity. A theory of religious soft power must also account for the "baseline of religion" in any interactions to determine divergence from it and hence the onset of a religious soft-power dance versus any other kind of dance in international relations.

The reason for attending to the "baseline" carefully is also so as not to inadvertently reproduce Protestant assumptions about what is "religion"

(Asad 1993) in analysis of "religious soft power." If we accept there are no boundaries between religion and other areas of life like politics, the economy, or the military, then this also fundamentally problematizes what we say we are looking at and for when we study religious soft power in international affairs. Are we not just studying the multivectored workings of power?

References

Abu Hanieh, Hassan. 2008. *Women and Politics: From Islamists' Movements Perspectives in Jordan*. Amman: Friedrich Ebert Stiftung.

Abu Rumman, Mohammed, and Hassan Abu Hanieh. 2013. *The Islamic Solution in Jordan*. Amman: Friedrich Ebert Stiftung.

Adely, Fida J. 2012. "God Made Beautiful Things: Proper Faith and Religious Authority in a Jordanian High School." *American Ethnologist* 39 (2): 297–312.

Al-Khalidi, Suleiman. 2015. "Jordanian King Vows 'Relentless' War on Islamic State's Own Ground." *Reuters*. February 4, 2015. https://www.reuters.com/article/us-mideast-crisis-killing/jordanian-king-vows-relentless-war-on-islamic-states-own-groundidUSKBN0L71XE20150204.

Asad, Talal. 1993. *Genealogies of Religion: Disciplines and Reasons of Power in Christianity and Islam*. Baltimore, MD: Johns Hopkins University Press.

Ayesh, Mohammad. 2018. "Why Jordan Needs Saudi Arabia." *Middle East Eye*. June 12, 2018. https://www.middleeasteye.net/opinion/why-jordan-needs-saudi-arabia.

Baldwin, David. 2016. *Power and International Relations: A Conceptual Approach*. Princeton, NJ: Princeton University Press

Bayrakli, Enes, and Farid Hafez, eds. 2019. *European Islamophobia Report 2019*. Ankara: SETA the Foundation for Political, Economic and Social Research. https://www.islamophobiaeurope.com/wp-content/uploads/2020/06/EIR_2019.pdf.

Bettiza, Gregorio. 2019. *Finding Faith in Foreign Policy: Religion and American Diplomacy in a Postsecular World*. New York: Oxford University Press.

Boum, Aomar. 2016. "Morocco's Program for Securing Religious Toleration: A Model for the Region?" *University of Chicago Divinity School*, March 18, 2016. https://divinity.uchicago.edu/sightings/articles/moroccos-program-securing-religious-toleration-model-region.

Brannagon, Paul Michael, and Richard Giulianotti. 2018. "The Soft Power-Soft Disempowerment Nexus: The Case of Qatar." *International Affairs* 94 (5): 1139–1157.

Catto, Rebecca. 2017. "Islam in Europe and the Amman Message: Overview, Challenges and Potentials." In *Muslim Identity in a Turbulent Age: Islamic Extremism and Western Islamophobia*, edited by Mike Hardy, Fiyaz Mughal, and Sarah Markiewicz, 64–97. London: Jessica Kingsley Publishers.

Cifti, Sabri, and Günes Murat Tezkür. 2014. "Soft Power, Religion and Anti-Americanism in the Middle East." *Foreign Policy Analysis* 12: 374–394.

El Husseini, Rola. 2010. "Hezbollah and the Axis of Refusal: Hamas, Iran and Syria." *Third World Quarterly* 31 (5): 803–815. doi:https://doi.org/10.1080/01436597.2010.502695.

Grand List of Endorsements of the Amman Message and Its Three Points. https://amman message.com/grand-list-of-endorsements-of-the-amman-message-and-its-three-points/.

Gutkowski, Stacey. 2016. "We Are the Very Model of a Moderate Muslim State: The Amman Messages and Jordan's Foreign Policy." *International Relations* 30 (2): 206–226.

Gutkowski, Stacey. 2022. "Playing Host Since 1948: Jordan's Refugee Policies and Faith-Based Charity." *The Journal of the Middle East and Africa* 13 (2): 163–184.

Harik, Iliya. 2003. "Towards a New Secularism in Multicultural Societies." In *Lebanon in Limbo, Postwar Society and State in an Uncertain Regional Environment*, edited by Theodor Hanf and Nawaf A. Salam. Mainz, Germany: Conference Proceedings World Conference of Middle Eastern Studies, 2002.

Kavaler, Tara. 2019. "The Israel-Jordan Relationship: Cold, Cyclical and Complicated." *The Media Line*, October 30, 2019. https://themedialine.org/by-region/the-israel-jor dan-relationshipcold-cyclical-and-complicated/.

Kayaoglu, Turan. 2015. "Explaining Interfaith Dialogue in the Muslim World." *Politics and Religion* 8 (2): 236–262.

Kishi, Katayoun. 2019. "Assaults Against Muslims in U.S. Surpass 2001 Level." *Pew Research Centre*, November 15, 2017. https://www.pewresearch.org/fact-tank/2017/11/15/assaultsagainst-muslims-in-u-s-surpass-2001-level/.

Koppa, Maria Eleni. 2020. "Turkey, Iran and Gulf States in the Western Balkans: More Than the Islamic Factor?" *Journal of Contemporary European Studies* 29 (2): 251–263.

Kourgiotis, Panos. 2020. "'Moderate Islam' Made in the United Arab Emirates: Public Diplomacy and the Politics of Containment." *Religions* 11 (43): 1–17.

Mandaville, Peter and Shadi Hamid. 2018. "Islam as Statecraft: How Governments Use Religion in Foreign Policy." New Geopolitics, Foreign Policy at Brookings. https://www.brookings.edu/wpcontent/uploads/2018/11/FP_20181116_islam_as_statecr aft.pdf.

Markiewicz, Sarah L. 2019. "Preaching to the Converted? Interfaith Dialogue versus Interfaith Realities." In *Emergent Religious Pluralisms*, edited by Jan-Jonathan Bock, John Fahy, and Samuel Everett, 251–278. Basingstoke: Palgrave.

Nye, Joseph S. 2019. "Soft Power and Public Diplomacy Revisited." *The Hague Journal of Diplomacy* 14 (1–2): 7–20.

Pinto, Paulo Gabriel Hilu. 2017. "The Shattered Nation: the Sectarianizaiton of the Syrian Conflict." In *Sectarianization: Mapping the New Politics of the Middle East*, edited by Nader Hashemi and Danny Postel, 123–142. New York: Oxford University Press.

Reuters. 2017. "Jordan's King Rejects Change in Status of Jerusalem, Its Holy Sites." *Reuters*. December 13, 2017. https://www.reuters.com/article/us-usa-trump-israel-jordan/jordansking-rejects-change-in-status-of-jerusalem-its-holy-sites-idUSKB N1E715J.

Ryan, Curtis R. 2009. *Inter-Arab Alliances: Regime Security and Jordanian Foreign Policy.* Gainesville: University of Florida Press.

Ryan, Curtis R. 2018. *Jordan and the Arab Uprisings: Regime Survival and Politics Beyond the State.* New York: Columbia University Press.

Sadeghi-Boroujerdi, Eskander. 2017. "Strategic Depth, Counterinsurgency, and the Logic of Sectarianization: the Islamic Republic of Iran's Security Doctrine and its Regional Implications." In *Sectarianization: Mapping the New Politics of the Middle East*, edited by Nader Hashemi and Danny Postel, 159–184. New York: Oxford University Press.

Schmitt, Kenny. 2018. "Ribat in Palestine: The Growth of a Religious Discourse alongside Politicized Religious Practice." *Jerusalem Quarterly* 72 (1): 26–36.
Sheline, Annelle R. 2017. "Middle East Regimes Are Using 'Moderate' Islam to Stay in Power." *The Washington Post*, March 1, 2017. https://www.washingtonpost.com/news/monkeycage/wp/2017/03/01/middle-east-regimes-are-using-moderate-islam-to-stay-in-power/.
Sheline, Annelle R. 2020. "Shifting Reputations for 'Moderation': Evidence from Qatar, Jordan and Morocco." *Middle East Law and Governance* 12 (1): 109–129.
Tauber, Lillian. 2020. "Realms of Influence: The Dynamics of Social Entrepreneurship in the Kingdom of Jordan." PhD dissertation, Durham University.
The Royal Aal al-Bayt Institute of Islamic Thought. 2020. "The Hashemite Custodianship of Jerusalem's Islamic and Christian Holy Sites 1917–2020 CE: White Paper." Amman: The Royal Aal al-Bayt Institute for Islamic Thought. https://www.aalalbayt.org/wp-content/uploads/2020/07/WhitePaper_Jerusalem_3rdEd_web.pdf.
Times of Israel A. 2019. "King Abdullah: Israeli-Jordanian Relations Are at 'An All Time Low.'" *The Times of Israel*, November 22, 2019. https://www.timesofisrael.com/king-abdullah-israeli-jordanianrelations-are-at-an-all-time-low/.
Times of Israel B. 2019. "Jordanian King Says Pressured to Alter Custodianship of Jerusalem Holy Sites." *The Times of Israel*, March 21, 2019. https://www.timesofisrael.com/jordanian-kingsays-pressured-to-alter-custodianship-of-jerusalem-holy-sites/.
Tobin, Sarah A. 2018. "Vernacular Politics, Sectarianism, and National Identity Among Syrian Refugees in Jordan." *Religions* 9 (225): 1–13.
US State Department—Bureau of Democracy, Human Rights and Labor. 2004. "Reports on Religious Freedom: Jordan (2004)." https://www.jewishvirtuallibrary.org/jordan-religious-freedom-report-2004.
US State Department—Bureau of Democracy, Human Rights and Labor. 2017. "Reports on Religious Freedom: Jordan (2017)." https://www.state.gov/wp-content/uploads/2019/01/Jordan-2.pdf.
Wainscott, Ann Marie. 2017. *Bureaucratizing Islam: Morocco and the War on Terror*. Cambridge: Cambridge University Press.
Wastnidge, Edward. 2015. "The Modalities of Iranian Soft Power: From Cultural Diplomacy to Soft War." *Politics* 35 (3–4): 364–377.

12
Israel's Religious Soft Power
Within and Beyond Judaism

Claudia Baumgart-Ochse

Introduction

When Joseph Nye first introduced the term "soft power" into foreign policy research, he defined it as the ability of states "to set the political agenda and determine the framework of debate in a way that shapes others' preferences" (Nye, Jr. 1990, 166). While hard power is the ability to coerce and "grows out of a country's military and economic might," soft power, Nye argues, "arises from the attractiveness of a country's culture, political ideals, and policies" (Nye, Jr. 2004, 265). Soft power, therefore, is "the ability to get what you want through attraction rather than coercion or payments" (Nye, Jr. 2004, 265).

Does the State of Israel have such an ability to attract others and shape their preferences? According to "The Soft Power 30," an annual index which measures the soft power of states by combining data across six categories (Government, Culture, Education, Global Engagement, Enterprise, and Digital) and international polling, Israel ranked 26th among the 30 countries with the greatest resources for soft power in the index's first edition in 2015; the United Kingdom, Germany, the United States, France, and Canada were the top five countries in that year. However, Israel did not appear among the 30 countries with highest scores in soft power in subsequent years; it dropped from the index altogether.

That fact that Israel does not rank high among the states which employ soft power in their foreign policy may not be surprising. Due to its specific history and its geopolitical position in the region, Israel has set other priorities than exercising soft power. The rather short history of the Jewish state has seen a long sequence of wars and military conflicts with its Arab neighbors and the local Palestinian population. The perception of this unstable and hostile security situation is aggravated by the experience of the Nazis' attempt to extinguish the Jewish people in the Holocaust. The State of Israel, though it was conceived by the early Zionists before the Holocaust, is seen as the immediate response to the plight of the Jewish people in 1930s and 1940s Europe and beyond. For the first time in modern history, the founding of the state provided political sovereignty and power to a hitherto dispersed, persecuted and existentially threatened people. Therefore, security has become a core concern of Israeli governments as well as of the Israeli public[1]— so much so that some observers argue that national security has obtained the status of a religion in Israel. A team of researchers at the Jaffee Center for Strategic Studies at Tel Aviv University (today renamed Institute for National Security Studies) has conducted public opinion surveys on national security in Israel since the mid-1980s. They found that Israel's security was such a pervasive issue that the Israeli public developed unique ways to deal with it: "On the symbolic and psychological levels, there are the Almighty and the Jewish people; on the level of rationality and professionalism, there are the Israel Defence Forces, the Mossad, the Shin Bet Kaf (General Security Service) and Israel's other security institutions. Together, they make up a complex mosaic which is at the heart of the religion of security" (Arian 1995, 164).

Against the backdrop of this religion of security, soft power is not regarded the prime foreign policy strategy by Israeli officials. Speaking at the Munich Security Conference in 2017, Israel's defense minister Avigdor Lieberman explicitly denied the value of soft power and said that the chaos and instability in the Middle East today were a result of leaders who lacked 'political determination' and opted for softer, non-kinetic means of diplomacy" (Opall-Rome 2017). The defense minister instead supported a policy toward Iran and other actors in the region which according to Nye's conceptualization qualifies as hard power: "a combination of economic pressure and a very tough policy" (Opall-Rome 2017). Henry Kissinger's famous quote that "Israel has no foreign policy, only domestic politics" (Holbrooke 1976, 157) would thus need to be qualified by the claim that Israel at least has no foreign policy based on soft power. Its preferred currency in foreign policy is hard power which is not least measured in its military capabilities (International Institute for Strategic Studies 2020).

Contrary to this conventional wisdom, I argue that the State of Israel, despite its strong emphasis on national security in a regional and international environment which it perceives as overwhelmingly hostile and untrustworthy, does in fact employ soft power in order to achieve foreign policy goals and shape others' preferences. In particular, Israeli governments have been addressing two distinct civil society audiences in the United States, Israel's most important ally. Israel is the largest recipient of US foreign aid in history and heavily relies upon the US administration's military as well as diplomatic support, for example in the United Nations. Therefore, Israeli governments take great care to maintain this relationship. Both the US American Jewish community as well as US Evangelical Christians are regarded by Israeli officials as being highly influential in setting the political agenda and determining the framework of debate with regard to the State of Israel in a way that shapes the US administration's preferences. Therefore, Israeli governments seek to influence these communities' opinions and actions regarding the Jewish state and its security concerns.

A country's soft power, according to Nye, arises from the attractiveness of its culture, political ideals, and policies. Although religion does not figure separately in Nye's conception, it may constitute an important component of culture as a resource for some states' soft power. In the cases of soft power discussed here, religion is indeed very important—although in different shades of its meaning. Concerning the *Jewish* state's relationship with American *Jewish* diaspora, the word "Jewish" seems to suggest a connection that is exclusively grounded in religion; however, given the ambiguity of the term "Jewish," this relationship encompasses religion, but also goes well beyond religious identity and belief to include secular and ethno-national variants of Jewishness (Waxman and Lasensky 2013, 233). Israel's attractiveness to US American Jews is grounded in its being a cultural-religious symbol for Jewish peoplehood as well as providing a safe haven in times of endangerment of the safety of Jews worldwide.

The State of Israel's projection of soft power into the Evangelical community in the United States also comprises different shades of the culture-religion axis. The Jewish state's attractiveness to Evangelicals in the United States is first and foremost grounded in the significance of the Jewish people and the 'holy land' for the Christian faith; not least is Israel/Palestine the geographical region where Jesus actually lived. At the same time, the State of Israel is also attractive for a certain portion of Evangelical Christians who wish to overcome centuries of Christian contempt for Judaism and seek reconciliation with the Jewish people by way of supporting the Jewish state.

Interestingly, both the literatures on the relationship between Israel and US American Jews and on Israel and US Evangelical Christians have so far focused on the US American side of the equation. Studies on Jewish and Evangelical communities in the United States and their respective relationships with the State of Israel describe the origins, formation and development of these communities and their organizations, their theological and political backgrounds, their shared beliefs and convictions as well as their internal controversies, and the strategies they employ in order to reach out to the United States and, more recently, to the State of Israel.[2] When analyzing the two triangles of actors—US American Jews or US American Evangelicals, the US government, and the Israeli government—most studies look at them from the perspective of the nonstate civil society actors. Both Jews and Evangelicals are depicted as the driving forces in these relationships while the governments are the addressees of their advocacy and actions. The portrayal of these communities as energetic advocates and activists for what they think is good for the State of Israel and the Jewish people is certainly correct; however, the role of the Jewish state in this equation remains somewhat underexposed. In the remainder of this article, I seek to highlight the Israeli government as an actor who intentionally employs the Jewish state's cultural-religious significance for both communities in order to wield soft power and shape not only their preferences, but eventually also the preferences of the US administration on Israel.

From Consensus to Contention: Israel and the American Jewish Community

US American Jews make up the largest Jewish community outside the State of Israel. As of 2019, it comprised around 5.7 million people. This estimate, published by the Jewish People Policy Institute—a branch of the Jewish Agency—relies on findings from the 2013 Pew Report on Jewish Americans (Pew Research Center 2013) and assessments of demographic trends among US Jews since then (Rosner 2019, 22). However, other estimates see the American Jewish population at about 6.7 or even 7 million due to different definitions of "Jewishness," that is, of who should be included in the count (Rosner 2019, 22). For comparison, Israel's population for the first time reached 9 million persons in March 2019. Roughly 79 percent of them were Jews—about 6,66 million (Rosner 2019, 21).[3]

The sheer size of the Jewish community in the United States as well as its location in Israel's most important international ally state make it imperative for the Israeli government to reach out to US American Jews and rally for their support. As Waxman argues, "American Jewish politics directly affects American politics in general, particularly when it comes to Israel. For Israel itself, American Jewish politics is of even greater significance. Indeed, it is perhaps no exaggeration to say that Israel's very future depends in part on whether, and how, American Jews support it" (Waxman 2016, 6). The American Jewish community's advocacy for Israel has become an issue of American domestic politics—"so much so, in fact, that both political parties routinely compete over which one is more pro-Israel [...]" (Waxman 2016, 7). Therefore, Israeli officials and diplomats pay a lot of attention to the American Jewish community as they know how important a source of economic, political, and psychological support it is (Waxman 2016, 7).

Israel's attractiveness to American Jews, the foundation of its soft power, has several sources. Waxman argues that American Jewish "Israelism" rests on five pillars. *Familism* denotes a deep sense of kinship which in turn nurtures a strong sense of responsibility and solidarity among Jews. *Fear* for the safety of Israeli Jews in a hostile Arab environment as well as for the safety of Jews worldwide in the face of anti-Semitism elevates the State of Israel to a safe haven for persecuted Jews which deserves all possible support. *Functionality* describes how supporting Israel has become a "substitute religion" for many secular American Jews—a way "of being Jewish without having to be religious" (Waxman 2016, 26). The religiously grounded attachment is, on the other hand, very important for religious Jews: in the Jewish *faith*, the promised land, given by God to the Jewish people, is of utmost importance and features prominently in theology, belief, rituals and liturgy. Waxman adds one more pillar—*fantasy*—which points to the fact that many American Jews have a romantic and idealistic idea of Israel, of a mythical, imaginary land which has little to do with the real Israel (Waxman 2016, 26–28).

These themes and motives of *Israelism* run through the history of the relationship between Jewish Americans and the State of Israel from the state's founding until today. However, the degree of their importance to American Jews varies depending on their denominational background as well as on the historic-political circumstances. In general, religious Jews—as mentioned above—attach higher value to the State of Israel as the embodiment of Biblical prophecies about the land and people of Israel (Pew Research Center 2013, 13). US American religious Jews' connection to Israel is also affected by historic-political events and developments, but to a lesser degree than secular or traditional Jews' relationship. Under the leadership of rabbis like Joseph B. Soloveitchik, a considerable portion of Orthodoxy in the United

States opened up to modern life and other Jewish denominations—and modern Orthodoxy embraced Israel and Zionist positions on the matter. The Conservative and Reform movements also stressed the religious and ethnic ties to the Jewish State and acknowledged the responsibility to help build the state and secure its existence (Wertheimer 2008, 12–14).

For secular American Jews, on the other hand, their attachment to the Jewish state served as an important way to express their Jewish identity without having to practice the Jewish faith. Rosenthal (2001) describes how American Jews in the post–World War II era moved into the mainstream of American life. Their assimilation entailed the decline of religious observance, and Judaism for many became "increasingly nostalgic and sentimental [. . .]. Israel's image as a secular, progressive, pragmatic, and democratic state accorded with American Jews' self-conceptions and provided a convenient way to present their identity to the larger society" (Rosenthal 2001, XV).

American Jews' support for Israel has seen different stages since World War II. Although Zionist ideology did never take hold among American Jews to a significant degree, they actively supported the establishment of the State of Israel in 1948. Their support consisted of large amounts of money and arms as well as of intensive lobbying of the US administration and Congress on behalf of the fledgling state. However, the interest in Israel declined quickly after 1948; once the state was established, US American Jews returned to their own problems and issues. Among other things, they were concerned about being accused of having "dual loyalties" (Waxman 2016, 34). This concern was fed by declarations made by Israeli officials and Zionist leaders that all Jews should immigrate to Israel at this historic moment in time. Only in the sovereign state of Israel, they argued, could Jewish survival and flourishing be assured. Such statements stemmed from classic Zionism's negative view of the Diaspora which it assumed was doomed to wither. From this perspective, Diaspora communities were expected to play a minor role in Jewish affairs while the State of Israel now took center stage in the future development of the Jewish people. Therefore, Zionists focused on promoting aliyah—immigration to Israel. These calls for immigration, combined with the often articulated claim of Israeli officials to speak on behalf of all Jewry, caused considerable irritation in the American Jewish community who felt quite secure and at home in the United States: American Jews have "maintained an undiminished allegiance and profound gratitude to their land of residence, whose ethos from its inception has been shaped by the belief that America is the new Promised Land" (Wertheimer 2008, 3). It was only after the establishment of the State of Israel that Zionist ideological attitudes softened: "Although *aliyah* remained a core objective, the State of Israel preferred to develop relations with the Jewish communities as a whole [. . .]. Ideological considerations came second to the need to maximise the financial and political support of the Diaspora, which was especially important in the early years of statehood" (Rynhold 2007, 151).

As the Israeli government knew how important and indispensable the financial and political support from American Jews was for the young Jewish state, Prime Minister Ben-Gurion in 1950 consented to publicly announce a policy that was designed to accommodate the American Jewish perspective—he "swallowed his Zionist pride," as Wertheimer writes (Wertheimer 2008, 5). In an agreement with Jacob Blaustein, president of the American Jewish Committee (AJC)—one of the major Jewish organizations in the United States—Ben Gurion declared that American Jews were politically attached to the United States and did not owe political allegiance to the State of Israel; Israel would represent and speak only on behalf of its own citizens and not interfere with the internal affairs in Jewish communities abroad. "Any weakening of American Jewry, any disruption of its communal life, any lowering of its status, is a definite loss to Jews everywhere and to Israel in particular," Ben Gurion asserted. And he explained that Israel's "success or failure depends in large measure on our cooperation with, and on the strength of, the great Jewish community of the United States" (American Jewish Committee 1964, 55). Blaustein assured Ben Gurion of the Jewish community's support for the State of Israel, while at the same time stressing that American Jews repudiated "any suggestion or implication that they are in exile. American Jews—young and old alike, Zionists and non-Zionists alike—are profoundly attached to America" (American Jewish Committee 1964, 55).

The Ben-Gurion-Blaustein-agreement shows the readiness of the Israeli government to trade ideology for practical considerations and accommodate the concerns of the American Jewish community. Although Israeli politicians "retained a disdain for Diaspora lobbying" (Rynhold 2007, 152), they took into consideration the concerns and criticism of US American Jews because they needed their support; in other words, they adjusted their soft power as to keep the flame of Israelism burning.

Such diplomatic maneuvers were hardly necessary after 1967. The Six-Day war not only fundamentally changed the Israeli polity and its geography, it also had profound impact on the American Jewish community.

The fear of the imminent assault on Israel in the weeks preceding the war as well as the euphoria about the sweeping victory were closely followed by American Jews: "The widespread fear of a second Holocaust prior to the war, followed by the relief and jubilation felt after Israel's swift and stunning victory, led to a spontaneous outpouring of support for Israel from American Jews" (Waxman 2016, 35). The 1967 war forged a new Jewish American unanimity on Israel; the Jewish state had become the new civil religion of American Jews, and its heroes were Israeli officials like Moshe Dayan and Abba Eban (Rosenthal 2001, xvi). Israel's soft power reached its peak. The Jewish state was seen by American Jews as the culmination of Jewish history, as the highest expression of virtue and essential component of Jewish identity. Therefore, they were ready to provide all possible financial and political support "for whatever goals or policies the Jewish state chose to pursue. Critics of Israel were simply read out of the organized Jewish community" (Rosenthal 2001, 1).

But even in these days of unwavering support did Israel remain a religious-cultural symbol rather than a real country in the minds of most US American Jews. Few were actually interested in or had knowledge about Israel's actual society and politics. It was possibly this discrepancy between the imaginary, idealized Israel which figured so prominently in American Jewish identity and the real Israel which was largely unknown to Jews abroad that allowed for the unprecedented level of support to the State of Israel in the 1960s and 1970s. The Israeli government did not have to put much effort into its attractiveness to American Jews in order to exert soft power. Rather, it could build on the cultural and especially religious traditions, symbols and motives which elevated Israel to a special place in collective Jewish memory: "At different times, Israel symbolized very different aspects of Jewish civilization—liberation from exile, David fighting Goliath, Jewish cultural renaissance, concern for fellow Jews, and religious renewal" (Wertheimer 2008, 78).

The "American Jewish romance" (Finkelstein 2012) or "love affair" (Rosenthal 2001) with Israel began to wane in the late 1970s; since then, there has been increasing "trouble in the tribe" (Waxman 2016). The euphoria of the post-1967 period evaporated when in 1977 for the first time a right-wing government under Menachem Begin from the Likud party took power. Israel under Begin looked much more right-wing, religious, intolerant and expansionist than the egalitarian, progressive and peace-loving Israel that many US American Jews were attached to. A series of events changed the attitude of Jewish Americans toward the State of Israel. The occupation of Palestinian territories took on increasingly repressive and violent features. The massacre of Palestinian civilians in the refugee camp of Sabra and Shatila in the wake of the Lebanon war in 1982, carried out by Israel's allied Phalangist militias, profoundly shook Jewish Americans' perspective on Israel. The first Intifada and Israel's harsh crack down on it further spurred massive criticism and disillusionment with Israel. Israel, once revered for maintaining its democratic character and its moral army in the face of a hostile environment, now became the oppressor and occupier in the eyes of many Jews in the United States and beyond. This impression was reinforced by the fact that more US American Jews began to actually visit Israel and thus were confronted with the real Israel instead of its idealized version (Waxman 2016, 46). While general support of a Jewish state—be it as fulfilment of Biblical prophecy, culmination of Jewish civilization, or as a safe haven for threatened and persecuted Jews—remained an important element of Jewish identity in the United States, many American Jews began to view critically the actual day-to-day policies of the Israeli state and its institutions.

The Israeli-Palestinian conflict and its repercussions on the Jewish state began to take center stage in US American Jews' engagement with Israel. It changed both the terms of the debate among American Jews as well as the ways in which this engagement was operatively channeled. While the 1960s were largely characterized by a broad consensus among the American Jewish community and their lobby organizations on the Jewish state, the debate became successively more pluralistic and even polarized. The controversy about the right way of going forward with the Israeli-Palestinian conflict was accompanied by a profound change in the ways US American Jews organize and lobby on behalf of Israel. While US-Jewry/Israel-relations until the 1980s have been characterized by what Sasson calls mass mobilization, the new way of connecting with Israel is via direct engagement. Mass mobilization rested on "large, centralized core organizations of American Jewry" (Sasson 2010, 175), most notably the AJC, the Council of Jewish Federations (CJF), the Conference of Presidents of Major American Jewish Organizations (CPMAJO), and later the American Israel Public Affairs Committee (AIPAC). They raised funds and advocated politically for Israel along the lines of the Israeli government's policies. The State of Israel, for its part, used governmental as well as quasi-governmental institutions such as the Diaspora ministry and the Jewish Agency in order to facilitate cooperation and handle the huge amounts of donations from US American Jews as well as issues such as travel and immigration.

Sasson describes that the first crack in the united front of Jewish organizations was provoked by the right, not by the Israeli left. After the Oslo Accords were announced, Benjamin Netanyahu, head of the opposition Likud party, "traveled to the U.S. to rally American Jewish opposition to the pact" (Sasson 2010, 177). Netanyahu convinced right-leaning American organizations such as the Zionist Organization of America to lobby Congress to attach conditions to assistance to the Palestinian Authority—"against the wishes of the Israeli government and AIPAC" (Sasson 2010). Left-leaning organizations such as Americans for Peace Now in turn lobbied in support of the Accords. Since then, new organizations on both sides of the spectrum have emerged which depart from the consensual mode of the traditional Jewish American lobby organizations and pursue either hawkish or dovish policies in parallel to the Israeli divide over the conflict. "While mainstream lobbying organizations such as AIPAC typically seek to promote the policies favored by the Israeli government, the new partisan organizations have pursued their own political agendas, promoting more hawkish or dovish policies" (Sasson 2010, 177).[4] The new pattern of direct engagement is also reflected in fundraising for Israel. While the collecting of funds for Israel was mainly a centralized process handled by the United Jewish Appeal, now many smaller organizations raise money for specific projects and organizations in Israel which are in line with their political stances. In addition, American Jews increasingly spend time working and living part-time in Israel and regularly consume Israeli news and culture, thereby gaining a direct and individual impression of state and society in Israel (Sasson 2010, 186).

With the emergence of new organizations on the left and on the right, Israeli governments now had to deal with a range of organizations and diverging political positions within the American Jewish community. Against the background of the Israeli-Palestinian conflict, Israel's attractiveness for US American Jews has decreased. While most US American Jews still stand with Israel in general terms, they frequently voice criticism and diverging opinions on the Israeli government's policies, in particular with regard to the conflict with the Palestinians. An increasing camp of young American Jewish activists openly departs from former generations' uncritical advocacy for the Jewish state's policies. Instead, these activists participate in an emergent Jewish-Palestinian solidarity movement, merging ideas of social justice and human rights with a reframed Jewish identity which emphasizes the prophetic and social justice oriented character of Judaism (Omer 2019).

Israeli officials—the President, the Prime Minister, and other government ministers—still do not miss a single big conference of the traditional lobby organizations such as AJC, AIPAC, or CPMAJO in order to project the state's soft power by evoking Jewish solidarity. However, giving welcoming speeches at these conferences does not exhaust the repertoire of soft power deployed by the state.

Since the late 1990s, Israel has tried to adapt to the new plurality of views as well as the more direct and individual forms of engagement of American Jews with Israel. The Israeli government is among the major funders of the so-called Taglit-Birthright program. The homeland tourism program Taglit-Birthright is targeted at young Jewish adults at the age of 18 to 26. The program especially reaches out to Jews outside Israel who are not already involved in Diaspora organizations. Taglit-Birthright brings them to Israel for 10-day educational trips which are organized by several tour organizations. The organization oversees the program and, most importantly, designs and regulates its educational content. Since its inception, more than 750.000 young Jewish adults from around the world have visited Israel on one of these trips.

Based on the literature on diaspora politics, Abramson analyses homeland tourism "as an attempt to construct a diasporic identity"; such "diasporization" is "used by political actors within the state and outside of it to diasporize the participants—to transform a land into a homeland and create a sense of collective identity across borders" (Abramson 2017, 15). Taglit-Birthright was founded against the background of growing concerns among American Jewish organizations about Jewish continuity due to high rates of inter-marriage and processes of assimilation and secularization in the United States. However, the idea was first brought up by Israeli Deputy Minister of Foreign Affairs, Yossi Beilin, and then taken up by Jewish philanthropists as well as major US Jewish organizations. Today, the goals of Taglit-Birthright reach beyond the US context and explicitly include the relationship to and support of the State of Israel: "Birthright Israel seeks to ensure the future of the Jewish people by strengthening Jewish identity, Jewish communities, and connection with Israel via a trip to Israel for the majority of Jewish young adults from around the world. [. . .] Our hope is that our trips motivate young people to continue to explore their Jewish identity and support for Israel and maintain long-lasting connections with the Israelis they meet on their trip" (Birthright Israel 2012). In order to achieve these goals, the trips focus on three core themes: narratives of the Jewish people, contemporary Israel, and ideas and values of the Jewish people (Birthright Israel 2012, 6–7). The groups visit historical and religious sites in Israel such as Yad Vashem, the City of David, or Independence Hall. All groups also visit Masada, the Western Wall in the Old City of Jerusalem, as well as the Knesset or the Supreme Court.

The strategic attempt to construct a diasporic identity through direct, physical experience of the homeland and personal encounters with Israeli and other Jewish peers includes three processes according to Abramson: a certain territory is transformed into a homeland in parallel to the existing home at the country of residence; a narrative of dispersion is created and shared among co-ethnics or co-citizens across borders; and a group membership is demarcated—"crystallizing a group identity vis-à-vis excluded others" (Abramson 2017, 15). In addition to tools for diasporization such as storytelling (e.g., by the tour guide), physical engagement (e.g., hiking) and group crystallization, the program uses rituals in order to create attachment to the land. The borderlines between secular and religious rituals and ceremonies are being blurred—ranging from dancing at sunset in front of the Western Wall to lighting candles at Shabbat, group blessings or personal prayers upon reaching the top of Masada (Abramson 2017, 19). As one of the major funders of Taglit-Birthright, the State of Israel can certainly be said to employ some sort of religious soft power via these trips, seeking to build long-lasting support from American Jews by acquainting them with the "homeland," its culture, society, history, and, not least, its religious tradition.

Steadfast Support: Israel and US American Evangelical Christians

The intense lobby work of the American Jewish community certainly helps explaining why Israel plays such a prominent role in US foreign policy, at times even outdoing other major global concerns such as the rise of China or the Syrian war. However, as Miller argues, "the American constituency most supportive of Israel is not Jews but fundamentalist and evangelical Christians" (Miller 2014, 8). In 2013, the Pew Forum on Religion and Public Life reported that 82 percent of Evangelicals "believed that Israel was given to the Jewish people by God—more than double the percentage of American Jews who held this belief [. . .]" (Miller 2014). A recent Pew Research Center survey found that Jewish Americans, despite their strong attachment to Israel, are divided in their assessment of the Trump administration's policies toward Israel such as moving the US embassy to Jerusalem and recognizing Israel's sovereignty over the Golan heights: "Roughly four-in-ten (42%) say they think Trump is favoring the Israelis too much, while a similar share (47%) say he is striking the right balance between the Israelis and Palestinians" (Smith 2019). By contrast, 72 percent of Evangelical Protestants say they think Trump strikes the right balance between the Israelis and Palestinians, and 15 percent say that Trump favors the Israelis too much (Smith 2019).

The Evangelical supporters of the State of Israel are often called Christian Zionists, combining Christian belief and the specific Jewish nationalism which has its origins in 19th century Europe. The literature which seeks to explain Christian Zionists' strong attachment to Israel focuses predominantly on specific religious and theological beliefs and ideas. The theology of premillennial dispensationalism gets by far the most attention, probably due to its fascinating strangeness in the eyes of mostly secular social scientists.[5] Premillennial dispensationalism was conceived and disseminated in the mid-nineteenth century by the Anglican dissenter John Nelson Darby. Conventionally, the Christian tradition held by-and-large that the Jews had lost their status as a "chosen people" when they rejected Jesus as the Messiah; instead, the church inherited God's covenant. Darby and his successors rejected what is commonly known as "replacement theology." Based on his reading of the Bible, Darby divided salvation history in seven epochs which he called dispensations. The so-called Church Age or Great Parenthesis is the sixth and current dispensation. Once the church has fulfilled its role, Christian believers will be "physically carried off into the clouds to be safe with Christ in an event called the Rapture" (Spector 2009, 14). After this rapture and a so-called tribulation of seven years, Jesus is expected to destroy the enemy at Armageddon and install his throne in Jerusalem (Hummel 2019, 12). The Jews play an important role in that tribulation as there "will be an opening of the eyes of some Jews to the truth of Jesus Christ. These Jewish believers will then evangelize the remaining Gentiles" (Shapiro 2015, 11). Thus, the Jews are being ascribed a new centrality in the unfolding of divine history, quite contrary to previous replacement theology. God's covenant with the Jewish people has never been repealed, his promises to the Jewish people are still valid today.

In the United States, Christian Zionist ideas appeared already in the late 19th century, promoted by the dispensationalist William E. Blackstone (Shindler 2000, 157). The founding of the Jewish state in 1948 and the subsequent wars are seen by dispensationalists as clear signs that the end times are near. As Spector notes: "At the center of the dispensational system is the idea that the Jews would establish their own state. Without that, there would be no Antichrist, no tribulation, no battle of Armageddon, and no Second Coming" (Spector 2009, 14–15).

The majority of Christian Zionists believe in dispensationalism to some degree. Some observers argue that their support and attachment to Israel runs so deep that Christian Zionism has developed into an outsider diaspora nationalism. The performance of Zionism by Evangelical Christians, Sturm (2018) argues, is actually a performance of their religion and not just an instrumental use of religion for nationalist ideologies: Judaism, Jews and Israel "are essential parts to the performance, and therefore practice, of their religion, regardless of them serving an imminent/immanent function in the continuum of history" (Sturm 2018, 302). As Christian Zionists' perception of End Times draws closer, Sturm shows how their national loyalty is in the process of shifting from America to Israel.

However, there are also other currents in contemporary Evangelicalism. Many Evangelicals base their support for Israel less on sophisticated apocalyptic theories and more on basic biblical teachings. In the center of what Mohr (2013) calls Biblical Christian Zionism stands Genesis 12:3 which connects the welfare of peoples to the way they treat Israel: "And I will bless them that bless thee, And curse him that curseth thee: And in thee shall all families of the earth be blessed" (The Bible). Not least because critics argue that dispensationalists only support the Jewish people due to their pivotal role in the end times, knowing that many Jews will be killed during the tribulation, Christian Zionist organizations tend to downplay dispensational theology and instead emphasize scripture which highlights God's continuous covenant with the Jewish people. Therefore, Genesis 12:3 is like a common denominator of Christian Zionism today, allowing for interreligious cooperation with Jewish organizations and individuals.

At the progressive end of the Evangelical spectrum, Christian ethics play a more important role than apocalyptic scenarios in explaining support for modern Israel. Against the background of recent history in which the Jews of Europe suffered extraordinary cruelties at the hand of Christians, liberal churches seek to complete the work of the Reformation, fight anti-Semitism and make amends for past sins by protecting and supporting Jews and the Jewish state (Mead 2008, 31). Thus, the quest for reconciliation has become a driving force for pro-Israel activism (Hummel 2019).

The dominant focus in the literature on specific religious ideas has led to the impression that Christian Zionism is a direct consequence of Evangelical theology. In a recent book, Hummel posits instead that "the evangelical political movement to support Israel is a product of advocacy, organizing, and cooperation beginning after the founding of the state of Israel in 1948 and advancing significantly in the wake of the 1967 Arab-Israeli War" (Hummel 2019, 8). Instead of assuming a simplistic translation of religious ideas into political action, Hummel emphasizes a range of factors—and one of them is the active engagement of the State of Israel. The Christian Zionist movement, Hummel argues, is "built on three pillars of recent origin: interreligious encounter, support by the government of Israel and by American Jewish allies, and changing evangelical attitudes toward political mobilization. [. . .] The rise of the Christian Zionist movement required strategic leadership, theological interreligious cooperation, political mobilization, and state-to-state diplomacy." In his book, Hummel presents an impressive historical account of all of these factors—including the State of Israel's role: "Outside actors—the government of Israel chief among them—have been constitutive to creating modern evangelical Christian Zionism and, by extension, modern conservative evangelical politics" (Hummel 2019, 15).

Israel, which sought to improve its image and searched for international support, recognized early on the potential of Christian Zionist interest in Israel. When in the 1950s the American G. Douglas Young founded the American Institute of Holy Land Studies and began to call US-Evangelicals' attention to the political implications of dispensational theology, the Israeli government was at first concerned about possible missionary ambitions. Later on, after Young had moved to Israel and dispersed those concerns, he and his institute enjoyed the support of the Israeli government—and especially the foreign ministry—for their efforts to mobilize a new generation of Evangelicals for Israel. From 1967 through 1973, Hummel reports, "Young spoke as many as 200 times a month throughout Europe and North America, often under the auspices of Israel's Ministry of Tourism" (Hummel 2019, 49). During the same period, Israeli officials such as Yitzhak Rabin made first appearances before US Evangelical audiences, and prominent Evangelicals such as Billy Graham voiced their support for Israel and sought alignment with American Jews as well as the State of Israel.

Israel actively worked to gather Evangelical support for its policies after the 1967 war in which it had occupied the Golan Heights, the Gaza Strip, the West Bank and East Jerusalem with the Temple Mount and the Old

City. Confronted with increasing criticism—not only from states and international institutions, but also from Catholic and mainline Protestant churches—Israel, in cooperation with American Jewish defense organizations, sought to "create an evangelical pro-Israel movement that would advance Israeli national interests in the American public and apply electoral pressure in support of Israeli policies" (Hummel 2019, 65). Shortly after the war, Yona Malachy, deputy director of the Christian Desk in Israel's foreign ministry, undertook a study tour of US Protestant seminaries and colleges, including Ivy League universities such as Harvard and Princeton, but also conservative Evangelical colleges. There he found widespread belief in dispensational theology and Israel's prophetic significance, but little transfer of these beliefs into tangible political action on behalf of Israel (Hummel 2019, 70). Therefore, part of the effort to reach out to conservative Evangelicals was to convey the ample importance of the actual land to Jewish peoplehood. This was to be achieved by Jewish scholars who engaged in interreligious Jewish-Christian research and dialogue and taught their Christian counterparts about the centrality of the land and the State of Israel in Jewish self-understanding (Hummel 2019, 68–69). Among Evangelicals who believed that the 1967 war was a fulfilment of Biblical prophecy before the Second Coming, this outreach fell on fertile ground.

In 1971, conservative Evangelicals organized a Bible prophecy conference in Jerusalem. The conference was attended by 1400 US American Christians. Israel's government provided the Jerusalem Convention Center free of charge, and former Prime Minister David Ben-Gurion addressed the conference and talked about Israel as the land of the Jewish people. This conference is seen as helping to spur two important developments: large-scale Evangelical tourism to Israel and an increasingly close alliance between Israel's conservative party, Likud, and Christian Zionists (Belhassen and Ebel 2009, 363; Spector 2009, 146).

Interestingly, by vigorously promoting Evangelical tourism to the Holy Land, Israel used a similar strategy to employ religious soft power as it did later in the case of the Birthright Israel tours for American Jews discussed above: facilitating direct experience of the physical land, combined with the dissemination of a specific ideological-religious framing of this encounter. From the 1970s on, the Israeli Ministry of Tourism brought "hundreds of evangelical pastors to the Jewish state at no charge" (Spector 2009, 146). In the following decades, the number of organizers of Holy Land tours grew steadily. Belhassen-Ebel sees four different actors involved in this endeavor: Christian Zionist organizations such as the International Christian Embassy Jerusalem (ICEJ), grass-roots tour organizers in the United States, the tourists or pilgrims themselves, and Israeli officials who choose to promote Christian Zionist tourism due to its Zionist orientation and economical value (Belhassen and Ebel 2009, 367). The Ministry of Tourism worked closely with Christian Zionists; it acted

> as a gatekeeper, promoting familiar evangelical leaders and sidelining those who fell outside its political goals. Longtime evangelical allies helped marketing firms and government ministries develop strategies for Holy Land tourism, creating the Christian Zionist pitches to evangelical tourists: Israel as the homeland of Judaism and Christianity; the modern state of Israel as a sacred expression of biblical prophecy; Israel as a unique site of interreligious reconciliation. (Hummel 2019, 84)

Weber has called these tours "tour bus diplomacy," pointing to the instrumental value of this strategy of projecting religious soft power in order to influence American politics toward Israel (Weber 2005, 220–222).

In addition to this level of practical support for Christian Zionist Holy Land tourism, Israeli leaders sought to build and benefit from personal relationships to Christian Zionist leaders. Golda Meir, for example, sought the help of Billy Graham who was close to President Nixon when diplomatic relations were at a low during the Nixon years (Hummel 2019, 73). The relationship between Israel and Christian Zionists became even closer—or "symbiotic," as Shindler (2000, 156) argues—when Likud came into government in 1977. Despite the theological-political peculiarities of dispensationalism which saw the Jews as an instrument in bringing about the second coming of Jesus, the Likud nevertheless wished to strengthen the ties with the Christian right and the Republicans "in order to maintain a Congressional bulwark against Presidential moves toward a peace settlement in the Middle East" (Shindler 2000, 169). Prime Minister Menachem Begin cultivated a special relationship with Christian Zionist leaders, most notably the televangelist Jerry Falwell. The rise of the Likud and its embrace of the messianic traits of national-religious Zionism—epitomized in the settler movement in the occupied territories—coincided with the rise of conservative Evangelicalism in the United States, most visible in the increasing political influence of Falwell's organization "Moral Majority." Christian Zionist support, Shindler finds, "proved to be important for successive Likud governments because there was a common ideological denominator in retaining territory and a willingness vociferously to promote it in the White House and US government circles" (Shindler 2000, 165).

This special relationship between Israeli officials, mostly from the Likud, and Christian Zionists has endured up to the present age. Benjamin Netanyahu invested heavily in personal ties with Christian Zionist leaders in both his tenures as Prime Minister of Israel. Back in the 1990s, he enlisted them in his efforts to roll back the Oslo peace process which was based on territorial compromise. In his second stint as head of government from 2009 to 2020, he again sought Christian Zionists' support for his uncompromising stance on territorial issues. At a virtual conference of Christians United for Israel (CUFI), currently the most important Evangelical lobby organization for Israel in the United States, Netanyahu said that Biblical sites such as the Jewish settlements Beit El and Shiloh were "an integral part of the historic Jewish homeland" and "these places are also an integral part of Christian identity, part of your heritage and of our common civilization." He added that "under Israeli sovereignty, this heritage will be forever protected" (Tibon 2020). He praised then-US president Donald Trump for presenting a Middle East plan that would have allowed Israel to annex these territories which have been under military occupation since 1967. Netanyahu utilized the fact that Donald Trump rallied for the Evangelical vote in the 2020 election. During the Trump years, Evangelical Christians "reached the zenith of political power in Washington," shaping a range of US policies, including on Israel and the Israeli-Palestinian conflict (Lynch 2021). Therefore, the Israeli government had considerable incentives to influence the Evangelical constituency in its own direction by using the religious soft power at its disposal. Its zenith might now lie behind Christian Zionism. Naftali Bennett, who became Prime Minister in 2021, had a somewhat rough start regarding his government's standing in Christian Zionist circles. Evangelicals criticized the right-wing, religious-nationalist politician Bennett for joining a government with centrist Israeli parties and even an Arab Israeli party, thereby sparking fears of renewed chances for a two-state solution. In addition, polls show that the support for Israel among young US Evangelicals has considerably dropped in recent years (Lynch 2021). It remains to be seen how the new government will adjust its religious soft power in the light of these developments.

Israel's Religious Soft Power

The Israeli government is in a unique position for exercising religious soft power. The small territory at the Mediterranean has been the site of both the history of the Jewish people as well as the early history of Christendom. The stories of the Hebrew Bible and the New Testament—those pertaining to the past and those telling of the future—are deeply entwined with the landscape and locations which make up this territory. Both communities described above have their very own motivations and reasons to support the Jewish state. However, this paper has shown how Israeli governments skillfully use the religious traditions, beliefs, imagery, and hopes tied to Erez Israel/ the Holy Land in order to strengthen the bonds of these communities with the State of Israel. Given the size and importance of Jewish and Evangelical communities in the United States, they often prove to be crucial in US elections. Therefore, Israeli officials have a considerable interest in obtaining their support in order to determine the framework of debate in a way that shapes the US administration's preferences with regard to Israel.

Among a variety of strategies for employing religious soft power, the government's promotion and support of bringing both American Jews and American Evangelicals to Israel stands out. The government's financial and organizational involvement in these touristic trips is geared toward ensuring that visitors are provided with an image of Israel which reflects the state's ideological foundations as well as its policies on various issues. The trips are carefully designed to combine religious and cultural experiences with an overall political message to support the contemporary State of Israel. Therefore, the instrument of tourism seems to be an important tool for exercising Israel's religious soft power to these specific religious-cultural communities in the United States.

References

Abramson, Yehonatan. 2017. "Making a Homeland, Constructing a Diaspora: The Case of Taglit-Birthright Israel." *Political Geography* 58: 14–23.

American Jewish Committee. 1964. *In Vigilant Brotherhood. The American Jewish Committee's Relationship to Palestine and Israel*. New York: Institute of Human Relations.

Arian, Asher. 1995. *Security Threatened. Surveying Israeli Opinion on Peace and War*. Cambridge: Cambridge University Press.

Belhassen, Yaniv, and Jonathan Ebel. 2009. "Tourism, Faith and Politics in the Holy Land: An Ideological Analysis of Evangelical Pilgrimage." *Current Issues in Tourism* 12 (4): 359–378.
Birthright Israel. n.d. https://www.birthrightisrael.com/about-us.
Birthright Israel. 2012. *The Educational Platform: Standards and Requirements.* New York: Birthright Israel Foundation. www.birthrightisrael.com/TaglitBirthright IsraelStory/Documents/Educational-Platform.pdf.
Finkelstein, Norman. 2012. *Knowing Too Much: Why the American Jewish Romance with Israel Is Coming to an End* [eng]. New York: OR Books.
Haija, Rammy M. 2006. "The Armageddon Lobby: Dispensationalist Christian Zionism and the Shaping of US Policy Towards Israel-Palestine." *Holy Land Studies: A Multidisciplinary Journal* 5 (1): 75–95.
Holbrooke, Richard. 1976. "Censored in Israel." *New York Times*, May 30, 1976. https://www.nytimes.com/1976/05/30/archives/censored-in-israel-the-secret-conversations-of-henry-kissinger.html.
Hummel, Daniel G. 2019. *Covenant Brothers: Evangelicals, Jews, and U.S.-Israeli Relations.* Philadelphia: University of Pennsylvania Press.
International Institute for Strategic Studies. 2020. *The Military Balance 2020*. London.
Lynch, Colum. 2021. "What's Next for Christian Zionists?" *Foreign Policy*, July 19, 2021. https://foreignpolicy.com/2021/07/19/christian-zionists-israel-trump-netanyahu-evangelicals/.
Maoz, Zeev. 2006. *Defending the Holy Land: A Critical Analysis of Israel's Security & Foreign Policy*. Ann Arbor: University of Michigan Press.
Mead, Walter R. 2008. "The New Israel and the Old. Why Gentile Americans Back the Jewish State." *Foreign Affairs* (July/August) 87 (4): 28–46.
Mearsheimer, John J., and Stephen M. Walt. 2007. *The Israel Lobby and U.S. Foreign Policy*. New York: Farrar, Straus and Giroux.
Miller, Paul D. 2014. "Evangelicals, Israel, and U.S. Foreign Policy." *Survival* 56 (1): 7–26.
Mohr, Samuel. 2013. "Understanding American Christian Zionism: Case Studies of Christians United for Israel and Christian Friends of Israeli Communities." *Journal of Politics & International Studies* 9: 287–331.
Nye, Jr., Joseph S. 1990. "Soft Power." *Foreign Policy* (80): 153–171.
Nye, Jr., Joseph S. 2004. "Soft Power and American Foreign Policy." *Political Science Quarterly* 119 (2): 255–270.
Omer, Atalia. 2019. *Days of Awe: Reimagining Jewishness in Solidarity with Palestinians.* Chicago: The University of Chicago Press.
Opall-Rome, Barbara. 2017. "Israel Defense Minister Disses "Soft Power" at Munich Security Conference." *DefenseNews*, February 19, 2017. https://www.defensenews.com/global/mideast-africa/2017/02/19/israel-defense-minister-disses-soft-power-at-munich-security-conference/.
Pew Research Center. 2013. "A Portrait of Jewish Americans: An Overview." *Pew Research Center*, July 10, 2013. https://www.pewresearch.org/wp-content/uploads/sites/7/2013/10/jewish-american-beliefs-attitudes-culture-survey-overview.pdf.
Rodman, David. 2019. "Israel's Post-1948 Security Experience." In *Routledge Handbook on Israeli Security*, edited by Stuart Cohen and Aaron S. Klieman, 25–35. New York: Routledge Taylor & Francis.

Rosenthal, Steven T. 2001. *Irreconcilable Differences: The Waning of the American Jewish Love Affair with Israel* [eng]. *Brandeis series in American Jewish history, culture, and life.* Hanover, NH: University Press of New England.

Rosner, Shmuel. 2019. *Annual Assessment of the Situation and Dynamics of the Jewish People 2019/5779.* Jerusalem: Jewish People Policy Institute. www.jppi.org.il.

Rynhold, Jonathan. 2007. "Israel's Foreign and Defence Policy and Diaspora Jewish Identity." In *Israel, the Diaspora and Jewish Identity,* edited by Danny Ben-Moshe and Zohar Segev, 144–163. Brighton: Sussex Academic Press.

Sasson, Theodore. 2010. "Mass Mobilization to Direct Engagement: American Jews' Changing Relationship to Israel." *Israel Studies* 15 (2): 173–195.

Shapiro, Faydra L. 2015. *Christian Zionism: Navigating the Jewish-Christian Border* [eng]. Eugene: Wipf and Stock Publishers.

Shindler, Colin. 2000. "Likud and the Christian Dispensationalists: A Symbiotic Relationship." *Israel Studies* 5 (1): 153–182.

Smith, Gregory A. 2019. "U.S. Jews Are More Likely than Christians to Say Trump Favors the Israelis Too Much." *Pew Research Center*, May 6, 2019. https://www.pewresearch.org/fact-tank/2019/05/06/u-s-jews-are-more-likely-than-christians-to-say-trump-favors-the-israelis-too-much/.

Soft Power 30. 2020. https://softpower30.com.

Spector, Stephen. 2009. *Evangelicals and Israel: The Story of American Christian Zionism.* Oxford: Oxford University Press.

Sturm, Tristan. 2018. "Religion as Nationalism: The Religious Nationalism of American Christian Zionists." *National Identities* 20 (3): 299–319.

Tibon, Amir. 2020. "Netanyahu Makes Case for Israeli Annexation in Speech to U.S. Evangelical Group." *Ha'aretz*, June 26, 2020. https://www.haaretz.com/israel-news/.premium-netanyahu-presents-case-for-annexation-before-american-crowd-of-evangelicals-1.8954661.

Waxman, Dov. 2010. "The Israel Lobbies: A Survey of the Pro-Israel Community in the United States." *Israel Studies Forum* 25 (1): 5–28.

Waxman, Dov. 2016. *Trouble in the Tribe: The American Jewish Conflict over Israel.* Princeton, NJ: Princeton University Press.

Waxman, Dov, and Scott Lasensky. 2013. "Jewish Foreign Policy: Israel, World Jewry and the Defence of 'Jewish Interests.'" *Journal of Modern Jewish Studies* 12 (2): 232–252.

Weber, Timothy P. 2005. *On the Road to Armageddon: How Evangelicals Became Israel's Best Friend* [eng]. Grand Rapids, MI: Baker Academic.

Wertheimer, Jack. 2008. "American Jews and Israel: A 60-Year Retrospective." *American Jewish Yearbook* 108: 3–79.

13
Soft Power of the Catholic Papacy

Timothy A. Byrnes

Introduction

It is telling that in his seminal book on "soft power," Joseph S. Nye cites papal influence within the Catholic Church as a clear example of his subject matter before he even deigns to define what soft power is. "Some loyal Catholics may follow the pope's teaching on capital punishment," Nye notes at the outset, "not because of a threat of excommunication but [instead] out of respect for his moral authority" (Nye 2004, 2). Then, after defining soft power as "an intangible attraction that persuades us to go along with others' purposes without an explicit threat or exchange taking place" (Nye 2004, 7) Nye *immediately* returns to the papacy as a paradigmatic example of a global player wielding *outside* of its own institutional context the kind of political power he is seeking to explicate. "The Vatican," Nye insists "has soft power despite Stalin's mocking question 'How many divisions does the Pope have?'" (Nye 2004, 9).

For much of European political history, of course, the Pope *did* have divisions, lots of them, and he ruled over much of modern-day Italy as a temporal authority interacting with other sovereigns as a full, equal participant in military and diplomatic relations.[1] Even then, however, the Pope enjoyed a kind of exalted political status that was not justified merely by his territorial and military assets, regardless of how substantial they were. In modern parlance, the Pope always "punched above his weight" in European politics, largely by leveraging what Rodney Hall has termed "moral authority as power resource" (Hall 1997, 591–622). Nye began by emphasizing the Pope's exercise of moral authority *inside* his own community. But Crespo and Gregory saw moral authority as the basis of modern papal efforts to advance "temporal-political foreign policy objectives" (Crespo and Gregory 2019, 2) *outside* of the Catholic Church.

For many centuries, a long line of Popes grounded the papacy's central place in European geopolitics at least in part in their status as the authoritative spiritual leader of the largest single religious institution on the Continent. Other Kings and Princes sought support from the papacy not only, or even mainly, for the tangible resources Popes could supply, but rather for the religious and moral approbation they could impart.[2] E. H. Carr wrote in 1939 of the underappreciated significance of what he called "power over opinion" (1939, 2). It is not really very surprising that in a political system designated as "Christendom," the leading, most prominent spokesman for Christianity would wield a substantial amount of "power over opinion," or what Joseph Nye would define decades later as the "power of attraction" (2004, 5).

My focus here, however, will be on the power—entirely "soft"—that has been exercised by Catholic Popes *after* the loss of temporal power in the nineteenth century. In this modern era, Popes have wielded the resources and opportunities that their office affords them to exercise soft power in three closely related ways: to defend the institutional interests of their Church; to advance their tradition's moral and social teachings both inside and outside the confines of their own institution; and to influence political and social processes and structures across the globe in ways that will move the world closer to the realization of the Kingdom of God, as that kingdom is defined within the Apostolic Palace in Vatican City.

In drawing our attention to this particular form of Papal power, I will emphasize throughout that Popes have exercised their soft power through two distinct but related channels of influence. The first element of papal influence is through the *direct* application of Papal preferences to political dynamics on the world stage. In its most formal application, this direct role takes the form of the Holy See's enduring diplomatic relations with over 180 countries across the globe. Individual Popes, as the personal embodiment of the Holy See's status as a juridical actor, have been able to interject themselves and their preferences into International Relations in ways that no other global religious leader could even dream of.[3] But beyond this formal role, Popes also participate directly in global politics by leveraging their unparalleled global celebrity for the purposes of advancing the institutional, moral, and political interests of their Church. Once described as "the first citizen of Global Civil Society" (Casanova 1997, 131), Catholic Popes are able to access a global media platform from which to issue statements and launch initiatives designed to exercise soft power by claiming status as what Nye called a "global conscience" (2004, 90).

At the same time, however, Popes also exercise soft power through an *indirect* path by speaking to, influencing, and in an institutional sense "governing" the far-flung membership of their global Church. As the authoritative spiritual leader of over a billion souls, Popes have institutionalized access to a huge transnational population. And as the global pastor of this sprawling flock, Popes can exercise soft power indirectly by appointing local leaders of the Church, and by molding the preferences and priorities of individual Catholics. The papal hope, as it were, is that those individual Catholics will, in turn, advance the Pope's positions and initiatives through actualization of their own distinctly Catholic lay vocations in the secular world.

History

The papacy and its actual governing control of territory—or "temporal power"—got caught up in the revolutionary systemic transformations of European politics in the nineteenth century. The interconnecting forces of great power competition, democratic agitation, and Italian unification ("Risorgimento") combined to render papal control of much of the Italian peninsula controversial, contested, and in time unsustainable. By 1870 and the historic capture of Rome by the forces of the consolidating Italian state, the papacy had effectively ceased to govern any "papal territory" in any meaningful sense of the term.

Nevertheless, in the decades immediately following the loss of temporal power, a number of Popes struggled with accommodating themselves to new institutional circumstances and to the related requirement to conceptualize and project papal power in new ways. Self-styled "Prisoners of the Vatican" retreated in a number of ways from power politics as they vainly awaited a restoration of temporal authority over the Papal States that would never come.[4] These Popes of the late nineteenth and early twentieth centuries were at the center of the so-called Roman Question concerning the degree to which the leader of the global Catholic Church ought to be subject to the sovereign power of the Italian state. This question was settled, of course, through the Lateran Accords of 1929, when Benito Mussolini offered formal recognition of papal sovereignty over the Vatican city-state (Kertzer 2014). But even with their temporal sovereignty reduced to symbolic governance of a miniscule microstate situated within a city and country most decidedly not under their control, a series of Popes still tried (relatively ineffectively) to exercise traditional backroom political power in European affairs.[5]

For our purposes here, however, it is worthy of note that even during this transitional period at the turn of the nineteenth to the twentieth century, soft power was already being articulated in ways that pointed the way to the modern era and to the two-track structure of papal influence. Pope Leo XIII's 1891 encyclical, *Rerum Novarum* ("Of New Things"), for example, was an early and paradigmatic example of papal efforts to shape public discourse both inside and outside the Catholic Church.[6] Offered as an application of Catholic teaching to the politically freighted matter of industrial relations, or what Leo's text called "the rights and duties of capital and labor," *Rerum Novarum* was formally addressed to "ordinaries (bishops) of places having Peace and Communion with the Apostolic See" (Leo XIII 1891). This first "social encyclical's" broader purpose, however, was to contribute a distinctively Catholic contribution to the great debates then raging over the proper relationship between capital and labor in an industrial economy.

Leo firmly endorsed the concept of private property, noting that "when men know they are working on what belongs to them, they work with far greater eagerness and diligence" (Leo XIII, 1891, para.66). However, at the same time, he also called for "oppressed workers" to be "liberated from the savagery of greedy men" (Leo XIII, 1891, para.59). And he announced a papal endorsement of "measures . . .which seem in any way capable of benefiting the condition of workers" (Leo XIII, 1891, para.51). Thus offering a kind of "third way" between unfettered capitalism and state-centric socialism, Pope Leo carved out a Catholic moral space centered on the responsibilities of capital and the dignity of labor that would come to define in both form and content papal efforts to shape global economic relations for over a century.

Meaningful articulation of soft power, however, requires appropriate projection. And so the modern era of papal politics did not really hit its stride, as it were, until the papacy accommodated itself to the developments in communication and transportation technologies that revolutionized global politics in the second half of the twentieth century. Just as the backroom diplomacy and severe mien of Pius XII were singularly unsuited for modern projection of papal influence, the welcoming visage and open persona of John XXIII set an example that all of his successors—some haltingly—have been challenged to follow. We can see most clearly John's purposeful comingling of his dual roles as authoritative embodiment of authentic Catholicism, and a global pastor to a sprawling transnational congregation in his most famous encyclical, *Pacem in Terris*.[7]

Promulgated in 1963, *Pacem in Terris* ("Peace on Earth") was a masterful expression of the two-track approach of modern papal politics. Addressed explicitly to "All Men of Good Will," *Pacem in Terris* was an eloquent articulation of Catholic teaching on a wide spectrum of public issues including war, disarmament, economic development, and the centrality of human rights to any legitimate conception of justice. Pope John offered the encyclical at one and the same time as both a *direct* intervention in global affairs through papal admonition to world leaders, and an *indirect* exercise of political influence through papal instruction to the Catholic people concerning moral issues of central public import. Moreover, this was all handed down from a papacy that had been truly liberated from the "prison" of the Vatican.

John XXII, of course, also called the historic Second Vatican Council. This three-year meeting of the universal Church is known for ushering in significant changes in Catholic liturgical practices, most prominently in terms of the use of vernacular languages in celebrating the Mass. But Vatican II also dramatically recast the Church's approach to, and relationship with, the outside world. The Church Fathers called by John XXII issued documents like *Dignitatis Humanae* ("Of the Dignity of the Human Person") on religious freedom, *Nostra Aetate* ("In Our Times") on relations with Jews, and (most portentously) *Guadium et Spes* ("Joy and Hope") on the Church's evangelical mission to the world.[8] These statements were made in the name of the entire magisterium of the Church and not merely of the papacy. But in repositioning the Church's views on matters of central public importance, these documents also redirected papal soft power in new and fertile directions. Through his iconic encyclicals and through the ultimate fruits of the Vatican Council, the papacy emerged during John XXIII's reign as a uniquely prominent public entity: a religious office and moral authority characterized perhaps as much by global celebrity as by institutional position.[9]

Ironically, it was Pope Paul VI, John's awkward and inscrutable successor, who nevertheless embraced the other prong of the modern papal role: international travel. Venturing out from Rome to (among other destinations) the Holy Land, India, Africa, and perhaps most significantly, the United Nations in New York, Paul offered an early glimpse into what the modern papacy as global pastor would look like.[10] Imploring delegates at the United Nations General Assembly in 1965 to share his commitment to "No more war; war never again," Paul engaged in one of the most direct and public efforts of any modern Pope to shape global discourse and cajole global leaders into sharing his priorities (Paul VI 1965). And on the very night of his UN speech, Paul celebrated a Mass in Yankee Stadium amid a display of devotion that would have made a rock star blush in humility, or a political leader puff his chest out in triumph.[11]

The Polish Colossus

By the 1970s, then, all of the elements of the modern papacy were in place and all of the contours of the soft power were clearly defined. But it wasn't until the Fall of 1978 and the arrival on the papal throne of Poland's Karol Wojtyla that the world and the Church saw just how aggressively this structure could be leveraged for influence on the global stage.[12] Pope John Paul II energetically exercised papal soft power in both its direct and indirect senses. His personal voice and influence were felt most acutely in East Central Europe, of course, where his eloquent denunciations of Communism and his confident presumption that historic transformation was possible proved to be world historic in significance (Weigel, 2003). In this particular arena, he combined the direct and indirect exercise of soft power to devastating effect. He confidently offered himself in the corridors of power in Warsaw, Moscow, and Washington as the unrivaled representative of authentic Polish national aspiration, and by extension of aspiration for political revolution throughout the nations of the Warsaw Pact. At the same time, however, he also sought to inspire and challenge the people of Poland and beyond, in and through their Catholic identities and devotions, to "Be Not Afraid," and to demand political change and social transformation, not in his name, but in their own.[13]

In other national and global contexts, John Paul worked a similar two-pronged approach, albeit with less dramatic results. In terms of the perennial questions involving economic structures and their political implications, the Polish Pope redoubled and reemphasized the Church's public and universal opposition to socialism. He denounced any system based in inevitable class conflict as antithetical to fundamental tenets of human dignity and to Catholic notions of solidarity.[14] But he also cautioned against over-reliance on market economies and demanded that economic systems and commercial transactions be grounded in an over-arching commitment to justice and the rights of labor.

At the same time, however, John Paul II also aggressively applied his institutional authority against elements within his own Church who sought to articulate a more radical, liberationist relationship between Catholic teaching and the rights of workers and the dispossessed.[15] And to put it bluntly, John Paul's targeted efforts to silence leading figures of Liberation Theology within his own Church may have done as much to limit and forestall social revolutions in Latin America and elsewhere than any criticism the Pope himself may have registered against left leaning governments or politicians.

John Paul's ubiquitous media presence, ceaseless travel, and historically lengthy pontificate combined to transform the role of the papacy itself, both in terms of its external role in global affairs and of its internal role as leader of the Catholic Church. Over 28 long years, world leaders and the global media grew used to a Pope who confidently expressed his opinions and preferences on the full range of issues and developments that comprised the world's moral and political agendas. And all of it was expressed in Pope John Paul II's own voice, as his *direct* contributions to public dialogue and political contestation on a dizzyingly broad array of topics and issues.

But the Polish Pope was equally committed to the exercise of *indirect* influence on global discourse and outcomes by insisting in uncompromising terms that his Church—the one billion persons who comprise global Catholicism—accede to his preferences and priorities and work to advance them through lay participation in the political, social, and economic systems in which they lived. Using papal visits as a spur and a cudgel, John Paul traversed the globe imploring Catholics to redouble their commitments to Catholic teaching, and to work in every national, regional, and global context to bring to fruition moral practices, social structures, and political outcomes that would bear the distinctive stamp of the Catholic ethos that he was articulating.

One of the effects of this epochal project was to place the global leader of the Catholic Church directly at the center of its local institutional structures and communities. Through his mastery of modern communications and his unprecedented use of modern modes of transportation (the airplane!), John Paul came to supplant local clergy, individual bishops, and national bishops conferences and established himself as the first truly global pastor of the far-flung Catholic Church. For the period of his pontificate—and still now through the lasting echoes of his episcopal appointments—John Paul stood astride his Church as *the* unimpeachable, indispensable leader and spokesmen for the largest single religious community on earth. It is difficult to measure the degree to which this exalted institutional status translated into actual indirect political influence outside his Church. But in defining and assessing the soft power of the papacy, the potential influence of this *indirect* track—grounded in unprecedented access to the views, preferences and priorities of a billion people—must be taken prominently into account.

Francis

Jorge Mario Bergoglio differs from Karol Wojtyla as both man and bishop in countless ways. Nevertheless, Bergoglio occupies as Pope Francis I the contemporary papacy as constructed by John Paul II. Notwithstanding all of the Argentine Pope's rejections of the papacy's regal trappings, and despite his efforts to ground papal authority in collective processes of synodality and collegiality, Francis relies on the same avenues of communication and travel to spread his message and assert his power as did the John Paul II and his other immediate predecessors. In other words, Francis avails himself of the same *direct* and *indirect* tracks of soft power through which to assert his own personal role in public dialogue, and to shape the emphases and priorities of his Church and its global membership.

In fairly substantial distinction to his predecessors, however, it appears that all of the efforts of Latin America's first pontificate—direct and indirect, personal and institutional—are targeted on a single, if complex goal: to raise the profile of the poor and the otherwise marginalized in the life of the Catholic Church and on the agenda of global politics. Francis speaks clearly and persistently, both in words and in metaphorical action, about the sufferings of the poor. And he consistently and insistently challenges those with political, social, and economic power to hear that suffering and to act to ameliorate it. At the same time, Francis preaches ceaselessly to his Catholic people about reemphasizing the Church's divinely ordained mission to feed the hungry, welcome the migrant, heal the sick in body and spirit, visit the imprisoned, and in all ways place the poor at the center of the collective life of global Catholicism. Francis has made it unmistakably clear that he wishes to place the varied powers of his office at the service of those who have no power themselves.

In terms of his *direct* participation in global political discourse, Francis has been straightforward and aggressive in asserting and advancing his own personal priorities. His very first foray out of the Vatican as Pope, for example, was to the island of Lampedusa, a prominent point of entry for refugees seeking safety in Europe. The new Pope pointedly took advantage of his place at the center of a media frenzy to draw attention of the plight of migrants, and to amplify his denunciation of what he called "the globalization of indifference" to the refugee crisis of 2013 (Bianchi 2016). Pope Francis later used his sovereign status in international law to make a symbolic point about the need for Europe and other rich nations to be more welcoming to vulnerable migrants who arrived at their shores. After a much-publicized visit to the Greek Island of Lesbos, Francis brought twelve migrants back with him to Rome, and formally granted them asylum within the borders of the Vatican.[16]

Pope Francis also took up as a central emphasis of his pontificate the issue of global climate change, or what he would prefer to call the threat that human "plunder" and "irresponsible use and abuse" of the earth's "goods" poses to "our common home" (Francis 2015).[17] His most magisterial statement on this issue, the encyclical *Laudato Si'* ("Praise Be to You"), was more than merely another call to acknowledge anthropomorphic climate change as real and to respond aggressively to it, however. *Laudato Si'* was also a uniquely Catholic reading of the global crisis—one is tempted to say a uniquely *Southern* Catholic reading—as it stressed that ecological catastrophe fell most dramatically on the poor, those who had played the least role in causing it and who possessed the fewest resources with which to survive it. "A true ecological approach," the Argentine Pope intoned, "must integrate questions of justice in debates on the environment, so as to hear *both the cry of the earth and the cry of the poor.*" (Francis, 2015, para.49).

This way of defining global challenges and crises in terms of how they affect the poor and marginalized is the common leitmotif of Pope Francis's interventions in a broad array of policy debates and political contestation. It drives his unwavering call for developed societies to welcome those who arrive at their shores; it impels his impassioned cry for the world to attend to the ecological threats posed by industrial production and economic development; but it also informs his resistance to social evolutions on issues like gay rights, reproductive technologies, and (especially) gender identity. He tends to see these "progressive" trends as not only antithetical to Catholic teaching, but also as rooted, at least in part, in "ideological colonization" of traditional societies by global cultural forces that have rejected the "natural order" that should govern human sexuality (Horowitz and Povoledo 2019).

If anything, an emphasis on the needs and dignity of the poor have been even more characteristic of Pope Francis' exercise of *indirect* soft power through his efforts to shift the priorities of his institutional Church and of individual Catholics across the globe. His decision not to reside as Pope in the Apostolic Palace, and his rejection of so much pomp and finery traditionally associated with his office were more than simply expressions of personal preference. They were, instead, purposefully symbolic decisions meant to convey to his fellow bishops and to his Church at large that he wished to reorient the power of his office and of his Church and direct it toward the service of the poor. From his first days in Rome, Pope Francis spoke of the Catholic Church not as a citadel of righteousness but instead as a "field hospital after battle" (Coday 2013), charged with attending to the suffering of the physically and spiritually wounded. Denouncing what he called the "spiritual Alzheimer's" of clericalism (Ohlheiser 2014), he challenged the hierarchy and clergy of his Church to view themselves as servants rather than served, and to minister to their people as shepherds not afraid to acquire "the smell of the sheep."[18]

It would not be an overstatement to say that virtually *everything* Jorge Bergoglio has done as Pope Francis has been in service of his commitment to making his Church more outward looking toward the poor and less self-referential as an institution. His purposeful reinvigoration of synodality, for example, should be understood within his conception of a "poor Church, for the poor." Francis gathers bishops regionally and globally in order to formulate more inclusive policies and to grant local bishops a greater stake in implementing and managing the Church's global priorities. But clearly, Francis also sees these Synods as places to hear and amplify voices from outside the Vatican curia (or bureaucracy), and as opportunities to brand with papal approbation certain ways of being the Catholic Church among the poor and the marginalized.

Hedging the "So What" Question

One of the most difficult aspects of any discussion of soft power is the challenge of isolating and assessing the independent influence that can be reliably ascribed to the entity supposedly exercising the power. The results of hard power are in general relatively easy to identify: soldiers are killed in war; territory is occupied or pacified; economies are damaged by sanctions. But even these hard examples are subject to the confounding complexity of competing explanations, intervening variables, and the like. How much less exact is it to ascribe any specific outcome to "moral authority" or to the "power of attraction?" To cite the most recent examples, have there been concrete results of Pope Francis's direct efforts to center global policies surrounding migration around the principle of "mercy?" Has his clarion call to explicitly target responses to climate change on the needs of the poor been heeded by world leaders and led to changes in national or global regimes related to the use of fossil fuels or the response to climate change? Any affirmative responses to these questions would have to be deeply qualified, to say the least.

At the same time, we are learning anew through Francis' experience that change within the Catholic Church—change that might be the source of *indirect* soft power—does not come immediately through papal fiat. Pope Francis's rhetorical and symbolic efforts to reorient his Church's priorities have received wall-to-wall media coverage for seven years. Yet when the US Catholic Bishops met to identify their own priorities heading into the 2020 election, they once again listed abortion as their (enduring) top priority, and did not even deign to mention climate change a single time.[19]

And yet, we ought not limit our assessment of papal influence, either direct or indirect, to immediate, and immediately measurable effects. Pope John Paul II's insistence that Poland should be free (could be free!) of Soviet domination was probably the high point of modern, direct papal power. "Pope Wojtyla" envisioned an alternative future for a reconstituted Europe, and he applied enormous diplomatic and political energy into advancing that vision. But it would be inappropriate to hold up that very unusual set of circumstances as the standard against which all papal soft power would be measured. Direct papal power is more likely found in long-term influence on international discourse, norms, and what Catholics would call values. *Rerum Novarum* remains over a century later an iconic and nuanced account of how capital and labor should relate to each other in an industrial economy. Paul VI's *Humanae Vitae* ("On Human Life") reiterating his Church's unswerving opposition to birth control, and all the papal pronouncements that have staked out the Church's traditionalist grounds on questions of reproductive rights, sexual morality, and gender identity have been appealed to for decades by social conservatives both inside and outside the Church.

Pope Francis hopes, I presume, that his priorities and emphases will be viewed in the future as prophetic challenges to the governing norms of his time. He is in the process of articulating from the papal throne a broad-based moral ethos that when linked to the institutional resources of the Catholic Church may one day be seen as making it more difficult for the powerful to ignore the interests of the powerless and the marginalized. Presumably in this spirit, *Fortune* magazine has repeatedly listed Pope Francis among the "Greatest Leaders" of our time, and in 2017 ascribed his "enduring influence" to his critique of capitalism without conscience."[20] In what Jan Melissen has called the "fuzzy world of postmodern international relations" (Melissen 2005, 5) the "power of attraction" might be able to rise more readily above the din of traditional inter-state relations and articulate alternative approaches to global challenges.

Moreover, it is within this emerging "fuzzy world" that modern Popes also seek to exercise indirect soft power by leading their Church, its leadership, and its adherents in new and politically meaningful directions. The modern papacy, shaped by Saint John Paul II, is characterized by nearly constant global travel that allows Popes to "press the flesh" and explicitly call on the Catholic Church to follow and embody Papal vision and papal emphases. Again, the opposition to Francis' priorities, in the United States and elsewhere, demonstrates the complexity and uncertainties hidden within the workings of a seemingly authoritative office. But @pontifex has millions of followers on Twitter; the Pope remains a subject of intense fascination for religious and secular media; and perhaps more than any other lever of authority, Francis enjoys a power of episcopal appointment that allows him to personally select Cardinals, Archbishops, and Bishops who will do his bidding, and thereby work to create in the longer term the "poor Church for the poor" that he envisions and demands. As much as I hesitate to ground my argument in a question: what other leader of what other global body has institutionalized access to over a billion people to whom he or she can preach about the rights of migrants and about the responsibility of political leaders to care for our "common home?"

However—and this is a significant "however"—the presumptions underlying this question are based in an even deeper presumption that Catholics the world over listen to their Pope and give credence to Papal pronouncements on moral matters with direct political ramifications. Put in terms employed by Nye in his delineation of the sources of soft power, Pope Francis or any other Pope, is only able to exercise such power directly or indirectly if he is broadly perceived to be "living up to" the "values" that he expresses (Nye 2004, 11). It is not enough to assert values; those values need to be backed up with "credibility" (Melissen 2005, 4). And the moral credibility of the papacy has been powerfully compromised in recent years by the revelation of the hierarchy's repeated failures to respond effectively to the clerical sex abuse scandal that has consumed the Church in recent years. This is a complex institutional matter, of course, and detailed analysis of the ways in which this crisis has affected the Church would take us beyond the boundaries of this short essay.[21]

But Saint John Paul II's silent complicity in the monstrous crimes of Rev. Marcial Maciel as founder and leader of the Legionnaires of Christ has indelibly tarnished the moral legacy of the Polish Pope (Berry and Renner 2004); Maciel, a sexual abuser of epic proportions, acted with institutional and personal impunity for decades, and was supported and honored by John Paul II long after minimal levels of discretion and respect for Maciel's victims would have cautioned otherwise. Benedict XVI's determination both as Pope and as head (as Cardinal Ratzinger) of the Congregation for the Doctrine of the Faith to keep investigations and adjudications of criminal allegations against Catholic clergy inside the high walls of the Church militated against transparency and delayed by many years the Church's reckoning with the extent of abusive behavior in its midst. And Pope Francis' initial defensiveness in the face of accusations against Bishops he knew and trusted (particularly in Chile) sowed doubts that a new Pope was adopting an authentically new approach when it came to the enduring problem of holding accountable Bishops who had either covered up abuse or committed abusive acts themselves (Bonnefoy and Ramsey 2018).

This is a troubling note on which to end a discussion of papal soft power. But *direct* exercise of such power in the world arena by individual Popes has always been dependent on a widespread perception that when declaiming on moral, social and political issues Catholic Popes were speaking as the legitimate leaders of a massive, global religious community. And *indirect* exercise of papal soft power has always been dependent on members of that religious community granting credence to the priorities and emphases expressed by individual Popes. Both of these interrelated dynamics are in turn dependent on Popes being perceived, both inside and outside the Catholic Church, as credible advocates for a set of moral values and related policies. This entire edifice—the edifice on which Papal power resides—is today threatened by a scandal that has metastasized throughout the Church. All other efforts by Pope Francis to reorient his Church and exercise his influence are today subordinate to one primary task: reestablishing the credibility of the Papacy's moral voice through institutional reforms that will prevent further clerical abuse in the future, and hold accountable those who failed to prevent abuse in the past.

References

"Address of the Holy Father Paul VI to the United Nations Organization." 1965. The Holy See. https://www.vatican.va/content/paul-vi/en/speeches/1965/documents/hf_p-vi_spe_19651004_united-nations.html.
Berry J., and G. Renner. 2004. *Vows of Silence: The Abuse of Power in the papacy of John Paul II*. New York: Free Press.
Bianchi, Alessandro. 2016. "Pope Francis Commemorates Migrant Dead at Lampedusa." *Reuters*. July 7, 2016. https://www.reuters.com/article/us-pope-lampedusa/pope-francis-commemorates-migrant-dead-at-lampedusa-idUSBRE9660KH20130708.
Bonnefoy, P., and A. Ramsey. 2018. "Pope's Defense of Chilean Bishop in Sex Abuse Scandal Called Outrageous." *New York Times*. January 19, 2018. https://www.nytimes.com/2018/01/19/world/americas/pope-sex-abuse-chile.html.
Byrnes, Timothy A. 2020. "Catholic Bishops and Sexual Abuse: Power, Constraints, and Institutional Context." *Journal of Church and State* 62 (1): 5–25.
Byrnes, Timothy A. 2019. "Sovereignty, Supranationalism, and Soft Power: The Holy See in International Relations." In *Modern Papal Diplomacy and Social Teaching in World Affairs* , edited by Dennis R. Hoover, Robert J. Joustra, and Mariano Barbato, 6–20. Abington: Routledge.
Casanova, José. 1997. "Globalizing Catholicism and the return to a 'Universal' Church." In *Transnational Religion and Fading States*, edited by Hoeber Rudolph and James Piscatori, 131. Boulder: Westview Press.
Carr, Edward H. 1939. *The Twenty Years' Crisis 1919–1939*. New York: Perennial.
Chadwick, Owen. 1998. *A History of the Popes 1830–1914*. Oxford: Clarendon Press.
Coday, Dennis. 2013. "Pope Quotes: The Field Hospital Church." *National Catholic Reporter,* October 26, 2013. https://www.ncronline.org/blogs/francis-chronicles/pope-s-quotes-field-hospital-church.
Colvin, Geoff. 2017. "The World's 50 Greatest Leaders." March 23. https://fortune.com/2017/03/23/worlds-50-greatest-leaders-intro/.
Coppa, Frank J. 2013. *The Life and Pontificate of Pope Pius XII: Between History and Controversy*. Washington, DC: The Catholic University of America Press.
Crespo, R. A., and C. C. Gregory. 2019. "The Doctrine of Mercy: Moral Authority, Soft Power, and the Foreign Policy of Pope Francis." *International Politics* 57 (1): 115–130.
Duchesne, Louis. 1907. *The Beginnings of the Temporal Sovereignty of the Popes: A. D. 754–1073*. London: K. Paul, Trench, Trübner & Company.
Formicola , Jo Renee. 2002. *Pope John Paul II, Prophetic Politician*. Washington, DC: Georgetown University Press.
Francis. 2018. *A Stranger and You Welcomed Me: A Call to Mercy and Solidarity with Migrants and Refugees*. Edited by Robert Ellsberg. Maryknoll: Orbis Books.
Francis. 2015. *Laudato si'*. Vatican City: Vatican Press.
Gutierrez, Gustavo. 1988. *A Theology of Liberation: History, Politics, and Salvation (15th Anniversary Edition)*. Maryknoll: Orbis Books.

Hall, Rodney. 1997. "Moral Authority as Power Resource." *International Organization* 51 (4): 591–622.
Hebblewaite, Peter. 1985. *Pope John XXII: Shepherd of the Modern World*. New York: Doubleday.
Hebblewaite, Peter. 1993. *Paul VI: The First Modern Pope*. New York: Paulist Press.
Hoover, Dennis R., Robert J. Joustra, and Mariano Barbato. 2019. *Sovereignty, Supranationalism, and Soft Power: The Holy See in International Relations*. Abington: Routledge.
Horowitz, J., and E. Povoledo. 2019. "Vatican Rejects Notion that Gender Identity Can Be Fluid." *New York Times*, June 10, 2019. https://www.nytimes.com/2019/06/10/world/europe/vatican-francis-gender-identity-sexuality.html.
John Paul II. 1991. *Centesimus Annus*. Encyclical Letter. The Holy See. https://www.vatican.va/content/john-paul-ii/en/encyclicals/documents/hf_jp-ii_enc_01051991_centesimus-annus.html.
Kertzer, David I. 2004. *Prisoner of the Vatican: The Pope's Secret Plot to Capture Rome from the New Italian State*. New York: Houghton Mifflin.
Kertzer, David I. 2014. *The Pope and Mussolini: The Secret History of Pius XI and the Rise of Fascism in Europe*. New York: Random House.
Leo XIII. 1891. *Rerum Novarum*. Encyclical letter. The Holy See. https://www.vatican.va/content/leo-xiii/en/encyclicals/documents/hf_l-xiii_enc_15051891_rerum-novarum.html
Lyon, Alynna J, Christine A. Gustafson, and Paul Christopher Manuel. 2018. *Pope Francis as a Global Actor: Where Politics and Theology Meet*. Cham: Palgrave Macmillan.
M. Abbott, Walter. 1966. *The Documents of Vatican II*. New York: Guild.
Melissen, Jan. 2005. "The New Public Diplomacy: Between Theory and Practice." In *The New Public Diplomacy: Soft Power in International Relations*, edited by Jan Melissen. London: Palgrave Macmillan
Nye, Joseph S. Jr. 2004. *Soft Power: The Means to Success in World Politics*. New York: Public Affairs.
Ohlheiser, Abby. 2014. "Pope Francis Warns Vatican Leaders Against 'Spiritual Alzheimer's.'" *Washington Post*, December 22, 2014. https://www.washingtonpost.com/news/world/wp/2014/12/22/pope-francis-warns-vatican-leaders-against-spiritual-alzheimers/.
Pollard, John F. 1999. *The Unknown Pope: Benedict XV and the Pursuit of Peace*. London: Geoffrey Chapman.
Francis. 2015. "Laudato Si.' Vatican City: Vatican Press. https://www.vatican.va/content/francesco/en/encyclicals/documents/papa-francesco_20150524_enciclica-laudato-si.html
Francis. 2018. *A Stranger and You Welcomed Me: A Call to Mercy and Solidarity with Migrants and Refugees*. Maryknoll: Orbis Books.
Francis. 2017. *With the Smell of the Sheep: To Priests, Bishops, and Other Shepherds*. Edited by Giussepe Merola. Maryknoll: Orbis Books.
Smith, Christian. 1991. *The Emergence of Liberation Theology: Radical Religion and Social Movement Theory*. Chicago: University of Chicago Press.
Southern, R. W. 1970. *Western Society and the Church in the Middles Ages*. Harmondsworth: Penguin Books.
Thomson, John A. F. 1980. *Popes and Princes, 1417–1517: Politics and Polity in the Late Medieval Church*. London; Boston: Allen and Unwin.

Weigel, George. 2003. *The Final Revolution: The Resistance Church and the Collapse of Communism*. New York: Oxford University Press.
Whelan, Brett Edward. 2014. *The Medieval Papacy*. London: Palgrave-Macmillan.
Willey, David. 1992. *God's Politician: Pope John Paul II, the Catholic Church, and the New World Order*. New York: St. Martin's Press.
Yardley, Jim. 2016. "Pope Francis Takes 12 Refugees Back to Vatican with After Trip to Greece." *New York Times*, April 16.

14
"Brazil above Everything or God above Everyone?"

The Sources of Brazil's Religious Soft Power

Guilherme Casarões and Amy Erica Smith

Introduction

At a campaign stop in the northeastern city of Campina Grande in 2017, Brazil's right-wing congressman Jair Bolsonaro, then a precandidate preparing to launch a presidential campaign, proclaimed to his excited fans, "God above everything! Forget that little story about the state being secular. The state is Christian and the minority who's against it should move away. Minorities need to bow to majorities." When he launched his campaign a year later, Bolsonaro would adopt the first sentence for his campaign slogan: "Brazil above everything, God above everyone." Yet despite his bellicose declaration of loyalty to country first, Bolsonaro in the presidency would seek to position Brazil as a supportive player in a US-led, far-right international alliance to "spiritually regenerate" the West, in the words of then-Foreign Minister Ernesto Araújo (Araújo 2019). To this end, Christian nations should mobilize religious values to fight the so-called globalists, an alleged transnational network of sexual and racial minorities, progressive activists, and leftist politicians.

Bolsonaro foreign policy's embrace of religion came as a shock to observers at home and abroad. Prior to him, references to God and Christianity had never been a regular part of Brazil's diplomatic parlance. On the rare occasions previous presidents had hinted at religious values in the international sphere, it had been a way to reassert broader alignments, not to wage a global holy war. Let us take President Jânio Quadros as an example. More than half a century before Bolsonaro adopted his campaign slogan, Quadros described his "Independent Foreign Policy" doctrine in a 1961 article in

Foreign Affairs in the following terms: "Because of our historical, cultural and Christian background as well as our geographical situation, ours is a predominantly Western nation."[1]

Quadros' relatively bland declaration of religious affiliation was the exception in a highly secular era. More recently, however, President Luiz Inácio Lula da Silva (2003–2010) began evoking religion to justify regional integration. In remarks while visiting Argentina, Lula asserted that,

> As I finish my second term, I would like to leave a legacy of a president that has looked to the South American continent as if God had given us a sign. Why has God built us glued to one another? Even if we want to take separate ways, we cannot, because it is the same territory . . . For the entire 20th century we turned our eyes towards Europe and the United States . . . now, we have to look more to each other (. . .) and build the partnerships we must build (Ministério das Relações Exteriores 2008, 67).

On their face, these quotes from Brazilian presidents might appear similar. In context, however, they have very different connotations and meanings. Quadros' declaration was conceived as a domestically uncontroversial, inclusive, and nonpartisan description of national identity. His statement was aimed at foreign ears, pitched to reassure Western Cold War powers that Brazil was their natural and intrinsic ally, before declaring his intention to forge a depolarized middle path in foreign affairs. Along the same lines, Lula's God-talk sought to allay growing suspicions among neighbors of Brazil's emerging-power ambitions, thus reiterating the importance of regional integration—another supra-partisan endeavor. By contrast, Bolsonaro's statements are intended to be controversial, partisan, and divisive, setting up a culture war competition in order to win domestic supporters in a democratic, electoral conflict, as well as international allies against the backdrop of a changing world order.

This chapter seeks to explain Brazil's use of religious soft power in international affairs. We ask: In what ways have Brazilian presidents used religious soft power, how has this use changed over time, and what explains variation? While Brazil has long been a profoundly Catholic country, with a fast-growing Evangelical minority, its use of religious soft power in international affairs has transformed over the past several decades. Joseph Nye (1990) has defined soft power as a country's ability to get others to *want* what it wants. As opposed to hard or commanding power, which often involves the threat to use force or other forms of coercion, soft power is primarily about exerting attraction over other nations through culture, communications, institutions, or ideology. In a world of greater interdependence, traditional forms of power become less fungible, and the legitimacy that stems from soft forms of power gain relevance in world affairs.[2] As a core identity across global cultures and civilizations, religion naturally became one among several soft-power tools, exerted not only by states, but increasingly by religious leaders and groups (Haynes 2012; Steiner 2012).

We offer three explanations for Brazil's use of religious soft power, drawing on key theories of international relations. The first proposes that political leaders deploy religion in their international dealings as a means of creating a cohesive national identity. Alternatively, a second explanation postulates religious soft power as a tool for coalition building vis-à-vis international actors. Finally, our third take sees the use of religion in foreign affairs as a tool for maintaining domestic political coalitions in the context of democratic competition. All such explanations have obvious parallels to the use of religion in foreign affairs in other countries (Bettiza 2019, 9).

This chapter proceeds as follows. In the next section, we review Brazil's historical use of soft power, focusing on the constraints that would limit Brazil's use of religious (versus other forms of) soft power. Then, the following three sections lay out three alternative explanations that could explain the rise, and changes over time, of Brazil's use of religious soft power. We examine evidence for each hypothesis in turn. As we discuss in the conclusion, we believe that all three explanations make important contributions to our understanding of religious soft power.

Soft Power and Religion in Brazil

Brazil is arguably one of the earliest (and rare) examples of a major nation whose engagement in global affairs has relied primarily on soft power. This has been true since even before Brazil's independence, as the Portuguese chose diplomacy over military conquest in expanding colonial possessions across the Atlantic. The Brazilian borders were drawn in two treaties signed between Portugal and Spain, under the auspices of the Catholic Church: the Treaty of Tordesillas (1494), brokered soon after the first Iberian mission to the New World, and the Treaty of Madrid (1750), which recognized Portuguese territorial claims in South America's heartland, based on the long-standing custom of *Uti Possidetis*. A last treaty, signed in Petrópolis in 1903, gave Brazil its final contours in the early republican years. This is why many historians (and diplomats) claim that diplomacy has played a key role in forging the Brazilian national character.[3]

Good diplomacy skills have also been the ticket to Brazil's recognition in the concert of nations. Out of all continental-sized countries in the world—which US diplomat George Kennan neatly described as "monster countries" (Kennan 1993)—Brazil is perhaps the only one that has never been able to match its territorial assets with military or economic clout. Partly because it inhabits a low-conflict zone, and partly thanks to a set of strong foreign policy principles (such as pacifism and multilateralism) that have evolved over the last two centuries, Brazil's global presence has been indissociable from its diplomatic statecraft, as undertaken by the renowned and highly professional bureaucrats at the Brazilian Ministry of Foreign Affairs, also known as Itamaraty.

Only through diplomatic soft power could Brazil be recognized as part of the high circles of international affairs. If in the nineteenth century the Brazilian Empire (1822–1889) moved up the ranks among European monarchies by promoting itself as Europe in the Tropics (Vizentini 1999, 134–154). In the first decades of the twentieth century the Brazilian Republic's key soft-power asset was its multilateral engagement. By actively participating in the construction of the Pan-American Conferences, the League of Nations, and the United Nations, Brazil became a champion of multilateralism, or what used to be called "parliamentary diplomacy." In recent years, it has even become a "norm entrepreneur" in its own right, contributing to the creation of new rules and norms in issue-areas as diverse as free trade, nuclear non-proliferation, climate change, and human rights.[4]

Therefore, it was soft power that allowed Brazil to play the role of a *middle power* over most of the twentieth century. Middle powers have been conceptualized by Cooper et al. (1993) as countries that tend to "pursue multilateral solutions to international problems, [to] embrace compromise positions in international disputes, and [to] embrace notions of 'good international citizenship' to guide their diplomacy" (Cooper 1993). In a similar approach, Robert Keohane defines middle powers (or what he calls *system-affecting states*) as those countries that "cannot hope to affect the [international] system acting alone [but] can nevertheless exert significant impact on the system by working through small groups or alliances or through universal or regional international organizations" (Keohane 1969, 23).

Brazil's consistent set of diplomatic principles and its desire to play an autonomous role in world affairs lay at the heart of a soft-power driven universalist foreign policy strategy that gained ground in the early 1960s and that still resonated up until very recently (before being systematically attacked by Jair Bolsonaro's foreign minister, Ernesto Araújo; Araújo 2019). Unlike postcolonial neutralism adopted by African and Asian nations, Brazilian universalism was fundamentally pragmatic and nonideological, through which the country could preserve good relations with Washington while boosting trade and forging political and technological ties from Bonn to Moscow, and from Beijing to Baghdad. Not only has universalism widened the range of Brazil's foreign relations in terms of themes and partnerships, it also allowed it to forge issue-specific coalitions to increase its leverage in multilateral negotiations, such as the Cairns Group (1986), the Group of 15 (1989), and the New Agenda Coalition (1998), to name only a few.

Soft power has also allowed Brazil to build a regional integration project in South America. While regional powers' bid for hegemony or preeminence in their neighborhood often come through military threats or economic incentives, Brazil's plan to bring the region together involved the careful construction of a common narrative based on shared identities, worldviews, and foreign policy goals—a strategy Sean Burges has called *consensual hegemony* (Burges 2008). Even though several authors have already underscored the limits and flaws of such strategy, particularly in light of recent regional turmoil,[5] soft power has allowed Brazil to create and sustain regional institutions for trade (Mercosur), infrastructure promotion (Iirsa, Cosiplan), conflict resolution (Unasur), and even defense cooperation (South American Defense Council). As recent Brazilian administrations undermined the country's soft-power tools, notably Itamaraty's institution-building capabilities, the Brazil-led regional order has either been neglected or utterly abandoned.[6]

Finally, soft power has also been an integral element of Brazil's rise as an emerging power in the last two decades. Now, it is no longer used to safeguard multilateralism or to forge a regional order that begets stability in South America, but rather to make room for Brazil's growing international ambitions. Lula da Silva's diplomatic efforts, combined with a stronger, resource-rich Itamaraty over the 2000s, are often regarded as the pinnacle of Brazil's soft power, which has been deployed to advance a mildly revisionist agenda in international organizations (Valença and Carvalho 2014; Chatin 2016). Soft power has been the driving force behind Brazil's bold claims to UN Security Council reform, to greater participation in peacekeeping operations, and to reform the global financial and economic architecture to accommodate emerging power demands. Lula's foreign minister, Celso Amorim, often boasted that Brazil was about to usher in a new form of power, based on "the use of culture and civilization, not threats. It is a belief in dialogue, not force" (Lustig 2010).

Over time, however, Brazil's soft-power strategies have rarely resorted to religion. Since the beginning of the Republican era, in 1889, Brazilian governments have chosen to advance a secular agenda, which gave presidents and lawmakers independence from the Catholic Church, but that also allowed Brazil to construct a linear, stable, and supra-partisan foreign policy strategy. Unlike most other public policies, Brazilian foreign policy is presented as a state policy and does not subject itself to partisan or religious ideologies or incongruities. Diplomats and scholars often quote, as the cornerstone of such claim, Barão do Rio Branco's inaugural speech upon taking office as foreign minister in 1902: "I come not to serve a political party; I come to serve Brazil, which we all want to see united, integrated, strong, and respected" (Ministério das Relações Exteriores 2012).

Prior to Jair Bolsonaro, only two presidents have made explicit references to Brazil's religious character in the context of foreign affairs. As discussed in the introduction, in the early 1960s, as the Cold War came closer to Latin America, Jânio Quadros wrote about the country's Christian background and Western identity to reassure the US administration that Brazil was a loyal ally in the hemisphere. More recently, at the dawn of the new century, Lula da Silva made few and scattered mentions of religion, emphasizing commonalities and shared interests with diverse countries. Such examples beg the question: why and in what circumstances has Brazil used religion as a tool of its soft power, and why does the Bolsonaro administration represent such a significant break with Brazil's foreign policy traditions? In the next three sections, we present and discuss three explanations that draw on major International Relations theories.

Hypothesis 1: Religious Soft Power as a Nation-Building Project

First, we consider a potential explanation that is simultaneously constructivist and civilizational: that Brazilian leaders find religion a useful building material in the construction of a national image and foreign policy narrative.

Over Brazil's two centuries, political leaders and intellectuals have repeatedly sought to define the nation's identity, and to position the Brazilian nation in an imagined geopolitical space, in contradistinction to and relation with Western and colonial powers. Catholicism and Christianity have played a role in this process, serving not only as a historical link between Brazil and Portugal, but also ensuring prosperous relations with Western Catholic countries and the Holy See.

In this historically overwhelmingly Catholic country, thinkers envisioning the state and nation have never been able entirely to distance polity from religion. Constitutionally, Brazil has been a secular republic since its Constitution of 1891, which simultaneously ended the Brazilian monarchy and separated the monopolistic Roman Catholic Church from state functions such as public schools and elections. Nonetheless, the Brazilian version of secularism has, since its inception, been one that Kuru would classify as "passively secular"—allowing a robust religious presence in the public sphere and prioritizing state neutrality toward religion, rather than advancing a "comprehensive doctrine" entailing state dominance over religion.[7] Soper and Fetzer note that the form of nationalism a country adopts (whether secular nationalism, religious nationalism, or civil-religious nationalism) depends not merely on the institutional separation or fusion of religion and state.[8] Instead, religious demographics and the role of religious actors in society and politics—first at the founding national moment, and subsequently over the course of the nation's history—determine whether a constitutionally secular country *adopts* and then *maintains* secular nationalism or civil-religious nationalism. In Brazil's case, these forces have, on balance, tended to yield a civil-religious nationalism, in which a distinctly Brazilian variant of Catholic symbology and theology provide bones, flesh, and blood for the imagined nation.

Several instances exemplify religion's service to the Brazilian state and nation. The statesmen who authored Brazil's 1891 Constitution had forced a not-entirely-amicable divorce of state and Church. Nonetheless, five years later, the Church sided with the Brazilian state in the War of Canudos, a military campaign that extinguished a millenarian religious movement in the state of Bahia protesting that same divorce (Ramos 1974, 65–83). In the 1930s, the Church-state partnership drew closer, as the Church became an ally of Getulio Vargas' populist, fascist-leaning Estado Novo, and public religious education was reinstated (Azzi 1980, 49–71). The accommodationist nature of Brazilian secularism, as well as the central role of Catholicism in the nation, are symbolized in the fact that, to this day, seven of Brazil's twelve official holidays are Catholic—five of them commemorating moments in the life and death of Jesus Christ (Farias 2012). Yet perhaps nothing embodies the never-quite-settled partnership between Church and nation more than the iconic Christ the Redeemer statue, international symbol of Brazil. Catholic civil society organizations raised the funds to build the statue atop the Corcovado mountain in the 1920s, yet today the international icon is administered in an occasionally contentious and bureaucratically complex partnership between the Catholic Church and Brazilian federal agencies.[9]

The seminal intellectual project of nation-building in twentieth-century Brazil may be that of the anthropologist Gilberto Freyre. Rejecting Western colonialist, racist notions of civilization that saw Brazil's demographic diversity as an impediment to development and progress, Freyre instead promulgated a romanticized, sentimental image of Brazil as a mixed-race country. In works such as his 1933 tome *Casa Grande e Senzala*, Freyre argued that Brazil's nineteenth-century slave economy had created the conditions for a contemporary "racial democracy."[10] In Freyre's telling, romantic and familial relations between enslaved people and their enslavers in Brazil had created deeply rooted affections across lines of race and class. Not surprisingly, late twentieth and twenty-first century scholars reject Freyre's exceptionally rosy understanding of the history and sociology of race in Brazil.[11] Nonetheless, his vision of Brazil as a nation fortified through the mixing of races and cultures has deeply shaped Brazilian understandings of the national self today. Within this vision, Freyre saw Brazilian popular religion as a critical component of national identity. On Brazilian shores, he and subsequent thinkers argued, the Catholicism of the conquering Portuguese had absorbed rituals, practices, and beliefs from African as well as indigenous communities, creating a distinctively Brazilian form of "syncretic" Catholicism (Soares 2009, 200–224; Valente 1955). Perhaps nothing symbolizes this fusion more than that Brazilian's patron saint, Nossa Senhora Aparecida, is a black-skinned apparition of the Virgin Mary. To be Brazilian, in Freyre's and his followers' thinking, was to embrace a popular, locally distinct Catholicism.

What role did this civil-religious national identity play in Brazilian foreign policy? An analogy to the "civil religion" of the United States, as famously described by Robert N. Bellah, is imperfect.[12] Like in the United States, civil religion suffused Brazilians' sense of national belonging; images of Nossa Senhora Aparecida and the Christ the Redeemer statue, together with the Brazilian flag, served as powerful and unifying symbols. Unlike the US civil religion Bellah described, however, Brazil's variant was not typically interpreted as providing precepts for a national stance vis-à-vis other nations. Rather, Brazilian foreign policy largely remained a secular affair—although this is not unlike foreign policy in the United States itself until the 1990s.[13]

Nonetheless, in the mid-twentieth century, presidents returned to Freyre's notion that Brazil could define a middle path—one that celebrated Brazil's inheritance from Western colonial powers while also acknowledging its distinctiveness from those powers. Few statements capture this approach more fully than President Jânio Quadros' 1961 statement quoted in the introduction to this chapter. In the context of an essay that went on to argue that Brazil must establish relations with all countries, independently of Cold War politics, Quadros was likely seeking to send a reassuring signal to the states he perceived as Brazil's natural allies. Itamaraty's policy would remain staunchly secular, yet the declaration also stood as an indicator of an unquestioned national identity perceived as consensual.

Things were soon to change, however. In the following years, the Church would ally itself with the right-wing military dictatorship installed in 1964, before breaking with the dictatorship in the 1970s and becoming one of the most openly critical voices fighting for redemocratization, which ultimately came in 1985.[14] Simultaneously, the Church began to hemorrhage members, dropping from well over 90 percent of the population in 1970 to likely around 50 percent in the 2020 estimates, while Evangelicals and Pentecostals have risen to around a third of the Brazilian population.[15] With these changes, the Church's seemingly natural alliance with Brazilian nation began to falter, while a new form of politicized religion arose in the context of an increasingly pluralistic religious marketplace (Smith 2019).

Epitomizing a "modern" secular relationship between state and religious groups—in the plural—was the foreign policy of the left-leaning President Lula da Silva (2003–2010). Aiming to reposition Brazil as an emerging power in the context of what his Foreign Minister Celso Amorim predicted would be "a more multipolar order," Lula built South–South ties with other multicultural, religiously pluralistic democracies through the IBSA (India-Brazil-South Africa) Dialogue Forum (Amorim 2010, 215). He also sought ties to Muslim-majority nations, working with Turkey to broker a nuclear deal with Iran in 2010 and with Syria and Libya to bring South America and the Arab world closer together through an unprecedented biregional summit, launched in 2005 (Amorim 2010; Brands 2011, 28–49).

This approach would abruptly reverse with the ascent of the far-rightist Jair Bolsonaro, who made a sharp turn toward Christian nationalism the centerpiece of his governing strategy. As Bolsonaro's new Foreign Minister Ernesto Araújo argued in the conservative magazine *The New Criterion* in early 2019,

> I am convinced that President Bolsonaro's faith is instrumental, not accidental, to his electoral victory and to the wave of change that is washing over Brazil. Brazil is experiencing a political and spiritual rebirth, and the spiritual aspect of this phenomenon is the determinant one. The political aspect is only a consequence. (Araújo 2019)

Declaring his enmity to various ideologies including "cultural Marxism," "globalism," and "economic globalization," as well as all of Brazil's traditional parties, Araújo proclaimed his belief that "divine providence" was guiding Brazil, and had united the far-right pundit Olavo de Carvalho with "the determination and patriotism of Bolsonaro."

This new religious nationalism superficially revives, but more accurately revises, former Brazilian notions of religion's role in the nation. In their recent book *Taking America Back for God: Christian Nationalism in the United States*, Whitehead and Perry argue that the rise of Trump's right-wing base in the United States must be understood in the context of Christian nationalism, which is a distinct ideology from the country's historical civil religion (Whitehead and Perry 2020). While the latter posited a divine mandate for Americans to lead through "exemplary fairness, beneficence, and faithful stewardship," the former instead emphasizes the need for "allegiance to our national—almost ethnic—Christian identity" (Whitehead and Perry 2020, 25). Analogously, we argue, Bolsonaro's distinctive brand of religious nationalism views God as a partisan and patriot—a dramatic shift from the popular Catholicism that shaped Brazilian identity for most of its history. Bolsonaro's religious nationalism is deployed not to build commonality among Brazilians and define natural allies in the international arena, but as a tool for domestic and international competition and dominance. In an insightful recent essay, R. Scott Appleby suggests that this transition may result from the impact of "late modernity" on visions of national self and the divine, producing a "conflation of the petty machinations of mortals and the awesome grandeur of the sacred" (Appleby 2020, 55). As Appleby argues, modern "religious subcultures" have come to interpret "Divine Power as merely the extrapolation of earthly power, as the pure, unfettered essence of the kind of power wielded by the modern state—namely, the power to command, to control, to master, to dominate" (Appleby 2020, 54–55). At the same time, it is important to note that Bolsonaro's Christian nationalism is not simply a Brazilian copy of the American version. In contrast to the "America First" ideology of Trumpism, Bolsonaro's motto of "Brazil above everything" imagines Brazil as a supportive player in an international spiritual alliance of global rightists, together arrayed against enemies who are simultaneously domestic and foreign.

Hypothesis 2: Religious Soft Power as a Tool of Foreign Affairs

Our second explanation as to why Brazil has used religion as a form of soft power touches upon a realist, power-seeking perspective and refers to Brazil's attempt to expand its global reach. This has been particularly visible in the last two decades, when successive administrations pledged to turn Brazil into an emerging power. Religion, to be sure, has never been at the center of Brazilian foreign policy strategy, as we have previously discussed. However, it has proven to be a useful narrative tool in at least three power-related contexts.

The first is to increase Brazil's presence and influence across the Global South, especially in Latin America. This has been particularly true under Lula da Silva, who mentioned God and religious themes in several of his addresses to foreign leaders or audiences (unlike his predecessors back until the 1960s and successors up until Jair Bolsonaro). The way he evoked his faith varied greatly from country to country, though. While Lula virtually did not refer to religion when speaking to authorities from developed countries, he sounded particularly pious in his relationship with Latin American presidents, often describing those countries' resources and assets as "God-given." That was the case in his interactions with Bolivia ("the Bolivian gas is an extraordinary treasure God has given this country"; Ministério das Relações Exteriores 2004, 38), Venezuela ("we must create a deep strategic alliance so that both nations may benefit from the resources God has given us"; Ministério das Relações Exteriores 2005a, 52) and Panama ("we want to build a vigorous relationship with Panama, taking advantage of the strategic position God has placed Panama in our planet"; Ministério das Relações Exteriores 2007a, 150).

In his interactions with regional counterparts, Lula also attributed the great ideological convergence among presidents in the hemisphere—which is usually referred to as the Latin American "pink tide" of the 2000s—to divine work. "God wanted Latin America and South America [to have elected left-wing presidents]," Lula declared at the inauguration of a bridge over the Orinoco river in Venezuela (Ministério das Relações Exteriores 2006, 163). At the launching of the construction of the Inter-Oceanic Highway, which connected Brazil, Peru, and Bolivia in the tri-border Peruvian city of Puerto Maldonado, Lula declared to the Peruvian president Alejandro Toledo that "God wanted that you and me to start this construction . . . I am sure that someone will write in History [books] that it was exactly on this day that the South American Community of Nations was consolidated" (Ministério das Relações Exteriores 2005b, 83). The Brazilian president went so far as to describe South American integration as "a miracle" before a crowd in Caracas, at the inauguration ceremony of a Brazilian public bank in Venezuela: "if we look into a not-so-distant past, [South American integration], for those who believe in God like me, is a miracle—it is a miracle because there are so many adversaries out there" (Ministério das Relações Exteriores 2009b, 150).

We may hypothesize that Lula was tapping into Latin America's religious sentiments to allay neighboring countries' suspicion of Brazil's growing power. After all, before the "pink tide" swept across the hemisphere, the strong Christian (mostly Catholic) faith was perhaps the strongest bond that united countries, large or small. And most saw Brazil as a potentially destabilizing force in the region, either thanks to its occasional alignment with US interests (which many in South America denounced as "subimperialist" behavior, as theorized by Ruy Mauro Marini; Marini 1972, 4–24) or to Brazil's historical tendency to neglect the interests of neighbors in its international relations (Santos 2014).

Outside of Latin America, one situation has spurred the use of religion to justify new partnerships and alliances. Brazilian authorities have often brought up religion as a link between Brazil and India.[16] On their official trips to Delhi, presidents Lula and Rousseff have underscored the bonds of democracy as well as ethnic and religious pluralism as something that brought the two countries together (Ministério das Relações Exteriores 2007b, 158). This rare combination even explained their great convergence in multilateral issues and made both countries transformative forces toward a new world order (Rousseff 2012).

More recently, Jair Bolsonaro gave religion a different twist in a letter of gratitude to Prime Minister Narendra Modi for supplying Brazil with hydroxychloroquine amid the COVID-19 pandemic: "Just as Lord Hanuman brought the holy medicine from the Himalayas to save the life of Lord Rama's brother Lakshmana, and Jesus healed those who were sick and restored sight to Bartimeus, India and Brazil will overcome this global crisis by joining forces and sharing blessings for the sake of all people."[17] Although the message had the same rhetorical function of legitimizing the bilateral partnership, the shift in how national identities are portrayed, away from plurality and toward religious hegemony, is noteworthy as it reflects the current political moment in both countries.

The second context refers to Brazil's desire to raise its profile in international security matters. The idea was to offer the country's good offices as a conflict mediator, thanks to a long history of peaceful relations with the rest of the world. Brazil's "ethnic, religious and cultural harmony" (Ministério das Relações Exteriores 1996, 135) has been evoked as a unique asset that would allow Brazilian diplomacy to act as an honest broker in the Middle East and to therefore play a constructive role in the Israeli-Palestinian conflict. "Brazil is a country where various religious confessions live together: Jews, Christians, Sunni and Shia Muslims," said foreign minister Celso Amorim in 2006. Earlier that year, based on that same reasoning, President Lula posed a question at the UN General Assembly: "wouldn't it be time to summon a broad conference [on the Middle East] under the aegis of the United Nations (...) where countries could contribute through their capacity, and successful experience, in living peacefully with differences?" (Lula da Silva 2006). Variations on that same theme, especially those that praised Brazil as the land where Arabs and Jews could be friends, became commonplace across parties and ideologies of Brazilian administrations (Ministério das Relações Exteriores 2009a, 40).

Third, and lastly, religion has been used to increase Brazil's breadth of multilateral interests. In recent years, Brazil has vowed to lead discussions on religious intolerance from the perspective of a country that had successfully devised a model of ethno-religious coexistence.[18] The Lula administration enthusiastically embraced the Turkish-Spanish initiative "Alliance of Civilizations" because it was backed by the United Nations, in 2005, and offered to host the first Alliance summit outside of Europe, which took place in Rio de Janeiro in 2010. A few years later, in her UN speech, President Rousseff highlighted Brazil's leadership in the Alliance of Civilizations to legitimize the Brazilian position in fighting Islamophobia across the world.[19]

Under Bolsonaro, Brazil has joined the United States and other countries led by far-right leaders, such as Hungary and Poland, to advance a religious/Christian nationalist agenda. In the last two years, the Bolsonaro administration has joined conservative initiatives such as the Partnership for Families alliance and the US-led International Religious Freedom Alliance (Hartman, 2020). Together with the Hungarian government, Brazil has also promoted the panel "Rebuilding Lives, Rebuilding Communities: Ensuring a Future for Persecuted Christians" at the United Nations. While such initiatives reflect Brazil's new religious identity, they may also be understood as a form of jumping on the bandwagon with Trump while forging a new pattern of global alignment driven by religion.

Hypothesis 3: Religious Soft Power as a Tool for Building Domestic Coalitions

Finally, a third explanation for Brazilian presidents' deployment of religious soft power may be to shore up electoral and ideological support among varying domestic religious and political groups. As Haynes argues, "some [domestic] religious actors influence state foreign policy by encouraging policy makers to take into account religious beliefs, norms and values" (Haynes 2008, 143–165). This hypothesis has acquired particular relevance in Brazil's post-1985 democratic period, for two reasons. First, growing religious pluralism and interreligious competition has increased both the number of groups seeking advantages, as well as their interest in potentially enlisting the state's assistance. Second, the form of coalitional presidentialism that has evolved under conditions of extremely high multipartism has made presidents beholden to pluralistic, particularistic interest groups, typically without the "glue" of meaningful shared partisanship.[20]

In some cases, presidents have deployed foreign policy to support Evangelicals and Pentecostals as an interdenominational interest group. As part of Lula da Silva's alliance with Evangelical leaders, he used diplomatic channels to pave the way for Brazilian churches into Africa, notably the Universal Church of the Kingdom of God.[21] With the demise of the Workers' Party after President Rousseff's impeachment in 2016, Evangelical groups began scrambling for greater influence over foreign policy and have gained preeminence under the Bolsonaro administration. They focused on two main issues: human rights from a religious conservative perspective and improved relations with Israel along the lines of Christian Zionism.[22] As for the former, for instance, the National Association of Evangelical Jurists (in Portuguese, Anajure) has entered the foreign policy arena to a greater extent in recent years, and is currently seeking observer status at the United Nations.[23] The Bolsonaro administration has strongly supported Anajure's application, perceiving the association as an ally in its campaign against "gender ideology" within the UN (Chade 2020). As for the latter, President Bolsonaro has been the target of intense pressure from Brazilian Evangelical interest groups—as well as from the Trump administration—to move its Israeli embassy to Jerusalem.[24] In this case, however, the combined domestic and international lobbying has been matched by opposite domestic forces. While military leaders fear the national security implications of moving the embassy, Brazilian agribusiness fears that a breakdown in the country's relations with the Arab world could endanger the country's highly lucrative, export-oriented halal meat industry. Ultimately, the Bolsonaro administration followed a middle path that angered Evangelicals. On a visit to Israel in late March 2019, Bolsonaro announced his plan to open a trade office lacking diplomatic status in Jerusalem.

In other cases, Brazilian foreign affairs provide special recognition to one domestic religious group or another, instigating interreligious insecurity and competition among other groups. Most notable is the case of the 2008 Concordat quickly written and signed between the Lula government and the Holy See. While much of the text of the Concordat simply reaffirmed laws already in place, the convention granted the Catholic Church in Brazil certain rights not already stipulated in law. These included tax immunity for religiously affiliated organizations other than churches, the explicit right to confessional public school religious education, and recognition of the Church's special contribution to the Brazilian cultural heritage (Souza 2016). The legislative Evangelical Caucus, incensed that Lula would rather abruptly grant special privileges for the Catholic Church, responded by introducing a bill for a General Law on Religions in 2009, which was ultimately passed in 2016, stipulating many of the same rights and protections for Evangelical churches (Franco and Altafin 2016).

Similar dynamics are observed in the case of diplomatic passports. Until 2006, since the days of the Brazilian empire, Brazil had explicitly allowed diplomatic passports to be granted to "Brazilian Cardinals and other high authorities of a similar hierarchical level," supposedly in recognition of their special relationship with the Vatican.[25] In an executive decree promulgated in that year, the clause for Cardinals was removed. In its place has emerged a system in which diplomatic passports are granted as "special exceptions" to religious leaders of various denominations on an ad hoc, particularistic basis involving individual consideration from the foreign minister, which is generally considered to have benefitted Pentecostal and neo-Pentecostal leaders (Leitão 2011). Following a scandal in which President Lula's children were discovered to have received diplomatic passports, media attention provoked some formalization of the process, but no new decree spelling out the rights of religious leaders was promulgated. Under Foreign Minister José Serra, the practice of granting religious diplomatic passports was entirely ended in 2016; it was reinstated under President Bolsonaro in 2019 (Coletta 2019).[26] While a federal judge temporarily blocked his granting of a diplomatic passport to Bishop Edir Macedo of the Universal Church of the Kingdom of God, an appeals court reversed the injunction, effectively giving some legal protection to the informal practice.

Final Remarks

Despite being the world's largest Catholic country, Brazil's foreign policy establishment has historically resisted letting religious values strongly influence foreign policy. While the Vatican did exert some degree of political influence and moral authority over the Brazilian Empire throughout the nineteenth century, the Republican era has ushered in a secular, sovereign, and supra-partisan foreign policy strategy, which relied on values such as pacifism and multilateralism and on resources of soft power.

As a core identity across global cultures and civilizations, one would expect Brazil to use religion as an indissociable element of its soft-power toolkit. This has not been the case, however. Brazilian foreign policy has rarely invoked religious values, even when it only meant a mere statement of a consensual position (as the one of Brazil as a Western nation based on Christian values, as Quadros has put it). There have been almost no mentions of God, religion, or Christianity in Brazil's official foreign policy statements and documents.

Yet, something has changed in recent decades. Lula da Silva, a left-wing politician whose religious beliefs had never been a major political issue, began praising Brazil's religious composition as a means to justify a more ambitious and far-reaching foreign policy. While he spoke of the Christian God when addressing Latin American audiences, he also lauded Brazil's religious diversity and tolerance at multilateral negotiating tables. Bolsonaro, on the other hand, has transformed religion into the cornerstone of his political strategy, one based on a Christian nationalist ideology. His former foreign minister Ernesto Araújo (who left office in March 2021) is right to affirm that Brazil's "new" foreign policy does not shy away from talking about God. The question is how Brazil has moved from a secular and predictable foreign policy strategy toward a wholly religious one, where Christian conservatism has taken over pragmatic universalism.

Drawing on three international relations theories—constructivism, realism, and interest-group liberalism—we have presented hypotheses that shed light on the circumstances under which Brazil has resorted to religion as part of its soft power. It seems clear that they are all intertwined: the country has undergone a significant religious transition, in which Evangelicals, who now correspond to roughly 30 percent of the Brazilian population, have become a major political force. This has provoked a shift in how governments have addressed and constructed Brazil's national identity, moving from ethno-religious pluralism toward Christian nationalism. And, of course, these identities will be instrumentalized in foreign policy as a means to increase the country's power.

While Lula could cherry-pick elements of Brazil's religious identities with relative freedom as part of his emerging power strategy, Bolsonaro's use of religious soft power takes place under much greater constraints. Not only is Bolsonaro pressured by religious groups, but his administration is faithfully committed to a Christian nationalist platform at home and to far-right populist partners abroad. As discussed in this chapter, Brazil's use of religious soft power depends on both structural and conjunctural factors, with the former playing an increasingly greater role as religious shifts lead to deeper changes in Brazil's religious identity.

References

Aldrovandi, Carlo. 2014. *Apocalyptic Movements in Contemporary Politics: Christian and Jewish Zionism*. New York: Palgrave.
Amorim, Celso. 2010. "Brazilian Foreign Policy under President Lula (2003–2010): An Overview." *Revista Brasileira de Política Internacional* 53: 214–240.

Appleby, R. Scott. 2020. "Narrowing the Options: Power and Glory in the Late Modern Religious Imagination." *The Review of Faith & International Affairs* 18 (3): 53–59.
Araújo, Ernesto. 2019. Discurso de posse como Ministro das Relações Exteriores. http://funag.gov.br/index.php/pt-br/component/content/article?id=2913.
Araújo, Ernesto. 2019. "Now We Do." *The New Criterion*, January 2019. https://newcriterion.com/issues/2019/1/now-we-do.
Azzi, Riolando. 1980. "A Igreja Católica no Brasil Durante o Estado Novo (1937–1945)." *Síntese: Revista de Filosofia* 7 (19): 49–71.
Bebbington, David William. 1989. *Evangelicalism in Modern Britain: A History from the 1730s to the 1980s*. London and Boston: Unwin Hyman.
Bellah, Robert N. 1967. "Civil Religion in America." *Daedalus* 96 (1): 1–21.
Bettiza, Gregorio. 2019. *Finding Faith in Foreign Policy: Religion and American Diplomacy in a Postsecular World*. Oxford: Oxford University Press.
Brands, Hal. 2011. "Evaluating Brazilian Grand Strategy under Lula." *Comparative Strategy* 30 (1): 28–49.
"Brazilian President Invokes Ramayana While Seeking Hydroxychloroquine from India." 2020. *The Hindu*. April 9. https://www.thehindu.com/news/international/brazilian-prez-invokes-ramayana-while-seeking-hydroxychloroquine-from-india/article31295486.ece.
Burges, Sean. 2008. "Consensual Hegemony: Theorizing Brazilian Foreign Policy after the Cold War." *International Relations* 22 (1): 65–84.
Burges, Sean W. 2015. " Revisiting Consensual Hegemony: Brazilian Regional Leadership in Question." *International Politics* 52 (2): 193–207.
Casarões, Guilherme. 2017. "Geo-Economic Competition in Latin America: Brazil, Venezuela, and Regional Integration in the 21st Century." 33. UNISA Latin America Report.
Casarões, Guilherme. 2019. "Trump's Jerusalem Move in South America: Falling on Deaf Ears?" In *Trump's Jerusalem Move: Making Sense of US Policy on the Israeli-Palestinian Conflict*, edited by Kadir Üstün. Ankara: SETA Publications.
Casarões, Guilherme. 2020. "Leaving the Club Without Slamming the Door: Brazil's Return to Middle-Power Status." In *Status and the Rise of Brazil:Global Ambitions, Humanitarian Engagement and International Challenges*, edited by Paulo Esteves, Maria Gabrielsen Jumbert, and Benjamin de Carvalho, 89–110. London: Palgrave Macmillan.
Casarões, Guilherme, and Daniel Flemes. 2019. *Brazil First, Climate Last: Bolsonaro's Foreign Policy*. 5 vols. GIGA Focus: Latin America . https://pesquisa-eaesp.fgv.br/sites/gvpesquisa.fgv.br/files/arquivos/brazil_first.pdf.
Celso, Lafer. 2000. "Brazilian International Identity and Foreign Policy: Past, Present and Future." 129 (2).
Chade, Jamil. 2020. "Apoiadores do Itamaraty, juristas evangélicos querem voz em debates na ONU." *UOL*, January 10, 2020. https://noticias.uol.com.br/colunas/jamil-chade/2020/01/10/juristas-evangelicos-onu-brasil-governo-bolsonaro.htm.
Chade, Jamil. 2020. "China Freia Juristas Evangélicos Do Brasil Na ONU." *UOL*, January 20. https://noticias.uol.com.br/colunas/jamil-chade/2020/01/20/china-freia-juristas-evangelicos-do-brasil-na-onu.htm.
Chatin, Mathilde. 2016. "Brazil: Analysis of a Rising Soft Power." *Journal of Political Power* 9 (3): 369–393.

Coletta, Ricardo Della. 2019. "Itamaraty retoma prática do governo Lula e concede passaporte diplomático a Edir Macedo e sua mulher." *Folha de S.Paulo*, April 15, 2019. https://www1.folha.uol.com.br/mundo/2019/04/itamaraty-concede-passaporte-dipl omatico-para-edir-macedo-e-sua-mulher.shtml.

Cooper, Andrew Fenton, Richard A. Higgott, and Kim Richard Nossal. 1993. *Relocating Middle Powers: Australia and Canada in a Changing World Order.* Vancouver: University of British Columbia Press.

Danese, Sérgio França. 1999. "A Diplomacia No Processo de Formação Nacional Do Brasil." *Política Externa* 81 (1).

Duarte, Sérgio de Queiroz. 2017. "The Role of Brazil in Multilateral Disarmament Efforts." *Revista Brasileira de Política Internacional* 60 (2).

Engstrom, Par. 2012. "Brazilian Foreign Policy and Human Rights: Change and Continuity under Dilma." *Critical Sociology* 38 (6).

Farias, Cibele Guerra. 2012. "*A laicidade do estado brasileiro e os feriados nacionais.*" Master's Thesis, Universidade Lusófona. https://recil.grupolusofona.pt/handle/ 10437/4718.

Franco, Simone, and Iara Guimarães Altafin. 2016. "Lei Geral das Religiões é aprovada na Comissão de Justiça e vai a Plenário." *Senado Federal*, March 16, 2016. https://www12. senado.leg.br/noticias/materias/2016/03/16/lei-geral-das-religioes-e-aprovada-na-comissao-de-justica-e-vai-a-plenario.

Freyre, Gilberto. 1973. *Casa-Grande e Senzala*. Rio de Janeiro : Livraria José Olympio Editora.

Goes Filho, Synesio Sampaio. 1999. *Navegantes, Bandeirantes, Diplomatas: Um Ensaio Sobre a Formação Das Fronteiras Do Brasil.* São Paulo: Martins Fontes.

Hartman, Leigh. 2020. "U.S. Launches International Religious Freedom Alliance." *Share America*, February 6, 2020. https://share.america.gov/u-s-launches-international-religious-freedom-alliance/.

Haynes, Jeffrey. 2008. "Religion and Foreign Policy Making in the USA, India and Iran: Towards a Research Agenda." *Third World Quarterly* 29 (1): 143–165.

Haynes, Jeffrey. 2012. *Religious Transnational Actors and Soft Power.* London: Routledge.

Jansen, Roberta. 2018. "Igreja e Governo Disputam Receitas Do Cristo Redentor." *Terra*, August 30. https://www.terra.com.br/noticias/brasil/cidades/igreja-e-parque-nacio nal-disputam-receitas-do-cristo-redentor,ea5f8b54b54130af70c3eb08248eb330iug9d 6pm.html.

Kennan, George F. 1993. *Around the Cragged Hill: A Personal and Political Philosophy.* New York: W.W. Norton & Company.

Keohane, Robert. 1969. "Lilliputians' Dilemmas: Small States in International Politics." *International Organization* 23 (2): 291–310.

Kuru, Ahmet T. 2009. *Secularism and State Policies Toward Religion: The United States, France, and Turkey.* Cambridge: Cambridge University Press.

Layton, Matthew L., and Amy Erica Smith. 2017. "Is It Race, Class, or Gender? The Sources of Perceived Discrimination in Brazil." *Latin American Politics and Society* 59 (1): 52–73.

Leitão, Matheus. "Em 5 anos, Itamaraty deu 328 passaportes especiais." *Folha de S. Paulo*, February 16, 2011. https://www1.folha.uol.com.br/fsp/poder/po1602201102.htm.

Lula da Silva, Luiz I. *General Debate of the 61st Session of the United Nations General Assembly.* September 19, 2006. https://www.un.org/webcast/ga/61/pdfs/brasil-e.pdf.

Lustig, Robin. "Brazil emerges as a leading exponent of soft power." *BBC News*, March 23, 2010. http://news.bbc.co.uk/2/hi/americas/8580560.stm.
Mainwaring, Scott. 1986. *The Catholic Church and Politics in Brazil, 1916–1985*. Redwood City: Stanford University Press.
Malamud, Andres. 2011. "A Leader without Followers? The Growing Divergence between the Regional and Global Performance of Brazilian Foreign Policy." *Latin American Politics and Society* 53 (3): 1–24.
Marini, Ruy Mauro. 1972. "Brazilian Subimperialism." *Monthly Review* 23 (9), 14–24.
Mauerberg Junior, Arnaldo, Carlos Pereira, and Ciro Biderman. 2015. "The Evolution of Theories about the Brazilian Multiparty Presidential System." *Journal of Politics in Latin America* 7 (1): 143–61.
Ministério das Relações Exteriores. 1996. "Pronunciamento do Ministro de Estado das Relações Exteriores, Embaixador Luis Felipe Lampreia, por ocasião do almoço oferecido pelos Embaixadores dos Países Árabes acreditados junto ao Governo Brasileiro, Brasília, 28 de março de 1996." *Resenha de Política Exterior* 78 (1): 135–136.
Ministério das Relações Exteriores. 2004. "Discurso do Presidente da República, Luiz Inácio Lula da Silva, na cerimônia de comemoração dos vinte anos de relançamento da Câmara Nacional de Comércio Brasileiro-Boliviana, em Santa Cruz de la Sierra, em 8 de julho de 2004." *Resenha de Política Exterior* 95 (2): 37–39.
Ministério das Relações Exteriores. 2005a. "Discurso do Presidente da República, Luiz Inácio Lula da Silva, por ocasião do Encontro Empresarial Brasil-Venezuela, em Caracas, no dia 14 de fevereiro de 2005." *Resenha de Política Exterior* 96 (1): 51–53.
Ministério das Relações Exteriores. 2005b. "Discurso do Presidente da República, Luiz Inácio Lula da Silva, na cerimônia de início das obras da Rodovia Interoceânica, em Puerto Maldonado, Peru, em 8 de setembro de 2005." *Resenha de Política Exterior* 97 (2): 81–84.
Ministério das Relações Exteriores. 2006. "Discurso do Presidente da República, Luiz Inácio Lula da Silva, durante a inauguração da segunda ponte sobre o rio Orinoco, na Venezuela." *Resenha de Política Exterior* 99 (2): 163–166.
Ministério das Relações Exteriores. 2007a. "Discurso do Presidente da República, Luiz Inácio Lula da Silva, por ocasião da visita ao Brasil do Presidente da República do Panamá, Martín Torrijos." *Resenha de Política Exterior* 100 (1): 149–152.
Ministério das Relações Exteriores. 2007b. "Visita do Presidente da República Luiz Inácio Lula da Silva à Índia." *Resenha de Política Exterior* 100 (1): 155–160.
Ministério das Relações Exteriores. 2008. "Discurso do Presidente da República, Luiz Inácio Lula da Silva, durante a cerimônia de abertura do Encontro Empresarial Brasil-Argentina." *Resenha de Política Exterior* 103 (2): 61–68.
Ministério das Relações Exteriores. 2009a. "Discurso do Presidente da República, Luiz Inácio Lula da Silva, durante solenidade do Dia Internacional em Memória das Vítimas do Holocausto." *Resenha de Política Exterior* 104 (1): 39–42.
Ministério das Relações Exteriores. 2009b. "Discurso do Presidente da República, Luiz Inácio Lula da Silva, na cerimônia de inauguração do Consulado-Geral do Brasil e do Escritório da Caixa Econômica Federal em Caracas." *Resenha de Política Exterior* 105 (2): 149–152.
Ministério das Relações Exteriores. 2012. *Obras do Barão do Rio Branco IX—Discursos*. Brasília: FUNAG.
Nye, Joseph. 1990. "Soft Power." *Foreign Policy* 80.

O Estado de S. Paulo. 2012. "Crivella Acredita Que Evangélicos Ainda Vão Eleger Um Presidente." *Estado.* September 16. https://politica.estadao.com.br/noticias/eleic oes,crivella-acredita-que-evangelicos-ainda-vao-eleger-um-presidente-imp-,931355.

Power, Timothy J. 2010. "Optimism, Pessimism, and Coalitional Presidentialism: Debating the Institutional Design of Brazilian Democracy." *Bulletin of Latin American Research* 29 (1): 18–33.

Quadros, Jânio. 1961. "Brazil's New Foreign Policy." *Foreign Affairs* 40 (1): 19–27.

Ramos, Jovelino P. 1974. "Interpretando o Fenômeno Canudos." *Luso-Brazilian Review* 11 (1): 65–83.

Ricupero, Rubens. 2017. *A Diplomacia Na Construção Do Brasil: 1750–2016.* São Paulo: Versal.

Rousseff, Dilma. 2012. "BRICS Members Brazil and India Are Strategic Partners for a New World Vision." *The Economic Times,* March 29, 2012. https://economictimes.ind iatimes.com/news/politics-and-nation/brics-members-brazil-and-india-are-strate gic-partners-for-a-new-world-vision/articleshow/12450895.cms.

Sanchez-Badin, Michelle, Gregory Schaeffer, and Barbara Rosenberg. 2008. "The Trials of Winning at the WTO: What Lies behind Brazil's Success." *Cornell International Law Journal* 41 (2).

Santos, Luís Cláudio Villafañe G. 2014. *A América do Sul no Discurso Diplomático Brasileiro.* Brasília: FUNAG.

Serbin, Kenneth. 2000. *Secret Dialogues.* Pittsburgh: University of Pittsburgh Press.

Serbin, Kenneth P. 1996. "Church-State Reciprocity in Contemporary Brazil: The Convening of the International Eucharistic Congress of 1955 in Rio de Janeiro." *The Hispanic American Historical Review* 76 (4): 721–51.

Smith, Amy Erica. 2019. *Religion and Brazilian Democracy: Mobilizing the People of God.* Cambridge: Cambridge University Press.

Soares, Geraldo Antônio. 2009. "Religião, Cultura e Poder Na Obra de Gilberto Freyre." *Dimensões* 22: 200–224.

Soper, Christopher J., and Joel S. Fetzer. 2018. *Religion and Nationalism in Global Perspective.* Cambridge: Cambridge University Press.

Souza, Lidyane Maria Ferreira de. 2016. "The 2008 Concordat in Brazil: 'Modern Public Religion' or Neo-Corporatism?" In *The Social Equality of Religion or Belief,* edited by Alan Carling. New York: Palgrave MacMillan.

Spector, Stephen. 2009. *Evangelicals and Israel: The Story of American Christian Zionism.* Oxford: Oxford University Press.

"Speech by President Dilma Rousseff on the Occasion of the Opening of the General Debate of the 67th Session of the United Nations General Assembly." 2012. *Ministério Das Relações Exteriores.* Government of Brazil. September 25. https://www.gov.br/ mre/en/content-centers/speeches-articles-and-interviews/president-of-the-federat ive-republic-of-brazil/speeches/statement-by-h-e-dilma-rousseff-president-of-the- federative-republic-of-brazil-at-the-opening-of-the-general-debate-of-the-67th-sess ion-of-the-united-nations-general-assembly.

Steiner, Sherrie. 2016. "Is Religious Soft Power of Consequence in the World Today?" In *Religious Diversity Today. Goulet. In Religion Transforming Societies and Social Lives,* edited by Jean-Guy A. Goulet. New York: Praeger, 1–34.

Stuenkel, Oliver. 2019. "How Bolsonaro's Chaotic Foreign Policy Worries the Rest of South America." *Americas Quarterly,* June 18. https://www.americasquarterly.org/arti cle/how-bolsonaros-chaotic-foreign-policy-worries-the-rest-of-south-america/.

Whitehead, Andrew L., and Samuel L. Perry. 2020. *Taking America Back for God: Christian Nationalism in the United States*. New York: Oxford University Press.

Valença, Marcelo, and Gustavo Carvalho. 2014. "Soft Power, Hard Aspirations: the Shifting Role of Power in Brazilian Foreign Policy." *Brazilian Political Science Review* 8 (3): 1–29.

Valente, Waldemar. 1955. *Sincretismo Religioso Afro-Brasileiro*. São Paulo: Companhia Editora Nacional.

Vieira, Marco A. 2012. "Brazilian Foreign Policy in the Context of Global Climate Norms." *Foreign Policy Analysis*: 1–18.

Vizentini, Paulo F. 1999. "O Brasil e o Mundo: A Política Externa e Suas Fases." *Ensaios FEE: Porto Alegre* 20 (1): 134–154.

15

Religious Soft Power

Promises, Limits, and Ways Forward

Gregorio Bettiza and Peter S. Henne

Introduction

The Geopolitics of Religious Soft Power project is a groundbreaking initiative. No other research project has focused in such a sustained manner on conceptually and empirically investigating religion as a particular form of power in world politics. The project draws on Joseph Nye's notorious concept of soft power to explore, first through a series of reports, how a range of Muslim-majority states—like Turkey, Iran, or Morocco—draw on Islam as a soft-power tool to advance their interests and values in the international system. Thereafter this conceptual lens has been applied to explore a wider set of cases—such as those of the United States, Russia, China, Turkey, India, Iran, Morocco, Indonesia, Jordan, Israel, the Vatican, and Brazil—which populate the present volume. The project opens up a range of fascinating avenues for research on religion in world politics and more broadly also on power, soft or otherwise, in international relations.

While taking the present volume as this concluding chapter's main reference point, we also seek to reflect on *The Geopolitics of Religious Soft Power* project's theoretical and empirical contributions as a whole. We divide the chapter into three main parts, each divided into three subsections. The first part outlines what we see as the project and volume's major contributions. These include making power central to the analysis of religion in world politics; broadening a budding research agenda on the entanglements between religion and states' foreign policy; and challenging in important ways a number of ingrained secularist assumptions about the practice and theory of international relations. In the second section we sharpen our critical lenses and identify three shortcomings of the project. These include what we would label as a reductive approach to religion, as well as certain limits in its use of the concept of soft power, which is both at once too (conceptually) broad and (empirically) narrow. Finally, we conclude with three suggestions for future research that directly build on the valuable insights generated by the project and this volume. These include thinking about religious power beyond the notion of soft power; identifying in a more systematic way how the characteristics of different political actors and religions shape (soft) power resources and relations; and lastly addressing the challenge of how to measure religious (soft) power and influence.

Promises

The Geopolitics of Religious Soft Power project, which this volume is a key part of, is a pathbreaking initiative. It is so especially for the breadth of its case studies and the depth of its analysis into the entanglements between religion, states, and power in international relations. Most notably it makes, in our view, three distinctive scholarly contributions including placing power more centrally in the study of religion in world politics, broadening research on religion and foreign policy, and challenging enduring secularist assumptions in international relations (IR).

Brining Power "Back In" The Study of Religion

The most immediate contribution of *The Geopolitics of Religious Soft Power* project and this volume is to squarely position power analysis at the center of research on religion in world politics. That religion is a powerful political force has been very well understood by political and social theorists across the ages, whether it be Niccolò Machiavelli (Viroli 2010), Karl Marx (Raines 2002), or Michael Foucault (Carrette and Foucault 1999). Likewise, historically oriented scholarship has certainly been attentive to the complex entanglements between political power, empire, and religion (Carey 2008; Nexon 2009; Phillips 2010).

While scholarship on religion in comparative politics and IR has grown exponentially in past decades, the issue of power has generally been neglected in the field. Many studies certainly focus on *the power of* religion to produce dramatic effects in international relations, most notably in terms of conflict or peace. Nonetheless these hardly approach religion in explicit terms as a *form and source of power.* Furthermore, when power does enter the discussion, the study of religion is generally presented as a reaction to the significance of (military) power in the field of international relations. For example, the introduction to Johnston and Sampson's (1995) influential edited volume, *Religion, the Missing Dimension of Statecraft,* is entitled "beyond power politics." Others have similarly stressed how religious and ethical concerns could override considerations of power (Otis 2004). As Elshtain (2004, 116) has argued, religion has thus often been "seen in simplistic alternatives," as "either a source of sanctimonious aspirations . . . that are politely ignored in 'real' statecraft" or as "the source of all the terrorist extremism."

Accepting a dichotomy between religious and material factors problematically limits the applicability of the former to the study of power. As Nexon (2008, 151) puts it, many studies of religion have followed Constructivism's critique of materialist theories, creating a "misconception" that "the significance of religion should be evaluated by comparing the relative importance of material and ideational factors in any particular outcome." That is, generally studies try to uncover instances in which religious ideas mattered, even when we account for the role of material conditions. This dichotomy can be useful in demonstrating the significance of religion, but there are only so many clear-cut examples of religious actors overcoming limits placed on them by their lack of material power. As one of us has argued elsewhere, "religion and international relations scholars' tendency to [frame] their arguments . . . in contraposition to the dominant materialist ontologies and positivist methodologies of social scientists," leads this research to miss "the power of religion as an instrument" (Bettiza 2013, 22).

Overall, both approaches—either overlooking religion as a source of power or singularly presenting faith in opposition to (material) power—have had the unintended consequence of cutting somewhat this research program off from many important areas of debate in international relations. By making power an explicit focus of research on faith, *The Geopolitics of Religious Soft Power* project and this volume provide both an avenue for deepening our understanding of religion in world politics and connecting this research program to key discussions about power, security, and international order taking place in the discipline.[1] We will now unpack in more detail what we mean by this.

First of all, attention to power is valuable because it provides a foundational lens to explain in greater detail why and how religion matters in world politics. In other words, we cannot fully make sense of why religion becomes entangled with violence, why it is such a helpful resource for peace, or why states seek to govern, manage, or mobilize it in global affairs—as the multiple case studies in this volume show—if we do not understand the type of power resources and dynamics that are constituted and enabled by religion.

Conversely, this volume provides us a wider and more nuanced understanding of power and especially of soft power in international relations. It pushes forward existing efforts seeking to broaden the boundaries of this concept beyond the current overwhelmingly Western- and liberal-centric understandings offered by Nye (e.g., Keating and Kaczmarska 2019). It vividly demonstrates how the international sphere is marked by considerable value and cultural pluralism, itself shaped by distinct religious traditions in their complex local and global manifestations, which a multiplicity of states and communities embrace and find attractive around the world. Many of these dynamics go well beyond the supposedly unique attractiveness of secular liberal norms which much of the "soft power" literature focuses on.

Furthermore, the various cases connect—mostly implicitly—with new and important work opening up the study of power politics to include cultural and symbolic instruments alongside conventional military and economic ones. Goddard and Nexon (2016) have argued that scholars need to separate Realism from power politics, paying as much attention to symbolic and cultural instruments of power as they do to military and economic ones. They mention religious sites and rhetoric as examples of these. Their article is mainly a framework for analysis, and the contributions to this volume do not draw on them, but this may be a useful framework for future studies on religious soft power.[2]

Finally, a power perspective provides a valuable lens for analyzing numerous high-stakes areas of international relations, from geopolitical struggles to counterterrorism, highlighting the important role of religion in all these cases. By doing so, the project makes it increasingly difficult for security studies to continue ignoring religion. Informed by variants of Realism or classical geopolitics, international tensions and hostilities are generally analyzed in IR by focusing on military power and self-interest, effectively ignoring beliefs and identities. Thus, even in countries with a strong role for religion—such as Saudi Arabia—security studies tend to overwhelmingly emphasize material factors like oil wealth and geopolitics (Mabon 2018, 3).

The chapters in this volume provide a different story. Iranian geopolitical struggles in the Middle East against regional and global rivals, Wastnidge ("Shi'i Diplomacy: Religious Identity and Foreign Policy in the Axis of

Resistance") shows, cannot be completely divorced from the role that Shi'a narratives of resistance and transnational networks of coreligionists play. Henne and Bettiza ("Tragedy or Irony: Geopolitical Grand Narratives, Religious Outreach, and US Soft Power") highlight how religious grand narratives and outreach activities have been an integral part of America's efforts to generate legitimacy and mobilize allies during the Cold War and the recent War on Terror. Baumgart-Ochse ("Israel's Religious Soft Power: Within and Beyond Judaism") unpacks how Israeli religious soft-power strategies, especially targeting the Jewish diaspora and Christian Zionists in the United States, are central for securing American backing and support. Blitt ("'Putin-phonia': Harnessing Russian Orthodoxy to Advance Russia's Secular Foreign Policy") explores how the resurgence of Russia as a great power is deeply entangled with the ideological legitimacy and appeal the Russian Orthodox Church provides it. Muslim-majority states like Jordan (Gutkowski, "Moderation as Jordanian Soft Power: Islam and Beyond"), Indonesia (Hoesterey, "Indonesian Islam as Model for the World? Diplomacy, Soft Power, and the Geopolitics of 'Moderate Islam'"), Pakistan (Sheline, "Religious Diplomacy in the Arab Gulf and the Politics of Moderate Islam"), and Morocco (Wainscott, "Hassan II and the Foundations of Moroccan Religious Soft Power") seek to present themselves as the embodiment and promoters of "Moderate Islam" to align themselves with the West and supress domestic Islamist challengers in the context of the War on Terror. These examples of religion's importance cannot be confined to "low politics" or "cultural exchanges" but are crucial security issues that scholars and policymakers ought to take more seriously.

Broadening Research on Religion and Foreign Policy

The project speaks also to a more specific research agenda that has emerged in recent years exploring the interactions between states and religion in foreign policy, with particular reference to international religious freedom, counterterrorism, faith-based humanitarianism, or religious engagement. Work here has taken multiple directions. Some have been quite active in advocating for the operationalization of religion in American and European foreign policy (Albright 2006; Appleby and Cizik 2010; Birdsall, Lindsay, and Tomalin 2015; Farr 2008; Johnston and Sampson 1995; Petito et al. 2016; Seiple and Hoover 2004). Others have adopted a decidedly critical stance on this agenda conceptualizing it as a modern attempt to "govern" religious difference and dissent according to the needs of political power (Hurd 2015; Mahmood 2015; Sullivan et al. 2015). A further strand of scholarship takes a more analytical—rather than policy or normative—stance, seeking to explain the origins and effects, whether positive or negative, of making religion an object of foreign policy (Bettiza 2019, 2015; Henne 2019b, 2017; Henne, Saiya, and Hand 2019; Kolbe and Henne 2014; Wainscott 2017).

Against this scholarly backdrop, the present volume speaks most consistently to this third strand of research. In other words, it is less concerned with providing policy prescriptions or conceptually focused on the power of states themselves in governing religion. By developing the concept of religious soft power, instead, the volume shows in ways that have not yet been done as comprehensively thus far, how multiple states seek to advance their interests and values in the international system not only through well-known instruments like economic resources, military capabilities, and diplomatic skills. But also, and possibly increasingly so in an era defined by the return of the sacred (Sandal and Fox 2013; Toft, Philpott, and Shah 2011), through the power of religious discourses, norms, authority, actors, and networks.

The rich tapestry of cases proves to be quite eye opening, demonstrating how state practices seeking to mobilize religion as a soft-power resource are diffused. One may be hardly surprised to find religious states like the Vatican or Iran, and to some extent also Israel or Morocco, mobilizing religion to pursue their international and domestic interests. Yet all of this becomes more surprising when seeing that supposedly secular states like India, the United States and Turkey or even nominally communist ones like China engage in similar practices as well. Likewise, one finds that religious soft power is a potentially useful foreign policy tool for states with very different power resources and status. These include materially weak states like Jordan seeking to survive in a conflict-ridden region, large developing countries seeking to increase their international status like Brazil or Indonesia, or major powers engaged in international geopolitical struggles like Russia.

Challenging Secularist Assumptions in IR

By placing power at the center of the study of religion in IR and showing the extent to which a multiplicity of states draw upon the sacred to pursue their interests globally, this volume challenges in important ways a number of ingrained secularist assumptions about global politics. The field of IR has, by now, a well-known "secularist bias" (Hurd 2008; Philpott 2002), with its assumptions about rationality and modernity leaving little room for faith and religious practice. Even the emergence of Constructivism as one of the main theoretical paradigms in IR did little to change this, as most Constructivist studies emphasized secular norms and knowledge, ignoring religion (for important exceptions, see Bettiza and Dionigi 2015; Sandal 2011).

This volume pushes back on these secularist limitations in a number of ways. First, it shifts the focus away from approaching state-religion relations in mutually exclusive and zero-sum terms. Underpinned by certain secularist and modernist assumptions, a voluminous scholarship exists which treats the relationship between the Westphalian nation-state and religion, whether at the domestic (Anderson 2006; Carlson and Owens 2003; Fox 2015; Juergensmeyer 1993) or international level (Byrnes 2011; Philpott 2001; Mendelsohn 2012; Rudolph and Piscatori 1997; Shani 2008; Thomas 2005), as conflictual. Such a view is not wrong a priori. The issue we take is with the generally one-sided emphasis in the scholarship on the separate and antagonist, rather than entangled and cooperative aspects of this relation. This project—along with a few other exceptions (Cesari 2018)—bucks the trend by highlighting, instead, the positive-sum and mutually reinforcing dynamics, which may potentially exist between states and religions in today's international system.

Second, the volume pushes us to think about world politics beyond the well-worn secularist narratives of the "end of history" (Fukuyama 1992) and the "liberal international order" (Ikenberry 2009). In its exploration of the role of religion as a powerful cultural, ethical, and ideational force in our contemporary world, this volume gives further substance to Shmuel Eisenstadt's (2000) intuition that modernity expresses itself in multiple, not necessarily liberal and secular, forms (see also Casanova 2011). As Peter Mandaville and Shadi Hamid (2018, 27) argue in their agenda-setting article for this project, a focus on religious soft-power sheds important light on how we may be "moving toward a post-liberal or post-Western world order." If we are indeed heading towards such an international order, one that is likely to be also postsecular (Barbato and Kratochwil 2009; Bettiza and Dionigi 2015), it is not unreasonable to assume that religious soft power will have an ever greater weight and influence in international relations. Put differently, this project highlights certain particular global power relations and dynamics that we expect are likely to be increasingly important in the decades to come.

Limits

In this section we engage in a friendly, immanent critique of *The Geopolitics of Religious Soft Power* project. One that shares many of the project's premises and operates within the logics and parameters set out by it. We aim through critique to be constructive as well as self-reflective given that both of us contributed to this project.[3] Our intent is therefore to open up avenues for further research rather than closing them down.

Reductive Approach to Religion

The project has a tendency to adopt somewhat of a *reductive*, as we would put it, approach to religion. While the project's strength is certainly its narrow, laser-like, focus on the way states have (ab)used religion as a form of soft power, we find it does run the risk of oversimplifying the complex and nuanced ways religion matters in international relations. Such reductivism expresses itself in two ways.

The first reductive assumption permeating the project and this volume are their general neglect of the independent force of religious actors, institutions, and ideas themselves. There are some exceptions. For instance, in the Russian case (Blitt, "Russia's 2020 Constitutional Amendments and the Entrenchment of the Moscow Patriarchate as a Lever of Foreign Policy Soft Power"), the Moscow Patriarchate is seen as having some degree of independence and agency with respect to Vladimir Putin's intentions. Yet, overall, there is a sense that religion is reduced to a tool of statecraft that is instrumentally deployed by states according to their whims. This is of course partly understandable, given that the main concern here is with the religious soft power of states rather than faith-based actors themselves. Yet, it is also possible and worthwhile investigating how religious institutions and agents, understood as acting with a certain degree of autonomy from the state, can either: (a) generate soft-power resources for it; or (b) undermine and delegitimize states' ability to mobilize religion effectively as a soft-power tool of foreign policy.

A second form of reductionism relates to the project's implicit understanding of "geopolitics," which basically refers to interstate competition and power political practices employing religious tools. What is left out here, is the geographical and spatial dimension of this concept and how religion—once again understood more substantively as an independent social force—may relate to "geopolitics." We are thinking here, for example, of a growing and interesting body of research which explores the role of religion in shaping our geopolitical imaginaries (Agnew 2006; Dittmer and Sturm 2010) or how sacred sites and landscapes profoundly affect political dynamics (Cesari 2021; Dumper 2020; Hassner 2009). Once again there are some exceptions, with both the Israeli (Baumgart-Ochse, "Israel's Religious Soft Power: Within and Beyond Judaism") and Indian (Ganguly, "India and the Geopolitics of Religious Soft Power") cases unpacking how holy places and spatial imaginaries are integral to these countries' religious soft power. Yet, overall, these insights remain underexplored in the volume. We are conscious that one project cannot do everything. Nonetheless this is a missed opportunity given the centrality of the concept of "geopolitics" to it and we hope that future work will take the spatial element of religion further into account.

Soft Power and Conceptual Stretching

This project incurs a number of familiar problems which most analyses that draw on the concept of soft power fall into. Many are rooted in the concept's often vague characteristics. Soft power, as defined by Nye (1990), is the ability of an actor to get others to want what it wants through attraction. Despite Nye emphasizing that soft power is principally a relational concept, there is a tendency in his own work to refer back to it as an attribute or resource—like military or economic power—that states have or seek to possess. Hence, while soft power should be expressed in terms of relations and effects, much analysis instead focuses on how states attempt to increase their soft-power stock by expanding the attractiveness of their culture or demonstrating its attractiveness through public diplomacy campaigns (Melissen 2011; Parmar and Cox 2010). There has also been some ambiguity in works on soft power about how states attain it, and how it relates to "hard power" in international relations (Nye 2010; Bially Mattern 2007; Kearn 2011; Wilson 2008). Additionally, in popular and policy discussions, any nonmilitary use of power—especially involving culture or ideals—is often described as "soft." For example, some calls for an approach to ISIS that includes strategic narratives and economic development discuss such a strategy as "soft power" (Stavridis 2015).[4]

These ambiguities come somewhat inevitably to permeate this project. Throughout the volume soft power is used in multiple and, admittedly, disparate ways. Including as the generator of positive attitudes toward a particular state, as a shorthand for the spreading of religious beliefs, as the shaping of religious and political ideas and practices in foreign societies in ways that benefit a particular state, as a resource states have and cultivate, as a tool that states deploy, and as a relational concept rather than an attribute that depends very much on social interactions and perceptions. Notable, for instance, is the fact that only Gutkowski's chapter on Jordan approaches in a sustained manner soft power principally as the relational concept it is supposed to be. Ultimately, soft power seems to suffer from conceptual overstretching. Most often it tends to become a shorthand for showing that states engage in some kind of "religious statecraft."

To be clear, we are not suggesting that the concept of soft power has no value. Indeed, there is a sense that it is probably one of the most appropriate concepts for capturing the power of faith in world politics (see, e.g., Haynes 2012). This project is therefore in good company. A clearer sense of what constitutes and what does not constitute religious soft power when it comes to religious statecraft, however, would be desirable. As Goddard and Nexon (2016) discuss, power politics involves conventional military and economic instruments of power, but also "cultural" and "symbolic" instruments. Cultural instruments of power, in their framework, correspond to soft power, the elements of a state's culture that attract others to it and grant it influence in international relations. But symbolic instruments of power are distinct from soft power. They are the *active use of symbolic appeals*—such as, in the case of this volume, religious rhetoric or historical references—to undermine support for rivals and attract allies in international crises. Yet, symbolic religious appeals are often conflated with soft power, leading to the problems of conceptual overstretching in both policy and academic discussions. As Henne (2021) discussed, it may be useful to think of soft power as one among several cultural-symbolic instruments of power. Their specific nature depends on whether the power is direct or diffuse, and whether it integrates or fragments international coalitions.

Soft Power as a Narrow Power Concept

Paradoxically while on the one hand too broad and generic, the concept of soft power appears on the other hand too narrow and specific. In fact, the notion of soft power does not seem to capture all the different and complex forms of power and influence that religion can generate for states in world politics as they also transpire from this volume's own country cases. This is not simply to suggest, somewhat unfairly, that the project should have focused on an understanding of power that was not exclusively "soft." Having said this, it is evident from the multiple and rich case studies conducted in the context of *The Geopolitics of Religious Soft Power* project that religion matters in a complex set of ways not always immediately or clearly reducible to soft power.

Let us go beyond this volume's chapters and consider here for instance some of the reports tied to the wider project. In some cases, religion matters to the extent that it enables the mobilization of informants and networks on the ground (Öztürk 2019); it provides important economic and business opportunities (Biard 2019); it constitutes a resource through which violent or antiestablishment Islamist narratives can be contested and suppressed (Sakthivel 2019); it enables to strengthen the domestic authority of particular rulers (Alaoui 2019); and it allows to signal a particular foreign policy orientation and to positively "brand" a country (Philippon 2018). All of these cases show how religion produces some form of international influence, without necessarily generating any deeper ideological convergence with or attractiveness toward the countries in question.

In other words, what we are dealing with here are phenomena and dynamics that cannot be captured only with the concept—however stretched this can become—of soft power. One way, for example, could be to approach this issue through Barnett and Duvall's (2005) taxonomy of power in international relations. Specifically, they identify four concepts of power: compulsory, institutional, structural, and productive. These forms of power vary according to the kinds of social relations through which power works—whether relations of interaction or constitution—and the specificity of social relations through which effects are produced—whether direct or diffused. Those interested in how religion constitutes a form of power for states may want to think more expansively at how it may fall into one or more of Barnett and Duvall's (2005) categories.

Ways Forward

In this section we build on the project's strengths and limits identified so far to reflect on some of the most promising avenues for future research. Above all, rather than seeing *The Geopolitics of Religious Soft Power* project as the final word on the complex relationship between religion and power—soft or otherwise—in world politics, we instead view it as the most substantive contribution as of yet to an emerging, exciting, and promising research agenda on these issues.

Beyond Power as "Soft"

There is certainly space to improve our understanding and conceptualization of religion as a form of soft power as we suggested in the previous section. Having said this, we also think there is much promise in going beyond this concept, to explore the multifaceted ways in which religion constitutes a particular form of power. As noted earlier, future research could connect religion more explicitly to the analytically eclectic framework on the "dynamics of global power politics" developed by Stacey Goddard and Daniel Nexon (2016). In such a framework, political actors—state and nonstate alike—pursue their interests in the international system by mobilizing a series of instruments, including cultural and symbolic ones, in ways that are not just "soft." For example, in addition to exploring religion as a cultural instrument of power—that is, soft power—we could also explore whether and how different actors can use religion as a symbolic instrument of power, appealing to religious beliefs and symbols to legitimize their actions and undermine rivals' appeal and support in international crises. Henne's (2021) work on soft power, which relates this concept to Goddard and Nexon's (2016) theory, provides a further avenue for analyzing various ways states mobilize religion as a form of power (see also Bettiza and Lewis 2020).

Scholarship on religion as a form of power could also connect to a range of novel theoretical efforts approaching religions from a more relational, constitutive and material angle. Fascinating literature is emerging on faith from a practice (Alexseev and Zhemukhov 2017; Schwarz 2018), new materialist (Hazard 2013; Vásquez 2011), and network (Everton 2018) perspectives. These theoretical and methodological perspectives reconceptualize the sacred not solely in terms of ideas and identities but as a set of practices, objects, sacred sites, and networks, which shape world politics in complex ways.

It is against this conceptual backdrop that, for instance, Bettiza (2020) proposes to think about religion in terms of multiple forms of sacred capital: symbolic, cultural, and network. Hassner's (2009, 2016) work is seminal for suggesting an approach to religion that goes beyond the supposedly causal role of "beliefs," focusing instead on the sacred as a constitutive element of time, space, institutions, and rituals with "force-multiplying" or "force-dividing" effects on military practices and conflicts. By moving beyond the usual focus on religion as a cultural force, which is the currency of soft power, these alternative understandings of religion open up a host of different possibilities for theorizing and exploring the power of faith in world politics.

Variance in State and Religious Characteristics

With research on religion as a form of power expanding to include a broad range of cases and power concepts, we will need to understand in a more systematic manner how different state and religious characteristics affect practices and outcomes. The international system is populated by a great variety of states whose characteristics will likely shape how they exercise global influence through religion. These may include regime type, whether a state is democratic or authoritarian, or anything in between; the nature of state-religion relations, ranging from having an established religion, to strict separation from or even hostility towards religion; and distinct religious demographics and identity, including whether a state hosts or not major religious sites and institutions.

Likewise, religious traditions, denominations, and communities exhibit profound differences between and within them, which are likely to lead to substantial variations in terms of the power resources and effects they generate. These characteristics may vary in terms of a religion's historical trajectory and evolution; its geographical distribution and concentration; its foundational beliefs, theology, and traditions; whether it actively seeks converts or not; and the kind of organizational structure it exhibits, from a more hierarchical and centralized one to a more flat and decentralized one instead.

Contributors to the project already acknowledge that some of these characteristics have a bearing on the practices and narratives adopted by different actors and the forms of influence these are likely to generate. As Mandaville and Hamid's (2018, 26) introductory framework suggests,

> It is clear that while religious soft power has been a constant in the foreign policy of Middle Eastern states over the past decades, there are significant

differences in how it is used; the mechanisms through which it operates; and the kinds of outcomes associated with its deployment.

Elsewhere, Mandaville (quoted in Berkley Center 2020) points out how Iran has mobilized "the strong religious discourse on resistance and dispossession that is part of the Shia tradition," which despite its religious connotations has nonetheless been able to resonate with wider antiimperialist narratives and audiences in the Global South (see also Wastnidge, "Shi'i Diplomacy: Religious Identity and Foreign Policy in the Axis of Resistance"). Ashiwa and Wank ("Chinese Buddhism and Soft Power: Geopolitical Strategy and Modality of Religion") show how Chinese efforts to cultivate soft power are increasingly relying on Buddhism. That's because, compared to other major local traditions such as Confucianism and Daoism, Buddhism has an important presence across many Asian countries and growing popularity in the West. Shifts in Brazil's religious demographics, especially with the rise of more socially conservative Evangelicals, constitute an important premise of Jair Bolsonaro's electoral success and his attempts to form a "populist international" with the likes of Donald Trump and Viktor Orbán (Casarões and Smith, "'Brazil above Everything or God above Everyone?' The Sources of Brazil's Religious Soft Power"). Shifts between democratic and authoritarian forces as well as secular and Islamic ones in Turkey, influence the kind of audiences that are most receptive to Turkey's soft power (Ozturk, "Turkey's Ambivalent Religious Soft Power in the Illiberal Turn"). Henne and Bettiza, Ganguly, and Baumgart-Ochse in this volume unpack how the complex religious history and diversity of the United States, India, and Israel, respectively, constitute a resource for reaching out to multiple distinct global communities.

Future research should aim to shed greater and more systematic light precisely on how these context specific factors enable and constrain particular practices and outcomes. Moreover, paying greater attention to different state and religious characteristics can allow us to make useful comparisons and refine our conceptual models further. Let's take the issue of soft power, for instance. Scholars and policymakers could examine whether certain types of states and certain religious traditions are more likely to generate greater religious soft-power resources and outcomes compared to others. They could also determine which audiences are most likely to be receptive and influenced by these kinds of cultural dynamics and practices. This, of course, may vary greatly.

Assessing and Measuring Influence

Ultimately does religion as a form of power, soft or otherwise, really matter in world politics? The contributors to *The Geopolitics of Religious Soft Power* project certainly think so, but they are also—correctly in our view—careful in their assessments to avoid overly ambitious claims. Mandaville and Hamid (2018, 25–26) crucially set the tone in their agenda-setting report as follows:

> The challenge, as many of these examples tell us, is in striking a balance between, on the one hand, over-emphasizing the power of religious ideas to produce certain kinds of foreign policy outcomes and, on the other, reducing all religious soft power to just another expression of *realpolitik*.

Indeed, cases across the volume do not shy away from highlighting the limits of soft-power strategies. Sheline and Henne and Bettiza discuss how certain religious soft-power strategies adopted by the United States in the context of the War on Terror were not only ineffectual but also potentially counterproductive. Ganguly concludes on a cautious note regarding the extent to which India's religious soft power has yielded international results in the context of countervailing material pressures and charges of hypocrisy leveled against Narendra Modi. Hoesterey suggests that despite considerable efforts, Indonesia's religious soft-power strategy has made little inroads in the Middle East. Gutkowski reaches similar conclusions when it comes to assessing Jordan's ability—or, better, lack thereof—to shape positive perceptions about Islam in the West.

Having said this, the issue of systematically showing and measuring whether religion as a form of power does bring about specific outcomes largely remains moot in this volume. It is certainly the case that explaining power and influence remains one of the thorniest tasks of social scientists to this day. Conventional power analysis involves demonstrating that an actor changed or initiated behavior in response to the intervention of another actor; the intervening agent is then said to have exerted power (Baldwin 2016). This is difficult enough to do when looking at military or economic instruments of power, and many studies resort to indirect measures. It is even more difficult when analyzing something as intangible as religious soft power. Moreover, religious soft power often exists alongside military and economic influence and it is rare to find a materially weak state exerting power through religious outreach (although exceptions certainly exist, see especially the case of the Pope and the Holy See (Byrnes, "Soft Power of the Catholic Papacy"). As a result, it is hard to disentangle the relative impact of religious soft power from other instruments of power. Additionally, the impact of religious soft power is often indirect: religious soft power increases the attractiveness of a state or nonstate actors to international partners, enabling greater influence as a result. This is harder to account for and measure than an agent changing its behavior in response to the use of coercive measures and military threats.

Having said this, a range of useful methodological tools—for example, statistical analysis, surveys, interviews, ethnography and participant observation, discourse analysis, and network analysis—do exist that can aid in this enterprise. Future research should definitely find more consistent ways of establishing causal connections and measuring effects. We highlight two methodological approaches and tools in particular that are especially useful.

First, process tracing is an increasingly accepted tool of qualitative causal inference. One particular variant, Bayesian process tracing, may be particularly effective in measuring the impact of soft power (Bennett and Checkel 2014). Rather than isolating religious soft power's impact from material power, a scholar would instead point to evidence that would be unlikely to exist if religious soft power was irrelevant. For example, a state may invest significant resources into deploying religious soft power, or a state's leader may express concerns about the soft-power efforts of another. Neither of these would be likely if religious soft power was irrelevant.

Second, social network analysis can capture the diffuse nature of religious soft power. States acquire influence through religious soft power not from tangible resources, but from drawing others to them. Social network analysis is one useful tool that is gaining greater acceptance in international relations (Hafner-Burton, Kahler, and Montgomery 2009). There have also been some applications to the study of religion and politics (Everton 2018; Asal and Rethemeyer 2008; Henne 2019c). Social network analysis provides several measures of influence that may be useful for the study of religious soft power: brokerage between different groups of states, popularity measured by connections, and centrality in networks. One way to measure the impact of soft power—which is, as we note above, difficult to do—is to analyze the effects of religious soft-power efforts on these measures of network influence.

Conclusion

The Geopolitics of Religious Soft Power is an important and ambitious project, which the breadth and depth of the cases in this volume demonstrably attests to. It productively places power at the center of analysis of religion in world politics, sheds light on the multiple and complex ways that states draw upon and mobilize religion to exercise influence globally, and challenges enduring secularist biases in political science. Yet the project's contributions also go beyond the limited subfield of scholars engaged in the study of religion in political science, they also make—in our view—wider interventions into broader debates in IR about power, foreign policy, security, and the future of international order.

Some of the areas we are most critical about—the project's generally reductive approach to religion, and issues with its conceptualization and empirical application of soft power—are intended to spur further thinking and research in this area rather than invalidating the whole enterprise. In fact, we view this edited book as pathbreaking. It provides the foundations for a productive research program on the complex role that religion plays as a source of power in international relations. Future research could think more expansively about the multifaceted ways in which religion constitutes different forms of power that are not only "soft"; it could unpack further how distinct state and religious characteristics feed into our analyses of religious (soft) power; and it could draw more rigorously on a variety of research methods—we suggested process tracing and network analysis—for assessing and measuring religious (soft) power's impact.

Finally, this volume and the wider project it is part of offer much food for thought to practitioners as well, potentially helping to improve European and American policymakers' ability to understand and engage religion in foreign policy. While religion never appears to be as central to foreign policy as nuclear doctrine or trade flows, states around the world persistently adopt various forms of religious statecraft in their interactions with the international community. Being attuned to such practices and their consequences is vital in order to succeed in a changing international order marked by new forms of religious geopolitics. A better grasp of these dynamics is likewise pivotal in a context where European and American foreign policymakers are themselves investing greater energy in advancing international religious freedom, promoting interfaith dialogues, and engaging with religious actors to solve international crisis. There has been little work, however, testing the impact of such efforts. The study of religious soft power can aid Western policymakers by showing the promises, but also the many pitfalls, that these sort of initiatives and practices can generate.

References

Agnew, John. 2006. "Religion and Geopolitics." *Geopolitics* 11 (2): 183–191.
Alaoui, Sarah. 2019. "Morocco, Commander of the (African) Faithful?" In *The Geopolitics of Religious Soft Power Project*. Washington, DC: The Brookings Institution.
Albright, Madeleine K. 2006. *The Mighty and the Almighty: Reflections on America, God, and World Affairs*. New York: Harper.
Alexseev, Mikhail A., and Sufian N. Zhemukhov. 2017. *Mass Religious Ritual and Intergroup Tolerance: The Muslim Pilgrims' Paradox*. Cambridge: Cambridge University Press.
Anderson, Benedict. 2006. *Imagined Communities: Reflections on the Origin and Spread of Nationalism*. London: Verso.
Appleby, R. Scott, and Richard Cizik. 2010. "Engaging Religious Communities Abroad: A New Imperative for U.S. Foreign Policy." In *Report of the Task Force on Religion and the Making of U.S. Foreign Policy*. Chicago: Chicago Council on Global Affairs.
Asal, Victor, and R. Karl Rethemeyer. 2008. "The Nature of the Beast: Organizational Structures and the Lethality of Terrorist Attacks." *Journal of Politics* 70 (2): 437–449.
Baldwin, David A. 2016. *Power and International Relations: A Conceptual Approach*. Princeton, NJ: Princeton University Press.
Barbato, Mariano, and Friedrich Kratochwil. 2009. "Towards a Post-Secular Political Order?" *European Political Science Review* 1 (3): 317–340.
Barnett, Michael, and Raymond Duvall. 2005. "Power in International Politics." *International Organization* 59 (1): 39–75.
Bennett, Andrew, and Jeffrey Checkel. 2014. "Process Tracing: From Philosophical Roots to Best Practices." In *Process Tracing: From Metaphor to Analytic Tool*, edited by Andrew Bennett and Jeffrey Checkel, 3–37. New York: Cambridge University Press.
Berkley Center. 2020. "Islamic Soft Power in the U.S.-Iran Crisis: A Conversation with Peter Mandaville." https://berkleycenter.georgetown.edu/posts/islamic-soft-power-in-the-u-s-iran-crisis-a-conversation-with-peter-mandaville.Washington, DC: Berkley Center for Religion, Peace & World Affairs.
Bettiza, Gregorio. 2013. "Religion and American Foreign Policy in the Context of the Postsecular Turn in World Politics and the Social Sciences." *International Politics Reviews* 1 (1): 11–26.
Bettiza, Gregorio. 2015. "Constructing Civilisations: Embedding and Reproducing the 'Muslim World' in American Foreign Policy Practices and Institutions since 9/11." *Review of International Studies* 41 (3): 575–600.
Bettiza, Gregorio. 2019. *Finding Faith in Foreign Policy: Religion and American Diplomacy in a Postsecular World*. New York: Oxford University Press.
Bettiza, Gregorio. 2020. "States, Religions, and Power: Highlighting the Role of Sacred Capital in World Politics." In *The Geopolitics of Religious Soft Power*. Washington, DC: Berkley Center for Religion, Peace & World Affairs.

Bettiza, Gregorio, and Filippo Dionigi. 2015. "How Do Religious Norms Diffuse? Institutional Translation and International Change in a Postsecular World Society." *European Journal of International Relations* 21 (3): 621–646.

Bettiza, Gregorio, and David Lewis. 2020. "Authoritarian Powers and Norm Contestation in the Liberal International Order: Theorizing the Power Politics of Ideas and Identity." *Journal of Global Security Studies* 5 (4): 559–577. Online first.

Bially Mattern, Janice. 2007. "Why Soft Power Isn't So Soft: Representational Force and Attraction in World Politics." In *Power in World Politics*, edited by Felix Berenskoetter and Michael J. Williams, 98–120. New York: Routledge.

Biard, Aurélie. 2019. "'We Pray for Our President': Saudi-Inspired Loyalist Salafism and the Business Sector in Kazakhstan." In *The Geopolitics of Religious Soft Power*. Washington, DC: Berkley Center for Religion, Peace & World Affairs.

Birdsall, Judd, Jane Lindsay, and Emma Tomalin, eds. 2015. "Toward Religion-Attentive Foreign Policy: A Report on an Anglo-American Dialogue." In Centre for Religion and Public Life at the University of Leeds, Religious Freedom Project at Georgetown University, and Institute for Global Engagement.

Byrnes, Timothy A. 2011. *Reverse Mission: Transnational Religious Communities and the Making of US Foreign Policy*. Washington, DC: Georgetown University Press.

Byrnes, Timothy A. 2017. "Sovereignty, Supranationalism, and Soft Power: The Holy See in International Relations." *The Review of Faith & International Affairs* 15 (4): 6–20.

Carey, Hilary, ed. 2008. *Empires of Religion*. Basingstoke: Palgrave MacMillan.

Carlson, J. D., and E. C. Owens. 2003. *The Sacred and the Sovereign: Religion and International Politics*. Washington, DC: Georgetown University Press.

Carrette, Jeremy R., and Michel Foucault, eds. 1999. *Religion and Culture*. Manchester: Manchester University Press.

Casanova, José. 2011. "Cosmopolitanism, the Clash of Civilizations and Multiple Modernities." *Current Sociology* 59 (2): 252–267.

Cesari, Jocelyne. 2018. "Unexpected Convergences: Religious Nationalism in Israel and Turkey." *Religions* 9 (11): 1–20.

Cesari, Jocelyne. 2021. "Time, Power, and Religion: Comparing the Disputes over Temple Mount and the Ayodhya Sacred Sites." *Journal of Law, Religion and State* 9 (1): 95–123.

Dittmer, Jason, and Tristan Sturm. 2010. *Mapping the End Times*. Aldershot: Ashgate.

Dumper, Michael. 2020. *Power, Piety, and People: The Politics of Holy Cities in the Twenty-First Century*. New York: Columbia University Press.

Eisenstadt, Shmuel N. 2000. "Multiple Modernities." *Daedalus* 129 (1): 1–29.

Elshtain, Jean Bethke. 2004. "Military Intervention and Justice as Equal Regard." In *Religion and Security: The New Nexus in International Relations*, edited by Robert Seiple and Dennis R. Hoover, 115–131. Lanham, MD: Rowman and Littlefield.

Everton, Sean F. 2018b. *Networks and Religion: Ties that Bind, Loose, Build-up, and Tear Down*. Vol. 45. Cambridge: Cambridge University Press.

Farr, Thomas F. 2008. *World of Faith and Freedom: Why International Religious Liberty is Vital to American National Security*. New York: Oxford University Press.

Fox, Jonathan. 2015. *Political Secularism, Religion, and the State: A Time Series Analysis of Worldwide Data*. Cambridge: Cambridge University Press.

Fukuyama, Francis. 1992. *The End of History and the Last Man*. New York: Free Press, Maxwell Macmillan.

Goddard, Stacie E., and Daniel H. Nexon. 2016. "The Dynamics of Global Power Politics: A Framework for Analysis." *Journal of Global Security Studies* 1 (1): 4–18.

Hafner-Burton, Emilie M., Miles Kahler, and Alexander H. Montgomery. 2009. "Network Analysis for International Relations." *International Organization* 63: 559–592.
Hassner, Ron E. 2009. *War on Sacred Grounds*. Ithaca, NY: Cornell University Press.
Hassner, Ron E. 2016. *Religion on the Battlefield*. Ithaca, NY: Cornell University Press.
Haynes, Jeffrey. 2012. *Religious Transnational Actors and Soft Power*. Aldershot: Ashgate.
Hazard, Sonia. 2013. "The Material Turn in the Study of Religion." *Religion and Society* 4 (1): 58–78.
Henne, Peter. 2019. *The Geopolitics of Religious Soft Power Project*. Washington, DC: Berkley Center for Religion, Peace & World Affairs.
Henne, Peter S. 2017. *Islamic Politics, Muslim States, and Counterterrorism Tensions*. New York: Cambridge University Press.
Henne, Peter S. 2019b. "Government Interference in Religious Institutions and Terrorism." *Religion, State and Society* 47 (1): 67–87.
Henne, Peter S. 2019c. "The Role of Islam in Post-Arab Spring International Relations: A Social Network Analysis." American Political Science Association, Washington, DC.
Henne, Peter S. 2021. "What We Talk About When We Talk About Soft Power." *International Studies Perspectives* 23 (1): 94–111.
Henne, Peter S., Nilay Saiya, and Ashlyn W. Hand. 2019. "Weapon of the Strong? Government Support for Religion and Majoritarian Terrorism." International Studies Association, Toronto, Canada, March.
Hurd, Elizabeth Shakman. 2008. *The Politics of Secularism in International Relations*. Princeton, NJ: Princeton University Press.
Hurd, Elizabeth Shakman. 2015. *Beyond Religious Freedom: The New Global Politics of Religion*. Princeton, NJ: Princeton University Press.
Ikenberry, G. John. 2009. "Liberal Internationalism 3.0: America and the Dilemmas of Liberal World Order." *Perspectives on Politics* 7 (1):71–87.
Johnston, Douglas M., and Cynthia Sampson, eds. 1995. *Religion, the Missing Dimension of Statecraft*. New York: Oxford University Press.
Juergensmeyer, Mark. 1993. *The New Cold War? Religious Nationalism Confronts the Secular State*. Berkeley: University of California Press.
Kearn, David. 2011. "The Hard Truths about Soft Power." *Journal of Political Power* 4 (1): 65–85.
Keating, Vincent Charles, and Katarzyna Kaczmarska. 2019. "Conservative Soft Power: Liberal Soft Power Bias and the 'Hidden' Attraction of Russia." *Journal of International Relations and Development* 22 (1): 1–27.
Kolbe, Melanie, and Peter S. Henne. 2014. "The Effect of Religious Restrictions on Forced Migration." *Politics and Religion* 7 (4): 665–683.
Mabon, Simon, ed. 2018. *Saudi Arabia and Iran: The Struggle to Shape the Middle East*. London: The Foreign Policy Center.
Mahmood, Saba. 2015. *Religious Difference in a Secular Age: A Minority Report*. Princeton, NJ: Princeton University Press.
Mandaville, Peter, and Shadi Hamid. 2018. "Islam as Statecraft: How Governments Use Religion in Foreign Policy." In *Foreign Policy at Brookings*. Washington DC: Brookings Institution.
Melissen, Jan. 2011. *Public Diplomacy and Soft power in East Asia*. New York: Palgrave MacMillan.
Mendelsohn, Barak 2012. "God vs. Westphalia: Radical Islamist Movements and the Battle for Organizing the World." *Review of International Studies* 38 (3): 589–613.

Nexon, Daniel H. "Religion and International Relations: No Leap of Faith Required." In Religion and International Relations Theory, edited by Jack Snyder, 141–168. New York: Columbia University Press, 2011.

Nexon, Daniel H. 2009. *The Struggle for Power in Early Modern Europe: Religious Conflict, Dynastic Empires, and International Change*. Princeton, NJ: Princeton University Press.

Nye, Joseph S. 1990. "Soft Power." *Foreign Policy* 80: 153–171.

Nye, Joseph S. 2010. "Responding to My Critics and Concluding Thoughts." In *Soft power and US Foreign Policy*, edited by Inderjeet Parmar and Michael Cox, 215–228. New York: Routledge.

Otis, Pauletta. 2004. "Religion and War in the Twenty-First Century." In *Religion and Security: The New Nexus in International Relations*, edited by Robert Seiple and Dennis R. Hoover, 11–25. Lanham, MD: Rowman and Littlefield.

Öztürk, Ahmet Erdi. 2019. Turkey: An Ambivalent Religious Soft Power. In *The Geopolitics of Religious Soft Power Project*. Washington, DC.

Parmar, Inderjeet, and Michael Cox, eds. 2010. *Soft Power and US Foreign Policy: Theoretical, Historical and Contemporary Perspectives*. London: Routledge.

Petito, Fabio, Daniel Philpott, Silvio Ferrari, and Judd Birdsall. 2016. "FoRB—Recognising our Differences Can Be Our Strength: Enhancing Transatlantic Cooperation on Promoting Freedom of Religion or Belief." In *Policy Briefing*. Brighton: University of Sussex.

Philippon, Alix. 2018. Positive Branding and Soft Power: The Promotion of Sufism in the War on Terror. In *The Geopolitics of Religious Soft Power Project*. Washington, DC: The Brookings Institution.

Phillips, Andrew. 2010. *War, Religion and Empire: The Transformation of International orders*. Cambridge: Cambridge University Press.

Philpott, Daniel. 2001. *Revolutions in Sovereignty: How Ideas Shaped Modern International Relations*. Princeton, NJ: Princeton University Press.

Philpott, Daniel. 2002. "The Challenge of September 11 to Secularism in International Relations." *World Politics* 55 (1): 66–95.

Raines, John C., ed. 2002. *Marx on Religion*. Philadelphia: Temple University Press.

Rudolph, Susanne Hoeber, and James P. Piscatori, eds. 1997. *Transnational Religion and Fading States*. Boulder, CO: Westview Press.

Sakthivel, Vish. 2019. Moderate Islam in the Maghreb: How US Foreign Policy Shapes Islamist Contention. In *The Geopolitics of Religious Soft Power Project*. Washington, DC: The Brookings Institution.

Sandal, Nukhet A. 2011. "Religious Actors as Epistemic Communities in Conflict Transformation: the Cases of South Africa and Northern Ireland." *Review of International Studies* 37 (3): 929–949.

Sandal, Nukhet A., and Jonathan Fox. 2013. *Religion in International Relations Theory: Interactions and Possibilities*. Abingdon: Routledge.

Schwarz, Tanya B. 2018. "Challenging the Ontological Boundaries of Religious Practices in International Relations Scholarship." *International Studies Review* 20 (1): 30–54.

Seiple, Robert A., and Dennis Hoover, eds. 2004. *Religion and Security: the New Nexus in International Relations*. Lanham, MD: Rowman & Littlefield.

Shani, Giorgio. 2008. "Toward a Post Western IR: The Umma, Khalsa Panth, and Critical International Relations Theory." *International Studies Review* 10 (4): 722–734.

Stavridis, James. 2015. "Killing the Islamic State Softly." *Foreign Policy*, December 28.

Sullivan, Winnifred Fallers, Elizabeth Shakman Hurd, Saba Mahmood, and Peter G. Danchin, eds. 2015. *Politics of Religious Freedom*. Chicago: The University of Chicago Press.

Thomas, Scott. 2005. *The Global Resurgence of Religion and the Transformation of International Relations: The Struggle for the Soul of the Twenty-First Century*. New York: Palgrave Macmillan.

Toft, Monica Duffy, Daniel Philpott, and Timothy Samuel Shah. 2011. *God's Century: Resurgent Religion and Global Politics*. New York: W.W. Norton and Company.

Vásquez, Manuel A. 2011. *More than Belief: A Materialist Theory of Religion*. New York: Oxford University Press.

Viroli, Maurizio. 2010. *Machiavelli's God*. Princeton, NJ: Princeton University Press.

Wainscott, Ann Marie. 2017. *Bureaucratizing Islam: Morocco and the war on terror*. Cambridge: Cambridge University Press.

Wilson, Ernest J. III. 2008. "Hard Power, Soft Power, Smart Power." *The Annals of the American Academy of Political and Social Science* 616 (1): 110–124.

Notes

Chapter 2

1. To learn more about the Vatican's own soft power efforts against Communism, see Chapter 13 of this text.

Chapter 3

1. Article 14(1) of the 1993 Russian Constitution specifies that Russia "is a secular state. No state or obligatory religion may be established" (Orthodox Christianity 2020).
2. See http://doc.ksrf.ru/decision/KSRFDecision459904.pdf.
3. See Luzgin v Russia (2017).
4. See Stabile and Grimm Arsenault (2020).
5. Russia's efforts

    "to distort historical facts and whitewash crimes committed by the Soviet totalitarian regime [are] a dangerous component of the information war . . . that aims to divide Europe" (European Parliament 2019).

6. Laruelle describes Russian law as defining the term compatriot "in an utterly extensive way" (Laruelle 2015).
7. "Putin Address to World Russian People's Council," November 1, 2018, http://en.kremlin.ru/events/president/news/59013.
8. See for example, Nerses Isajanyan, "Russia: Decriminalization of Domestic Violence," *Law Library of Congress*, June 2017. https://tile.loc.gov/storage-services/service/ll/llglrd/2017299008/2017299008.pdf, 5.
9. This legislation already includes an anti-gay "propaganda" law that imposes "hefty fines on same-sex couples who are affectionate in public." Alina Polyakova, "Strange Bedfellows: Putin and Europe's Far Right," *World Affairs* 177, no. 3 (2014): 36–40, 39, www.jstor.org/stable/43555253.
10. For example, Russia was one of four non-Organization of Islamic Cooperation (OIC) states that voted against the UNHRC's landmark 2011 resolution opposing violence and discrimination of the basis of sexual orientation and gender identity (SOGI). Five years later, in its own version of cancel culture, Russia joined a failed attempt to torpedo the UNHRC's endorsement of an Independent Expert on SOGI. Blitt, "The Organization of Islamic Cooperation's (OIC) Response to Sexual Orientation and Gender Identity Rights: A Challenge to Equality and Nondiscrimination Under

International Law," *University of Iowa Transnational Law & Contemporary Problems* 28, no. 89 (2018), 160 and 178.
11. See https://www.rt.com/russia/494869-montenegro-church-crackdown-patriarch/.
12. See https://tass.com/society/1105033.
13. For example, see UN, "Security Council Fails to Adopt Draft Resolution Condemning Syria's Crackdown on Anti-Government Protestors, Owing to Veto by Russian Federation, China," UN Doc. SC/10403, Oct. 4, 2011. https://www.un.org/press/en/2011/sc10403.doc.htm.
14. For example, see "Report of the Independent International Commission of Inquiry on the Syrian Arab Republic (Advanced Unedited Version)," UN Doc. A/HRC/44/61, July 2, 2020, paragraph 40.
15. *Russian Orthodox Church representatives attend conference of compatriots in Shanghai*, Mar. 21, 2019. https://mospat.ru/en/2019/03/21/news171759/.
16. See https://vrns.ru. Patriarch Aleksii II established the WRPC in 1993 and the organization is currently led by Patriarch Kirill.
17. Under the guise of promoting the Russian language, Russkiy Mir busies itself "strengthening the spiritual unity of the Russian world" and operating as "a bulwark against the threat of globalization." The organization reserves a seat on its board of directors for the Moscow Patriarchate, and also has been accused of serving as "one of the structural divisions of Russia's Foreign Intelligence Service" (Blitt 2011).
18. See also Atanas Slavov, "The Bulgarian Orthodox Church: An Instrument For Russian Influence in the Region," *Bulgaria Analytica*, June 28, 2017. https://bulgariaanalytica.org/en/2017/06/28/the-bulgarian-orthodox-church-an-instrument-for-russian-influence-in-the-region/.
19. The meeting was the first of its kind since the Great Schism of 1054 divided eastern and western Christianity.
20. See, for example, "Bishop Pitirim of Jakarta meets with the head of Indonesian diplomatic mission in Moscow," Sep. 29, 2020. http://www.patriarchia.ru/en/db/text/5699285.html.
21. See, for example, Mark Silk, "The Other Russian Collusion Story." *Religion News Service*, March 25, 2019. https://religionnews.com/2019/03/25/the-other-russian-collusion-story/.

Chapter 4

1. The project is "Chinese Buddhism in Globalization: States, Communities, and the Practice of Religion" funded by the Henry Luce Foundation Program on Religion in International Affairs.
2. This analysis and insights expressed in this brief draw from an ongoing research project and are tentative. In particular, the insights of the fourth and fifth section are based only on preliminary fieldwork and should be considered hypothetical.

3. For historical uses of Buddhism in international relations see Tambiah (1976) and Tansen (2015); John S. Strong, *Relics of the Buddha* (Princeton, NJ: Princeton University Press, 2004).
4. The Pew Research Center puts the number of Buddhists in China at 244,130,000 in 2010. Luis Lugo et al. 2012. *The Global Religious Landscape: A Report on the Size and Distribution of the World's Major Religious Groups as of 2021*. Washington, DC: The Pew Form on Religion & Public Life, 32.
5. From its founding in 1953 until 1997, it was called the Religious Affairs Bureau. To avoid confusion, we refer to it by its current anacronym SARA.
6. For the changing role of the UFWD see Sonny Shiu-Hing Lo et al, *China's New United Front Work in Hong Kong: Penetrative Politics and it Implications* (Singapore: Palgrave Macmillan, 2019).
7. Xinhua News Agency, "Hu Jintao's Speech at the 8th Artists' Conference," November 17, 2006 (Zhang 2013). For the concept of soft power in PRC policy circles see Hongyi Lai, "Introduction: The Soft Power Concept and a Rising China," *China's Soft Power and International Relations*, ed. Hongyi Lai and Yiyi Lu (Abingdon: Routledge, 2012), 1–20.
8. Xinhua News Agency, "Senior Official Stresses Need for Developing Soft Power," April 8, 2007. Quoted in Zhang, *China's Faith Diplomacy*.
9. For public diplomacy under Xi Jinping, see Yihua Xu. 2015. "Religion and China's Public Diplomacy in the Era of Globalization," *Journal of Middle Eastern and Islamic Studies (in Asia)* 9 (4): 14–35.
10. See, for example, Xi Jinping's speech at UNESCO Headquarters (March 27, 2014), www.fmprc.gov.cn/mfa_eng/wjdt_665385/zyjh_665391/t1142560.shtml.
11. For soft power promotion activities during the time of COVID, see Yoshiko Ashiwa and David L. Wank, "COVID-19 Impacts Chinese Buddhism, State Control, and Soft Power." Coauthored with Yoshiko Ashiwa. *Religion & Diplomacy*, April 20 (2020), https://religionanddiplomacy.org.uk/2020/04/20/special-report-impact-of-covid-19-on-chinese-buddhism-and-soft-power/.
12. For a discussion of friendship networks, see Jichang Lulu, "Repurposing Democracy: The European Parliament China Friendship Cluster," *Sinopsis*, November 26 (2019): 28.
13. Interviews with administrator and students at Berlin Shaolin Temple by David Wank, September 22, 2018.
14. For more information on India and China's competing claims of Buddhism, see this text's Chapter 6: "India and the Geopolitics of Religious Soft Power."
15. For the relationship of the UWFD to overseas Chinese business persons see, Gerry Groot. 2018. "Understanding the Role of Chambers of Commerce and Industry Association in United Front Work," *China Brief* 18, 11, https://jamestown.org/program/understanding-the-role-of-chambers-of-commerce-and-industry-associations-in-united-front-work/.
16. This Yinshun is different from the influential cleric Yinshun (1906–2005) on Taiwan.
17. For further discussion, see Jackson (2019).
18. For further discussion of such third-party actors, see Lim and Bergin (2018).

19. Huieguang received a dharma transmission from Benhuan at Hongfa Temple. International Bodhisattva Sangha website, accessed October 2, 2021, https://www.ibstemple.org/who-we-are-2/master-hueiguang-founder-president/.
20. This statement reflects our idea of the mutual constitution of religion and modern states (Ashiwa and Wank 2009).

Chapter 5

1. To learn more about the continued importance of religion in Iran's soft power foreign policy, see Chapter 7.

Chapter 6

1. For a discussion of the evolution of Nehru's attitudes toward religion see Rajeev Bhargava. 2017. "Nehru against Nehruvians: On Religion and Secularism." *Economic and Political Weekly* 52 (8).
2. The Harvard theologian, Harvey Cox, cites an episode where Nehru chased away a Hindu mendicant who sought to bless an edifice that Nehru was about to inaugurate. See Harvey Cox. 2014. *The Secular City*. Princeton, NJ: Princeton University Press.
3. For a thoughtful discussion of the ideological shift within the party and its impact on Indian security policy see Chris Ogden. 2014. *Hindu Nationalism and the Evolution of Contemporary Indian Security: Portents of Power*. New Delhi: Oxford University Press.
4. For an excellent analysis see Meera Nanda. 2003. *Prophets Facing backwards: Postmodern Critiques of Science and Hindu Nationalism*. New Brunswick, NJ: Rutgers University Press.
5. I am grateful to Dr. Chris Ogden for this insight. Personal correspondence with Dr. Chris Ogden, University of St Andrews, July 22, 2020.
6. See: http://southasia.ucla.edu/religions/avatars-divinities/avatars-of-vishnu/
7. For a discussion of the policy and its promises and limits see Sumit Ganguly and Karen Stoll Farrell, eds. 2016. *Heading East: Security, Trade and Environment between India and Southeast Asia*. New Delhi: Oxford University Press.
8. On the evolution of the Indo-Israeli relationship see Nicolas Blarel 2014. *The Evolution of India's Israel Policy: Continuity, Change and Compromise Since 1922*. New Delhi: Oxford University Press.
9. See, for example, Shyam Saran, "The Fall into Infamy," *The Tribune*, March 12, 2020; K.C. Singh, "The Diplomatic Cost," *The Indian Express*, March 7, 2020.

Chapter 7

1. Private audience with Ayatollah Ali Sistani's representative in Iran, Javad Sharestani, Qom, Iran. Ayatollah Sistani is perhaps the highest ranking marja' (source of emulation) in the Shi'i world, acting as the spiritual leader for the vast majority of Iraqi Shia, and Shia globally. In contrast to Khomeini and his successor Khamenei, he does not advocate direct clerical involvement in politics, but his pronouncements have significant political weight in Iraq due to his widespread following.
2. See, for example, Iranian news agency *Fars News*' report on *Emdad's* charitable activities in Gaza: "Imam Khomeini Relief Committee's assistance to needy Palestinian families in Gaza," *Fars News*, July 2013, https://www.farsnews.ir/photo/13920509001 164 (*in Persian*).
3. For detailed analyses of how the Saudi-Iran rivalry plays out across time and space, see the work of Simon Mabon, most notably *Saudi Arabia and Iran: Power and Rivalry in the Middle East* (London: I. B. Tauris, 2015), and Wastnidge and Mabon (eds.), *Saudi Arabia and Iran: The Struggle to Shape the Middle East* (Manchester: Manchester University Press, 2021).
4. For further detail on these incidents in Tajikistan, see Wastnidge, "Central Asia and the Iran-Saudi Rivalry," *POMPES Studies* 38 (2020): 47–51.
5. See https://aawsat.com/home/article/958941.
6. See announcement on *Emdad* website, September 30, 2019 (in Persian): https://news.emdad.ir/fa/newsagency/171023/.
7. See news item from Iranian Embassy in France, July 2021, https://france.mfa.gov.ir/portal/newsview/644476 (in Persian).
8. Author interview with Iranian cultural attaché's office, Beirut.
9. Ibid.
10. Ibid.
11. See ICRO website (in Persian): https://icro.ir/index.aspx?fkeyid=&siteid=261&pageid=32255&newsview=746069.
12. Attended by author.
13. See, for example, the Iranian cultural attaché in Lebanon's comments in his meeting with Lebanon's Grand Mufti Sheikh Abdul Latif Daryan, *Islamic Republic News Agency (IRNA)*, September 5, 2019. https://www.irna.ir/news/83466620.
14. Interview with Sheikh Ali Daher, Beirut.
15. Ibid.
16. Ibid.
17. Ibid.
18. Ibid.
19. Ibid.

Chapter 8

1. Safi, Omid. 2018. *Radical Love: Teachings from the Islamic Mystical Tradition.* New Haven, CT: Yale University Press.
2. Nye, Joseph S. 1990. *Bound to Lead: The Changing Nature of American Power.* New York: Basic Books.
3. See (in Arabic): http://www.edhh.org/index.php/etablissement/intro.
4. "Maghribīyāt Yalqīn Durūsān Dīniyya Fī Ḥaḍrat Jalālat Al-Malik." *Al-Itiḥād Al-Ishtirākī,* April 9, 2010. http://www.maghress.com/alittihad/114213.
5. "A la Grande mosquée de Dakar, les prières surérogatoires jettent des ponts de communion entre Marocains et Sénégalais." *Agence Marocaine De Presse,* Mai 2019, p. 4.
6. For more information on how Iran's 1979 Cultural Revolution shaped its use of religion in its politics, see this text's Chapter 7.
7. *Discours de SM le Roi à l'occasion de la tenue à Tétouan de la Session ordinaire du Conseil supérieur des Oulémas.* http://www.habous.gov.ma/fr/discours-royaux/665-27-septembre-2008-discours-de-sm-le-roi-a-l-occasion-de-la-tenue-a-tetouan-de-la-session-ordinaire-du-conseil-superieur-des-oulemas.html.
8. See Wainscott (2017, 113).
9. See: https://2m.ma/fr/news/senegal-les-tijanes-de-dakar-celebrent-leur-40e-ziara-annuelle-sous-le-haut-patronage-de-sm-le-roi-20210111/.
10. See: https://www.facebook.com/Barhamday/posts/3266631643375959/.
11. The author visited the offices of the Ligue in 2015 in Dakar, finding them still functional but largely in disrepair.
12. To learn about the Papacy's own religious soft-power efforts, see this text's Chapter 13.
13. For more on contemporary efforts to reach out to the Jewish population see the section beginning on page 87 of Wainscott (2017).
14. See: "Le Maroc envoie 700 imams de par le monde pour encadrer le ramadan de sa diaspora." *Telquel.ma,* https://telquel.ma/2019/05/06/france-canada-gabon-le-maroc-envoie-pres-de-700-psalmodieurs-et-predicateurs-encadrer-le-ramadan-de-sa-diaspora_1637471?fbrefresh=3.
15. For an overview of this effort, see: Ann Marie Wainscott. "Morocco's AU Bid Builds on Years of Strategic Diplomacy." *IPI Global Observatory,* July 27, 2016. https://theglobalobservatory.org/2016/07/morocco-african-union-western-sahara-mohammed-vi/.
16. "Infographie: Mohammed VI, un roi voyageur—Jeune Afrique." *JeuneAfrique.com,* November 28, 2016. https://www.jeuneafrique.com/mag/376906/politique/infographie-mohammed-vi-roi-voyageur/.

Chapter 9

1. See, e.g., Tarek Masoud, *Counting Islam: Religion, Class, and Elections in Egypt.* New York: Cambridge University Press, 2014; Ann Marie Wainscott, *Bureaucratizing Islam: Morocco and the War on Terror.* New York: Cambridge University Press, 2017.

NOTES 299

2. See: Sahih Al-Bukhari, Volume 8, Hadith 470; Sahih Al-Bukhari, Volume 7, Hadith 127; Sahih Al-Bukhari, Volume 7, Book 62, Number 1.
3. See: State Department Country Reports on Terrorism 2015—Jordan. http://www.state.gov/j/ct/rls/crt/2015/257517.htm.
4. See: https://ammanmessage.com/.
5. See also Chapter 11 in this volume.
6. General Secondary Education Certificate Examination Textbook. *Tawjīhī* ("Guided") 2014. Amman: Jordan Ministry of Education: 48–50. [Translation by author].
7. From notes taken by the author at the event, "U.S. Foreign Policy and International Religious Freedom: Recommendations for the Trump Administration and the U.S. Congress," coordinated by the Religious Freedom Institute and the Institute for Global Engagement, Kennedy Caucus Room (SR-325) Russell Senate Office Building, 3 p.m., March 20, 2017.
8. International Religious Freedom Roundtable webinar attended by the author, 11 a.m. EST, December 15, 2020.
9. See Chapter 3 in this volume.
10. See Chapter 12 in this volume.
11. Phone interview with author, 4:30 p.m., August 31, 2020.

Chapter 10

1. For more information on Obama's broader engagement with Muslim countries, see Chapter 2.
2. See "Remarks by the President at the University of Indonesia in Jakarta, Indonesia."
3. See Landler, "Clinton Praises Indonesian Democracy."
4. In this chapter, I focus mostly on how Nahdlatul Ulama coordinated with various religious diplomacy programs. Without the space to elaborate, it must be noted also that leaders of the modernist organization Muhammadiyah, especially former Chair Din Syamsuddin, were also (and continue to be) civil society figures who collaborated with the state to develop a far-reaching religious diplomacy.
5. See "Indonesian Foreign Minister Wirajuda on the U.S.-Indonesian Comprehensive Partnership."
6. This historical retelling neglects to mention Darul Islam, the Indonesian militia group that fought both Dutch and Indonesian Republican soldiers in its efforts to establish an Islamic State (see Formichi 2012). Beyond Darul Islam, the drafting of the constitution proved difficult, with the stipulation of Islamic law for Muslim citizens finally being omitted from the constitution.

Chapter 11

1. For further information on post–9/11 US cooperation efforts with Arab states, see Chapter 2 of this text.
2. Also see Chapter 5 of this work to learn more about Turkey's religious soft-power ambitions.
3. To learn more about Morocco's moderate Islamic identity and how it utilizes this in its foreign policy, see Chapter 8 of this text.
4. For more of Bettiza's discussion of US religious soft power within its CVE efforts, see Chapter 2 in this text.
5. For further details on Morocco's moderate Islam interpretations, see Chapter 8 of this text.
6. For more from Bettiza on US religious soft power in its foreign policy, see Chapter 2 in this text.
7. Elsewhere, I have used Deleuze and Guattari's *assemblage* concept to describe how domestic public policy works within Jordan (Gutkowski 2022).

Chapter 12

1. See for an overview Rodman (2019) and Maoz (2006, 6–7).
2. For the Jewish American community, see, for example, Waxman (2016), Sasson (2010), Rosenthal (2001), Finkelstein (2012), and Wertheimer (2008); for the Evangelical American community, see Spector (2009), Hummel (2019), and Weber (2005). Some authors have treated these communities as part and parcel of an overarching so-called Israel Lobby, in which Evangelicals, however, play a minor role; see Walt and Mearsheimer (2007) and Waxman (2010).
3. However, the Jewish population according to the Jewish People Policy Institute's report also includes residents with no religion "based on the assumption that they are socially and culturally settled in the majority society (without them the ratio of Jews to non-Jews would be 74 and 26 percent, respectively)" (Rosner 2019, 21).
4. Organizations on the left include Israel Policy Forum, Brit Tzedek V'Shalom, J Street; on the right, Zionist Organization of America, Jewish Institute for National Security Affairs, and Americans for a Safe Israel.
5. See, for example, Haija (2006).

Chapter 13

1. The literature on this history, of course, is vast. Particularly helpful on the early years are the classic Duchesne (1907), Southern (1970), and the compact Whelan (2014). The later years are covered well in Chadwick (1998).
2. See, on this dynamic, Thomson (1980).

3. There is a growing literature on the role of the papacy and the Holy See in International Relations. Two valuable introductions are Lyon, Gustafson, and Christopher Manuel (2018) and Hoover, Joustra, and Barbato (2019). See Byrnes (2019) for my contributions to the latter.
4. See, on this dynamic, Kertzer (2004).
5. The Most prominent examples here were Benedict XV's failed attempt to forestall World War I and Pius XII's notoriously controversial public silence in the face of the Holocaust. For judicious treatments of these cases, see Pollard (1999) and Coppa (2013).
6. Text available at vatican.va.
7. Text available at vatican.va.
8. These documents are all collected in M. Abbott (1966).
9. An indispensable account of John XXIII and his impact is Hebblewaite (1985).
10. An aptly named biography is Hebblewaite (1993).
11. Life magazine, then a leading barometer of cultural interest, had on its cover the week of the papal visit a dazzling picture of the Mass at Yankee Stadium.
12. There is a huge literature on John Paul II and politics. Two representative examples are Willey (1992) and Formicola (2002).
13. An excellent way to grasp the tone of John Paul II's historic visit to Poland in 1979 is simply to read his speeches at Gniezno and Warsaw during that trip. They are both available at vatican.va.
14. See John Paul II (1991).
15. For a founding perspective on Liberation Theology, see Gutierrez (1988). A useful analysis of the theology's direct political ramifications can be found in Smith (1991).
16. See Yardley (2016). Francis has spoken so frequently and passionately in the issue of migration that Orbis Books was able to publish a book of his statement on it Francis (2018).
17. See Francis (2015).
18. Again, this characterization of the priesthood was so emblematic of Pope Francis in his early days in Rome that Orbis published a book of these kinds of statements as well (Francis 2017).
19. This came in an updated "Introductory Letter" appended to their 2015 statement "Forming Consciences for faithful Citizenship." Both can be found at usccb.org.
20. Francis was 3rd on this list, but interestingly, *Fortune* ranked him *the* greatest leader in 2014, the first year after his elevation to the papacy (Colvin 2017).
21. For my own treatment of the scandal, see Byrnes (2020).

Chapter 14

1. While this piece was written during his presidency, ironically, it was published after he had resigned from office in the midst of political intrigue. Nonetheless, the article embodies a broader approach to foreign policy in the era (Quadros 1961).

2. Nye conceptualizes "fungibility" as the capacity to transform one form of power into another (Nye 1990).
3. Goes Filho (1999); Danese (1999); Celso (2000); Ricupero (2017).
4. Sanchez-Badin, Schaeffer, and Rosenberg (2008); Vieira (2012); Duarte (2017); Engstrom (2012).
5. Malamud (2011); Burges (2015); Casarões (2017).
6. Stuenkel (2019); Casarões (2020).
7. Kuru (2009). Note that Kuru's book codes Brazil as "secular," but does not elaborate the form of secularism (assertive v. passive). The coding is our own; see further discussion in Smith (2019).
8. Soper and Fetzer (2018). The classification is, again, our own. Note that Soper and Fetzer's typology and theory would seem to predict that Brazil might go the way of Turkey under Ataturk in adopting assertive secularism, as a secular constitutional framework coincided with demographic religious uniformity. The reason Brazil seems to defy Soper and Fetzer's soft predictions is a very interesting question beyond the scope of this chapter.
9. Jansen (2018). For a further example of Church-state partnerships for religious and tourism development purposes during the democratic-populist era, see Serbin (1996).
10. Freyre (1973). The book is translated in English as *The Masters and the Slaves*.
11. For a review of scholarship disconfirming Freyre's understanding of race relations in Brazil, see, e.g., Layton and Smith (2017).
12. See Bellah (1967).
13. On the US transition from a secular to a more religiously infused foreign policy, see Bettiza (2019).
14. On the Church's relations with the military, see Serbin (2000), Mainwaring (1986), and Mainwaring and Wilde (1989).
15. In the Brazilian context, the term "Evangelical" is the most common overarching category used to refer to all Protestants; given the limited reach of theological liberalism within Brazilian Protestantism, the vast majority of Brazilian Evangelicals would meet common definitions of Evangelicalism from anglophone societies (Bebbington 1989).

    Within the broader category of "Evangelicalism," Brazilian scholars and demographers typically distinguish between Pentecostalism and non-Pentecostal (or "historical") Evangelicalism/Protestantism.
16. For more information on India's religious soft power efforts, see Chapter 6 in this text.
17. "Brazilian President Invokes Ramayana While Seeking Hydroxychloroquine from India" (2020).
18. Brasil (2009). *Plano Nacional para a Aliança de Civilizações*. Available at https://sistemas.mre.gov.br/kitweb/datafiles/Alianca/pt-br/file/Plano%20Nacional1803.pdf.
19. "Speech by President Dilma Rousseff on the occasion of the opening of the general debate of the 67th session of the United Nations General Assembly" (2012).
20. For review of the literature on Brazil's coalitional presidentialism, see Mauerberg Junior, Pereira, and Biderman (2015) and Power (2010).

21. O Estado de S. Paulo (2012).
22. The Christian Zionist ideology refers to the relentless defense of Israel among Evangelicals—and the recognition of the Holy City of Jerusalem as Israel's "complete and united" capital—as part of the biblical prophecy of the second coming of Christ. Although it was born in the United States, it has gained prominence across Latin America in the last decades. For further discussion, see Spector (2009) and Aldrovandi (2014).
23. Since January 2020 [as of this writing in October 2020], China has temporarily blocked Anajure's application; see Chade (2020).
24. For further discussion, see Casarões (2019, 111–144) and Casarões and Flemes (2019).
25. This text is from Decree 85.451/1980, which was replaced by Decree 5.798/2006.
26. Coletta (2019).

Chapter 15

1. In fairness *The Geopolitics of Religious Soft Power* project is neither the sole nor the first attempt to theorize and empirically investigate faith and the sacred as a form of "soft" power (see for example Byrnes 2017; Haynes 2012). Sandal and Fox (2013, 15), for instance, refer to religious legitimacy as a "potential source of power in the international system." Having said this, the present volume—in our view—constitutes the most comprehensive effort to this day in making power analysis an explicit element in the study of religion in world politics.
2. Some have partly begun this work. For instance, Bettiza and Lewis (2020) apply this power political framework to explore how Russia and China are ideologically contesting the liberal international order, which includes mobilizing a set of norms and identities that have their roots in religious traditions.
3. Along with coauthoring two chapters for this volume—the present concluding one and the chapter on US foreign policy—we also individually contributed to the wider project with two reports. See Bettiza (2020) and Henne (2019a).
4. For a recent useful overview of some of these critiques, see Henne (2021).

Index

For the benefit of digital users, indexed terms that span two pages (e.g., 52–53) may, on occasion, appear on only one of those pages.
Tables and figures are indicated by *t* and *f* following the page number

Abderrahim, Mohammed, 141
Abdullah II (Jordan), 157–58, 194, 196–97, 199
Abdullah (Saudi Arabia), 165
Abraham Accords (2020), 15–16, 164
Abramson, Yehonatan, 221–22
Abu Ghuddah, Abd al-Fattah, 134
Acharya, Amitav, 3–4
Afghanistan
    Iran and, 119–20
    Jordan and, 157
    Mujahideen, 2–3
    Soviet invasion of, 2–3, 28
    Taliban, 28
Afghanistan War, 30–31, 153
Africa–Asia Conference (1955), 172
African Union (AU), 147
Ahmad, Khurshid, 156–57
Ahmadinejad, Mahmoud, 121, 201–2
Albania, 85
Ali (Imam), 115
Alliance of Civilizations, 260–61
al-Qaeda
    generally, 20–21
    emergence of, 28, 35–36
    Jordan, bombings in, 196–97, 199
    moderate Islam and, 202–3
    9/11 attacks, 3, 29, 152, 154
Alshuaibi, Osama Mohammad Abdullah, 178–80, 179*f*
Amin, K.H. Ma'aruf, 187
Amnesty International, 138
Amorim, Celso, 252–53, 256, 260
Anwar, Dewi Fortuna, 187
Appleby, R. Scott, 257–58
Arab Spring/Arab Uprising (2011)
    Indonesia, impact in, 175–76, 182–83
    Iran, impact in, 121, 126–27
    Jordan, impact in, 194, 195
    moderate Islam and, 159
    Turkey, impact in, 90–91
Araújo, Ernesto, 248, 252, 257, 263–64
Ashiwa, Yoshiko, 8, 283
al-Assad, Bashar, 48
Asy'ari, K.H. Hashim, 183, 184–85
Ataturk, Kemal, 142–43, 302n.8
Australia, 71
Austria, 91
Azad, Maulana Abul Kalam, 99
Azerbaijan, 85
Azra, Azyumardi, 186–87

Bahrain, 15–16, 202
Baktiari, B., 116
Baldwin, David, 206
Barnett, Michael, 113, 280
Baumgart-Ochse, Claudia, 8, 273–74, 283
Bayyah, Bin (Sheikh), 163–64
Beers, Charlotte, 31–32
Begin, Menachem, 218–19, 227–28
Beilin, Yossi, 221–22
Belhassen, Yaniv, 226–27
Beling, Willard, 133
Bell, George, 25–26
Bellah, Robert N., 255–56
Benedict XV (Pope), 301n.5
Benedict XIV (Pope), 199, 244
Ben-Gurion, David, 217, 226
Benhuan, 73
Bennett, Naftali, 228
Ben-Porat, Guy, 80–81
Bergoglio, Jorge Maria. *See* Francis (Pope)

Bettiza, Gregorio, 12, 82–83, 197–98, 204–6, 273–74, 281–82, 283, 284, 303n.2
Bhutan, 101–2
Biden, Joe, 54, 165
bin Laden, Osama, 152
Blackstone, William E., 223–24
Blaustein, Jacob, 217
Blitt, Robert C., 8–9, 273–74
Bolivia, 258–59
Bolsonaro, Jair
  generally, 12
  Christian nationalism and, 257–58, 260–61
  foreign policy and, 260–61
  identity and, 14
  Israel and, 261–62
  Modi and, 260
  outreach and, 14–15
  religion and, 248–49, 263–64
  Trump and, 34–35, 283
Bond, Christopher S., 171–72
Bosnian War, 81
Brannagan, Paul Michael, 201, 205–6
Brazil
  Anajure (National Association of Evangelical Jurists), 261–62, 303n.23
  Bolivia and, 258–59
  Christianity in
    Catholic Church, 254–56, 262–63
    Christian nationalism, 257–58, 260–61, 264
    Evangelical Christianity, 261–62, 264, 283, 302n.15
    Pentecostals, 14–15, 256, 261–63
    Universal Church of the Kingdom of God, 261–63
  Christ the Redeemer statue, 254–56
  consensual hegemony and, 252
  Constitution, 254–55
  demographics of, 255
  domestic coalitions, religious soft power and, 250, 261–63
  Estado Novo, 254–55
  foreign policy, religious soft power in, 250, 258–61, 263–64
  General Law on Religions, 262
  historical background, 250–53
  identity and, 14
  India and, 259–60
  Iran and, 256
  Israel and, 261–62
  Libya and, 256
  middle power, as, 251
  Ministry of Foreign Affairs, 251
  nation-building, religious soft power in, 250, 253–58
  Nossa Senhora Aparecida (patron saint), 255–56
  outreach by, 14–15
  Panama and, 258–59
  Peru and, 259
  Portugal and, 250–51
  religious soft power generally, 12, 248–50, 263–64, 275
  secularism in, 254–55, 256
  Spain and, 250–51
  Syria and, 256
  Turkey and, 256, 260–61
  universalism in, 252
  Vatican and, 262–63
  Venezuela and, 258–59
  War of Canudos, 254–55
Brownback, Sam, 161–62
Buddhism. *See also specific country*
  Mahayana Buddhism, 62, 67–68, 70, 73–74, 103
  Theravada Buddhism, 62, 67–68, 70
  Vajrayana Buddhism, 62, 67–68, 70, 71–72, 73–74
Buddhist Compassion Relief Tzu Chi Foundation, 71–72
Bulgaria
  Bulgarian Orthodox Church, 53
  Russia and, 49, 53
  Turkish outreach in, 85
Burges, Sean, 252
Burma. *See* Myanmar
Bush, George W.
  faith-based ministries and, 32, 35–36
  Iraq War and, 153–54
  9/11 attacks and, 3
  religious soft power and, 20
  securing and advancing "civilization," 30–32

Byrnes, Timothy A., 10

Cairns Group, 252
Cambodia, 70–71, 74–75
Canada, 71, 211
Carr, E.H., 233
Carson, Ben, 161
Carter, Jimmy, 22
Carter Doctrine, 153
Casaröes, Guilherme, 12
Castro, Martin, 160
Catholic Church, 254–56, 262–63. *See also* Vatican
C-Fam, 54
Chao, Elaine, 161
Chehabi, H.E., 117–18
China
  analytical framework, 63–66
  Baoao Forum, 74
  Belt and Road Initiative, 14–15, 61, 72, 73–74
  Buddhism in
    generally, 8, 13–15, 283
    Buddhism Culture Park, 74–75
    Buddhist culture, 63–64, 70
    Chinese Buddhism, 63–64, 70
    Chinese Communist Party (CPC) and, 61–62, 63, 64–68, 70, 71–72, 74, 75
    clerics, 72
    Hainan Buddhist Academy, 74–75
    Hongfa Temple, 73, 74, 296n.19
    Mahayana Buddhism, 62, 67–68, 70, 73–74
    modalities of, 62, 70–75
    Nanhai Buddhist Academy, 74–75
    Nanshan Temple, 74–75
    people-to-people exchanges, 74
    Sinicized Buddhism, 63–64, 70
    state use of in foreign relations, 62, 66–70
    strategies of promotion, 62, 70–75
    Theravada Buddhism, 62, 67–68, 70
    Vajrayana Buddhism, 62, 67–68, 70, 71–72, 73–74
  Buddhist Association of China (BAC), 65, 66–68, 69–70, 73–74
  Chinese Communist Party (CPC)
    generally, 8
    Buddhism and, 61–62, 63, 64–68, 70, 71–72, 74, 75
  Chinese People's Political Consultative Conference (CPPCC), 65, 73
  communist revolution in, 2
  Confucianism in, 68, 283
  Confucius Institutes, 13, 64, 68
  Cultural Revolution, 66
  Daoism in, 68, 283
  Four Modernizations, 66–67
  Guanyin Park, 74–75
  India and, 99, 104
  Islam in, 161–62
  malignant forms of religion in, 15
  Ministry of Education, 64
  Nanshan Culture Tourism Zone, 74–75
  National People's Congress, 65
  outreach by, 14–15, 66–68, 70–71, 73–75
  Overseas Chinese Affairs Office, 65–66
  religious administration in, 64–65
  religious soft power generally, 8, 61–62, 75–76, 275
  "sharp power" versus religious soft power, 64
  South China Sea Buddhism Shenzhen Round Table, 74–75
  State Administration of Religious Affairs (SARA), 65–66, 295n.5
  Tang Dynasty, 61
  United Front Work Department (UFWD), 63, 65–66, 70–71, 72, 74
China-Korea-Japan Friendship Buddhist Exchange Association, 66–67
Christianity. *See also specific country*
  Bulgarian Orthodox Church, 53
  Catholic Church, 254–56, 262–63 (*see also* Vatican)
  Christian nationalism, 257–58, 260–61, 264
  Christian Zionism, 223–24, 225, 226–28, 261–62, 303n.22
  Church of Jesus Christ of Latter-Day Saints, 164, 200
  Evangelical Christianity, 8, 13–14, 161–63, 212–14, 222–29, 261–62, 264, 283, 302n.15

Christianity (*cont.*)
  Greek Orthodox Church, 23
  Moscow Patriarchate (Russian Orthodox Church) (*see* Russia)
  Pentecostals, 14–15, 256, 261–63
  Universal Church of the Kingdom of God, 261–63
"clash of civilizations," 5, 16, 29, 87
Clinton, Bill, 29
Clinton, Hillary Rodham, 173–74
Cold War
  Arab governments and, 154
  Soviet Union and, 2–3
  US and (*see* United States)
Comoros, 121
comparative approach, 12–14
Confucianism, 68, 283
constructivism, 272, 275–76
Cooper, Andrew, 251
Cox, Harvey, 296n.2
Crespo, R.A., 232
Croatia, 49
Cuba, communist revolution in, 2
cultural appeals, 279

Daesh, 20–21, 196–98, 202–3. *See also* Islamic State in Iraq and Syria (ISIS)
Daher, Ali (Sheikh), 125–26
Dalai Lama, 71, 73–74, 104
Daoism, 68, 283
Darby, John Nelson, 223
Daryan, Abdul Latif (Sheikh), 297n.13
Davos World Economic Forum, 74
Davutoğlu, Ahmet, 88–89
Dayan, Moshe, 217–18
Denmark, 200–1
Derviş, Kemal, 87–88
DeVos, Betsy, 161
Diem, Ngo Dinh, 27, 28, 35–36
Dignitatis Humanae (Papal encyclical), 236
Din Syamsuddin, 299n.4
Diop, Ibrahim Mahmoud, 139–40, 146
Diwan, Kristin, 6–7
Djala, Dino Patti, 175–76
Djukanovic, Milo, 46
Doran, Michael, 26–27

Drollinger, Ralph, 161
Dulles, John Foster, 24
Duvall, Raymond, 280

Eban, Abba, 217–18
Ebel, Jonathan, 226–27
Egypt
  Gulf Cooperation Council (GCC), in, 153
  Indonesia and, 175–76, 187–88
  Islam generally, 91–92
  Jordan and, 195
  nationalist revolution in, 2
Eisenhower, Dwight
  anti-communism and, 2, 21
  religious soft power and, 22, 23–24, 26
  Saudi Arabia and, 26–27, 28
  Vietnam and, 27
Eisenstadt, Shmuel, 276
El Hassan bin Talal (Jordan), 192, 198–99
Elshtain, Jean Bethke, 271–72
Elson, Edward, 26
Erbakan, Necmettin, 86–87
Erdoğan, Recep Tayyip
  generally, 9
  foreign policy and, 86–87, 88
  religious soft power and, 89, 90–92
European Court of Human Rights (ECtHR), 45

Faisal (Saudi Arabia), 28
Falwell, Jerry, 227–28
al-Fasi, 'Allal, 134–35
Fetzer, Joel S., 254, 302n.8
Fischer, Markus, 4
Fogg, Kevin, 172
Fo Guang Shan, 71–72, 74
foreign policy, religious soft power in, 1–4. *See also specific country*
Foucault, Michel, 271
Fox, Jonathan, 303n.1
France
  French Revolution, 1–2
  soft power in, 211
  Turkey and, 87–88, 91
Francis (Pope)
  climate change and, 240
  direct exercise of soft power, 239–40, 241–42

indirect exercise of soft power, 239, 241, 242
institution of Church and, 243, 301n.18
migrants and, 239–40, 241–42, 301n.16
Modi and, 107
Mohammed VI and, 140–41
opposition to, 243
poverty and, 239, 241, 242–43
religious soft power and, 239–41
sex abuse scandal and, 244–45
UAE and, 164
Freyre, Gilbert, 255
Fukuyama, Francis, 29

Gabon, 147
Gad al-Haq, Gad al-Haq 'Ali, 143
Gandhi, Indira, 99
Ganguly, Sumit, 9, 283, 284
Gautama, Siddhartha, 73–74
Gaza war, 203–4
Geneva Consensus Declaration (GCD) on Promoting Women's Health and Strengthening the Family, 54
Germany
  Buddhism in, 71
  Jordan and, 200–1
  Nazism in, 2
  soft power in, 211
  Turkey and, 87–88, 91
  US outreach to, 23
Ghazi bin Muhammad bin Talal (Jordan), 192, 196–97
Giuliannotti, Richard, 201, 205–6
Glendon, Mary Ann, 162
Global War on Terror (GWOT). *See* United States
Goddard, Stacey, 273, 279, 281
Golwalkar, Sadashiv, 103
Görmez, Mehmet, 87–88
Graham, Billy, 24, 26
Great Tafsir Project, 192–93
Greece
  Greek Orthodox Church, 23
  Jordan and, 201
  US outreach to, 23, 25
Gregory, C.C., 232
Group of 15, 252
Guadium et Spes (Papal encyclical), 236

Guantanamo Bay, 31, 33
Gülen, Fethullah, 85–86
Gulf Cooperation Council (GCC), 153, 163, 195
Gulf War, 195
Gutkowski, Stacey, 11, 157–58, 278–79, 284

Hadi, Umar, 174
Haga, Allison, 27
Hall, Rodney, 232
Hamid, Shadi, 3–4, 6–7, 19–20, 82, 171, 182–83, 193, 202–3, 276, 282–83, 284
Harsono, Andreas, 187
Hassan II (Morocco)
  generally, 10, 130–31
  accession to throne, 132–33
  Casablanca riots (1965) and, 137
  Conseil supérier des Oulémas (High Council of 'Ulema) and, 139
  Dar al-Hadith al-Hassaniya (Hassan's House of Hadith) and, 130, 135–36
  Durus Hasaniya (Hassanian Lectures) and, 139–40, 142–46
  Great Mosque of Dakar and, 136–37
  "Green March" and, 137–38
  Hassan II Foundation for Moroccan Foreign Residents, 141–42
  Hassan II Mosque, 130, 141
  John Paul II and, 140–41
  League of Scholars of Morocco and Senegal and, 139–40
  leftist opposition, concerns regarding, 134–35
  religion and, 134, 138
  Union Nationaliste des Forces Populaires (UNFP) and, 134–35
  "Years of Lead" and, 138
Hassner, Ron E., 281–82
Hattar, Nahed, 196
Havana Declaration (2016), 53
Haynes, Jeffrey, 1–2, 5, 81–83, 261
Henne, Peter S., 8, 12, 36, 273–74, 279, 281, 283, 284
Hezbollah
  Iran and, 113–14, 118–19, 124–26
  Israel and, 123–24
  Risalat (cultural arm), 125–26

Hilarion (Metropolitan), 45–46, 49–50, 52
Hinduism. *See also specific country*
　generally, 102, 177–78
　Bharatiya Janata Party (BJP) and, 100–1
　International Day of Yoga, 102–3
　historical background, 1–4
Hoesterey, James B., 10–11, 284
Holocaust, 211–12, 301n.5
Holy See. *See* Vatican
Hsingyun, 74
Hughes, Karen, 31–32
Huieguang, 74, 296n.19
Hu Jintao, 67–68
Humanae Vitae (Papal encyclical), 242
Human Rights Watch, 187
Hummel, Daniel G., 225
Hungary, 162, 260–61
Huntington, Samuel P., 5, 16, 29, 87
Hussein, Saddam, 115–16, 157, 195
Hussein (Imam), 115–16, 125–26
Hussein (Jordan), 195

Inboden, William, 21–22, 25–26
India
　"Act East" initiative, 103
　Bajrang Dal, 107
　Bharatiya Jana Sangh, 100
　Bharatiya Janata Party (BJP)
　　generally, 9
　　Buddhism and, 103
　　Christianity and, 107
　　Hinduism and, 100–1
　　Islam and, 106
　　Judaism and, 104–5
　Bhutan and, 101–2
　Brazil and, 259–60
　Buddhism in
　　Bharatiya Janata Party (BJP) and, 103
　　China and, 71–72, 73–75
　　Mahayana Buddhism, 103
　　soft power resource, as, 103–4
　Center for Media Studies Academy, 99–100
　China and, 99, 104
　Christianity in, 107–8
　Citizenship Amendment Act, 106
　Division of Public Diplomacy, 99
　"Festivals of India," 99

Hinduism in
　Bharatiya Janata Party (BJP) and, 100–1
　International Day of Yoga, 102–3
Hindutva ("Hinduness"), 101
identity and, 14
Indian Council for Cultural Relations (ICCR), 99
Indian National Congress (INC), 99, 100, 101
Indonesia and, 105
International Day of Yoga, 102–3
Iran and, 106
Islam in
　geopolitics, 105–7
　persecution of Muslims, 161–62
　Sufism, 106
Jamia Milia Islamia incident, 107
Japan and, 103
Judaism in, 104–5, 108–9
Malaysia and, 106
malignant forms of religion in, 15
Ministry of External Affairs, 99
Ministry of Tourism, 99
"Muslim Question," 105–7
Myanmar and, 103
Nalanda University, 103–4
National Democratic Alliance (NDA), 100
nationalist revolution in, 2
National Register of Citizens (NRC), 106
Nepal and, 102, 103
nonalignment and, 97–98
outreach by, 103, 104–5, 108–9, 283
Pakistan and, 98
Panchshila (five pillars of peaceful coexistence), 97–98
Rashtriya Swyamsevak Sangh (RSS), 107
reductionism and, 277–78
religious soft power generally, 9, 97–100, 108–9, 284
Saudi Arabia and, 106
secularism in, 100
South Korea and, 103
Sri Lanka and, 103, 108–9
Thailand and, 103

United Arab Emirates and, 105
United Progressive Alliance (UPA), 99,
  100, 101, 103–4
US and, 108
Vatican and, 107
India–Brazil–South African Dialogue
  Forum, 256
Indonesia
  Arab Spring/Arab Uprising, impact of,
    175–76, 182–83
  Bali bombing (2002), 169, 173
  Bali Democracy Forum (BDF), 176–80,
    177f, 178f
  Christianity in, 173
  Darul Islam, 299n.6
  Egypt and, 175–76, 187–88
  foreign policy, Islamic turn in,
    171, 172–76
  Hinduism in, 177–78
  India and, 105
  Indonesian Council of Ulama, 181
  Indonesian exceptionalism, 180–86
  Institute for Peace and Democracy
    (IPD), 175–76
  International Summit of Moderate
    Islamic Leaders (ISOMIL), 182–
    86, 182f
  Islam in
    "Arabization" of, 181
    Bali Democracy Forum (BDF) and,
      176–80, 177f, 178f
    Darul Islam, 299n.6
    foreign policy, Islamic turn in,
      171, 172–76
    Indonesian exceptionalism
      and, 180–86
    International Summit of Moderate
      Islamic Leaders (ISOMIL), 182–
      86, 182f
    Islamic school tours, 176
    Islam Nusantara (Islam of the
      Archipelago), 171, 180–
      86, 187–88
    moderate Islam, 170–71, 173–74,
      181–82, 187–88
    Sufism, 170–71, 180–81, 182–
      83, 185–86
    Wahhabism, 171
  Islam Nusantara (Islam of the
    Archipelago), 171, 180–86, 187–88
  Jaringan Islam Liberal (Liberal Islam
    Network), 181
  Jordan and, 187–88
  Laskar Jihad, 169
  Ministry of Foreign Affairs, 173, 187–88
  Ministry of Religion, 187–88
  moderate Islam and, 10–11, 170–71,
    173–74, 181–82, 187–88
  Morocco and, 187–88
  Muhammadiyah, 175, 299n.4
  Nahdlatul Ulama (NU), 171, 175, 180–
    83, 184–86, 187, 299n.4
  National Agency for the Eradication of
    Terrorism (BNPT), 182–83
  nationalist revolution in, 2
  New Order, 172–73
  Obama and, 169–70, 175
  Partai Keadilan Sejahtera (Prosperous
    Justice Party), 173
  power analysis and, 273–74
  reform in, 173
  religious soft power generally, 10–11,
    169–72, 173–74, 186–88, 275, 284
  Saudi Arabia and, 178–80, 179f
  Tunisia and, 175–76
International Bodhisattva Sangha, 74
International Christian Embassy
  Jerusalem (ICEJ), 226–27
International Conference on Islamic
  Studies (ICIS), 175
International Organization of the Family
  (IOF), 54
International Relations (IR)
  neglect of religion in, 4
  9/11 attacks, impact of, 5
  secularist assumptions,
    challenging, 275–76
  secular nature of, 5
International Religious Freedom
  Alliance, 261
International Religious Freedom
  Roundtable, 161–62
Iran
  Afghanistan and, 119–20
  Arab Spring/Arab Uprising, impact of,
    121, 126–27

Iran (*cont.*)
  Brazil and, 256
  Comoros and, 121
  Constitution, 117
  cultural diplomacy and exchange, 120
  Emdad (Imam Khomeini Relief Foundation), 113–14, 120, 121–22
  hawza (Shi'i seminaries), 113–14, 120
  Hezbollah and, 113–14, 118–19, 124–26
  identity and, 14
  India and, 106
  Iraq and, 118–20, 122–23
  Islamic Culture and Relations Organization (ICRO), 113–14, 122–24
  Islamic Revolution (1979), 2–3, 81, 113, 114–18, 138, 154
  Islam in
    generally, 91–92
    Shi'i Islam (*see below*, Shi'i Islam)
    Wahhabism, 118–19
  Israel and, 123, 127, 212
  justice, foreign policy and, 114–17
  Lebanon and, 118–19, 124–26
  maslaha (common good), 124
  Middle East conflict and, 118–20
  Ministry of Foreign Affairs, 122
  mostzafin (oppressed), 116–17
  outreach by, 13–14, 113–14
  Pakistan and, 119–20
  power analysis and, 273–74
  religious soft power generally, 9–10, 113–14, 126–27, 205, 275
  Saudi Arabia and, 119–20, 121, 127
  Shi'i Islam in
    generally, 9–10, 13–14, 117–18, 283
    cultural diplomacy and exchange, 120
    justice, foreign policy and, 114–17
    Middle East conflict and, 118–20
  Special Forces, 119
  Syria and, 118–19, 120, 122–23, 126
  Tajikistan and, 121, 122–23
  Tehran Symphony Orchestra, 126
  US versus, 123, 127
  velayat-e-faqih (guardianship of the jurist), 116
Iran–Iraq War, 115–16

Iraq
  Gulf War and, 195
  Iran and, 118–20, 122–23
  Jordan and, 191–92
  Shi'i Islam in, 13
Iraq War, 30–31, 153–54
Islam. *See also specific country*
  moderate Islam (*see* moderate Islam)
  Ramadan, 142
  Salafism, 84–85, 194–95, 196, 197, 202–3
  Shi'i Islam
    Iran, in (*see* Iran)
    Sunni Islam versus, 115–16, 119–20
  Sufism, 106, 137, 170–71, 180–81, 182–83, 185–86
  Sunni Islam
    generally, 13, 79–80, 83–84, 194
    Shi'i Islam versus, 115–16, 119–20
  Wahhabism, 10–11, 84–85, 118–19, 171, 202–3
"Islamic Awakening," 126–27
Islamic State in Iraq and Syria (ISIS), 3, 20–21, 81, 118–19, 159–60, 196–98. *See also* Daesh
Islamofascism, 30–31
Israel
  Abraham Accords and, 15–16
  Al-Aqsa Mosque, 194, 202–3
  Brazil and, 261–62
  Gaza war, 203–4
  Haram al-Sharif and, 203–4
  Hezbollah and, 123–24
  identity and, 14
  Indian outreach to, 104–5, 108–9
  Institute for National Security Studies, 211–12
  Iran and, 123, 127, 212
  Islamic Movement in Jerusalem, 203
  Israel Defence Forces, 211–12
  Jordan and, 190, 191–92, 203–4, 206
  Judaism generally, 8, 13–14
  Lebanon, war with, 218–19
  Likud Party, 226, 227–28
  Ministry of Tourism, 225, 226–27
  Mossad, 211–12
  origins of, 211–12
  outreach by, 13–14, 283

INDEX 313

Palestinian conflict, 33, 218–19, 220
power analysis and, 273–74
reductionism and, 277–78
religious soft power generally, 8, 211–14, 229, 275
Shin Bet Kaf, 211–12
Six-Day War and, 217–18, 225–26
Taglit-Birthright Program, 221–22
Temple Mount, 225–26
US and
    Christian Zionism, 223–24, 225, 226–28
    Evangelical Christians, 8, 13–14, 162–63, 212–14, 222–29
    foreign aid from, 212–13
    "Israelism," 215–16
    Jewish community, 212–22, 229
    tourism, 225–28
Zionism and, 215–17
al-Issa, Muhammad, 165
Italy
    Christian Democrats, 23, 24–25
    Fascism in, 2
    Jordan and, 201

Jakarta Declaration, 186–87
Japan
    Buddhism in, 62, 68, 71–72, 75–76
    India and, 103
Jesus, 213, 223, 254–55
John Paul II (Pope)
    generally, 2–3
    direct exercise of soft power, 237, 238
    Hassan II and, 140–41
    indirect exercise of soft power, 237, 238–39
    institution of Church and, 243
    Liberation Theology and, 238
    Mohammed VI and, 140–41
    Poland and, 242
    religious soft power and, 237–39
    sex abuse scandal and, 244
Johnston, Douglas M., 271–72
John XXIII (Pope), 235–37
Joko Widodo (Jokowi), 105, 176–77, 182–83
Jordan
    Afghanistan and, 157

al-Qaeda and, 196–97, 199, 202–3
al-Qaeda bombings in, 196–97, 199
Amman Message (2004), 199, 200–2
Arab Spring/Arab Uprising, impact of, 194, 195
Bahrain and, 202
Baptism Site of Jesus Christ—Bethany Beyond the Jordan, 192–93
Catholic Center for Media Studies, 193
Christianity in, 191–92, 193, 200, 203–4
civil society organizations in, 193
Community Ecumenical Center, 193
countering jihadist activism in, 194
Daesh and, 196–98, 202–3
Denmark and, 200–1
Du'a Party, 194–95
"ecosystem" in, 191–92, 193
Egypt and, 195
foreign policy, religious soft power in
    generally, 198
    Europe and, 190, 200–1, 206
    Gulf States and, 190, 201–3, 206
    Israel and, 190, 191–92, 203–4, 206
    US and, 190, 191–92, 198–200, 206
General Intelligence Directorate, 158, 197
Germany and, 200–1
Greece and, 201
Gulf Cooperation Council (GCC), in, 153
Gulf War and, 195
Haram al-Sharif and, 203–4
Hirak Movement, 194
Hizb al-Tahrir, 194–95
Indonesia and, 187–88
Iraq and, 191–92
Islamic Action Front, 194–95
Islam in
    generally, 203–4
    legitimacy and, 194–96
    moderate Islam, 157–58, 190, 205
    Salafism, 194–95, 196, 197, 202–3
    Sunni Islam, 194
    Wahhabism, 202–3
Italy and, 201
Jordanian Interfaith Coexistence Research Centre, 193
Jordan Interfaith Coexistence Research Center, 13

Jordan (*cont.*)
  Middle East Council of Churches, 193
  Ministry of Education, 158
  Ministry of Islamic Affairs, 194–95, 197
  moderate Islam and, 157–58, 190, 205
  Morocco and, 195, 201–2
  Muslim Brotherhood in, 194–95
  "omni-balancing" in, 190
  power analysis and, 273–74
  Qatar and, 195, 201–3
  religious coexistence in, 194
  religious soft power generally, 11, 190–91, 196–98, 205, 275, 284
  Royal Aal al-Bayt Institute of Islamic Thought, 13, 192–93, 203–4
  Royal Court, 192–93
  Royal Institute for Interfaith Studies (RIIFS), 192–93
  Royal Islamic Strategic Studies Center, 13, 192–93
  Russia and, 199
  Saudi Arabia and, 201–3
  soft power analysis, 278–79
  Syria and, 191–92, 198, 201, 202
  Trump and, 203–4
  Turkey and, 195
  UAE and, 201–2
  UK and, 200–1
  wasatiyya (centrism), 197–98
  Wasat Party, 194–95
Judaism. *See also specific country*
  Conservative Judaism, 215–16
  Orthodoxy, 215–16
  Reform Judaism, 215–16
Juexing, 68–69

al-Kasabeh, Muath, 196–97, 207
Kébé, Abdul Aziz, 142
Kennan, George, 251
Keohane, Robert, 251
Khamenei, Ali (Ayatollah), 122, 124, 125–26
Khan, Hazrat Inayat, 10, 130, 131
Khatib, Abdelkrim, 134
Khomeini, Ruhollah (Ayatollah), 114–18, 124, 125–26
Kirby, Dianne, 21–22, 24–25

Kirill (Patriarch), 41–42, 45, 46, 47, 49, 51–52, 53
Kissinger, Henry, 212
Kmich, Abdul Ghafoor, 146
Korean War, 25–26, 28
Kuru, Ahmet T., 254, 302n.7

Lackner, Helen, 165–66
Laos, 74–75
Laruelle, Marlene, 293n.6
Lateran Accords (1929), 234–35
Laudato Si (Papal encyclical), 240
Lavrov, Sergei, 47, 48, 49–50
League of Nations, 251
Lebanon
  Hezbollah in, 113–14, 118–19, 124–26
  Iranian influence in, 113–14, 118–19, 122–26
  Islamic Culture and Relations Organization (ICRO) in, 113–14, 122–24
  Israel, war with, 218–19
Leo XIII (Pope), 235
Lewis, David, 303n.2
Liberation Theology, 238
Libya, 256
Lieberman, Avigdor, 212
Ligue des oulémas du Maroc et du Sénégal (League of Scholars of Morocco and Senegal), 139–40
Lowery, Charles, 27
Lula da Silva, Inácio
  foreign policy and, 252–53, 256, 258–61
  religion and, 249, 253, 261–62, 263–64
  Vatican and, 262

Macedo, Edir, 262–63
Machiavelli, Niccolò, 271
Maciel, Marcial, 244
Mahathir Mohammed, 106
Malachy, Yona, 225–26
Malaysia, 106
Mali, 147
Malofeev, Konstantin, 54
Mama Dedeh, 181
Mandaville, Peter, 3–4, 6–7, 19–20, 82, 113, 171, 182–83, 193, 202–3, 276, 282–83, 284

INDEX 315

al-Maqdisi, Muhammad, 197
Markham, James, 138
Markiewicz, Sarah L., 199, 201–2
Marx, Karl, 271
al-Mawdudi, Abu al-A'la, 143
M'Daghri, Abdelkébir Alaoui, 135–36
Meir, Golda, 227–28
Mekkaoui, Rajaa Naji, 136
Melissen, Jan, 242–43
Miller, Paul D., 222–23
Mneimneh, H.I., 117–18
moderate Islam
  generally, 10, 151–52, 165–66
  Abraham Accords and, 164
  Arab Spring/Arab Uprising and, 159
  Biden and, 165
  Global War on Terror (GWOT)
    and, 153–54
  Indonesia and, 170–71, 173–74, 181–82, 187–88
  Jordan and, 157–58, 205
  9/11 attacks and, 151
  Obama and, 158–60
  Pakistan and, 156–57
  power analysis and, 273–74
  Qatar and, 163
  reasons for, 152–55
  Saudi Arabia and, 165
  Trump and, 160–63
  UAE and, 163–65
  Yemen and, 165–66
modern state system, 1–2
Modi, Narendra
  generally, 9, 100
  Bolsonaro and, 260
  Buddhism and, 103–4
  Christianity and, 107–8
  criticism of, 284
  Francis and, 107
  Hinduism and, 100–1
  International Day of Yoga
    and, 102–3
  Islam and, 105–7
  Judaism and, 104–5
  political career of, 101–2
  religious soft power and, 109
  Trump and, 34–35
Mohamed bin Zayed (UAE), 164

Mohammad (Prophet), 115, 142–43, 155, 158, 159
Mohammad Reza Pahlavi (Shah), 115–16
Mohammed bin Salman (Saudi
  Arabia), 165
Mohammed VI (Morocco)
  generally, 10, 130, 139–40
  Durus Hasaniya (Hassanian Lectures)
    and, 143
  Francis and, 140–41
  John Paul II and, 140–41
  Mohammed VI Foundation for African
    'Ulama, 140
  Mohammed VI Foundation for Quranic
    Recitation, 146
  Vatican and, 140–41
Mohammed V (Morocco), 132–33
Mohr, Samuel, 224
Mongolia, 70–71
Montenegro, Law on Freedom of Religion
  or Beliefs, 46–48
Morocco
  1963-1981 period, 132–38
    Casablanca riots (1965), 137
    Dar al-Hadith al-Hassaniya (Hassan's
      House of Hadith), 135–36
    "Green March," 137–38
    "Years of Lead," 138–39
  1981-2003 period, 138–42
    Casablanca riots (1981), 138–39
    Conseil supérier des Oulémas (High
      Council of 'Ulema), 139
    foreign policy, religious soft power
      in, 139–40
    Hassan II Foundation for Moroccan
      Foreign Residents, 141–42
    Hassan II Mosque, 141
    Mohammed VI Foundation for
      African 'Ulama, 140
  Attijariwafa Bank, 147–48
  Banque Centrale Populaire
    (CBP), 147–48
  BMCE Bank of Africa, 147–48
  Conseil supérier des Oulémas (High
    Council of 'Ulema), 139
  Constitution, 133–34
  Dar al-Hadith al-Hassaniya (Hassan's
    House of Hadith), 130, 135–36

Morocco (*cont.*)
　Durus Hasaniya (Hassanian
　　Lectures), 142–46
　　generally, 130, 132–33, 134
　　Diop and, 139–40
　　format of, 143
　　functions of, 146
　　invitations, 142–43
　　lists of, 143–46, 144*t*, 145*t*
　　themes of, 146
　　women and, 136
　economic outreach by, 147–48
　Gabon and, 147
　Hassan II Foundation for Moroccan
　　Foreign Residents, 141–42
　Hassan II Mosque, 130, 141
　Indonesia and, 187–88
　Islam generally, 137
　Istiqlal Party, 134–35
　Jordan and, 195, 201–2
　Judaism in, 140–41
　Koutoubia Mosque, 137
　Mali and, 147
　Marrakesh Declaration, 201–2
　Ministry of Endowments and Islamic
　　Affairs, 146
　Mohammed VI Foundation for African
　　'Ulama, 140
　Mohammed VI Foundation for Quranic
　　Recitation, 140
　Mohammed V Mosque, 137
　Mourchida program, 146
　Movement for Unity and Reform
　　(MUR), 143
　Niger and, 147
　Nigeria and, 147
　Party of Justice and Development, 143
　power analysis and, 273–74
　Qarawiyyin University, 134, 135–36
　religious soft power generally, 10, 130–
　　31, 132, 147–48, 275
　Senegal and, 130–31, 136–37, 139–40,
　　146, 147
　Sufism is, 137
　Vatican and, 140–41
　women in, 130–31, 136, 141
Moshirzadeh, H., 117–18

Moskalkova, Tatyana, 44
Mother Teresa, 107–8
Mrili, Amina, 141
Mubarak, Hosni, 201–2
Musharraf, Pervez, 156, 157
Muslim Brotherhood, 90–91, 154,
　173, 194–95
Muslim World League, 165
Mussolini, Benito, 234–35
Muzadi, K.H. Hasyim, 175
Myanmar
　Chinese outreach to, 67–68, 70–71
　India and, 103
　Islam in, 161–62

al-Nabhan, Mohammad Farouk, 136
Nahyan, Khalifa bin Zayed Al
　(UAE), 201–2
Nasser, Gamal Abdel, 28, 143, 154, 185
Nehru, Jawaharlal, 9, 97–99, 296n.2
Nepal
　Buddhism in, 73–75
　Chinese outreach to, 67–68, 70–
　　71, 73–75
　Hinduism in, 102
　India and, 102, 103
Nerses Bedros XIX (Patriarch), 51–52
Netanyahu, Benjamin, 105, 220, 228
Neumann, Franz L., 131–32
New Agenda Coalition, 252
New International Economic Order
　(NIEO), 98
Nexon, Daniel, 272, 273, 279, 281
Niasse, Tijani Sheikh
　Ibrahim, 140
Niger, 147
Nigeria, 147
al-Nimr, Nimr, 121
9/11 attacks
　generally, 3, 29, 81, 154
　importance of religion and, 3, 5
　moderate Islam and, 151
　reasons for, 152
Nixon, Richard, 227–28
North Macedonia, 85
Nostra Aetate (Papal encyclical), 236
Nowi-Aghdam, Rahim, 119

INDEX 317

Nye, Joseph S., 6, 7, 19–20, 29, 63, 80–82, 131–32, 148, 156, 206, 211, 212, 213, 232–33, 243–44, 249–50, 270, 273, 278

Obama, Barack
   engaging religion and Muslims, 30, 32–33, 35–36, 158–60
   Indonesia and, 169–70, 175
   moderate Islam and, 158–60
   religious soft power and, 20
Orbán, Viktor, 34–35, 36–37, 283
Organization for Islamic Cooperation (OIC), 172–73, 186–87
Orientalism, 81, 87, 155, 170–71
Orthodox Christianity
   Bulgarian Orthodox Church, 53
   Greek Orthodox Church, 23
   Moscow Patriarchate (Russian Orthodox Church) (*see* Russia)
Oslo Accords, 220, 228
Öztürk, Ahmet Erdi, 9

Pacem in Terris (Papal encyclical), 235–36
Pakistan
   India and, 98
   moderate Islam and, 156–57
   US outreach to, 27, 28
Panama, 258–59
Pan-American Conferences, 251
Papacy. *See* Vatican
Paul VI (Pope), 236–37
Peace of Westphalia (1648), 1–2, 5
Pence, Mike, 161
Perdue, Sonny, 161
Perry, Rick, 161
Perry, Samuel L, 257–58
Peru, 259
Pew Forum on Religion and Public Life, 222–23
Pew Report on Jewish Americans, 214
Pew Research Center, 214, 222–23
Philippines, "progressive imperialism" in, 1–2
Philpott, Daniel, 81–82
Pinto, Paulo Gabriel Hilu, 207
Pius XII (Pope), 235–36, 301n.5

Poland
   Christianity in, 162
   Christian nationalism in, 260–61
   John Paul II and, 242
Pompeo, Mike, 34, 161, 162–63
Portugal, 250–51
Prandith, Farah, 158–59
Preston, Andrew, 21–22
Price, Tom, 161
process tracing, 285
Pruitt, Scott, 161
Putin, Vladimir
   generally, 8–9, 277
   compatriots and, 43
   Constitutional Amendments (2020) and, 41–42
   historical revisionism and, 42–43
   multipolarity and, 42
   sovereignty and, 42
   "traditional values" and, 43–44
   Trump and, 34–35

al-Qaradawi, Yusuf, 163–64
Qatada, Abu, 197
Qatar
   Jordan and, 195, 201–3
   moderate Islam and, 163
   Saudi Arabia and, 164
   UAE and, 163–64
Quadros, Jânio, 248–49, 253, 256, 263, 301n.1

Rabin, Yitzhak, 225
Raïssouni, Ahmed, 143
Ramazani, R.K., 117–18
RAND Foundation, 170–71
Rawls, John, 114–15
Raymond, Gregory V., 63
Reagan, Ronald, 22
realism, 273
Rebeiro, Julio, 107
reductionism, 277–78
Religious Freedom Institute, 160
religious soft power. *See also specific country or topic*
   generally, 81–82
   ballroom dancing metaphor, 190–91

religious soft power (*cont.*)
  centers and organizations, 13
  comparative study of, 204–8
  competition with other religious institutions, 13
  concept of, 7
  context of, 12
  debates regarding, 80–83
  defined, 6
  emergence of, 81–82
  foreign policy, in, 1–4
  future research, 286
  future trends
    generally, 14–16, 280–81
    beyond power as "soft," 281–82
    influence, assessing and measuring, 284–85
    process tracing and, 285
    social network analysis and, 285
    variance in state and religious characteristics, 282–83
  historical background, 1–4
  holistic analysis, 191, 205–6
  identity and, 14
  interstate competition and, 191, 207
  limitations of
    generally, 277
    conceptual stretching, 278–79
    narrow power concept, soft power as, 279–80
    reductive approach to religion, 277–78
  outreach, 13–14
  preexisting baseline, 191, 207–8
  promises of
    generally, 271, 286–87
    foreign policy, broadening research on religion and, 274–75
    power analysis in study of religion, 271–74
    secularist assumptions, challenging, 275–76
  scholarship on, 4–7
  state, role of, 6–7
Rerum Novarum (Papal encyclical), 235, 242
Retno Marsudi, 177–78
Rhodesia, 97
Rio Branco, Barão do, 253

Rizal Sukma, 172–73, 186
Roberson, Jennifer, 141
Rosenthal, Steven T., 216
Rousseff, Dilma, 259–62
Rushdie, Salman, 155
Russia. *See also* Soviet Union
  Bulgaria and, 49, 53
  Christianity in, 162
  Constitutional Amendments (2020), 41–45
    compatriots and, 43
    historical revisionism and, 42–43
    multipolarity and, 42
    sovereignty and, 42
    "traditional values" and, 43–45
  Croatia and, 49
  identity and, 14
  Jehovah's Witnesses in, 49–50
  Jordan and, 199
  LGBTQ persons and, 44, 293n.9, 293–94n.10
  Ministry of Foreign Affairs, 48, 49
  Montenegro and, 46–48
  Moscow Patriarchate (Russian Orthodox Church)
    generally, 8–9, 45, 277
    compatriots and, 50–52
    historical revisionism and, 48–50
    multipolarity and, 45–48
    sovereignty and, 45–48
    "traditional values" and, 52–54
  Muslim Tatars in, 49–50
  outreach by, 13–15
  power analysis and, 273–74
  reductionism and, 277
  religious soft power generally, 8–9, 54–55, 275
  Rossotrudnichestvo (Federal Agency for Compatriots Abroad and International Humanitarian Cooperation), 50–51
  Russian Revolution, 2
  Russkiy Mir, 50–51, 294n.17
  Serbia and, 47
  Syria and, 48, 51–52, 53–54
  Ukraine and, 48, 53
  World Russian People's Council (WRPC), 50–51

Saad, A., 124–25
al-Sadr, Musa, 115–16
Safavid Dynasty, 115–16
Salman (Saudi Arabia), 165, 178–79, 186
Sambi, Ahmed Abdallah Mohamed, 121
Sampson, Cynthia, 271–72
Sandal, Nukhet A., 303n.1
Sasson, Theodore, 219–20
Saudi Arabia
   "ecosystem" in, 193
   India and, 106
   Indonesia and, 178–80, 179f
   Iran and, 121
   Islam generally, 91–92
   Jordan and, 201–3
   moderate Islam and, 165
   Qatar and, 164
   religious soft power generally, 205
   Sunni Islam in, 13
   US outreach to, 26–27
   US troops in, 152
Saud (Saudi Arabia), 26–27, 28
Savarkar, Vinayak Damodar, 103
scholarship on religious soft power, 4–7
secular nationalism, 2
Senegal
   Great Mosque of Dakar, 136–37, 139
   Islamic Institute, 137
   L'association pour l'édification de la Grande Mosquée de Dakar (Association for the Construction of the Great Mosque of Dakar), 137
   Morocco and, 130–31, 136–37, 139–40, 146, 147
Senghor, Léopold Sédar, 136–37
Serbia, 47
Serra, José, 262–63
Sessions, Jeff, 161
Shariati, Ali, 115–17
"sharp power," 15, 64, 206
Sheline, Annelle, 10, 196, 284
Shindler, Colin, 227–28
Simons, Lewis M., 171–72
Singapore, 66–67
Siraj, Sa'id Aqil, 181–86
Sistani, Ali (Ayatollah), 118–19, 297n.1
Six-Day War, 217–18, 225–26

Smith, Amy Erica, 12
Snyder, Jack, 3
social network analysis, 285
soft power. *See also specific country or topic*
   generally, 270
   conceptual stretching and, 278–79
   culture and, 63, 213
   defined, 6, 80–81, 211, 232, 249–50
   description of, 148
   emergence of concept, 131–32
   religious soft power (*see* religious soft power)
   turn toward, 6
   US ideals and, 7, 156
Soft Power 30, 211
Soloveitchik, Joseph B., 215–16
Soper, J. Christopher, 254, 302n.8
South Africa, apartheid in, 97
South Asian Association for Regional Cooperation (SAARC), 101–2
South Korea
   Buddhism in, 68
   India and, 103
   US outreach to, 27, 28
Soviet Union. *See also* Russia
   Afghanistan, invasion of, 2–3, 28
   Cold War and, 2–3
   historical revisionism regarding, 293n.5
Spain, 87, 250–51
Spector, Stephen, 223–24
Sri Lanka
   Belt and Road Initiative and, 14–15
   Chinese outreach to, 70–71
   India and, 103, 108–9
Staines, Graham, 107
Stalin, Josef, 232
Sturm, Tristan, 224
Suharto, 169, 172–73
Sukarno, 172, 173
Suryadinata, Leo, 172
Susilo Bambang Yudhoyono (SBK), 173–74, 175–76, 187
Swaraj, Sushma, 107–8
Sweden, 87–88
symbolic appeals, 279
Syria
   Brazil and, 256
   Christianity in, 51–52, 53

Syria (*cont.*)
  civil war in, 207
  Jordan and, 191–92, 198, 201, 202
  Russia and, 48, 51–52, 53–54
  Syrian Muslim Brotherhood, 134

Taiwan, Buddhism in, 68, 69, 71–72, 74
Tajikistan, 121, 122–23
al-Tamimi, Iz al-Din (Sheikh), 199
Tan, Morse, 162
Tantaoui, Mohamed Sayed (Sheikh), 143
Taskhiri, Mohamed (Sheikh Ayatollah), 146
Tauber, Lillian, 197–98
Taylor, Myron, 19, 23
Telhami, S., 113
Thailand, 14–15, 103
Thirty Years' War, 1–2
Tocqueville, Alexis de, 19
Toledo, Alejandro, 259
Toufiq, Ahmed, 143–46
Treaty of Madrid (1750), 250–51
Treaty of Tordesillas (1494), 250–51
Truman, Harry
  anti-communism and, 21, 24–25
  religious soft power and, 19, 21–22
Trump, Donald
  abortion and, 54
  Bolsonaro and, 34–35, 283
  Christian nationalism and, 257–58
  explicit turn to "clash of civilizations," 30, 34–35
  international religious freedom and, 34, 36–37, 160–63
  Israel and, 34, 222–23, 228, 261–62
  Jordan and, 203–4
  moderate Islam and, 160–63
  Muslim travel ban and, 200
  Qatar and, 164
  religious soft power and, 20
  Saudi Arabia and, 165
  strongmen and, 34–35
  UAE and, 164
Tunisia, 175–76, 187–88
Turkey
  Adalet ve Kalkinma Partisi (Turkish Justice and Development Party) (AKP)
    generally, 9, 79
    state use of religion in foreign policy and, 80, 86–89, 92–93
    Sunni Islam and, 79–80
    transformation of religious soft power and, 89–92
  Anavatan Partisi (Motherland Party), 86–87
  Arab Spring/Arab Uprising, impact of, 90–91
  Austria and, 91
  Brazil and, 256, 260–61
  Diyanet İşleri Başkanlığı (Presidency of Religious Affairs)
    generally, 9, 13
    historical background, 83–86
    state use of religion in foreign policy, 87–88, 89–90
    transformation of religious soft power and, 91
  Doğru Yol Partisi (True Path Party), 86–87
  France and, 87–88, 91
  Furkan Foundation, 91–92
  Germany and, 87–88, 91
  Gezi Protests, 90–91
  Gülen Movement, 85–86, 88–89, 91–92
  Hagia Sophia, 91–92
  historical background, 82–85
  India and, 106
  Islam in
    Salafism, 84–85
    Sunni Islam, 79–80, 83–84
    Wahhabism, 84–85
  Jordan and, 195
  Kemalists, 2, 85–87, 88–89, 91
  Milli Görüş (National Vision), 86–87, 88
  Naksibendi Movement, 84–85
  Nur Movement, 84–86
  outreach by, 85–86, 87–88, 89–90, 91
  political uncertainty in, 182–83, 187–88
  populist authoritarianism in, 90–91
  religious soft power generally, 9, 79–80, 92–93, 275, 283
  Revolution, 2
  secularism in, 83–86
  state use of in foreign policy, 80, 86–89, 92–93

INDEX 321

Sweden and, 87–88
transformation of, 89–92
US outreach to, 23
Wahhabism in, 84–85

Ukraine, 48, 53
Umayyad Dynasty, 115
United Arab Emirates
  Abraham Accords and, 15–16, 164
  Francis and, 164
  India and, 105
  Jordan and, 201–2
  Ministry of Tolerance, 163–64
  moderate Islam and, 163–65
  Muslim Council of Elders, 163–64
  Qatar and, 163–64
  Vatican and, 164
United Kingdom
  Jordan and, 200–1
  missionary activities and, 1–2
  soft power in, 211
  US outreach to, 23
United Nations
  generally, 251
  Alliance of Civilizations and, 260–61
  Charter, 172–73
  Human Rights Council (UNHRC), 43, 293–94n.10
  Security Council, 48, 252–53
  UNESCO, 73–74, 123–24
  UNICEF, 54
  World Interfaith Harmony Week, 192–93, 196
United States
  Affordable Care Act, 160
  Afghanistan War and, 30–31, 153
  American Israel Public Affairs Committee (AIPAC), 219–20, 221
  American Jewish Committee (AJC), 217, 219, 221
  American Revolution, 1–2
  Americans for a Safe Israel, 300n.4
  Brit Tzedek V'Shalom, 300n.4
  Bureau of Democracy, Human Rights, and Labor, 162
  Carter Doctrine, 153
  Christian nationalism in, 257–58, 260–61
  Christians United for Israel (CUFI), 228
  Cold War and
    generally, 2, 8, 19–22, 35–36
    Europe, outreach to, 22–26
    grand narratives, 21–22
    missionary activities, 24
    non-Western states, outreach to, 26–28
    propaganda, 23–24, 26
    success of, 24–26, 28
    Vatican, outreach to, 23, 24–25
  Commission on International Religious Freedom (USCIRF), 108, 161–62
  Commission on Unalienable Rights, 162
  Conference of Presidents of Major American Jewish Organizations (CPMAJO), 219, 221
  Council of Jewish Federations (CJF), 219
  counterinsurgency (COIN) operations, 153
  Evangelical Christianity in, 13–14, 161–63
  Faith-Based and Community Initiative, 32
  Federal Bureau of Investigation (FBI), 161
  Food for Peace, 23–24
  foreign policy, religious soft power in, 204–5
  Foundation for Religious Action in the Social and Civil Order (FRASCO), 27
  Global War on Terror (GWOT) and
    generally, 8, 20–21, 29–30, 35–36, 284
    Bush and, 30–32
    engaging religion and Muslims, 30, 32–33
    explicit turn to "clash of civilizations," 30, 34–35
    grand narratives, 29–30
    institutionalized statecraft, 30
    moderate Islam and, 153–54
    9/11 attacks and, 29
    Obama and, 30, 32–33
    propaganda, 31–32
    securing and advancing "civilization," 30–32
    Trump and, 30, 34–35

United States (*cont.*)
  India and, 108
  International Religious Freedom Act, 31
  Iran versus, 123, 127
  Iraq War and, 30–31, 153–54
  Islamophobia in, 160
  Israel and
    Christian Zionism, 223–24, 225, 226–28
    Evangelical Christians, 8, 13–14, 162–63, 212–14, 222–29
    foreign aid to, 212–13
    "Israelism," 215–16
    Jewish community, 212–22, 229
    tourism, 225–28
  Israel Policy Forum, 300n.4
  Jewish Institute for National Security, 300n.4
  Jewish People Policy Institute, 214, 300n.3
  Jordan and, 190, 191–92, 198–200, 206
  J Street, 300n.4
  Judaism in, 214–16
  Justice Department, 161
  Manifest Destiny, 1–2, 19
  Marshall Plan, 22
  "Moral Majority," 227–28
  Muslim Affairs Council, 160
  Muslim travel ban, 34, 160, 200
  Office of Religion and Global Affairs (RGA), 33
  outreach by, 23, 25, 26–28, 283
  power analysis and, 273–74
  President's Emergency Plan for AIDS Relief (PEPFAR), 32
  Radio Free Europe, 23–24
  Religious Freedom Report (2005), 199
  religious soft power generally, 8, 19–21, 35–37, 275
  Republican Party, 227–28
  Saudi Arabia, US troops in, 152
  soft power in, 211
  Special Representative to Muslim Communities, 32–33
  State Department, 158–59, 162
  Strategy on Religious Leader and Faith Community Engagement, 33
  United Jewish Appeal, 220
  US Information Agency (USIA), 23–24
  Washington Islamic Center, 26
  Zionist Organization of America, 220, 300n.4
US–Jordan Free Trade Agreement, 198

Vajpayee, Atal Behari, 101, 102
van Bruinessen, Martin, 186
Vargas, Getulio, 254–55
Vatican
  Brazil and, 262–63
  diplomatic relations, 233
  direct exercise of soft power, 236, 237, 238, 239–40, 241–42, 243–45
  historical background, 234–37
  India and, 107
  indirect exercise of soft power, 234, 236, 237, 238–39, 241, 242, 243–45
  Lateran Accords and, 234–35
  loss of political power, 234
  moral authority of, 232–33, 241–42
  moral credibility, loss of, 243–45
  Morocco and, 140–41
  outreach by, 13–14
  religious soft power generally, 10, 232–34, 275
  Second Vatican Council, 2–3, 236
  sex abuse scandal and, 243–45
  UAE and, 164
Venezuela, 258–59
Vietnam
  Chinese outreach to, 70–71
  US outreach to, 27, 28

Wadi Arab Treaty (1994), 191–92
Walker, Christopher, 15, 64
Wank, David L., 8, 283
Washburn, Abbott, 26
Wastnidge, Edward, 9–10, 205–6, 273–74
Waxman, Dov, 214–15
Weber, Timothy P., 227
Welch, Holmes, 66
Wertheimer, Jack, 217
Whitehead, Andrew L., 257–58
Wirajuda, Hasan, 173–76
Wojtyla, Karol. *See* John Paul II (Pope)
Wolf, Frank, 161
World Buddhist Forum, 67–68
World Congress of Families, 54

World Sufi Forum, 106

Xi Jinping
   generally, 8
   Buddhism and, 61–62, 63–64, 68, 75–76
   Buddhist Association of China (BAC) and, 68
   United Front Work Department (UFWD) and, 65–66
Xuecheng, 69–70

Yemen, moderate Islam and, 165–66

Yin, Kai, 27
Yinshun, 72–75
Young, G. Douglas, 225
Yugoslavia, civil war in, 2–3, 29

Zakaria, Fareed, 156–57
Zia ul-Haq, 27, 156
Zinke, Ryan, 161
Zionism
   Christian Zionism, 223–24, 225, 226–28, 261–62, 303n.22
   Israel and, 215–17